The Home Design

Source Book

BARRIE & JENKINS

LONDON

Barbara Chandler

**For my daughters Abigail Chandler and
Catherine Morris, stalwart shoppers both**

First published in Great Britain in 1989 by
Barrie & Jenkins Ltd
289 Westbourne Grove, London W11 2QA

British Library Cataloguing in Publication Data

Chandler, Barbara, 1942-
    The home design source book.
    1. England. Household furnishings
    I. Title
    645'.0942

ISBN 0 7126 3018 X

Editors: Michael Coultas and Neelam Sharma

Designer: Sarah Menon

Computer Management: Helen Brown

Research Assistants: Vera Fearn, Linda Mundy, Deborah Tubb and Jan Smith

Typeset by SX Composing Ltd, Rayleigh, Essex
Printed and bound in Great Britain by Butler & Tanner Ltd,
Frome and London.

CONTENTS

PART ONE

What to Buy Where

PART TWO

Where to Buy What

INTRODUCTION

"There's no place like home." This common tag sums up perfectly my philosophy as specialist writer on home design, decorating, furnishing and DIY. At a time when the outside world is getting increasingly mass-produced, standardised, computerised, and vandalised, it's a relief to get back home. Here at least is maybe the only place left to create surroundings we feel are beautiful, comfortable and efficient.

As writer of *Ideal Home* magazine's 'London Shopping Digest', and as weekly design columnist for the *Evening Standard*, I spend a lot of time tracking down where to buy what for my readers' homes (and my own!), and publishing the results. There have been many requests for this information in a more permanent book form.

Here it is.

I have divided the book into two parts. The first, **What To Buy Where**, splits home merchandise into 24 chapters. Each chapter is divided, for convenience, into numbered sections. Inevitably, you must cross-refer a fair amount; and I am sorry when this gets tedious. For example, **Soft Furnishings** (divided into sections which include **1/Fabrics, 2/Lace & Nets, 3/Made-to-measure**, and so on), is also relevant to **Living & Diningrooms, Bedrooms, Interior Design, Services** and so on.

So many of the sections overlap it's worth browsing around over and above the sections you first highlighted.

Cross-references give the chapter heading in bold lettering, followed by the section number and name. Section headings are printed clearly down the side of each page.

If you get lost at any point, at the back there's an index which lists subjects in alphabetical order, together with their page numbers. There is also an index of shops, in alphabetical order, to help you track down old or new favourites.

The second part of the book, **Where To Buy What**, overlaps with the first. It indicates the strength and interest of the department stores, out-of-town superstores, larger independent furnishers, and store groups. Paradoxically, other shopping guides have often concentrated on smaller 'specialist' shops and devoted little space to the big names.

Most people shop for their homes from multiple sources, ranging from huge central department stores, through to their own local High Streets. Then they make special journeys to out-of-town superstores, or to specialist shops which cater for particular needs or interests. *The Home Design Source Book* attempts to reflect this diversity of shopping patterns.

This book only covers London, the Home Counties, and the South-East. Although coverage is not nationwide, distances between entries can be substantial. So I have divided each section geographically into All Districts (where applicable), London Postal Districts, Outer Ring (which is the area that falls roughly within the M25), and Home Counties/S.East, which is roughly Bucks, Berks, Herts, Hants, Middx, Surrey, and parts of Oxon, Cambs, Essex, Kent and Sussex. Where places are particularly jolly to visit, and fall outside these areas, I've included them under the heading Worth a Trip.

Where a shop has several branches, they are placed under the appropriate geographical sections, with a cross-reference to the main entry, where goods/services are described.

Exclusively mail order services have been listed separately within each section. Special items are often available only or more easily by mail order. And some mail order sources are cheaper than shops. Once again, I have selected the businesses that seem most interesting. Mail order services also operated by shops are listed under entries in the geographical areas. The term Mail Order denotes those goods which can be ordered by telephone or letter, regardless of how they are delivered.

At the back, there is a **Help!** section, which states your consumer rights, and other miscellaneous advice to make shopping more satisfactory.

All information is correct insofar as I have been able to ascertain. Mentions should not be taken as endorsements of quality of products or services. No fee or condition has been or will be accepted for the insertion or exclusion of any name. Things change very fast in retailing: always check before making a special journey. Postcodes and opening hours have been included where information was available.

Although there are getting on for 3,000 entries in this book, obviously there are still very many worthwhile businesses I have been unable to mention. Selection has been what I personally feel merits inclusion, judged on uniqueness of stock, popular appeal, prices, individual or special service, and so on.

Onus for selection in all sections rests on me, and my judgement. Please allocate praise/blame accordingly. I can only hope readers share my interests and values. I have been much encouraged by readers' responses to my articles in magazines and newspapers.

But if you run a shop or are its customer, and you feel an inclusion is merited, please do write and tell me at *The Home Design Source Book*, c/o Barrie & Jenkins Ltd. Updated and expanded issues are planned.

Barbara Chandler
London 1989

PART ONE

WHAT TO BUY WHERE

LIVING & DINING-ROOMS

For show and for blow, living rooms work hard for their keep. Comfort, style, practicality and durability are key considerations. It's not easy to get the right balance, but shops below can help.

1/SPECIALISTS

"Today is the age of the interiors' 'specialist': kitchens, bathrooms and bedrooms shops are prominently displayed on any High Street. But you might feel justifiably stumped if asked to name a specialist for livingrooms. Just stop and think a minute: who could be a better expert on your furnishings' needs downstairs than your local furniture store?" **Hugh Calder-Jones OBE**, *National Association of Retail Furnishers (NARF), 17/21 George Street, Croydon CR9 1TQ.*

Mr Calder-Jones has anticipated me: well, he would, wouldn't he. He's been in the industry for 14 years, initiating, steering, guiding, arbitrating. Send sae to NARF at the address above for excellent leaflets on choosing and caring for home furnishings. For planning/colour advice, consult firms listed under **Interior Design** and **Furnishing Stores**. For carpets, see **Floors**; for curtains etc., see **Soft Furnishings**. See also **Lighting**, **Accessories**. **Department Stores** can also help: many have furnishing consultants.

2/UPHOLSTERY & SUITES

"I can assure readers that new British upholstered furniture is the safest in the world, thanks to regulations in-troduced in Spring 1989 which ensure that combustion modified high resilient (cmhr) foam is used throughout. The foam contains particles which inhibit combustion and resist ignition for longer periods than the previous types of foam." **John Dunthorne**, *managing director, Silentnight.*

Do remember, to a certain extent nothing can be made completely safe and that furniture cannot set fire to itself. It needs a flame, match, candle, ember or cigarette. So take care. You are buying what the eye can't see – so it's worth purchasing from reputable retailers and manufacturers. Specialist firms abound, with a welcome return to traditional methods. Check delivery dates: these can range from immediate to 14 weeks! Shop also for upholstery at larger **Interior Design** firms, and **Furnishing Stores**.

London Postal Districts

Delcor Furniture 65 Tottenham Court Road, W1P 8PA. (*2 mins Goode Street tube*). *Tel*: 01-580 7900. *Open*: 9.30am to 6pm. Late night Thurs 7.30pm. Sofas/chairs; classic designs to order from firm's workshops (6 to 8 weeks). Huge choice of fabrics. Colour brochure/fabric swatches. *Tel*: 091 237 1303.
Also at: 279 King's Road, Chelsea, SW3 5EW. (*10 mins Sloane Square tube*). *Tel*: 01-352 5551. *Open*: Mon to Sat 9.30am to 6pm.

Peter Dudgeon Brompton Place, Knightsbridge, SW3 1QE. (*2 mins Knightsbridge tube*). *Tel*: 01-589 0322. *Open*: Mon to Sat 9.30am to 5.30pm. Trading since 1947. Top-quality handmade upholstery, over 30 styles. No foam: hand-tied springs/horsehair/cane seat edges. Beech frames, dowelled joints. Wonderful classic/traditional designs, e.g. wing/leather club chairs. Plus simple modern shapes. Colour catalogue.

Highly Sprung 549 Battersea Park Road, SW11 3BL. (*10 mins Clapham Junction BR*). *Tel*: 01-924 1124. *Open*: Mon to Fri 10am to 7pm. Sat 10am to 6pm. Keenly-priced classic upholstery designs, including Knole settee, chesterfield. Supply your own fabric. Orders: 2 to 3 weeks. Bedheads, cushions, accessories. Loose covers, reupholstery.

Kingcome Sofas 305 Fulham Road, SW10 9EP. (*10 mins Fulham Broadway tube*). *Tel*: 01-351 3998. *Open*: Mon to Fri 9.30am to 5.30pm. Sat 10am to 2pm. 20 years ago, Brian and Lesley Kingcome pioneered made-to-measure upholstery. Over 40 standard models made in firm's own workshops. Settees, sofabeds, chaises longues, corner units, chairs. Choose from a host of practical/stylish variations: self-piping, kick- or box-pleats, fabric-covered plinths or legs, castors, ball feet, gathered skirts or fringes. Cushions: Dacron-wrapped fire-retardant foam or feathers-and-down. On-site assembly where access is tricky.

Multiyork 25/28 Thurloe Place, SW7 2HQ. (*5 mins Gloucester Road tube*). *Tel*: 01-589 2303. *Open* (all branches): Mon to Sat 9.30am to 5.30pm. Sun 10am to 5pm. Traditionally-made upholstery; classic designs; natural fillings. Removable covers. Co-ordinated soft furnishings/accessories. *Also at*: 309 Green Lanes, Palmers Green, N13. *Tel*: 01-886 7514. *And at*: 13 Harben Parade, Finchley Road, Swiss Cottage, NW3 6JP. *Tel*: 01-722 7810.

Norfolk Furniture 632 King's Road, SW6 2DV. (*5 mins Fulham Broadway tube*). *Tel*: 01-836 4840. *Open*: Mon to Fri 10am to 6pm. Sat 10am to 2pm. Upholstery made to order in firm's workshops. Commissions for any fabric/style.

Omega Furniture 27 Wright's Lane, Kensington High Street, W8. (*2 mins High Street Kensington tube*). *Tel*: 01-938 2817. *Open* (both branches): Mon to Sat 10am to 6pm. Late night Thurs 8pm. Made-to-measure sofas, sofabeds, armchairs, corner units at ready-made prices. Expert advice, thousands of fabrics.

Simply Sofas 258/260 Lavender Hill, SW11 1LJ. (*2 mins Clapham Junction BR*). *Tel*: 01-228 4588. *Open* (both branches): Mon to Sat 10am to 6pm. Late night Thurs 8pm. Sun 11am to 6pm. *Also at*: 130 Notting Hill Gate, W11 3QG. (*1 min Notting Hill Gate tube*). *Tel*: 01-221 1816. See also Outer Ring below.

Sofaland North Circular Road, Brentside Works, NW10 7SX. (*5 mins Hanger Lane tube*). *Tel*: 01-965 4242. *Open*: 7 days 10am to 7pm. Vast showroom; around 150 sofas (many exclusive) from European designers. Thousands of fabrics. Orders take 12 to 14 weeks; some models available immediately. Occasional tables/lamps. Sofabeds. Coffee bar and children's play area.

Sofas and Sofabeds 219 Tottenham Court Road, W1P 9AF. (*Opposite Goodge Street tube*). *Tel*: 01-580 4287. *Open*: Mon to Sat 10am to 6.30pm. Late night Thurs 7pm. Sun viewing 12 noon to 5pm. Over 60 models sofas/sofabeds/chairs. Available immediately or made-to-measure. Top name fabrics. Reasonable prices. *Also at*: 3 Fulham Broadway, SW6 1AA. (*Opposite tube*). *Tel*: 01-381 3708. *Open*: Mon to Sat 10am to to 5.30pm. Sun viewing 12 noon to 5pm. *And at*: 296/298 Upper Richmond Road, Putney SW15 6TH. (*10 mins East Putney tube*). *Tel*: 01-789 8108. *Open*: Mon to Sat 10am to 6.30pm. Late night Mon 7pm. Sun viewing 12 noon to 5pm. *And at*: 3B Standard Industrial Estate, Henley Road, Docklands E16 2JJ. (*Off Pier Road*). *Tel*: 01-511 1431. *Open*: Mon to Fri 9am to 5.30pm. Sat 9am to 1pm.

Sofa So Good 2/10 Jerdan Place, Fulham SW6 1BH. (*2 mins Fulham Broadway tube*). *Tel*: 01-385 4719. *Open* (all branches): Mon to Fri 10am to 6pm. Late night Wed 7.30pm. Sat 9.30am to 6pm. Sun 12 noon to 5pm. Largest independent supplier sofas/sofabeds in UK, they say. 220 stock designs, many available immediately; or made-to-measure, 8 weeks. 15,000 fabrics. Stain- and soil-proof treatments. Curtains/cushions to order. Exclusive cane furniture. Colour brochure. *Mail order*. *Also at*: 32/38 Battersea Rise, South Circular, SW11 1EE. (*3 mins Clapham Junction BR*). *Tel*: 01-228 4546. Late night Tues 7.30. *And at*: 147 Chiswick High Road, Chiswick W4 4DT. (*5 mins Turnham Green tube*). *Tel*: 01-994 9399. Late night Thurs 7.30pm.

Sofa Workshop Ealing Broadway Centre, 8 High Street, W5 5DB. (*5 mins Ealing Broadway tube/BR*). *Tel*: 01-579 0693. *Open*: Mon to Sat 10am to 6.30pm. Large choice sofas/convertibles, wide fabric range. Exclusive fire-retardant treatment for any fabric.

Tulleys of Chelsea 289/297 Fulham Road SW10 9PZ. (*20 mins South Ken-* *sington tube*). *Tel*: 01-352 1078. *Open*: Mon to Sat 9am to 5.30pm. Over 20 classic designs sofas/chairs made to traditional standards in firm's workshops. Trading for over 100 years. Over 8,000 covering fabrics. Or "in the white" (unbleached calico) for your own loose covers. Some models tight upholstery/calico available immediately. Promotional fabrics (50% discount) 6 to 8 weeks. Other fabrics, tight upholstery, 10 to 12 weeks. Loose covers 12 to 14 weeks.

Wesley-Barrell 86 Tottenham Court Road, W19 9HD. (*3 mins Goodge Street tube*). *Tel*: 01-580 6979. *Open*: Mon to Sat 9.30am to 6pm. Late night Thurs to 7pm. Oxfordshire family business, trading for close on 100 years. Custom-made handcrafted upholstered/occasional furniture. Interior design/colour schemes. Co-ordinating cushions, curtains and upholstery. Handpainting for furniture and accessories. Free colour catalogue. *Tel*: 0608 810481. *Also at*: 198 Walton Street, SW3 2JL. (*7 mins South Kensington tube*). *Tel*: 01-584 3423. *And at*: 409 Upper Richmond Road West, East Sheen SW14 4NX. (*10 mins Richmond tube/BR*). *Tel*: 01-878 4001.

Outer Ring

Calico Furniture 15 Brookhill Close, East Barnet, Herts EN4 8SH. *Tel*: 01-440 2708. *Open*: Mon to Fri 10am to 5pm. Showroom with factory behind. To order: upholstery in white calico for loose covers. They supply patterns/instructions. Also dining tables, chairs, decor tables, sideboards and screens, with thin foam layer for your own covering fabric. Glass table tops available. Brochure.

Multiyork High Street, Bromley, Kent. *Tel*: 01-464 2253. See London Postal Districts above.

Simply Sofas 159 Clarence Street, Kingston-upon-Thames, Surrey KT1 1TQ. (*1 min Kingston BR*). *Tel*: 01-549 8383. *Open* (all branches): Mon to Sat 10am to 6pm. Late night Thurs 8pm. Sun viewing 11am to 6pm. Kingston open 9.30am. Sofas, armchairs, sofa-

3/Sofabeds

beds, over two floors, with section for leather. Attractive settings with soft furnishings/accessories. Reasonable prices. Stock lines immediate delivery. Orders from 2 weeks. Brochures. *Mail order.*

Spadesbourne 59 High Street, Ruislip, Middx HA4 7BD. (*3 mins Ruislip tube*). *Tel*: 0895 630577. *Open* (both branches): Mon to Sat 10am to 5.30pm. Sun 11am to 4pm. Made-to-measure upholstery from firm's Leamington Spa workshops. Sofas, chairs, sofabeds, corner units, 6 to 8 weeks. 8,000 fabrics. Some showroom models off the floor. Brochures/enquiries: 0926 882881.
Also at: 26/30 London Road, Twickenham, Middx TW1 3RR. (*2 mins Twickenham BR*). *Tel*: 01-891 5344.

Wesley-Barrell 2 Market Street, Watford WD1 7AD. *Tel*: 0923 229825. See London Postal Districts above.

Home Counties/S.East

Delcor Furniture 50 High Street, Tunbridge Wells, Kent TN1 1XF. *Tel*: 0892 47233. *Open* (both branches): Mon to Sat 9.30am to 5.30pm.
Also at: 10/12 Market Street, Guildford, Surrey GU1 4LB. *Tel*: 0483 570171. See London Postal Districts above.

Multiyork 16 St Christopher Place, St Albans, Herts AL3 5DG. *Tel*: 0727 38588.
Also at: Unit 2, Safeway Complex, Grove Road, Sutton, Surrey. *Tel*: 01-643 3242.
And at: 66/68 Church Street, Weybridge, Surrey. *Tel*: 0932 859390.
And at: Wickes Development, Weldale Street, Reading, Berks. *Tel*: 0734 583052.
And at: 1 Villa Road, Stanway, Colchester, Essex CO3 5RH. *Tel*: 0206 42007.
See London Postal Districts above.

The Old Bakery Punnetts Town, Nr Heathfield, East Sussex TN21 9DS. (*About 2 miles from Heathfield on B2096*). *Tel*: 0435 830608. *Open*: Mon to Fri 9am to 5pm. Sat 9am to 4pm.

Converted Victorian workshops. Antique chairs/sofas restored or ready for restoration by traditional methods. Handbuilt English sofas/adaptable sizes/styles. Friendly professional design advice. Fabrics, wallpapers. Made-to-measure soft furnishings.

Omega Furniture Delamare Road, Cheshunt, Herts EN8 9TF. *Tel*: 0992 26686.
And at: 21 High Street, Old Town, Stevenage. *Tel*: 0438 722412. See London Postal Districts above.

Sofas and Sofabeds 58 Western Road, Hove, East Sussex BN4 1JD. *Tel*: 0273 736003. *Open*: Mon to Sat 10am to 5pm. Sun viewing 12 noon to 5pm (phone first).

Sofa Workshop The Great Hall, Mount Pleasant Road, Tunbridge Wells, Kent. (*Opposite Tunbridge Wells BR; park at rear*). *Tel*: 0892 34381. *Open*: Mon to Sat 9am to 5.30pm. See London Postal Districts above.

Spadesbourne Wheatsheaf House, Tunsgate, Guildford, Surrey GU1 3QT. *Tel*: 0483 506445. *Open* (both branches): Mon to Sat 10am to 5.30pm. Sun 11am to 4pm.
Also at: The Bishop Centre, Bath Road, Taplow, Maidenhead, Berks SL6 0NY. *Tel*: 06286 67530. See London Postal Districts, above.

Tulleys of Chelsea 1 Ward Street, off North Street, Guildford. *Tel*: 0483 64643. *Open*: Mon to Sat 9am to 5.30pm. Closed 1pm to 2pm. See London Postal Districts above.

Wesley-Barrell 33 High Street, Tunbridge Wells, TN1 1XL. *Tel*: 0892 36286. No late night.
Also at: 12 Parsons Street, Banbury, OX16 8LW. *Tel*: 0295 51971.
And at: 73 North Street, Guildford, Surrey GU1 4AW. *Tel*: 0483 37717.
And at: 3/11 Bridge Street, Witney, Oxon OX8 6BY. *Tel*: 0993 776682. See London Postal Districts above.

Mail Order

Chesterfields Unit 1, 139a London Road, Shardlow, Derbyshire DE7 2HA. *Tel*: 0332 792575. Handmade chesterfields, wing/club chairs, suites, traditional deep-button styles, using whole skin leathers, not "stitched-up" pieces. Plain/antiqued finishes. Hardwood frames, fully-sprung seat platforms/arms. Colour brochure.

Kirkdale Mail Order Gwalia Works, Factory Road, Brynmawr, Gwent NP3 4DP. *Tel*: 0494 311147. Brochure/fabric samples. Classic/modern upholstery.

Worth a Trip

A Barn Full of Sofas and Chairs Furnace Mill, Lamberhurst, Kent. *Tel*: 0892 890285. *Open*: Thurs to Sat 10am to 5pm. Sun viewing 10am to 12.30pm. Or by appointment. Trading over 15 years. Sally Symons packs old 3-storey mill with antique, period and good second-hand furniture. Original Victorian/Edwardian selections. 3-piece suites, 2-/3-seater sofas, chaises longues, spoon back/iron frame chairs, dining/wing/easy chairs. Good range fabrics for reupholstery/loose cover service. Or buy as are, for reupholstering yourself.

3/SOFABEDS

Many upholstery firms listed above also offer sofabeds. Sofabeds for regular use must provide a proper sleeping surface. Check converting mechanisms for ease of use/durability. Think where you will store bedding. See also 2/Upholstery above, and Bedrooms 11/Futons.

London Postal Districts

Estia 5/7 Tottenham Street, W1P 9PB. (*5 mins Goodge Street tube*). *Tel*: 01-636 5957 (24 hours). *Open*: Mon to Sat 10am to 6pm. Late night Thurs 7.30pm. Ingenious fire-retardant foam flip-over designs for chairs/sofas/corner units which turn into beds. Catalogue. *Mail order.*

3F Functional Furniture Factory 23/27 Pancras Road, NW1 2QB. (*2 mins King's Cross tube*). *Tel*: 01-833 3945. *Open*: Mon to Sat 10am to 6pm. Chunky good-looking sofabeds, your fabric or theirs. Home assembly if access is restricted. Five-year guarantee. Stain-protection service. Also pine beds, handmade mattresses. Futons.
Also at: 149 St John's Hill, SW11 1TQ. (*5 mins Clapham Junction BR*). *Tel*: 01-924 2517. *Open*: Tues to Sat 10am to 5.30pm.
And at: 56 Chalk Farm Road, NW1 8AN. (*4 mins Chalk Farm tube*). *Tel*: 01-485 1000. *Open*: Wed to Sun 11am to 5.30pm.

London Sofa-Bed Centre 185 Tottenham Court Road, W1P 9LE. (*5 mins Warren Street tube*). *Tel*: 01-631 1424. *Open*: Mon to Sat 9.30am to 6pm. Late night Thurs 7.30pm. Over 300 designs for immediate delivery, or made-to-order (6 to 8 weeks). Durable, comfortable wooden slats to support mattress.
Also at: 236 Fulham Road SW10. (*South Kensington tube plus bus*). *Tel*: 01-352 1358. *Open*: Mon to Sat 10am to 6pm.

Simply Sofa Beds 130 Notting Hill Gate, W11 3PG. (*3 mins Notting Hill Gate tube*). *Tel*: 01-221 1816. *Open* (both branches): Mon to Sat 10am to 6pm. Late night Thurs 8pm. Sun viewing 11am to 6pm.
Also at: 258/260 Lavender Hill, SW11 1LJ. *Tel*: 01-228 4588.

The Sofabed Shop 43a Colney Hatch Lane, Muswell Hill N10 1LJ. (*Highgate tube plus bus*). *Tel*: 01-444 7463. *Open* (all branches): Mon to Sat 10am to 6pm. Late nights Thurs & Fri 8pm. Sun viewing 11am to 6pm. Over 100 models, many for immediate delivery. Special shapes/sizes to order (6 to 8 weeks). Well-arranged showrooms.

West One Sofabeds 14 Golden Square, W1R 3AG. (*2 mins Piccadilly Circus tube*). *Tel*: 01-439 1065. *Open*: Mon to Fri 10am to 6pm. Sat 10am to 1pm. Chair/sofabeds, for regular or guest use. Good fabric choice, or supply your own. Some models from

stock; orders 6 to 8 weeks.

Outer Ring

Dreams Head office/enquiries: *Tel*: 0494 461146. Claim largest selection sofabeds in the country! Huge choice styles. Occasional or regular use. "Guaranteed lowest prices". 7 day trading. Interest free credit. Nationwide deliveries. Also trading as The Sofa-Bed Centre.

The Sofa-Bed Centre 14/15 New Broadway, Uxbridge Road, Hillingdon, Middx UB10 0LJ. *Tel*: 0895 53666. *Open*: Mon to Sat 9am to 5.30pm. Sun viewing 11am to 4.30pm.
And at: Thames Seating, 5/7 Hercies Road, Hillingdon, Middx UB10 9LS. *Tel*: 0895 56096. *Open*: Mon to Sat 9am to 5.30pm. Sun viewing 11am to 4.30pm.

The Sofabed Shop 100 Tolworth Broadway, Tolworth, Surrey KT6 7JD. *Tel*: 01-390 0775. See London Postal Districts above.

Home Counties/S.East

Dreams 156/158 Cowley Road, Oxford. *Tel*: 0865 792555. *Open*: Mon to Wed 10am to 6pm. Late nights Thurs & Fri 8pm. Sun viewing 11am to 5pm.
Also at: The Sofa-Bed Centre, 22/24 Watling Street, Bletchley, Milton Keynes, MK2 2BL. *Tel*: 0908 78557. *Open*: Mon to Sat 9am to 5.30pm. Sun viewing 11am to 4.30pm.
And at: The Sofa-Bed Centre, 20 Hosier Street, Reading, Berks RG1 7JL. *Tel*: 0734 393555. *Open*: Mon to Sat 9am to 5.30pm. Sun viewing 11am to 4.30pm. See Outer Ring above.

The Sofabed Shop 182 Hornchurch Road, Hornchurch, Essex RN11 1QL. *Tel*: 04024 45555. See London Postal Districts above.

4/STORAGE & SHELVING

Shop for DIY shelving at **DIY Superstores** *and* **Home Improvement Specialists**. *Find freestanding furniture at*

Furniture shops, **Interior Design** *firms, and* **Furnishing Stores**. *Also listed below are firms that can help with custom-made built-in units.*

London Postal Districts

CubeStore 58 Pembroke Road, W8. (*5 mins Earls Court tube*). *Tel*: 01-994 6016 (24 hours). *Open*: Tues Wed Fri 10am to 4pm. Thurs 10am to 7pm. Sat 10am to 5pm. First tentative cube in 1964 has grown into comprehensive range of cupboards, cubes, drawer units, wardrobes, record storage, etc. For home, office, studio. Finishes include plain chipboard, white/grey melamine, beech veneer. Colour brochure. *Mail order*.

Estia See **3/Sofabeds** above. Adjustable wall shelving with tubular frames and melamine-faced shelves. Wide range of sizes.

Charles Hurst Workshop Unit 21, Bow Triangle Business Centre, Eleanor Street, E3 4NP. *Tel*: 01-981 8562. *Open*: by appointment. Bespoke cabinetry: fitted/freestanding. Designed/made/installed.

The London Alcove 103 Lavender Hill, Battersea SW11 5QL. (*10 mins Clapham Junction BR*). *Tel*: 01-585 1481. *Open*: Mon to Sat 9.30am to 5.30pm. Built-in alcove cupboards/shelving. Choice of styles and finishes. Fitted in one day. Colour brochure. Design/install.

Michel & Polgar 41 Blandford Street W1H 3AE. (*5 mins Baker Street tube*). *Tel*: 01-935 9629. *Open*: Mon to Fri 9am to 5pm. Sat 9am to 1pm. Ladderax (on market 25 years) storage/shelving specialists. Majority parts available instantly. Brochure.

Shelfstore 160 Finchley Road, NW3 5HH. (*2 mins Finchley Road tube*). *Tel*: 01-794 0313. *Open*: Mon to Sat 10am to 6pm. Scandinavian storage/shelving systems. Attractive solid woods. Wardrobes (plus accessories): made-to-measure shelving. Free leaflets. *Mail order*.

Shelvex *Tel*: 06285 22476. Home

5 / Diningroom Furniture

visits by appointment. Established 14 years. Made-to-measure shelving, display units for books, TV, hi-fi, computers. Fitted in alcoves or along walls. Wood finishes or white. Design/install.

Themesetter 1/3 Becket Road, Montagu Industrial Estate, Montagu Road, N18. (*Off North Circular*). *Tel*: 01-803 8330 (24 hours). *Open*: Mon to Fri 9.30am to 5pm. Sat 10am to 4pm. Sun viewing 10.30am to 1pm. Make/display fitted storage for living/dining rooms. Mahogany, teak, oak, lacquers any colour. Design/install. Brochures.

Outer Ring

Hyperion Fitted Furniture 166 Oatlands Drive, Weybridge, Surrey KT13 9ET. *Tel*: 0932 844783. *Open*: Mon to Sat 9.30am to 5.30pm. Freestanding bookcases, wall-hunt storage units, panelling, study/corner units. Teak, rosewood, oak, walnut, mahogany. Colour brochure.

Marble Hill Fireplaces See **Heating 2/Fireplaces**. Storage and breakfront bookcases made-to-measure.

Stylus Furniture Pegwyn, The Green, Hampton Court, Surrey KT8 9BP. *Tel*: 01-979 1008. Made-to-measure storage/shelving: small alcove or whole wall. Mahogany, oak, colours. Home visits with samples, to measure/plan.

Upstairs Downstairs The Old Bakery, rear of 404 Staines Road, Bedfont, Middx. *Tel*: 01-890 8813. Design/make/install fitted storage furniture for living room, office, bedroom. To fit any space, wide range finishes.

Home Counties/S.East

Hyperion Fitted Furniture 71 Market Street, Watford, Herts WD1 7AG. *Tel*: 0923 243298. See Outer Ring above. *Mail order*.

Mail Order

G&B Shelving Progress Road, Whitewalls Industrial Estate, Nelson, Lancs. *Tel*: 0282 63757/695014. Industrial plastic-coated steel shelving, variety heights/depths. Genuine high-tech!

5/DININGROOM FURNITURE

"It's your party: you can do as you want to. Maybe you've invested in haut couture and haute cuisine so make sure your furniture lives up to it." **Bill Blake**, *Public Relations Consultant to the Furniture Industry for over 20 years.*

Besides listings below, find selections at **Furniture** *shops,* **Furnishing Stores,** *and* **Department Stores**.

London Postal Districts

Adeptus See **Furniture 1/General**. Sleek modern shapes for Italian dining furniture in glossy lacquers and natural ash.

Astrohome See **Furniture 1/General**. Home of high tech: essential for furniture fashion devotees. Go café continental with Spanish silver aluminium Casa collection. Textured burnished stainless steel table tops, round/rectangular. Arm/dining chairs in polished silver aluminium tube. Grey/blask plastic-coated nylon cord for seats/back (weather-resistant); or natural wicker. Good selections other dining chairs. Canvas/leather cantilever designs copy modern classics. Sculptural Costes Café chair in black bent lacquered plywood. Top pop is light-weight stackable Noodle, black tube/black plastic wire.

Bonomi Designs London House, 100 New King's Road, SW6. New shop opening shortly. (*10 mins Putney Bridge tube*). *Tel* (mobile): 0836 699983. *Open*: by appointment. Sharp, classy no-frills affordable café furniture. Domestic/contract, designed by Andrew Hilton/Paul Newman, art school graduates. Dining chairs: slatted seats in natural English ash; steel frames, metallic finishes/any BS colour. Rectangular cast-aluminium glass-topped tables. Matching bar stools. To order: 6 weeks.

The Dining Room Shop 62/64 White Hart Lane, Barnes, SW13. (*Hammersmith tube plus bus*). *Tel*: 01-878 1020. *Open*: Mon to Sat 10am to 5.30pm. Around 75% is antique: furniture, glass, china: everything for the dining room. Services: furniture finding, repro and modern, furniture made to measure; dinner services to customer's designs.

Estia See **3/Sofabeds** above. Choice of 5 rectangular and 4 circular melamine tabletops, supported by metal pedestals, trestles or legs. Tubular-framed chairs with canvas seats to match.

Glass Distinction See **Furniture 7/Glass & Marble**. Dining/console/side tables, sideboards; made-to-measure, high density fibreboard. Any colour lacquer, speckled/satin.

Kodama Woodwork 203 Avro House, Havelock Terrace, SW8 4AS. *Tel*: 01-627 0210. *Open*: by appointment. Designer made-to-measure tables/sideboards in solid hardwoods/specialist veneers/coloured lacquers. Distinctive shapes/detailing.

Meuble Espanol See **Ethnic**. Distinctive carved Spanish dining designs, limed (white, grainy) finish.

Tempus Stet See **Lighting 2/Traditional**. Massive Corinthian columns in cast resin support square/rectangular/octagonal tops. Also simple classical circular designs.

Home Counties/S.East

British Antique Interiors School Close, Queen Elizabeth Avenue, Burgess Hill, near Brighton. (*5 mins Burgess Hill BR*). *Tel*: 04446 45577. *Open*: Mon to Fri 9am to 5.30pm. Closed lunch 1 to 2pm. Antique/reproduction dining furniture: 18th, 19th, 20th centuries.

Fowler and Brace The Workshop Castle, Ditch Lane, East Sussex, Lewes, East Sussex BN7 1YJ. *Tel*: 0273 479680. *Open*: by appointment. Elegant designer tables in finely-worked hardwoods/lacquers, to order.

Mail Order

Deutschland Direkt Furnishing Horns Oak Farm, Horns Oak Road, Meopham, Kent. *Tel*: 0836 225388/ 0474 813981. Brochure. Traditional German corner-bench wooden dining units.

Oak Design See **Kitchens 3/Accessories**. Simple modern-styled tables from USA. Oblong, circular, extension models. Seating 2 to 14. Custom finishes, including limed oak.

United Systems Clipfix Unit 5, Bath Place, Royal Leamington Spa CV31 3AQ. *Tel*: 0926 450815. Clip together in seconds trestles to support table tops for extra guests. Easily dismantled.

6/OCCASIONAL FURNITURE

A low coffee table can make a dramatic focal point for your livingroom. Here are some more unusual ideas, with more in **Furniture 11/Designer**. *Besides listings below, consult* **Interior Design, Furniture, Antiques, Furnishing Stores**.

London Postal Districts

Adeptus See **Furniture 1/General**. Sculptural shapes for clear acrylic coffee tables; shiny brass frames.

Atrium See **Furniture 7/Glass & Marble**. Coffee table with glass tops on black marble bases.

Brandt Oriental Antiques 771 Fulham Road, SW6 7HD. *Tel*: 01-731 6835. *Open*: Mon to Fri 10am to 6pm. Sat 10am to 4pm. Low tables made by craftsmen; copies of 18th-century designs from temples of Northern Thailand. Traditional English woods: oak, ash, cherry, walnut, or colour lacquers. Height 14½ in; tops any size to order.

Glass Distinction See **Furniture 7/Glass & Marble**. Glass coffee tables made to order in any size/shape. Also made-to-measure designs in high density fibreboard sprayed in tough lacquer, speckled or satin, any colour.

Charlie Meaker 25 Randolph Crescent, W9. *Tel*: 01-286 8024. *Open*: by appointment. Handmade glass for table tops, decorative accessories, and unique coloured art glass. Charlie's art glass is collectable and found in numerous public museums.

Meubles d'Art 127 Fernhead Road, W9 3ED. *Tel*: 01-968 4552. *Open*: by appointment. Marlon Hayes (furniture designer) and Kathy Dalwood (fine art) have translated Cubist-style paintings into wonderful and a little weird tables wrapped round with vibrant images. Functional, surprising, sometimes bizarre.

The Mosaic Studio See **Accessories 3/Mirrors**. Handmade table tops in glass mosaic; to commission in colours to suit your room.

Tempus Stet See **Lighting 2/Traditional**. Delicate console/side tables in classic styles inspired by England's great country houses. Low coffee table on chunky Corinthian column with glass top.

Home Counties/S.East

Cardavia Terrarium Tables Sceptre House, 57 The Hundred, Romsey, Hants SO15 8BZ. (*Romsey BR*). Tel: 0794 830222. *Open*: Mon to Fri 9am to 5pm. Elegant wood-framed coffee tables. Glass panels enclose miniature indoor terrarium garden.

Nicholas Dyson Furniture Unit 2, Home Farm, Ardington, Wantage, Oxon OX12 8PN. *Tel*: 0235 834311. *Open*: by appointment. Intricate veneer/inlay techniques for modern designer tables. Exotic woods/extravagant shapes.

Mail Order

Grandisson See **Doors 1/Front & Interior**. Coffee/lamp tables in highly original forms. Rose table in white limed finish; carved flower cluster supports circular glass top. Oriental Chippendale is bold and square with corner column clusters. Simpler Valencia features 4 arching scrolls under circular glass.

7/CHINA, GLASS & CUTLERY

"The making of china and glass represent two of Man's oldest crafts. The finest works in these two materials achieve an aesthetic excellence that is unrivalled in human artefacts. There has never been a wider choice of products available to the consumer than today. In England you can buy china and glass from at least 10 European countries and also many countries in the Far East. The choice can be from a simple well-designed 20-piece starter set in Habitat for £20 to a Royal Copenhagen's Flora Danica dinner set at Thomas Goode for thousands of pounds. The same choice exists in glass from excellently designed and extraordinarily cheap automated glass to the finest crystal from firms like Baccarat and Dartington. For those who do not want industrially made products there are works to be had from excellent craftsmen. Sometimes these works are not as expensive as would be imagined. To live with beautiful china and glass is always a pleasure. Fine wine must be drunk from a good glass but even plonk tastes better. Food is appreciated by the eyes as well as the taste buds. My preference is towards simplicity: white china, uncut glass, quality materials, lead crystal, bone china and porcelain. It is interesting to reflect that the cost of four servings of smoked salmon will buy you a beautiful bone china plate and a crystal glass costs only the same as two or three bottles of modest wine." **David Queensberry,** *former Professor of Ceramics & Glass, Royal College of Art, and partner of Queensberry Hunt design group.*

Well-known are larger china store groups with comprehensive selections. **Department Stores** *are also fruitful sources and many have 'concessions' with stock/service controlled by big-name manufacturers. Below, extra inspiration. See also* **Antiques, Fine Art, Crafts** *and* **Kitchens 9/Kitchenware**.

7/ China, Glass & Cutlery

London Postal Districts

Astrohome See **Furniture 1/General** International café-style table/kitchenware. Lots of chrome. Unusual plastics.

Ceramica Blue 117 Clarendon Road, W11. (*10 mins Holland Park/Ladbroke Grove tubes*). *Tel*: 01-727 0288. *Open*: Tues to Sat 10.30am to 6.30pm. Modern Italian ceramics. Handmade handpainted English plates, vases, tiles etc. Practical/decorative; unusual, bold colours. Commissions.

Divertimenti See **Kitchens 3/Kitchenware**. Wide range cutlery/tableware. Mainly Italian/French charming provincial patterns; handdecorated modern/traditional designs. Good for large bowls/platters.

Garrard 112 Regent Street, W1A 2JJ. (*5 mins Oxford Circus/Piccadilly Circus tubes*). *Tel*: 01-734 7020. *Open*: Mon to Fri 9am to 5.30pm. Sat 9.30am to 5pm. Another glittering Central London haunt of Royals and lesser folk hunting cutlery, antiques/modern silver, classy gifts. Catalogue. Commissions. Free deliveries Central London. *Mail order*.

Gered Wedgwood 173/174 Piccadilly, W1V 0PD. (*5 mins Green Park/Piccadilly tubes*). *Tel*: 01-629 2614. *Open*: Mon to Fri 9am to 6pm. Sat 9am to 4pm. Spacious one-floor showroom for top table makes: Worcester, Spode, Wedgwood, Coalport, Masons, Doulton, Minton, Derby. Also glass: Edinburgh, Stuart, Brierly. Catalogue.

Thomas Goode & Co 19 South Audley Street, W1Y 6BN. (*2 mins Bond Street tube*). *Tel*: 01-499 2823. *Open*: Mon to Sat 9.30am to 5.30pm. Possibly grandest of posh tableware shops in W1. Fine china, glass and silver-plated tableware. Browsing is inspirational. Antecedents are impeccable: wealthy Mayfair cognoscenti have been shopping here since 1827. Now an international and frequently royal clientele beat a path to their door, for their claim to be "the most famous china and glass retailer in the world" has a great deal of credibility. The exotic pair of Minton elephants that grace the façade are tourist landmarks. Nevertheless, atmosphere is not intimidating. Still independent family concern (5th generation) with courteous, knowledgeable, friendly staff: "we call it service". Royal Doulton, Herend, Minton, Royal Crown Derby, Wedgwood, Royal Worcester, Spode, etc. From cosy willow pattern to finest, thinnest gilded bone. Plus crystal from Baccarat, Crystal de Sèvres, Royal Brierly, Waterford, Stuart. Goodewse Cumberland: superbly simple quality plain tumblers/wine glasses. Silverware: coffee/teapots, covered vegetable dishes, jugs, bowls, champagne buckets, coasters, hotplates, napkin rings, nutcrackers. Silver-plated cutlery holder keeps 24 pieces easily accessible. Classic cutlery in sterling silver and silver plate. Accessories/gifts. Awash with royal warrants. Goode's execute commissions for crests/monograms. Antique/modern ornaments/plates/vases. Lavish colour catalogue. Deliveries, Engraving service. Glass repairs.

Graham & Green See **Accessories 10/General**. Good selections attractive tableware at reasonable prices, including plain/decorated ranges from Poland.

Ikea See **Furnishing Stores**. Well worth braving crowds (try and shop off-peak) for rock-bottom prices. Plain no-nonsense shapes/patterns for chinaware: e.g. white glazed chunky stoneware, dishwasher/microwave safe. Stainless steel simple modern cutlery. Good choice of glasses, including party packs. Glazed flintware plates/bowls in bright shades with designer feel. Imaginative plastics.

Mappin & Webb 170 Regent Street, W1R 6BQ. (*5 mins Piccadilly Circus tube*). *Tel*: 01-734 3801. Major name in London's table talk. Silver specialists. International reputation. History dates back to Jonathan Mappin's small Sheffield workshop. Mappin Plate classic designs such as gadroon/capstan for bowls, dishes, cruets, condiment sets, candlesticks, grape scissors, sauce boats, sugar dredgers. Holloware sterling silver/Mappin Plate tea/coffee sets with elegant matching trays. Classic plated or solid silver cutlery individually or in 7-piece place settings; designs from simple Rattail to ultra-ornate Russell. Stag horn meat carvers. Watches/clocks. Jewellery with custom design workshop. Repairs/cleaning/restorations. Colour gift catalogue. Expert valuations. Special commissions for china/porcelain, silver, glass. Crystal engraving. Gift vouchers. Wedding service. New personal stationery service.
Also at: 65 Brompton Road, Knightsbridge, SW3 1DB. (*5 mins Knightsbridge tube*). *Tel*: 01-584 9361.
And at: 2 Queen Victoria Street, EC4N 4TL. *Tel*: 01-248 6661.
And at: 125/6 Fenchurch Street, EC3 5DL. *Tel*: 01-626 3171.

Molino Coffee Shop 16 Leeland Road, West Ealing, W13 9HH. (*Just off West Ealing Broadway*). *Tel*: 01-567 2853. *Open*: Mon to Sat 9am to 5.30pm. Excellent coffee! Emilia Castro also stocks wide range of Italian coffee machines, plus all sizes French cafetières and Bistro green/gold china.

The Reject China Shop 33/35 Beauchamp Place, SW3 1NU. (*10 mins Knightsbridge tube*). *Tel*: 01-581 0737. *Open*: Mon to Sat 9am to 6pm. Late night Wed 7pm. This stylish tableware shop started years ago with seconds; but now stock is first quality fine china/crystal at good prices through bulk buying. Still some seconds worth hunting down.
Also at: 134 Regent Street, W1. (*5 mins Oxford Circus tube*). *Tel*: 01-434 2502. *Open*: Mon to Sat 9am to 6pm. Late night Thurs 8pm.
And at: 74 Southampton Row, WC1. (*5 mins Holborn tube*). *Tel*: 01-242 3271. *Open*: Mon to Fri 9am to 6pm. Late night Thurs 7pm. Sat 9am to 5.30pm.

Rosenthal Studio House 102 Brompton Road, SW3 1JJ. (*5 mins Knightsbridge tube*). *Tel*: 01-584 0683. *Open*: Mon to Sat 9am to 6pm. Late night Wed 7pm. Quality modern china, glass, crystal, cutlery and silver plate, with some furniture.

Also at: Wilson & Gill, 136 Regent Street, W1R 8ND. *Tel*: 01-734 3076.

The Tea House 15a Neal Street, WC2H 9PU. (*3 mins Covent Garden tube*). *Tel*: 01-240 7539. *Open*: Mon to Sat 10am to 7pm. Over 200 teapots from traditional/antique to unusual or even bizarre. Trays, tea infusers, caddies, mugs, strainers, stirrers, cosies, milk jugs, jumbo cups and saucers. Many pots escape tea table to become collector's items.

Villeroy & Boch 155 Regent Street, W1R 7FD. (*5 mins Oxford Circus/Piccadilly Circus tubes*). *Tel*: 01-434 0249. *Open*: Mon to Sat 9.30am to 6pm. Late night Thurs 7pm. Distinctive decorated china from Luxembourg. Fresh modern feel contrasts with rich traditional colours/styles of Regent Street tableware neighbours. Expensive but eminently covetable. Even gold patterns are overglazed for dishwashers. Crystal/cutlery. Gift wrapping. Leaflets. Wedding lists. *Mail order*.

Outer Ring

Ashton House 181B High Street, Hampton Hill, Middx TW12 1NS. *Tel*: 01-979 0027. *Open*: Mon to Sat 9am to 5.30pm. Pretty shop overflowing with china, glass, table linen, cookware. Also stationery/gifts. Helpful staff. Gift wrapping.

Obsidan 17 Broad Street, Teddington, Middx TW11 8QZ. (*10 mins Teddington BR*). *Tel*: 01-977 9332. *Open*: Mon to Sat 9.30am to 6pm. Quality china/glass; varied stock/prices. Aynsley, Royal Doulton, Lladro, Swarouski, Villeroy & Boch. Gift wrapping. Wedding lists.

Worth a Trip

Carrington Interiors 23 Market Street, Cambridge CB2 3NS. *Tel*: 0223 62106. *Open*: Mon to Sat 9am to 5.30pm. Extensive tableware, plus full interior design samples/service. Basement coffee house: snacks/meals. Favourite meeting place, with waiter service from directors.

Mail Order

Lace Lady Fiddlebridge Centre, Unit 4, Lemsford Road, Hatfield, Herts AL10 0DE. *Tel*: 07072 75966. Catalogue. Affordable selections exquisite lace/embroidered table linens.

8/DESIGNER TABLEWARE

We have had designer jeans, designer perfume and designer bedlinens, but most of these products are in fact made for the mass market with the designer's name as a promotional tag. Below I list just a few of the many studios around London who can supply designer tableware which is truly designer in that each piece is unique.

Authentics See **Furniture 1/General**. 20th-century tableware classics including the Swid Powell Collection designed by international architects.

Beryl Sedgwick 14 Fabyc House, Cumberland Road, Richmond, Surrey TW9 3HH. *Tel*: 01-948 5804. *Open*: by appointment. Painted bowls/jugs/teapots in bolt bright under-glaze designs. Tea sets to order.

Golden Section Studio 24, 90 Lots Road, Chelsea SW10 0QA. Entrance in Overdale Road). *Tel*: 01-351 9567. Stylish tableware direct from designers' studio, including innovative screen-printed mats to set off designer tables (see **Furniture 11/Designer Furniture**).

Lisa Katzenstein 17 Belsize Park Gardens, NW3 4JG. *Tel*: 01-722 5795. *Open*: by appointment. Slipcast tableware.

Andy Lloyd South Hill Park Arts Centre, Bracknell, Berks, RG12 4PA. *Tel*: 0344 427272. *Open*: by appointment. Domestic pottery.

Mac Products 44 St. Mark's Rise, E8 2NL. *Tel*: 01-254 5928. *Open*: by appointment. Exciting ultra-modern designs on bone china tableware. Screen-printed/handpainted.

Derek Northfield Ceramics 7 Laburnham Road, Epsom, Surrey KT18 5DT. *Tel*: 03727 23908. *Open*: by appointment. Striking/functional tableware. Cup and saucer, creamer, sugar, breakfast plate, dinner plate and water jug.

Timney Fowler See **Soft Furnishings 8/Designer Fabrics**. Black-and-white ceramics with striking classical motifs.

Rob Turner 2 Taymount Grange, Taymount Rise, SE23 3UH. *Tel*: 01-291 6515. *Open*: by appointment. Bone china tableware. Pretty all-over floral design and wonderful lustre.

Prue Venables 7 Windus Road, N16 6UT. *Tel*: 01-806 2591 or 01-806 1872. *Open*: by appointment. Hand-thrown/turned functional ceramics. Lively patterns using coloured slips/underglaze colours.

Deborah Windsor 18 Portobello Green, W10 5TD. *Tel*: 01-968 5800. *Open*: by appointment. Classic porcelain tableware, decorated with colourful handpainted designs. Images of sun/moon, amusing fishes, leaves/flowers, painted with a watercolour effect. Slipcast miniature urns/vases. Commemorative pieces, dinner services, mosaic panels, tile murals.

BEDROOMS

Beds are really pretty boring – except when you are tired and long for the fine crisp white cotton and the super spring interior, or when you are feeling rotten with aching limbs and a throbbing head, or when your sexual fantasies are about to come true, or when you haven't got one! Beds aren't really all that boring at all!

1/SPECIALISTS

See also: **Furniture Stores, Interior Design, Soft Furnishings, Floors, Lighting, Accessories.**

London Postal Districts

Domain 42 Newman Street, W1P 3PA. (*8 mins Goodge Street tube*). *Tel*: 01-255 3264. *Open*: Mon to Sat 9.30am to 5pm. The Living Bedroom Centre for B&B Italia stylish lacquered beds; plus sheets, duvets, quilts, bedspreads.

Duxiana 46 George Street, W1H 5RE. (*5 mins Baker Street tube*). *Tel*: 01-486 2363. *Open*: Mon to Fri 10am to 6pm. Sat 10am to 5pm. Ultra-stylish Swedish bedrooms; slim-line Dux beds, with double-layer springs for firm but resilient support; cotton-wadding mattresses. All-cotton bed linens: choice of 20 colours. Down-filled pillows/duvets. Headboards include upholstered/lacquered cane. Bedside tables match overall scheme. Wardrobes: black/chrome frames or choice of 3 woods. Doors lacquered in colours. Leaflet.

Hulsta 22 Bruton Street, W1X 7DA. (*5 mins Green Park tube*). *Tel*: 01-629 4881. *Open*: Mon to Fri 9am to 5pm. German modern fitted furniture/beds. Also living/dining rooms. Wood veneers/lacquers. Sophisti-cated, flexible high quality systems. You can also find Hulsta Studios at the following stores in Greater London and the Home Counties:
EKO Furnishings 130/132 Fortress Road, NW5 2HP. *Tel*: 01-485 2735.
Also at: 100 South Street, Romford, Essex. *Tel*: 0708 767811.
And at: **Harrods**. See **Department Stores**.
And at: **Heals**, W1; Guildford; Kingston-on-Thames; Reading. See **Furnishing Stores**.
And at: **CH Furniture**, 19/20 North Street, Guildford, Surrey. *Tel*: 0483 573405.
And at: **Charles Page**, NW1; Brighton. See **Furnishing Stores**.
And at: **Clement Joscelyne**, Bury St Edmunds. See **Furnishing Stores**.
And at: **Stockwell & Oxford**, Croydon; Sutton. See **Furnishing Stores**.

Master Bedrooms 39 Burnt Ash Hill, Lee SE12 9JQ. (*2 mins Lee BR*). *Tel*: 01-851 5533. *Open*: Tues to Sat 9.30am to 5.30pm. Mon to 3pm. Everything for the bedroom from own nearby workshops. Friendly unpressurised design advice. Fitted wardrobes. Matching stools, chairs, ottomans, headboards, chaises longues in velvets, moires or your own fabrics. 11 finishes, hundreds of mouldings. Window seats. Fitted dressing tables.

Home Counties/S.East

Domain 89 High Street, Esher, Surrey KT10 9QA. (*15 mins Esher BR*). *Tel*: 0372 68189. *Open*: Mon to Sat 9am to 6pm. See London Postal Districts above.

2/BEDS

"You can't see for yourself the damage normal wear and tear does to your bed, so give your bed a deadline. If it's more than ten years old, it's time for it to go. For a healthier life after a healthier night, choose a good new bed that's right for you on the basis of expert advice, comfort and support – not price." **Patrick Quigley**, *chief executive, National Bed Federation.*

The golden rule: lie before you buy! Quality is essential. Buy the best, even if you must arrange credit. Try out selections at **Furnishing Stores** *and* **Department Stores.**

London Postal Districts

Beaumont Beds 238/240 Lewisham High Street, Lewisham SE13 6JU. (*10 mins Lewisham BR; plentiful parking*). *Tel*: 01-852 4515. *Open*: Mon to Sat 9.30am to 6pm. Good stocks/same day or 24-hour deliveries. Mattresses/divans sold separately. Custom-made beds. Special/odd sizes. Brass/pine. Experienced advice.

Beds Beds Beds 629 Market Place, Kingston-upon-Thames KT1 1JT.

(*Kingston BR*). *Tel*: 01-549 0111. *Open*: Mon to Fri 9am to 5.30pm. Sun 9am to 6pm. Price promise plus guaranteed delivery from stock of all well-known makes: Vi Spring, Dunlopillo, Rest Assured, etc. Londoners will be familiar with their catchy jingle. They share their Superstore premises with pine furniture/sofa bed shops.

Bargains!

Myers Warehouse 39/49 The Broadway, Crouch End N8. (*5 mins Finsbury Park tube*). *Tel*: 01-340 9488. *Open*: Mon to Sat 9am to 5.30pm. Discounts for branded beds: Slumberland, Relyon, Myers, Sleepeezee. Orthopaedic/pine beds; king-sizes.

S & M Myers See **Floors 3/Carpets**. Government/hotel surplus beds/bedding, soft furnishings. Constantly changing stocks.

Tranquilty 162 Fortis Green Road, Muswell Hill N10 3DU. (*Highgate tube plus bus*). *Tel*: 01-883 7700. *Open*: Mon to Sat 10am to 6pm. West End quality beds/bed linens at "suburban prices". Expert advice, personal service.

Tulleys of Chelsea See **Living & Diningrooms 2/Upholstery & Suites**. Ground floor bedding department with 35 beds on show. Brass beds, pine beds, folding beds, sofabeds, bunks, storage beds, ottomans, headboards, firm beds, mattresses, mattress covers, pillows. Wide range sizes/prices; hundreds in stock for immediate delivery.

Outer Ring

Bargains!

The Bedpost 7 Station Approach, Hayes, Bromley, Kent BR2 7EQ. (*Opposite Hayes BR*). *Tel*: 01-462 5544. *Open*: Mon to Sat 9am to 5.30pm. Discount prices major brands: Relyon, Sleepeezee, Sealy, Silent Night, Myers. 2,500 sq ft; divan bases, mattresses, brass/lacquered bedsteads, headboards. From spare room models to luxurious pocket springs.

3/PINE BEDS

Mostly styles are pleasantly informal, chunky and robust; but many of the firms below offer elegant colour stains, or hardwood models.

London Postal Districts

Alphabeds 16 Broadway Market, Hackney E8 4QJ. (*10 mins Bethnal Green tube*). *Tel*: 01-249 6100. *Open*: Mon to Sat 10am to 6pm. Closed Thurs. Strong jointed bolted frames, guaranteed 15 years. Free delivery. Own make spring-interior mattresses. Illustrated price list.
Also at: 8 Foscote Mews, W9 2HH. (*2 mins Royal Oak tube*). *Tel*: 01-289 2467. *Open*: Tues to Sat 10am to 6pm.

Big Table Furniture Coop 56 Great Western Road, W9 3NT. (*1 min Westbourne Park tube*). *Tel*: 01-221 5058/ 229 6032. *Open*: Mon to Sat 10am to 6pm. Sun viewing 2pm to 5pm. Well-established maker of pine beds (despite name!). Brochure.

Litvinoff & Fawcett 9 Chalk Farm Road, NW1. (*5 mins Chalk Farm tube*). *Tel*: 01-482 0066. *Open*: 7 days 10am to 6pm. In stock: sturdy strong plain pine beds. Other designs to order; various colours/finishes. Guaranteed. Choice of handmade mattresses. Brochure with sae.

McQueen Pine 725 Garratt Lane, SW17 0PD. (*10 mins Tooting Broadway tube/Earlsfield BR*). *Tel*: 01-879 7324. *Open* (all branches): Mon to Sat 10am to 6pm. Closed Wed. Handmade solid pine beds direct from workshop. Under-bed drawers, blanket boxes, bedside tables. Any size to order. Sprung/foam mattresses. Water beds. Free illustrated leaflet. Nationwide deliveries.
Also at: 365 St John Street, EC1V 4LB. (*8 mins Angel tube*). *Tel*: 01-278 6905. *And at*: The Viaduct Workshops, St James's Lane, Muswell Hill N10 3AX. (*Highgate tube*). *Tel*: 01-883 4811.

Stokecroft 88/89 Caledonian Road, N1 9DN. (*5 mins King's Cross tube*). *Tel*: 01-278 6874. *Open*: Mon to Fri 9.30am to 5.30pm. Sat 10am to 5.30pm. Wide choice. Simple platform or box designs, or exotic Egyptian, Hollywood, Rio models. Pine or hardwoods: oak, iroko, afrormosia, mahogany. Choice of 5 handmade mattresses from foam to pocket springs: any size, available separately.

Taurus Pine Beds 333 Kilburn High Road, NW6 7QB. (*2 mins Kilburn tube*). *Tel*: 01-624 3024. *Open*: Mon to Sat 10am to 6pm. Handmade solid pine bed frames direct from workshop. Quality mattresses.

Warren Evans 1A Hawley Road, NW1. (*10 mins Camden tube*). *Tel*: 01-267 5354/6198. *Open*: Mon to Fri 9am to 7.30pm. Sat Sun 9am to 6pm. Workshop/showroom quality pine beds. Various styles/finishes. Futons, old pine furniture, orthopaedic mattresses.

Worth a Trip

Moriarti's Workshop High Halden, Nr Ashford, Kent TN26 3LY. *Tel*: 023385 214. *Open*: Mon to Sat 9am to 5pm. Master craftsman Ian de Fresnes (alias "Moriarti") masterminds country showroom/workshop: designer-maker par excellence. 38 bed styles, each in up to 8 sizes. Solid pine, slatted bases. Exclusive mattresses. Goldpine bedroom furniture. Brochure. *Mail order.*

4/SPACESAVING BEDS

*Where space is tight, beds can fold or stack; or leave them standing, but pack in extra storage. See also **Living & Diningrooms 3/Sofabeds**.*

London Postal Districts

Golden Plan 14 Golden Square, W1R 3AG. (*2 mins Piccadilly Circus tube*). *Tel*: 01-434 2066. *Open*: Mon to Fri 10am to 6pm. Sat 10am to 1pm. Beds that fold (fully made-up) flat against the wall vertically (on end) or horizontally (widthways). Firm-based with proper mattresses to take standard bedding. Five-year guaran-

Bedrooms

tee. Catalogue. *Mail order.*

James Harland Design 263 The Vale, Acton, W3 7QA. (*Customer collection service from Acton Town/Shepherd's Bush tubes*). *Tel*: 01-743 1174. *Open*: Mon to Fri 10am to 6pm. Sat 11am to 4pm. Small showroom with folding wall beds, mirrored wardrobes, fitted bedrooms. Personal service.

Rest-Rite Bedding 51/55 High Road, Willesden Green, NW10 2SX. (*2 mins Willesden Green tube*). *Tel*: 01-459 6138. *Open*: Mon to Fri 9.30am to 5pm. Half-day Thurs 12.30pm. Sat 10am to 4.30pm. Strongly-made metal beds which fold flat (vertically or horizontally) against wall complete with bedding. Spring bases/mattresses for regular use. Brochures. *Mail order.*

The Space Bed Centre 90 Lots Road, SW10 0QD. (*Earl's Court tube plus Hopper bus to Chelsea harbour*). *Tel*: 01-376 3345. *Open*: Mon to Fri 9am to 6pm. Sat 10am to 4pm. Swiss high quality counter-balanced beds that fold away neatly into lounge/bedrooms storage units. Standard styles, or any style to order. Design/install.

Mail Order

The German Bedding Centre 138 Marylebone Road, NW1 5PH. *Tel*: 01-935 0196. Callers by appointment: no displays. 7 ranges of apartment/studio furniture each containing wide range of units for maximum flexibility of arrangements. 8 finishes (laminates/veneers), 6 heights. Fold-away beds in various sizes, horizontal/vertical. Flexible slat base, adjustable headboard, built-in shelf with reading light, radio/alarm clock. Single/double sofabeds, some with built-in containers for bedlinens.

5/BRASS BEDS

Redolent of Victorian values, antiques are still plentiful; reproductions also proliferate.

London Postal Districts

And So To Bed 638/640 King's Road,

Fulham SW6 2DU. (*10 mins Fulham Broadway tube*). *Tel*: 01-731 3593. *Open*: Mon to Sat 10am to 6pm. Best known for brass beds: originals, and reproductions made in own factory. Also beautiful wooden bedsteads. Divans and mattresses. Wonderful linens (many natural fibres), bedcoverings and accessories. Interior design service.
Also at: 18/20 Baker Street, W1M 1DE. (*5 mins Baker Street tube*). *Tel*: 01-487 4460. *Open*: Mon to Sat 9.30am to 6pm.
And at: 96B Camden High Street, NW1 0LT. (*5 mins Camden Town tube*). *Tel*: 01-388 0364. *Open*: Mon to Fri 9.30am to 5.30pm. Closed Thurs. Sat 10am to 6pm.
For sumptuous free Book of the Bedroom, telephone 01-731 3593, or write 638/640 King's Road, SW6 2DU.

Brass Beds 48 Bell Street, NW1 5BU. (*2 mins Edgware Road tube*). *Tel*: 01-262 2036. *Open*: Mon to Sat 11am to 7.30pm. Antique brass/iron bedsteads; new mattresses. Also reproductions.

Dreams 34 Chalk Farm Road, NW1. *Tel*: 01-267 8107. *Open*: Mon to Fri 10.30am to 6pm. Sat and Sun 11am to 6pm. Two floors of repro/Victorian brass beds, plus modern Italian beds/accessories. Mr and Mrs Amato are brass specialists.

Home Counties/S.East

And So To Bed 5 The Pantiles, Tunbridge Wells, Kent TN1 5TZ. (*10 mins Tunbridge Wells BR*). *Tel*: 0892 515099. *Open*: Mon to Sat 9am to 5.30pm. Closed Wed. See London Postal Districts above.

Victorian Brass Bedsteads 37a Broad Street, Canterbury, Kent. (*7 mins Canterbury East BR*). *Tel*: 0227 69055. *Open*: Mon to Sat 9am to 5pm. Iron/brass antique bedsteads.

Worth a Trip

The Antique Bedstead Company The Baddow Antique Centre, The Bringy, Church Street, Great Baddow, near Chelmsford, Essex. (*A12

from London*). *Tel*: 0245 71137. *Open*: Mon to Sat 10am to 5pm. Sun viewing 12 noon to 5pm. Large selections original Victorian bedsteads, brass, black, white. Singles; or 4ft/4ft 6in/5ft widths. Good investments. Modern spring-bases/mattresses to fit. Photo sheet of current stock. Nationwide deliveries.

The Victorian Brass Bedstead Company Hoe Copse, Cocking, Sussex. (*A286 Midhurst/Chichester Road*). *Tel*: 073081 2287. *Open*: 7 days by appointment. 18th-century 60ft Sussex barn filled with hundreds of Victorian bedsteads. Full restoration service. New bed bases if required.

Mail Order

Brass Bed Manufacturing Co Jubilee House, West Street, Sowerby Bridge, West Yorks HX6 3AP. *Tel*: 0422 834457. *Showroom open*: Mon to Fri 9.30am to 5.30pm. Brochure. Traditional brass bedsteads, four-posters, half-testers, headboards. Mattresses/bedbases.

6/BEDS FOR BAD BACKS

Back pain is one of the country's most widespread and misunderstood complaints. The DHSS calculate that it costs Britain some 33.4 million working days a year. Just as important as the economic cost is the human misery it causes. It can result in people losing their jobs; it can prevent them from participating fully in family and social activities; and it can lead to chronic depression. A great deal of back pain can be prevented by education – learning to treat the body sensibly. Ensuring good posture, not becoming overweight, lifting and handling objects with care. Further attention should be given to furniture and equipment at home and in the workplace. A good firm bed is most important. It should offer firm (not hard) support with enough resilience to allow for the body's natural curves. A variety of beds should be examined and compared, one with the other. Most large departmental stores have a wide range and should welcome the interest of potential customers. Your spine needs rest and time to "recharge" the discs. A bed cannot cure back pain but it can make life more comfortable and provide relief from discomfort. The National Back Pain Association funded research into beds and mattresses which was carried out at the University of Surrey and completed in 1985. It was found that the most popular bed consisted of a wooden base (allowing for ventilation) and a foam mattress made up with two resiliences – one hard one soft. For information send sae to the Association at 31-33 Park Road, Teddington, Middx TW11 0AB.

London Postal Districts

Orthopaedic Bedding Advisory Service (OBAS) Obas House, 6 Bow Common Lane, E3 4AX. *Tel*: 01- 538 1361. First, trained consultant visits to assess your comfort needs. Beds are designed/made accordingly with combination of 4 different spring types. Double beds combine 2 different mattresses to suit needs of each partner.

Mail Order

Contour Beds Unit 7/8, Anglesey Bus Park, Littleworth Road, Hednesford, Cannock, Staffs WS12 5NR. *Tel*: 05438 79777. Remote control beds that adjust position at touch of button; fire-resistant mattress, 2-year guarantee.

Foam for Comfort See **Services 17/ Reupholstery**. *Tel*: 0532 678281 or 673770. Colour brochure. But if your bed's too hard, use their "soft overlay".

Bay Jacobsen Freepost 644, Slough SL1 6BT. *Tel*: 06286 4049. Mattress "topper"/pillow ergonomically designed to relieve back stress. Colour brochure.

7/HEADBOARDS

Many standard bed ranges (see 2/Beds above) feature headboards. See also:

Furniture *(in particular 6/Cane and 8/Painted)*; Soft Furnishings firms can usually provide upholstered headboards, as can **Interior Design**.

London Postal Districts

The Choumert Upholstery Co See Services 17/Reupholstery. Specialists in padded fabric-covered headboards in pretty shapes.

Mail Order

Anka Fabrics 59 King Street, Darlaston. West Mid WS10 8DE. *Tel*: 021 526 7409/0902 353310/0785 715271. Brochure. Anne Bartlett and Kath Wright design/make/supply delightful designer soft furnishings. Dress bedheads with half-tester where space prohibits full four-poster. High-density chipboard canopy frame supplied complete with fixing instructions; drapes any style/fabrics, including Laura Ashley/Dolly Mixture. Less lavish: corona (half-circle gathered fabric, flowing drapes) complete with fixings/made-up fabrics. Reasonable prices.

The Dormy House See **Soft Furnishings 6/Tables & Cloths**. Foam padded headboards with pattern for your own slip-cover.

Grandisson See **Doors 1/Front & Interior**. Distinctive carved hardwood headboards; Chippendale has ornate fretwork; Victorian is a pretty scrolled semi-circle.

8/TRADITIONAL BEDS

"And so home again, staying nowhere, and then up to her chamber, there to talk with pleasure of this day's passages and so to bed." **Samuel Pepys** 1668.

The modern divan has been reduced to a boring slab. Traditional styles return the bed to furniture status. See also 5/Brass Beds above and 9/Fourposters below.

London Postal Districts

And So to Bed See 5/Brass Beds above. Beautiful wooden traditional style bedsteads, complete with head/foot boards, imported from France.

Simon Horn 117/121 Wandsworth Bridge Road, Fulham SW6 2TP. (*Entrance in Broughton Road; 5 mins Parsons Green tube*). *Tel*: 01-731 1279. *Open*: Mon to Sat 9.30pm to 6pm. Spacious showrooms. Impressive French wooden classical beds. The famous "lit de bateau" daybed has curved head and foot of equal height. Place single version along wall, dress with sweep of fabric suspended from central coronet of wood/brass. Cherrywood, oak, cane or upholstered. Country pine/English reproductions.

Mail Order

Dreamtime Pine 77 Dovedale Avenue, Long Eaton, Nottingham NG10 3HT. *Tel*: 0602 721251. Handcrafted solid pine beds in traditional country styles.

Screens & Scenes 2 Skinner Street, Wolverhampton, West Mid WV14 L4. *Tel*: 0902 23901. Traditional hardwood bedhead designs, 3ft and 4ft 6in, from range of 5 designs. Also beech table lamps, shoe racks, stools.

Worth a Trip

Seventh Heaven Chirk Mill, Chirk, Clwyd, North Wales. (*About 3 hours drive from London. M1, M6, M54, A5*). *Tel*: 0691 777622/773563. *Open*: 7 days Mon to Sat 9am to 5pm. Sun 10am to 5pm. Possibly largest UK selection antique beds. Wooden, upholstered, brass, iron. Beautifully restored. New bases/mattresses. Exclusive bed linens. National deliveries. Catalogue.

9/FOUR-POSTERS

This style will dominate your bedroom even more strongly than brass. Do you really have the space? Yes? Results can be stunning!

Bedrooms

London Postal Districts

Beaudesert 8 Symons Street, SW3 2TJ. (*2 mins Sloane Square tube*). Tel: 01-730 5102. *Open*: Mon to Fri 9.30am to 5.30pm. Joinery workshop for expensive up-market four-posters, in handcrafted mahogany complete with hangings. Interior design. Own range of country-house style fabrics.

Dragons See entry under **Children's Rooms 2/Furniture**. Four-posters for children/adults with turned wooden posts and finials, handpainted with sprigged flowers. Fabric drapes to order in any fabric.

Home Counties/S.East

Beds of Distinction 190/192 High Street, Hornchurch, Essex. (*7 mins Hornchurch tube; 12 mins Upminster BR*). Tel: 04024 77096. *Open*: Mon to Sat 9am to 6pm. Design/make/deliver/assemble hardwood four-poster beds. Up to 10ft wide! Can incorporate water beds. *Mail order*.

Post 4 Beds 14 Thorney Lane North, Iver, Bucks SL0 9AR. (*1m Iver BR*). *Tel*: 0753 654874. *Open*: by appointment. Wooden four-posters, elegant drapes made to order. Posts can be simply hand-turned in pine or mahogany; reeded, fluted or carved with acanthus leaves. Brass rods take drapes in various styles. Painted, distressed, stencilled finishes to order. Leaflets. *Mail order*.

Mail Order

Barco Joinery See **Windows 1/Replacements**. Self-assembly kit to convert 4ft 6in double bed into fourposter. Finishes: dark oak/mahogany/pine. Turned 4in-thick posts with ball finials. White cotton canopy; white lace drapes with matching tie-backs. Shaped headboards. Part also available separately. Leaflet.

Pinecraft Beds 9 Wingate Drive, Didsbury, Manchester M20 8RT. *Tel*: 061 434 1432/446 2372. Colour brochure. Established maker pine fourposters; sturdy self-assembly design, lacquered plain, or stained any colour.

Choice head/foot boards. To order: 4 to 8 weeks.

10/WATERBEDS

Popular in the USA, sleeping on water (aka "flotation") is gaining British acceptance.

London Postal Districts

The London Waterbed Company 99 Crawford Street, W1H 1AN. (*10 mins Baker Street tube*). Tel: 01-935 1111. *Open*: Mon to Fri 10am to 6pm. Sat 11am to 4pm. Wide range stylish designs for water beds, including Japanese, pine, American Colonial, brass.

The Waterbed Company 57 New King's Road, SW6 4SE. (*5 mins Fulham Broadway tube*). Tel: 01-731 0606. *Open*: Mon to Fri 10am to 6pm. Sat 11am to 4pm. Water beds are an acquired taste: converts are addicted. All mattresses have heater, and are stabilised for different support/heat requirements. Favoured by back sufferers. Mattress weight makes special frame essential: 40 different frame styles in good choice wood/colour finishes. Mattress/heater guaranteed five years; fill with garden hose. Add water conditioner twice a year. Nationwide delivery/installation service.

Home Counties/S.East

Twilight Sleep Factory Unit 2/3, Ringwood Trading Estate, Christchurch Road, Ringwood, Hants BH24 3BB. (*Christchurch Road, M27*). Tel: 0425 470200. *Open*: 7 days 9am to 5pm. Manufacturers/sell direct. Wide range water bed styles.

11/FUTONS

A firm feel, natural fibres, and simple styling provide oriental allure.

London Postal Districts

Beau Regard 662 Old Kent Road, SE1 1JF. (*Elephant & Castle tube*). Tel: 01-

639 4220. *Open*: Mon to Sat 10am to 6pm. Sun viewing 1pm to 4pm. Closed all day Wed. Late night Thurs 7pm. Slatted base with futon cotton mattress made in their own workshops; lacquer/wood finishes, good selection of colours.

Futon Company 138 Notting Hill Gate, W11 3QG. (*2 mins Notting Hill Gate tube*). Tel: 01-221 2032. *Open* (all branches): Mon to Sat 10.30am to 6pm. Late night Thurs 7pm. Sun viewing 11am to 5pm. Robert Pearce pioneered futons in Britain, at first making them himself with friends. Now his shops sell futons/sofabeds, duvets, bed linen. Natural fibres. Matt black ultra-elegant modern tables, chairs, shelving, storage units. 300 furnishing fabrics; trendsetting glassware, ceramics, gifts. Most available immediately. Interior design service/wedding lists.
Also at: 82/83 Tottenham Court Road, W1P 9HD. *Tel*: 01-636 9984. *And at*: 654a Fulham Road, SW6 5RU. *Tel*: 01-736 9190. No late night or Sun.

Futon Palace 134/136 West End Lane, West Hampstead NW6 1SB. (*2 mins West Hampstead tube*). Tel: 01-624 1528. *Open*: Mon to Sat 10am to 6pm. Late night Thurs 8pm. Sun viewing 11am to 5pm. Japanese-style sofabeds, with futon cotton-filled mattresses. Also Japanese tatami mats, shoji screens, light shades and incense burners. Brochures, colour samples. *Mail order*.

Futon South 109 Balham High Road, SW12 9AP. (*5 mins Balham tube*). Tel: 01-675 6727. *Open*: Mon to Sat 10am to 6pm. Sun viewing 11am to 4pm. Slatted base plus six-layer cotton futon/cover at reasonable price. Curtains to match; cotton cushions, bolsters, pillows to order in any size.

Take 45/46 Chalk Farm Road, Camden Lock, NW1 8AJ. (*4 mins Chalk Farm tube*). Tel: 01-267 3937. *Open*: 7 days 10am to 6pm. Futon sofabeds; removable cotton satin covers.

12/BED LINEN

*Widely available, of course, from **Department Stores** and **Furnishing Stores**. Often offered as part of co-ordinated furnishings ranges: see **Decorating Materials, Interior Design, Soft Furnishings**.*

London Postal Districts

Boutique Descamps 197 Sloane Street, SW1X 9QX. (*3 mins Knightsbridge tube*). *Tel*: 01-235 6957. *Open*: Mon to Sat 9.30am to 6pm. Late night Wed 7pm. Exclusive bed linens/fabric by talented French designer Primrose Brodier. Towels, baby/nightwear.

Futon Company See entry under **11/Futons** above. Bed linens in natural fibres, including pure white sheets/duvet covers.

John Lewis See **Department Stores**. Sheeting by the metre; ground floor, Oxford Street.

The Linen Cupboard 21 Great Castle Street, W1. (*5 mins Oxford Circus tube*). *Tel*: 01-629 4062. *Open*: Mon to Sat 9am to 6pm. Late night Thurs 8pm. Small, but well-stocked. Bed linen, towels, table linen at very reasonable prices.

Lunn Antiques 86 New King's Road, SW6 4LU. (*5 mins Parsons Green tube*). *Tel*: 01-736 4638. *Open*: Mon to Sat 10am to 6pm. Bed/table linen, mainly in white. Well-known for antique lace.

Monogrammed Linen Shop 168 Walton Street, SW3 2JL. (*7 mins South Kensington tube*). *Tel*: 01-589 4033. *Open*: Mon to Fri 10am to 6pm. Sat 10am to 5pm. Linen, cotton, cotton satin sheets. Bedspreads, blanket covers. Creams, whites, patterns, plains with coloured bindings. Baby pillowcases. Monogramming service takes 3 days.

Bargains!

Pillow Talk 11/13 Temple Fortune Parade, Finchley Road, Temple Fortune NW11. (*15 mins Golders Green tube*). *Tel*: 01-458 9138. *Open*: 7 days 9am to 6pm. On-going promotions/discounts on wide selections branded sheets, duvet covers etc. Plain dyes/prints/frills/children's designs. Perfects/good quality seconds.
Also at: Kingsbury Circle, Kenton Road, NW9. (*Kingsbury tube*). *Tel*: 01-204 3366. *Open*: Mon to Fri 9am to 8pm. Sat Sun 9am to 6pm.

The Sleeping Company 68 Wigmore Street, W1H 9LG. (*10 mins Bond Street tube*). *Tel*: 01-486 3150. *Open* (both branches): Mon to Sat 10am to 6pm. Late night Thurs 7pm. Exclusive extensive bed linens mainly natural fibres. Linens, cottons, seersuckers, stripes, lace, frills, patterns. Lots of white. Matching robes, slippers, bedroom accessories. Free catalogue. Mail order.
Also at: 123 & 143 Fulham Road, SW3 6RT. (*10 mins South Kensington tube*). *Tel*: 01-581 2058.

The White House 51/2 New Bond Street, W1Y 0BY. (*10 mins Piccadilly Circus tube*). *Tel*: 01-629 3521. *Open*: Mon to Fri 9am to 5.30pm. Sat 9am to 1pm. Established 1906; London's premier stockist of fine (but expensive) bed linens. Printed, embroidered luxury sheet sets, co-ordinating well. Bedcovers. Tablecloths, tablemats. Monogramming. Commissions.

Mail Order

Satin Sheets PO Box 475, Ascot, Berks SL5 8BN. Polyester satin in 9 colours, including black, cream, grey, peach. Samples. Plain/frilled styles, including valance. Duvet has cotton back.

Keys of Clacton Stephenson Road, Gorse Lane Industrial Estate, Clacton-on-Sea, Essex CO15 3AJ. *Tel*: 0255 43251. Catalogue: send stamp. Warehouse/shop for personal callers: 132 Old Road, Clacton. *Open*: Mon to Sat 9am to 5pm. Bed linen for unusual bed sizes/shapes. Luxury percales, cosy flannelettes (including duvet covers). 20 sizes in fitted bottom sheets.

Limericks Limerick House, 117 Victoria Avenue, Southend-on-Sea, Essex SS2 6EL. *Tel*: 0702 343486. Colour catalogue: send stamp. Specialist in unusual sizes. Good-value own-brand sheets, pillowcases, quilt covers. Sheeting by-the-metre, deep-dye and pastel shades. Egyptian cottons, flannelettes.

13/DUVETS

*Also known as continental quilts. Buy the best you can afford. Find selections also at **Department** and **Furnishing Stores**. The warmth of duvets is measured in "tog" values: the higher the tog, the warmer the quilt. Summer weight is 4.5. 12 is warm; 13.5 extra warm. Fillings can be synthetic or natural. At the bottom end of the market, cheapest synthetics are made from low-grade polyesters; at the upper end, branded polyesters have hollow fibres for greater warmth and lightness. Natural fillings vary from cheaper feathers/down to down/feathers and the luxury of pure down. It's all a matter of personal preferences and budget. But a quality quilt is virtually a lifelong investment. Watch out for bargains in the sales.*

London Postal Districts

Karo-Step The German Bedding Centre, 138 Marylebone Road, NW1 5PH. (*Opposite Baker Street tube*). *Tel*: 01-935 0196. *Open*: Mon to Thurs 9.30am to 5.30pm. Fri 9.30am to 5pm. Closed Sat. Here they really do sell continental quilts: in Europe, they've had around 300 years of experience. Expert guidance on quilt suitability. 4 fillings: new feather/down (good quality feathers mixed with fine down); new down/feather (quality resilient down mixed with fine small feathers); new duck down (the most popular); and new goose down (blissful luxury, warm/light). After sales service: fillings adjusted if quilt is too warm/cold. Also available: professional cleaning/reconditioning service for duvets. Unique machine washes/dries/sterilises. Fillings topped up if necessary. Recovering service.

Mail Order

Sundown Quilts Kirk Clough, Brogden, Barnoldswick, Colne, Lancs BB8 5XE. *Tel*: 0282 813741. Excellent explanatory leaflets. 12 (many shops only stock 3) standard sizes continental quilts. Natural fillings from duck feather to luxury white goose down.

14/QUILTS & SPREADS

Not easily combined with a duvet, but can provide a wonderful focal point. See also **Interior Design**, *and* **Soft Furnishings**.

London Postal Districts

Ann Chiswell Designs 34 Queens Drive, W3 0HA. *Tel*: 01-992 0196. *Open*: by appointment. Beautifully handpainted and quilted designs for bedcovers, cushions and other soft furnishings. An exclusive range of tablelinen. Decorative ideas for any surface.

Contemporary Textile Gallery 10 Golden Square, W1R 3AF. (*8 mins Piccadilly Circus tube*). *Tel*: 01-439 9070/1. *Open*: Mon to Fri 10am to 6pm. Sat 11am to 5pm. Unique spacious (2 floors) gallery for handmade contemporary British furnishing textiles. Quilts/rugs/ tapestries/ embroideries/felt/mixed media.

Dreams See **Bedrooms 5/Brass Beds**. Good selection patchwork spreads plus throwover/fitted intricate white lace designs.

Norma Kitson c/o The Mosaic Studio, 43 Vallance Road, N22. (*Alexandra Palace BR; Bounds Green tube plus bus*). *Tel*: 01-889 0190. *Open*: by appointment. Commissions taken for all kinds of patchwork quilts to suit your bedroom/colour scheme. Wide choice of patterns includes Art Deco and Jewel of the Crown. Cushions to match. Wall hangings.

John Lewis See **Department Stores**. Quilted throwover bedspreads with curtaining/wallpapers to match.

Museum Quilts Susan Jenkins. *Open*: by appointment only. *Tel*: 01-833 0671. Original American patchwork quilts; each tells a story. Finest workmanship; good investment.

The Patchwork Dog and The Calico Cat 21 Chalk Farm Road, NW1. (*5 mins Chalk Farm tube*). *Tel*: 01-485 1239. *Open*: Tues to Sun 10am to 6pm. 3 floors, with made-up patchwork quilts/cushions; patchwork quilting supplies, including fabrics.

Mail Order

Keys of Clacton See **Bedrooms 12/ Bed Linen** above. Huge range of bedspreads, including nonstandard widths: 2ft 6in, 4ft, 6ft. Four valance drops cover bulky duvets or deep drawer divans. Also luxurious pure new wool blankets.

Rainbow Quilts 21 Cricketfield Road, E5 8NR. *Tel*: 01-986 8846. Brochures, 50p. Quilts to co-ordinate with your schemes. Outline/Italian quilting, appliqué.

15/BUILT-IN

You can't take them with you when you move, but they may add value to your house. Specialist firms mostly offer a home service: they design/ make/install, and this is usually included in the price. Find freestanding alternatives under **Bedroom Furniture** *below.*

London Postal Districts

Exclusive Bedrooms 489 Finchley Road, NW3 6HS. (*10 mins Finchley Road tube*). *Tel*: 01-431 1222. *Open*: Mon to Sat 9.30am to 5.30pm. Sun viewing 11am to 2pm. London's largest supplier fitted mirror wardrobes, they claim. Competitive prices, myriads of models. Plan/make/install. Brochures: dial 100, ask for Exclusive Bedrooms. Or write Freepost 1697, Watford WD1 8FP.
Also at: 448 Chiswick High Road, W4 5RG. (*2 mins Chiswick Park tube*). *Tel*: 01-994 2513.

GKD Lanrick House, Lanrick Road, E14 0JF. *Tel* (for nearest branch): 01-515 5151 (24 hours). Trading for over 25 years; largest fitted bedroom manufacturers in Europe, they tell me. Variety of styles. Plan/fit. Free 40-page colour brochure.

Harvey Jones and Roy Griffiths 293 New King's Road, SW6. (*3 mins Parsons Green tube*). *Tel*: 01-736 9761. *Open*: Mon to Fri 9am to 5.30pm. Sat 10am to 4pm. Made-to-measure wood and painted wardrobes from successful kitchen duo. (See **Kitchens 3/Wood**.)

Options 915 Fulham Road, SW6 5HU. (*7 mins Putney Bridge tube*). *Tel*: 01-384 1171. *Open*: Mon to Sat 9am to 5.30pm. Over 30 ranges fitted bedrooms, hundreds of colour combinations, from sliding mirrors to handpainted furniture and en suite bathrooms.

Personal Touch 39 Fairfax Road, Swiss Cottage, NW6 4EL. (*4 mins Swiss Cottage tube*). *Tel*: 01-328 5462. *Open*: Mon to Sat 9.30am to 5pm. Craft-based bespoke furniture individually designed/made-to-measure. Personal service. Plan/fit. Colour brochure.

Peter Jones See **Department Stores**. Complete service for bedroom built-ins. Design/supply/install. Many ranges on display include Living in Style featuring American Cherry and Light Oak. Optional mirrored doors. Matching chests, dressing/bedside tables, headboards.

Staton Fitted Furniture Ltd 719 North Circular Road, NW2 7AH. (*Near Brent Cross*). *Tel*: 01-450 6581. *Open*: Mon to Fri 9am to 5.30pm. Sat 9am to 5pm. Sun 10am to 4pm. Factory showroom, selling direct. Fitted wardrobes with backs, shelves, double hanging and shoe rails. Various door styles, with mirrors, mouldings, etc. Plan/fit.

Wickes See **Home Improvements Specialists**. Frameless wall-to-wall/ floor-to-ceiling mirrored doors from stock. Stripped/antique finish for attractive DIY planked pine doors, plain or with framed mirrors, standard sizes.

Outer Ring

Exclusive Bedrooms 81 Joel Street, Northwood Hills, Middx HA6 1LU. *Tel*: 09274 27514. See London Postal Districts above.

Personal Touch 55 Beckenham Lane, Bromley, Kent. *Tel*: 01-464 2196. See London Postal Districts above.

Sharps Bedrooms Albany Park, Frimley, Camberley, Surrey GU15 2PL. *Tel* (for nearest branch): 0276 685366. Also claim to be UK's largest maker of fitted bedroom furniture. Over 80 stores nationwide. Wide variety styles. Plan/make/install. Colour catalogue.

Home Counties/S.East

Gibbons Built-in Furniture Unit 2, Station Industrial Park, Oxford Road, Wokingham, Berks RG11 2YQ. (*Adjacent Wokingham BR*). *Tel*: 0734 793911. *Open*: Mon to Fri 8am to 5pm. Sat 9am to 12 noon. Fitted bedroom, kitchen, lounge furniture; melamine, medium density fibreboards, natural woods.

Mail Order

David Emerson See **Kitchens 6/Worktops**. Tailor-made sliding/bifold door wardrobes in wide choice finishes. In-home visits. Design/supply/install.

Sovereign Sliding Mirror Wardrobes 33a Torton Hill Road, Arundel, West Sussex BN18 9HF. *Tel*: 0243 552123. Free catalogue. Made-to-measure sliding mirror wardrobe fronts. Bottom track fits to floor, top to ceiling. Doors fit gap exactly. Mirror safety-backing to BS 6262. DIY installation, or hire local carpenter.

16/BEDROOM FURNITURE

"Style today is not just a question of showing people into the 'kept tidy for that purpose' front room. Style today permeates through the whole house. Make sure your bedroom doesn't miss out on style." **Jim Walsh**, *managing director*, Living in Style.

Like a kitchen, a bedroom that's fully fitted can become bland and boring. Add at least one or two piece of freestanding furniture: a pretty chair (use-ful for discarded clothing), and perhaps a dressing table and stool. See **Furniture 6/Cane** *for ideas. And a completely unfitted bedroom has its advantages. You can move the furniture around, to change positions/ room/homes. Shapes can be interesting. And, of course, a capacious wardrobe is the original junkshop best buy. But . . . cleaning is not minimised and space is not maximised. For attractive bedroom freestanding furniture, explore* **Furniture**: *in particular* **2/Pine & Country;** **4/Classics & Reproduction;** *and* **8/Painted**.

Mail Order

Ardenco Rosebery Avenue, Melton Mowbray, Leics LE13 1BL.Cheapo self-assembly square tube hanging rail; ideal spare room/temporary hanging space.

Country Furniture Stuart House, Arnold Street, Nantwich, Cheshire CW5 5QB. Tel: 0270 629974. Leaflet. Opposite of built-ins! Decorative handmade pine freestanding racks with hanging/shoe rails.

The Dormy House See **Soft Furnishings 6/Tables & Cloths**. Classic kidney shaped dressing tables with frilly fabrics.

KITCHENS

Kitchens are often the least planned part of a house or flat. After all, you use them every day, so when can they be altered? Be brave, take a long hard look, and act: it will always be worth the trouble. A happy kitchen makes a happy home.

1/SPECIALISTS

Two or even three on every High Street, including cowboys. How to choose? Membership of the Kitchen Specialists Association (KSA) is reassuring (see **Help!**)*, as are local references (take them up). Top makers, whether British, German, Spanish, or French, usually watch over stockists' service standards. It is not advisable to buy a kitchen sight unseen. Firms listed below almost universally offer home service as part of their deal; they will plan/install. The best can refit your whole kitchen, to include plumbing, electrics, decorating and even structural alterations.*

All Districts

In-toto *Tel (nearest branch)*: 0532 524131. National franchise chain of 37 kitchen specialists, with kitchens from Wellmann, one of Germany's largest manufacturers. Range of 142 kitchens, plus 60 in Contessa designer collection. Appliances from Philips and Bauknecht. Customer deposits, kitchen units, appliances and accessories all protected by Wellmann guarantees. Free catalogue. For individual addresses see below.

Roma Jay Design 2A Bartholomew Road, NW5. (*Dalston Kingsland BR*). *Tel*: 01-267 1428. *Open*: by appointment. Roma Jay offers impartial objective design services for kitchens; you pay for expertise, rather than "free" design with plump profits on furniture/appliances. Efficient, pleasant, practical, enthusiastic: she could actually save you money. Consultants travel nationwide.

Schreiber Fitted Kitchen & Bedroom Centres. Nearest Branch/Enquiries, *Linkline* 01-200 02000. Large modern Cheshire factory supplies quality fitted kitchen/bedroom ranges to kitchen specialists nationwide. Parent company oversees product/delivery/service standards. Schreiber specialists plan/supply/deliver/install. Laminates, veneers, solid wood, including limed oak finish. New solid chestnut, with raised and fielded cathedral panels. Wide choice Schreiber built-in appliances including Domino range combined gas/electric rings plus deep-fat frier.

London Postal Districts

Alternative Plans 185 New King's Road, Parsons Green, SW6. (*5 mins Fulham Broadway tube*). *Tel*: 01-731 1010. *Open* (all branches): Mon to Sat 9.30am to 5.30pm. Trading 7 years. Wide range kitchen styles from traditional oak to modern high-gloss polyesters. Appliances from most major makers. Design/install. Bathrooms, too.
Also at: 9 Hester Road, Battersea, SW11. (*Immediately over Battersea Bridge*). *Tel*: 01-228 6460.

Bulthaup 348/354 Kensington High Street, W14. (*10 mins Kensington High Street tube*). *Tel*: 01-602 4255/8168. *Open* (all branches): Mon to Fri 9am to 5pm. Sat 9.30am to 5pm. Other times by appointment. Extensive Bulthaup (top German make) room-settings: colours, finishes, layouts, accessories. Expert advice. Design/supply/install.
Also at: 37 Wigmore Street, W1. (*5 mins Oxford Circus/Bond Street tubes*). *Tel*: 01-495 3664.
And at: 93 Heath Street, NW3. (*2 mins Hampstead tube*). *Tel*: 01-431 0469.

Complete Kitchens 56 Springbank Road, Lewisham, SE13 6SN. (*Opposite Hither Green BR*). *Tel*: 01-852 5926. *Open*: Mon to Fri 9.30am to 6pm. Sat 10am to 4pm. Early closing Thurs. Design/supply/install. Mainly middle price bracket. Similar service for bathrooms. Leaflets.

The Fitted Kitchen Centre Selfridges, see **Department Stores**. Committed to customer satisfaction is the approachable manager of Selfridges 25 kitchen displays. British Wrighton (designer)/Elizabeth Ann (homely and cosy). German Bosch/Miele, with robust appliances. Home design/survey fee £35, deductible from order. Budget taken carefully into account. Deliveries from about 8 weeks. Carpentry/electrics/plumbing. No structural work, or decorating. "People like the reassurance of dealing with an established institution."

Hampstead Kitchens 3 The Market Place, Hampstead, NW11 6LB. *Tel:* 01-209 0042. *Open:* Mon to Fri 9.30am to 5.30pm. Sat 9.30am to 1.30pm. Sun 10am to 1pm. Extensive modern kitchens by allmilmö. Also English handpainted and wooden kitchens. Free measure/planning. Full installations. Personal service/advice.

Humphersons Heal's, 196 Tottenham Court Road, W1P 9I.D. (*3 mins Goodge Street tube*). *Tel:* 01-636 1666. *And at:* 227/229 High Road, Chiswick W4 2DW. (*5 mins Turnham Green tube*). *Tel:* 01-995 0733. *And at:* 66 Vivian Avenue, NW4 3XH. (*5 mins Hendon Central tube*). *Tel:* 01-202 4355. *And at:* 164 Brompton Road, SW3 1HW. ((*5 mins Knightsbridge tube*). *Tel:* 01-581 2271. See Outer Ring below.

In-House Supplies 236 North End Road, Fulham W14. (*3 mins West Brompton tube*). *Tel:* 01-385 9590. *Open:* Mon to Fri 8.30am to 5.30pm. Format designer German kitchens. Design/supply/install. AEG/Philips/Neff/Bauknecht appliances. Warehouse showroom, 7 kitchen sets. Partners Steve Holgate/Pat Murphy have been in kitchen business 8 years. Also popular bathroom brands.

In-toto Berners Street, W1P 4DE. (*10 mins Oxford Circus tube*). *Tel:* 01-436 2496/7. *Open:* Mon to Sat 9am to 5pm. Plan/supply/install: in heart of London's West End. A small frontage conceals deep, spacious showrooms with 24 roomsettings. Manager George Burrell can supply and fit a wide range of kitchens, from Wellmann laminate designs to luxury Tielsa models.

Kensington Lifestyle 203 North End Road, West Kensington W14 9NL. (*2 mins West Kensington tube*). *Tel:* 01-381 9625. *Open:* Mon to Fri 9am to 5pm. Sat 10am to 4pm. Sun 10am to 1pm. Large displays French Mobalpa

kitchens. Plan/design/install. Friendly personal service. Expert "faux" finishes: marbling, graining, dragging, etc.

JU Kitchen Consultants 160/162 Notting Hill Gate, W11 3QG. (*3 mins Notting Hill Gate tube; Parking, private road at back*). *Tel:* 01-221 0257. *Open:* Mon to Sat 9.30am to 5.30pm. Top quality German Miele units/ splendidly robust appliances. Plan/install.

Kitchen Design and Advice 254/256 Watford Way, Hendon, NW4 4UJ. *Tel:* 01-203 4162. *And at:* 818 High Road, North Finchley, N12 8PR. *Tel:* 01-445 1035. *And at:* 45 Chase Side, Southgate, N14 5BP. *Tel:* 01-886 3692. *And at:* 80 High Road, Woodford, E18 2NA. *Tel:* 01-530 6128. See Home Counties/S.East below.

Kitchen Design Centre 44 St Mary's Road, Ealing W5 5EN. (*6 mins South Ealing tube*). *Tel:* 01-840 2876. *Open:* Mon to Fri 9am to 5pm. Sat 10am to 4.30pm. Small showroom featuring 5 complete kitchens from Wellmann range. Established 5 years. Design/supply/install.

Kitchen Kraft 186 Chingford Mount Road, Chingford E4 9BS (*Walthamstow BR plus bus*). *Tel:* 01-524 1039. *Open:* Mon to Sat 9am to 6pm. Large double-fronted modern showroom, 5 roomset displays. Wellman kitchen specialist. Some working appliances. Husband and wife team Jaz/Sue Shogal are real enthusiasts, and delight in a kitchen challenge. Finance available.

Linward Interiors 135 Chiswick High Road, W4 2EA. (*10 mins Turnham Green tube*). *Tel:* 01-994 1030. *Open:* Mon to Sat 9am to 5.30pm. Closed all day Wed. Well-established family firm; personal service. Carmague/Jubilee fitted kitchens. Appliances by AEG, Neff, Bosch, Philips, Zanussi, Hotpoint. Complete installation service: from structural alterations to decorating. *Also at:* 68 Northfield Avenue, Ealing W13 9RR. (*5 mins Northfields tube*). *Tel:* 01-579 6291. *Open:* Mon to Sat

9.30am to 5pm. Closed Wed.

Norman Glenn Kitchens 477/481 Finchley Road, NW3 6HS. (*Finchley Road/West Hampstead tubes*). *Tel:* 01-794 7801. *Open:* Mon to Fri 5.30pm. Sat 10am to 5pm. Trading for 26 years. British Wrighton quality kitchens. Largest London showing for German Poggenpohl, plus Goldreif.

Pennybee Interiors 53/54 Wimbledon High Street, SW19 5AX. (*15 mins Wimbledon tube/BR*). *Tel:* 01-947 7224/5. *Open:* Mon to Fri 9.30am to 5.30pm. Sat 9.30am to 5pm. Extensive displays leading British/continental kitchens. Branded appliances. Also bathrooms, soft furnishings. Design and building service.

Ultimate Kitchens 107 Pimlico Road, SW1W 8PH. (*8 mins Sloane Square tube*). *Tel:* 01-730 7927. See Outer Ring below.

Outer Ring

Alternative Plans 7 Nork Way, Banstead, Surrey. *Tel:* 07373 61022. *Also at:* High Street, Epping, Essex. *Tel:* 0378 77737. See London Postal Districts above. Commissions for rugs etc. Small gift area.

Cheam Home Centre 17/19 High Street, Cheam, Surrey SM3 8RQ. (*2 mins Cheam BR; customer car park at rear*). *Tel:* 01-642 1788. *Open:* Mon to Sat 9.30am to 5.30pm. Halfday Wed. Largest displays of German quality Tielsa kitchens. 30 room displays (20 kitchens); working appliances. Wall tiles, flooring (marble, wood, cork), suspended and beamed ceilings, two brick-built home extensions. Planning, installations.

Humphersons 10 branches in and around London. Head office: 11-17 Fowler Road, Hainault Industrial Estate, Ilford, Essex IG6 3UU. *Open:* Mon to Sat 9am to 5.30pm. Kitchen, bedroom, bathroom specialists. Quality ranges, including SieMatic kitchens, Villeroy & Boch bathrooms, Olympus bedrooms. Professional and free planning service. Installations by own company. Free glossy colour

Kitchens

catalogues. Finance schemes available. *Also at*: 124/126 High Street, Barkingside, Essex. (*5 mins Barkingside tube*). *Tel*: 01-551 2666.
And at: Heal's, Drummond Place, Northend, Croydon, CR0 1TQ. *Tel*: 01-686 5767.
And at: 22 Hill Street, Richmond, Surrey. (*6 mins Richmond tube/BR*). *Tel*: 01-940 7140.
And at: 137/139 Station Road, Edgware, Middx. (*5 mins Edgware tube*). *Tel*: 01-951 1757.

In-toto 15/21 Headstone Drive, Harrow HA3 5QX. (*5 mins Harrow BR*). *Tel*: 01-861 1745. *Open*: Mon to Sat 9am to 6pm. Large modern frontage, featuring 17 kitchen displays. Knowledgeable staff, headed by enthusiastic, energetic director. Mac McCarthy and wife Inge pride themselves on designing for individuals, even making a comfy corner for the family pet! Plus prestigious Tielsa installations.

In-toto 18/20 Upper Mulgrave Road, Cheam. Surrey SM2 7AZ. (*Opposite Cheam BR*). *Tel*: 01-642 5097. *Open*: Mon to Sat 9.30am to 5.30pm. Early closing Wed 1pm. Large triple-fronted shop with 8 room displays. Working appliances. A husband-and-wife team, Peter and Phyllis Horner work with customers to design/supply/install kitchens for individual tastes. Gas integrated appliances including Bauknecht's built-in gas double oven.

In-toto 10/12 The Causeway, Teddington, Middx TE11 0HE. (*2 mins Teddington BR*). *Tel*: 01-943 2293. *Open*: Mon to Sat 9am to 5pm. Double-fronted exterior. Showroom contains 10 displays, including a full working kitchen. Owners Peter and Linda Ward design, free of charge, to individual requirements. Supply/install, including tiling/floors/ceilings.

Kitchen Design & Advice Eleys Estate, Angel Road, Edmonton N18 3BH. *Tel*: 01-803 9989. *Open* (all branches): Mon to Sat 9.30am to 5pm. Established 16 years; chain of 9 shops. Xey (Spanish), Olympic (British), Teisseire (French). Working ovens, hobs. Planning, installations.
Also at: 161 Shenley Road, Boreham-

wood, Herts WD6 1AH. *Tel*: 01-207 3828.
And at: 7 Genotin Road, Enfield, Middx EN1 2AA. *Tel*: 01-367 6464.

The Kitchen Company 23/7 Belmont Road, Uxbridge, Middx UB8 1QS. *Tel*: 0895 30600/58090. *Open*: Mon to Sat 9am to 5.30pm. With 20 displays, chic shop won French top brand Arthur Bonnet's award for best UK stockist. Design/supply/install. Plumbing/tiling/electrics. KSA members. Interior design advice. Floorings. Also central heating/windows/structural alterations. Appliances by Neff/De Dietrich.

Kitchen Concept 138/140 Upper Wickham Lane, Welling DA16 3DP. (*20 mins Welling/Bexley Heath BR*). *Tel*: 01-855 1298. *Open*: Mon to Sat 9.30am to 5pm. Refurbished double-fronted showroom with 6 displays. Established 15 years. Design/supply/install. Can advise on colours and co-ordination. Ceilings/tiles/floors a speciality. Enthusiastic proprietor, Steve Beaney, will pay taxi fare from station.

Kitchen Pleasure 17 Greenhill Parade, Great North Road, New Barnet, Herts EN5 1ES. (*Junction Great North Road/Station Road*). *Tel*: 01-449 0614/6734. *Open*: Mon to Sat 9am to 5.30pm. Top range kitchen/fitted furniture in 700 sq ft showroom. Plan/design/install.

Sigma Kitchens 47b Crown Road, St Margarets, Twickenham, Middx. (*St Margarets BR/Richmond tube plus bus*). *Tel*: 01-892 4593/891 3181. *Open*: Mon to Fri 10am to 5.30pm. Sat 10am to 4pm. Evenings by appointment. French Chabert Duval quality kitchens. Plan/install.

Stately Home Kitchens 54 Cannon Lane, Pinner, Middx HA5 1HW. (*Next to Whittington pub*). *Tel*: 01-866 0973. *Open*: Mon to Fri 9am to 5pm. Sat 9am to 1pm. Own factory for kitchens, bedrooms and bathrooms. Kitchens with laminate, polyester, wood doors. Most appliances supplied. Design/make/fit. Mail order brochure.

Ulteriors 80 High Street, Teddington, Middx TW11 8JD. (*5 mins Teddington BR*). *Tel*: 01-977 8287. *Open*: Mon to Fri 9.30am to 5.30pm. Sat 10am to 4.30pm. Flamboyant Italian Snaidero kitchens, plus handpainted British range. Owner David Smith, trained architect, advises on structural alterations.

Home Counties/S.East

AB Designs 13 Church Street, Reigate, Surrey RH2 0AA. (*Just off Junction 8 of M25*). *Tel*: 0737 249247. *Open*: Mon to Sat 9.30am to 5.30pm. German Rational/Tiffany in solid wood. Painted styles from England. Plan/install.

Harmony Interiors 46/50 Wellington Street, Luton, Beds LU1 2QH. (*Close to Town Hall*). *Tel*: 0582 25553. *Open*: Mon to Sat 9am to 6pm. Closed Wed. Trading for nine years; 12 international displays from Germany, France, Britain. Plan/install.

Humphersons Cardain House, Gregories Road, Beaconsfield, Bucks. (*3 mins Beaconsfield BR*). *Tel*: 04946 5316. *Open*: Mon to Sat 9am to 5.30pm.
And at: 123 Albert Street, Fleet, Hants. *Tel*: 0252 628605.
See Outer Ring above.

In-toto 37 Peter's Street, Bedford MK40 2PN. (*Public car park behind showroom*). *Tel*: 0234 328592. *Open*: Mon to Sat 9.30 to 5pm. Modern single-fronted studio, 10 roomsets. Tony and Joy Evans design/supply/install. Tiling, wall/floor/ceiling coverings etc. Tony has been in the kitchen industry for 23 years: can advise on all aspects of kitchen/interior design.

In-toto 2 The Links Business Centre, Raynham Road, off Dunmow Road, Bishops Stortford, Herts CM23 5NZ. (*½m Town Centre; junction 8 M11; ample parking*). *Tel*: 0279 757260. *Open*: Thurs to Tues 9.30am to 5pm. Sun viewing 11am to 4.30pm. Closed Wed. Showroom with 11 full roomsets, some with working appliances.

Roger and Joy Cunningham offer full design service. Supply/install. Finance available.

In-toto 211 High Street, Dorking, Surrey RH4 1RU. (*10 mins Dorking BR*). *Tel*: 0306 740509. *Open*: Mon to Sat 9am to 5.30pm. Single-fronted showroom in Dorking's busy High Street. Working appliances, and 9 roomsets. Plan/supply/install. Finance available. Manageress Gwynne Scaife can advise on co-ordination and interior design.

In-toto 38 Castle Street, Guildford, Surrey GU1 3UQ. (*10 mins Guildford BR*). *Tel*: 0483 502913. *Open*: Mon to Fri 9.30am to 5pm, Sat 9.30am to 4pm. Showroom with 10 roomsets, some with working appliances. Paul and Cherie O'Boyle offer a complete service: design/supply/fit. Finance available.

In-toto 6/7 Medwin Walk, Horsham, West Sussex RH12 1AG. (*Alongside new shopping centre; multi-storey car park*). *Tel*: 0403 66630. *Open*: Mon to Sat 9.30am to 5pm. Modern showroom displays, 11 complete kitchens. Mike Hodge and Carol Carter design/supply/install Wellmann kitchens with Philips/Bauknecht appliances.

In-toto (at Weekes) 2/12 Mount Pleasant Road, Tunbridge Wells, Kent TN1 1QT. (*Multi-storey car park at rear*). *Tel*: 0892 48341. *Open*: Mon 9.30am to 5.30pm, Tues to Sat 9am to 5.30pm. Situated within Weekes's department store, with 10 kitchen displays including examples from luxury Tielsa range. Owner Stephen Rigg was one of the first In-toto franchisees, formerly executive with parent company/supplier, Wellmann. Design/supply/install.

In-toto 47/50 Peascod Street, Windsor, Berks SL4 1DE. (*5 mins Windsor BR, pedestrian walkway off High Street*). *Tel*: 0753 854675. *Open*: Mon to Sat 9am to 5.30pm. Double-fronted. Large showroom, 12 displays. Working appliances include super-quiet dishwashers. Tielsa specialist, manager Peter Dobson designs/supplies Wellmann, Tielsa,

Philips and Baukenecht. Full installation service.

In-toto Unit 7, Station Road Industrial Estate, Oxford Road, Wokingham, Berks RG11 2VQ. (*5 mins Wokingham BR; free car park*). *Tel*: 0734 774949. *Open*: Tues to Sat 9.30am to 5pm, Sunday 11am to 4pm. Modern industrial unit. Large showroom, 9 kitchen displays. Laurie & Marial McGlone design/supply full Wellmann, Philips and Bauknecht range. Intallations. Finance available.

James Allen Interiors 202 Moulsham Street, Chelmsford, Essex CM2 0LG. (*Old town, off Parkway, parking at rear*). *Tel*: 0245 252325. *Open*: Mon to Sat 9am to 5.30pm. Or by appointment. German Rationale, and Cuisines Schmidt. Planning and installations.

The Kitchen and Bedroom Company 4 Saracen Close, Gillingham Business Park, Gillingham, Kent. (*Next to Ice Rink*). *Tel*: 0634 370100. *Open*: Mon to Sat: 9am to 6pm. Sun 10am to 5pm. KSA members offering full kitchen service for exclusive German Stormer; also Solent, Stoneham. Design/supply/install. Electrics/plumbing. Some working appliances. Interior design advice. New branch in Canterbury.

Kitchen Design & Advice 3 High Street, Fareham, Hants PO16 7AT. *Tel*: 0329 822002.
And at: 6 Market Street, Hertford, Herts SG14 1BD. *Tel*: 0992 553693. See Outer Ring above.

Ultimate Kitchens 120 South Street, Dorking, Surrey RH4 2EU. (*15 mins Dorking BR*). *Tel*: 0306 881814/76001. *Open* (all branches): Tues to Sat 9am to 5.30pm. Quality German brands: Poggenpohl/Goldreif. Laminates, wood veneers, solid woods, high-gloss polyesters. Design/install.
Also at: 45 South Street, Farnham, Surrey GU9 7RE. (*1 min Farnham BR*). *Tel*: 0252 727074.
And at: 78 High Street, Esher, Surrey KT10 9QS. (*10 mins Esher BR*). *Tel*: 0372 67776.
And at: 60 London Road, Southamp-

ton, Hants SO1 2AH. *Tel*: 0703 334281.

Edmund Vaughan 5 Tonbridge Road, Maidstone, Kent. (*3 mins Maidstone BR*). *Tel*: 0622 61661. *Open*: Mon to Fri 9am to 5pm. Sat 9am to 1pm. Come and meet your Waterloo! Established 1815 (is this a kitchen specialist record?) when present owner, Michael Vaughan's great-great-great-grandfather came from Wales to help build Martello towers.

2/BUDGET & SELF-ASSEMBLY

*Many kitchen specialists, above, run budget lines alongside the pricier ranges. Check out your High Street. For inexpensive self-assembly kitchens, shop at **DIY Superstores**, & **Home Improvement Specialists**.*

All Districts

B & Q See **DIY Superstores**. 21 styles in self-assembly Banquet range, displayed in roomsettings. Masterline and Q ranges especially good value for money. Appliances/sinks/worktops. Colour catalogue.

Magnet Super value stylish kitchens; free computer planning service with plan/3D printouts.

Wickes See **DIY Superstores**. Starter pack for everything you need for compact kitchen line-up: units, oven/hob/hood, sink, worktops, lighting, taps, waste.

Home Counties/S.East

Bargains!
STC Warehouse 7 Stepfield Industrial Estate, East Witham, Essex CM8 3DJ. (*1m Witham BR*). *Tel*: 0376 518715. *Open*: Tues to Sat 9am to 4pm. Sun viewing 10am to 3pm. Slightly-damaged or bankrupt ever-changing stock. Units, worktops, taps, sinks, appliances. Warehouse showroom. Bring kitchen size/plan for help with complete kitchen package!

3/WOOD KITCHENS

Most kitchen specialists offer British, French or German wood kitchens; below are firms that specialise.

London Postal Districts

The Danish Kitchen 106 Pitshanger Lane, Ealing W5 1QX. (*15 mins Ealing Broadway tube*). *Tel*: 01-998 4176. *Open*: Mon to Sat 10am to 6pm. Husband-and-wife team. Scandinavian solid wood styles (including worktops). Showroom recently enlarged. Plan/install.

Harvey Jones and Roy Griffiths 94 Waterford Road, King's Road, SW6. (*3 mins Fulham Broadway tube*). *Tel*: 01-736 1908. *Open*: Mon to Fri 9am to 5.30pm. Sat 10am to 4pm. This painter-and-artist partnership pioneered wood/painted finishes from 1977 onwards. Personal and individual service. Competitive prices.

Pine Unlimited 13a Greenwich South Street, SE10 8NW. (*Opposite Greenwich BR*). *Tel*: 01-858 0506. *Open*: Mon to Fri 8.30am to 5.30pm. Sat by appointment. David James takes endless trouble over original practical designs in solid wood with tiles, marble and clever storage. Unfitted sink unit resembles old washstand with inset brass bowl.

Sterling Kitchens & Bedrooms 234 Great Portland Street, W1. (*3 mins Great Portland Street tube*). *Tel*: 01-383 7141. *Open*: Mon to Sat 9.30am to 5.30pm. Late night Thurs 8pm. Solid wood furniture sold direct. Prices compete favourably with imported quality ranges. Oak, cherry, walnut, maple, pine, ash.

Wood Workshop 21 Canterbury Grove, SE27 0NT. (*West Norwood BR*). *Tel*: 01-670 8984. *Open*: Mon to Fri 8.30am to 5pm. Sat 10am to 2pm. Factory showroom. Kitchens in maple, mahogany, cherry, pine or oak, or made to your ideas. Timber work tops. Plan/install.

Outer Ring

Alpine Kitchens 715 Harrow Road, Wembley, Middx HA0 2LL. (*Sudbury Town tube; parking at rear*). *Tel*: 01-902 0855/9900/4135/0232. *Open*: Mon to Fri 8am to 6pm. Sat 8am to 12.30pm. Arthur Bonnet ranges from France: beautiful woods, keen prices. Also kitchens from England and Italy. Plan/install.

The Chartwell Kitchen Design Company Thames Corner, Thames Street, Lower Sunbury, Middx TW16 5QW. (*Opposite Lower Sunbury Swimming pool*). *Tel*: 0932 765611. *Open*: Mon to Fri 9am to 5pm. Sat 10am to 4pm. See Home Counties/ S.East below.

Home Counties/S.East

The Chartwell Kitchen Design Company Brook Lane (off The Street), Plaxtol, Nr. Sevenoaks, Kent TN15 0QR. (*6m Sevenoaks*). *Tel*: 0732 810285. *Open*: Mon to Fri 9am to 5pm. Sat 10am to 3.30pm. Kitchen furniture in solid pine or oak; or elegant handpainted finishes. Plan/install.
Also at: Sevenoaks Furniture Gallery, 53 High Street, Sevenoaks, Kent TN13 1JF. (*6 mins Sevenoaks BR*). *Tel*: 0732 453030. *Open*: Mon to Fri 9.30am to 5pm. Sat 9.30am to 5.30pm. Colour brochure: 128 Sovereign Way, Tonbridge, Kent TN19 1RS (head office/ workshop). *Tel*: 0732 357288.

Kitchen Splendour 1 Lord Street, Watford, Herts WD1 2LL. (*Service Road E, Watford High Street*). *Tel*: 0923 248235. *Open*: Mon to Sat 9am to 5.30pm. Natural pine/painted ranges; other woods available. Plan/install.

Naturally Wood Unit 4, Twyford Road, Bishops Stortford, Herts CM23 3JL. (*5 mins Bishops Stortford BR*). *Tel*: 0279 755501. *Open*: Mon to Fri 9am to 5.30pm. Sat 9am to 12 noon. Handmade kitchens to order. Antique pine, oak, limed oak, maple, ash, limed ash, painted. Plan/install.

Paula Rosa Kitchens 131/132 North Street, Brighton BN1 1RG. (*Below clock tower*). *Tel*: 0273 21516. *Open*: Mon to Sat 9am to 5.30pm. Sun 10am to 4pm. Traditional and contemporary designs/colours. Made in own workshops in Storrington. Plan/install.
Also at: 8/9 Friary Street, Guildford GU1 4EH. (*Off High Street*). *Tel*: 0483 502818. *Open*: Mon to Sat 9am to 5.30pm.
And at: 4 Phoenix Court, Guildford GU4 3EG. (*Off High Street*). *Tel*: 0483 31060. *Open*: Mon to Sat 9am to 5.30pm.
Factory showroom and brochures: Water Lane, Storrington, RH20 3DS. (*Water Lane Industrial Estate*). *Tel*: 09066 6666. *Open*: Mon to Thurs 9am to 5pm. Fri 9am to 4.30pm. Sat 9am to 5.30pm. Sun 10am to 5pm.

Pine Partners Kitchens 4 High Street, Barkway, Royston, Herts SG8 8EE. (*B1268*). *Tel*: 076384 764. *Open*: Tues to Fri 9.30am to 5pm. Sat 9.30am to 1pm. 18th-century wheelwright's shop now displays country kitchens from Cuisines Bonnet, plus pretty Country Diary Kitchen. Farmhouse tables, dressers, corner cupboards. Plan/install.

Sterling Kitchens and Bedrooms Smithbrook Kiln, Cranleigh, Guildford. *Tel*: 0483 275694. *Open*: 7 days 9.30am to 5.30pm. See London Postal Districts above.

Woodgoods Unit 40, Woolmer Industrial Estate, Bordon, Hants GU35 9AZ. (*8m south Farnham. Easy access M3, M25, M27 or A3*). *Tel*: 04203 7182/3. *Open*: Mon to Fri 9am to 5pm. Or by appointment. Limed old pine finish. Solid wood inside/out: no chipboard. Personal attention. Plan/install.

Worth a trip

Keith Gray & Co Great Priory Farm, Panfield, Braintree, Essex CM7 5BQ. (*2m Braintree*). *Tel*: 0376 24590. *Open*: 7 days 9am to 7pm but telephone for appointment. In medieval barns adjacent to their farmhouse home, Keith Gray and Lucy Tabor make/display solid wood kitchens with unlimited special features.

4/PAINTED KITCHENS

The softer, more delicate tones of painted finishes won't be as hardwearing as laminates or wood. But they're very fashionable! Factory-applied lacquered finishes are readily available from both continental and British firms, but handpainted effects are in the main uniquely British. Many of the kitchen companies listed under 1/Specialists and 3/Wood Kitchens above can offer handpainted finishes, as can their more expensive counterparts listed under 5/Luxury Bespoke Kitchens below.

London Postal Districts

Hampstead Kitchens See **1/Specialists** above. English handpainted kitchens.

Harvey Jones and **Roy Griffiths** See **3/Wood Kitchens** above. Painter/artist partnership which pioneered painted finishes at the end of the seventies.

Hygrove Kitchens 152/154 Merton Road, Wimbledon SW19 1EH. (*3 mins South Wimbledon tube; easy parking*). *Tel:* 01-543 1200. *Open:* Mon to Sat 10am to 6pm. Or by appointment. Custom-made kitchens in dragged/marbled paint finishes. Or pine, medium oak, limed oak. Spacious showroom. Attention to detail. Plan/install. Colour brochure.

Kensington Lifestyle See **1/Specialists** above. Expert "faux finishes": marbling, dragging, graining.

John Lewis of Hungerford See **5/Luxury Bespoke Kitchens** below.

Smallbone See **5/Luxury Bespoke Kitchens** below.

Outer Ring

Crabtree Kitchens See **5/Luxury Bespoke Kitchens** below. Special painted finishes that emulate exotic wood veneers.

Home Counties/S.East

AB Designs See **1/Specialists** above. Painted finishes for English units.

Kitchen Splendour See **3/Wood Kitchens** above. Good choice of painted ranges.

Naturally Wood See **3/Wood Kitchens** above. Painted finishes for hand-made kitchens.

5/LUXURY BESPOKE KITCHENS

Made to order in any size/finish, this is the top end of the trade/budget. Check out delivery dates: there is often a long queue.

London Postal Districts

John Lewis of Hungerford Connaught Street, W2 2BS. (*5 mins Marble Arch tube*). *Tel:* 01-402 7986. *Open:* Mon to Sat 9am to 5.30pm. Closed lunch 1 to 2pm. Factory/head office: 02357 68868. Perhaps the most original kitchen designer in Britain: 8 ranges in solid woods/painted finishes/gleaming lacquer. Inspirational roomsettings, tiled floors, lots of accessories.
Also at: **Liberty** Regent Street, W1R 6AH. *Tel:* 01-734 1234. *Open:* Mon to Fri 9.30am to 6pm. Late night Thurs 8pm. Sat 9am to 6.30pm.

Smallbone 103/105 Fulham Road, SW3 6RL. (*7 mins South Kensington tube*). *Tel:* 01-581 9989. *Open:* Mon to Fri 9am to 5.30pm. Sat 10am to 6pm. Smallbone is a trendsetter: first kitchens in old-pine, then painted finishes (stencils, too), then Gothic and the unfitted kitchen. For such celebrity, you have to pay substantially. All furniture built to order. Plan/make/install. Also bedroom, bathroom and sitting room furniture. Fulham is the largest, most lavish showroom. Brochure: *Tel:* 0734 868044.
Also at: 93 Wimpole Street, W1M 1DA. (*10 mins Bond Street tube*). *Tel:* 01-493 6298. *Open:* Mon to Fri 5.30pm. Sat 10am to 4pm. Bathrooms. *And at:* 91 Wimpole Street, W1M 1DA. *Tel:* 01-408 0026. *And at:* 17 Wigmore Street, W1H 9LA. *Tel:* 01-491 0515. Bedrooms.

Woodstock 23 Pakenham Street, WC1X 0LB. (*5 mins Russell Square tube*). *Tel:* 01-837 1818/3220. *Open:* Mon to Fri 9am to 6pm. Sat 10am to 2pm. Trading for 13 years, craftsman Alf Martensson has built a reputation as solid as the wood he works. Displays of working kitchens in unusual woods, workshops at back. Dressers, larders, chairs, benches, tables, stools, all made to order. Plan/make/install. *Also at:* 92 Lots Road, SW10 0QD. (*10 mins Fulham Broadway tube*). *Tel:* 01-837 1818/3220. *Open:* Mon to Fri 10am to 5.30pm. Sat 10am to 2pm.

Outer Ring

Crabtree Kitchens The Twickenham Centre, Norcutt Road, Twickenham, Middx TW2 6SR. (*Twickenham BR/Richmond tube plus bus; own car park*). *Tel:* 01-755 1121. *Open:* Mon to Fri 8.30am to 5.30pm. Or by appointment. Limed oak, ash, cherry or maple plus painted finishes that emulate exotic wood veneers.

Home Counties/S.East

John Lewis of Hungerford Hart Street, Henley, Oxon RG9 2AR. *Tel:* 0491 575376.
Also at: High Street & Park Street, Hungerford, Berks NG17 0DN. *Tel:* 0488 82066. See London Postal Districts above.

Smallbone 21 London Road, Tunbridge Wells, Kent. *Tel:* 0892 45918. *And at:* 11 North Street, Guildford, Surrey. *Tel:* 0483 300381. *And at:* 17 Holywell Hill, St Albans, Herts. *Tel:* 0727 37351. See London Postal Districts above.

6/WORKTOPS

Specialist suppliers offer a variety of materials.

Kitchens

London Postal Districts

Frederick 387/9 High Road, Wood Green, N22 4JA. (*15 mins Wood Green tube*). *Tel*: 01-888 8164. *Open*: Mon to Fri 8.15am to 5pm. Closed Thurs. Sat 9am to 5pm. Laminated worktops. Made-to-measure, cut-to-size. Mitring/cut-outs for sinks, hobs etc. 300 patterns/colours. Delivery anywhere London/northern home counties. Also sinks, taps, laminates.

Marble & Granite Trading Unit 4, Bush Industrial Estate, 15/25 Standard Road, Park Royal, NW10 6DF. (*7 mins North Acton tube*). *Tel*: 01-453 1166. *Open*: Mon to Fri 9am to 8pm. Sat 9am to 5.30pm. Sun 9.30am to 5pm. 40 colours marble/granite. Worktops cut to size with cut-outs for sinks, hobs etc.

Patrick Fireplaces See **Heating 2/Fireplaces**. Granite/marble worktops cut to size.

Quality Marble See **Tiles 3/Marble**. Work/vanity tops in marble/granite cut to size. Cut-outs for sinks hobs. Installations.

Ulteriors See **Specialists/1** above. Granite worktops a speciality.

Wood Workshop See **3/Wood Kitchens** above. Timber worktops made to order in various hardwoods.

Zarka Marble 41a Belsize Lane, NW3 5AU. (*5 mins Belsize Park tube*). *Tel*: 01-431 3042. *Open*: by appointment. Marble/granite worktops: samples in showroom. Also vanity tops, marble floors, walls, etc. Supply/ fix.

Home Counties/S.East

David Emerson King's Close, Yapton, Arundel BN18 0EX. *Tel*: 0243 552966 (24 hours). Made-to-measure worktops (takes 7 days) with optional fitting service. Duropal laminates, 26 colours/textures, exceptionally hardwearing. Cut-outs for sinks, hobs etc. Colour brochure.

7/SINKS

Large sizes and unusual materials come from specialist suppliers. Shop for sinks in stainless steel, vitreous/porcelain enamel, and new moulded resins at **Home Improvement Specialists** *and* **DIY Superstores**.

London Postal Districts

Bargett Kitchens & Interiors 347/349 King's Road, Chelsea SW3 5ES. (*Sloane Square tube plus bus*). *Tel*: 01-376 3484. *Open*: Mon to Fri 9.30am to 5.30pm. Sat 9am to 5pm. Large deep rectangular glazed fireclay sink by Thaxted Workshops: ideal for cumbersome oven racks/trays.

Mail Order

Brass Traditional Sinks Devauden Green, near Chepstow, Gwent NP6 6PL. *Tel*: 02915 738. Colour brochures. Old-fashioned rectangular Belfast ceramic sinks; capacious, robust. Also rectangular/round solid brass sinks (clean with water-soluble brass cream cleaner). Nationwide deliveries.

The French Collection Lower Green Farm, Felsham, Bury St Edmunds, Suffolk 1P30 0PP. *Tel*: 04493 7162. Leaflets. French farmhouse white porcelain sinks; generously-sized, robust. Nationwide deliveries.

GEC Anderson 89 Herkomer Road, Bushey, Watford, Herts WD2 3LS. *Tel*: 01-950 1826. Visitors by appointment only. Leaflets. Made-to-measure stainless steel worktops/integral sinks; also shelves, drawers, cupboards. Nationwide deliveries.

8/APPLIANCES

Buy appliances from kitchen specialists as a package deal, or shop for bargains.

London Postal Districts

Bargains!

All Gas 22 Lacy Road, Putney SW15. (*Putney BR; Putney Bridge tube*). *Tel*: 01-785 7126. *Open*: Mon to Fri 9am to 5pm. Sat 9am to 12 noon. New merchandise. Major brands. Discounts: 10 to 40%. Appliances (including boilers, fires) not in stock usually take 24 hours, maximum 4 days.

Bargains!

Appliances Direct 5/6 Burlington Parade, Edgware Road, NW2 6QQ. (*Kilburn tube plus bus*). *Tel*: 01-208 2672. *Open*: Mon to Fri 10am to 6pm. Sat 10am to 5pm. New cookers, fridges, dishwashers etc. Discounts up to 15%. Philips, Neff, Westinghouse, AEG. Philips machines ex-exhibition: up to 40% off.

Bargains!

Buyers & Sellers 120/122 Ladbroke Grove, W10 5NE. (*Opposite Ladbroke Grove tube*). *Tel*: 01-229 1947/8468. *Open*: Mon to Sat 9am to 5pm. Early closing Thurs 9.45 to 11.45am. Cynthia Coyne, wheeler-dealer par excellence, has constant supplies not-quite-perfect (tiny blemish) or end-of-line fridges, freezers, microwaves, ovens, hobs, washing machines etc. All brand new, guaranteed. All major brands: Electrolux/Zanussi/Philips/Ariston. Discounts up to 20%.

Bargains!

City Domestic Appliances 131 Essex Road, N1. (*Essex Road BR*). *Tel*: 01-837 6668. *Open*: Mon to Fri 9am to 5.30pm. Closed all day Thurs. Sat 9am to 4.30pm. Hoover near-perfect machines; full guarantee. Average 50 off. Also re-conditioned machines.

The Gas Shop 122/126 Kilburn High Road, NW6 4HY. (*5 mins Kilburn tube*). *Open*: Mon to Sat 9am to 6pm. Stylish new version of traditional gas showrooms. Explore over 2 floors: the Heat Shop, The Kitchen Shop, the Shower Shop, and the Money Shop (yours not theirs!).

Hartman Spare Parts 177 Drury Lane, WC2B. (*5 mins Covent Garden tube*). *Tel*: 01-379 0537. *Open*: Mon to Fri 9am to 5.30pm. Spare parts major brands. Elements, hot plates, switches, trims, handles, filters, hoses, pumps etc.

Bargains!

Hot & Cold Inc 13 Golborne Road, Notting Hill, W10 5NY. (*5 mins Westbourne Park tube*). Tel: 01-960 1300. *Open*: Mon to Sat 10am to 6pm. Very British, despite name. Smallish, rather scruffy, jam-packed shop. Owner Richard Fuchs tirelessly controls around hundreds of appliances on display, featuring 90 brands! – all discounted. Many more in stock. Speciality: posh built-ins; Miele, Scholtes, Neff, Gagganeau, Bosch etc.

J S Humidifiers Dufton Industrial Centre, 238 Green Lane, SE9 3TL. (*M25 Junction 3*). Tel: 01-851 7521. *Open*: Mon to Fri 8.30am to 5.30pm (showroom). Humidifiers to fight condensation. Also air purifiers and air conditioners.

Bargains!

Icetech Appliances 1/3 Barons Court Road, W14 9DP. (*Opposite West Kensington tube*). Tel: 01-381 2303/3119. *Open*: Mon to Fri 9.30am to 6pm. Sat 9.30am to 5pm. Early closing Thurs 1pm. All makes freestanding/built-in appliances from budget through to top range. 1,000 lines in stock, including sinks, taps, waste disposers. Very competitive prices. Bosch appliances with slight "cosmetic" faults (eg small chip or scratch). Save around £100 on e.g. washer/drier.

Bargains!

Stonecraft 988/992 Harrow Road, Kensal Green NW10 5NT. (*10 mins Kensal Green tube*). Tel: 01-968 8722. *Open*: Mon to Sat 9am to 6pm. Reconditioned fridges, cookers, washing machines. Servicing/repairs.

Outer Ring

Bargains!

GD Evans 331/333 High Street, Slough, Berks SL1 1TX. (*London side Slough, near large Co-Op*). Tel: 0753 24188/35138. *Open*: Mon to Sat 9am to 6pm. Sun viewing 10am to 1pm. Ex-exhibition/display built-in/freestanding ovens, hobs, cookers, washing machines, fridges, freezers, all colours. Over 2,000 appliances in stock. Mainly Neff/AEG. A few from Zanussi. Trading since 1956. Phone for current offers. Nationwide deliveries.

GasWorks Lakeside Retail Park, West Thurrock, Essex RM16. (*M25 Junction 30/31; ample free parking*). Tel: 0708 863366. *Open*: Mon to Fri 10am to 6pm. Late nights Thurs & Fri 8pm. Sat 9am to 6pm. Sun 10am to 5pm. British Gas Superstore! See wide range household goods in relaxed, spacious atmosphere. Look outside for the 30ft totem pole. Fitted kitchens, Be Modern and other leading brands. Design/supply/install. Bathrooms by The Bathroom Shop of George Lane, Woodford. Complete bathroom design/install service. Bathroom suites. Spa, whirlpools. Tiles, mirrors, shower trays, bathroom carpeting. Bathroom accessories. Towels, bathmats, shower curtains, roller and Austrian blinds. Cookers, fires. Central heating systems, showers.

RDO Bancroft Road, Reigate, Surrey RH2 7RP. (*M25 Junction 8; town centre, own car park*). Tel: 0737 240403. *Open*: Mon to Fri 9am to 5.30pm. Sat 9am to 1pm. Trading over 30 years. Enormous comprehensive stocks of AEG, Neff, Gaggenau, De Dietrich. Even manufacturers come to them when stuck for a particular model! Supply 70% trade, 30% public. Nationwide deliveries within 3 days.

Ruislip Appliances 70 Park Way, Ruislip Manor, Middx. (*Opposite Windmill Pub*). Tel: 0895 633837. *Open*: Mon to Sat 9am to 5.30pm. Early closing Wed 1pm. Most models Neff in stock. Servicing.

Home Counties/S.East

Lawrence Kitchens Unit C, Progress Road, Sands Industrial estate, Lane End Road, High Wycombe, Bucks. (*M40 Junction 4*). Tel: 0494 443474. *Open*: Mon to Fri 8.30am to 5.30pm. Built-in appliances/sinks at trade prices. Top brands, all models obtainable. Also self-assembly kitchens by Crosby, Kingswood, Symphony. No deliveries: customer must collect.

Stellison Kitchen Centre 11/13 Kents Hill Road, Benfleet, Essex SS7 5PN. (*2 free car parks nearby*). Tel: 0268 793729/758820. *Open*: Mon to Sat 9am to 6pm. Around 20 kitchen displays from Germany, Holland, Belgium and Britain. Built-in branded appliances at, they claim, unbeatable prices.

9/KITCHENWARE

Every kitchen needs an effective batterie de cuisine. *Take time off to browse round specialist suppliers: the equipment provides fresh cooking inspirations.*

London Postal Districts

Cookware & Cane 251 Upper Richmond Road West, East Sheen SW14 8QS. Tel: 01-878 8950. *Open*: Mon to Fri 9.30am to 5.30pm. Sat 9.30am to 6pm. Sun 10.30am to 4.30pm. Selections cookware, glass, china, earthenware; cane chairs, shelves, small tables etc.

Coppershop 48 Neal Street, Covent Garden WC2H 9PA. (*3 mins Covent Garden tube*). *Open*: Mon to Sat 10am to 6pm. Wonderful gleaming array copper pans/bowls/planters/fireside accessories/lamps/jugs and more. Most pans are lined, as acid in food reacts with copper. But unlined copper mixing bowls have stiffening effect on beaten egg whites! Catalogue £1.90.

David Mellor 4 Sloane Square, SW1W 8EE. (*3 mins Sloane Square tube*). Tel: 01-730 4259. *Open*: Mon to Sat 9.30am to 5.30pm. Spacious shop, tranquil atmosphere. Excellent general/specialist cookware. Tableware including elegant modern cutlery designed by owner. Emphasis on fine English crafts: woodware, ceramics, baskets. Beautiful catalogue: phone for price. *Mail order.*
Also at: 26 James Street, Covent Garden WC2E 8PA. (*2 mins Covent Garden tube*). Tel: 01- 379 6947. *Open*: Mon to Fri 10am to 6.30pm. Sat 10am to 6pm. As above, but more frantic!

Kitchens

Elizabeth David 46 Bourne Street, SW1W 8JD. (*5 mins Victoria tube*). *Tel*: 01-730 3123. *Open*: Mon to Sat 10am to 6pm. Definitive source for the complete cook. Porcelain, earthenware, copper, stainless steel, aluminium, woodware, basketware. Knives, pans, utensils, gadgets. Specialised equipment. Personal service, friendly advice. Cake tin hire. Wedding lists. Mail order catalogue. *Also at*: 3 North Row, The Market, Covent Garden WC2E 8RA. (*3 mins Covent Garden tube*). *Tel*: 01-836 9167. *Open*: Mon to Sat 10am to 8pm. Sun 12 noon to 5.30pm.

Divertimenti 139/141 Fulham Road, SW3 6SD. (*5 mins South Kensington tube*). *Tel*: 01-581 8065. *Open* (both branches): Mon to Fri 9.30am to 6pm. Sat 10am to 5pm. Specialist cookware. Also tableware, cookbooks, herbs & spices. Knife-sharpening; service for re-lining copper pans. *Also at*: 45/47 Wigmore Street, W1H 9LE. (*8 mins Bond Street tube*). *Tel*: 01-935 0689. Brochure, *Mail order* £2.50.

Leon Jaeggi & Sons 231 Tottenham Court Road, W1P 0BL. (*3 mins Goodge Street tube*). *Tel*: 01-631 1080. *Open*: (both branches): Mon to Sat 9.30am to 5.30pm. Caters for caterers, but individual shoppers welcome. Stacks of burnished copper stand beacon-like in the window, made by them in Staines. Most pans are lined with tin (retinning service available). But for very high temperatures (crepes, omelettes) lining is silver. Also own-make black iron omelette/fry pans. Season on first use: sprinkle with salt, heat gently for half-an-hour. Wipe out with kitchen paper. Rub over with cooking oil/more salt; heat again. Wipe out; thenceforth do not wash. Suits me!

Kerry's Kitchen Shop 118 High Street, Putney SW15 1RG. (*5 mins Putney Bridge/East Putney tubes*). *Tel*: 01-788 1745. *Open*: (both branches): Mon to Sat 9.15am to 5.30pm. Christopher Beresford keeps his supermarket-style shops strictly down-to-earth: no chi-chi apparatus for high cuisine. Just lots of goods ideas: brushes for teapot spouts/bottles; packs of dishcloths; kettle de-furrers; vegetable parers. Crockery/glass is sold individually, with stocks for replacements. Sensible pans ("no over-floral sets"): stainless steel, aluminium, non-stick. *Also at*: 119 King Street, Hammersmith W6 9JG. (*5 mins Hammersmith tube*). *Tel*: 01-748 5946.

Outer Ring

Peter Knight Cookshop 156 Walton Road, East Molesey, KT8 0HP. (*10/15 mins Hampton Court BR*). *Tel*: 01-979 8371. *Open*: Mon to Sat 9.30am to 5.30pm. Caters for the imaginative cook.

Mrs Sykes Kitchenry 146 High Street, Teddington, Middx TW11 8HZ. (*Teddington BR*). *Tel*: 01-943 2951. *Open*: Mon to Sat 9.45am to 5.30pm. Well-designed kitchenware, keen prices: casseroles, Sabatier knives, glass, earthenware, tinware, gifts. Small shop, friendly, knowledgeable service.

Mail Order

Lakeland Plastics Alexander Buildings, Windermere, Cumbria LA23 1BQ. *Tel*: 09662 2255. Free catalogue. 101 bright ideas for time/labour-saving in the kitchen, and around the house. Essential reading. Personal callers welcome at the Windermere Shop. *Open*: Mon to Fri 8am to 6pm. Sat 9am to 5pm. Open Bank Holidays. Closed Sun. The Miller Howe Kaff (run by famous chef/TV personality) has adventurous menu/affordable prices. Worth a trip?

10/ACCESSORIES

Extra visual and functional touches transform your kitchen from a brochure kit into real life. Here are just a few ideas.

Mail Order

Oak Design 48 Winkfield Road, Windsor, Berks SL4 4AF. *Tel*: 0753 830210. Mobile butcher's block/trolley/work station in super hard solid hickory. Oiled finish, flatpack.

Rackmaster 43 Russell Street, Wilton, Salisbury, Wilts SP2 0BG. *Tel*: 0722 744143. Leaflet. Attractive plain design for plate rack with solid beech frame/birch dowels. Drainage/storage. Oiled finish.

Spacefinder Design 7 Forest Drive East, E11 1JX. *Tel*: 01-558 2052. Hanging "batterie de cuisine" (rack for pans and implements). Measures 32 by 18in; frees cupboard space, puts everything easy to hand. Supplied with 6 butchers' hooks. Beechwood/brass or chrome.

Woodfit Kem Mill, Whittle le Woods, Chorley, Lancs PR6 7EA. *Tel*: 02572 66421 (24 hours). Invaluable catalogue professional kitchen/bedroom fittings to transform DIY/budget kitchen cupboards into streamlined storage/workstations.

The York Handmade Brick Co Forest Lane, Alne, North Yorks YO6 2LU. *Tel*: 03473 8881. Illustrated leaflet. York clay stacking wine racks made by traditional methods. Keeps wine at even temperature/right angle. Damaging ultra-violet light is excluded. Natural terracotta colours/two-bottle units.

BATHROOMS

The bathroom is a strange place, little used compared to other rooms, but for a few minutes a haven of peace where the cares of world and family wash warmly away, a reinvigorating, mystical, magical, secret chamber of dreams.

1/BATHROOM SPECIALISTS

Almost as common as kitchen shops, many can do the whole job with home service for design/supply/install. Ask for a local reference and check firms' efficiency right at the outset. Many builders' merchants (see Home Improvement Specialists) also offer similar services.

London Postal Districts

British Bathroom Centre 3 Portman Square, W1H 0JB. (*3 mins Bond Street tube*). *Tel*: 01-935 6938. *Open* (both branches): Mon to Sat 9am to 6pm. 30 luxurious displays of latest designs. Colour schemes, planning. Artists can decorate sanitaryware/tiles to match furnishings or personalise a room. Vanity units built to order. Special machinery for cutting marble. Plan/install.
Also at: 602/604 Seven Sisters Road, N15 6HT. *Tel*: 01-802 6493/6696. Open as above, plus Sun 10am to 2pm.

The David Neale Bathroom Centre 67/71 Abbey Road, St Johns Wood, NW8 0BU. (*10 mins Swiss Cottage tube*). *Tel*: 01-624 8126. *Open*: Mon to Fri 8am to 5pm. Sat 9am to 1pm. Bathroom displays include whirlpools. Top brand names: Bosch fitted bathrooms, Villeroy & Boch, Sanitan, Sbordoni, Twyford, Nordic etc.

Godwins 28 Rushgrove Avenue, The Hyde, Colindale NW9 6QS. (*10 mins Colindale tube*). *Tel*: 01-200 0508. *Open* (all branches): Mon to Fri 8am to 5pm. Sat 9am to 4pm. Around 80 bathroom settings: the largest bathroom/kitchen displays in NW London, they claim. Emphasis on traditional styles.
Also at: 49 Church Road, Hendon, NW4 4DU. (*Hendon Central tube, restricted parking*). *Tel*: 01-203 1095.
And at: 176 High Road, East Finchley N2 9AS. (*5 mins East Finchley tube, restricted parking*). *Tel*: 01-444 2311.

Just Showers 155 Beacontree Avenue, Dagenham, Essex RM8 2UL. (*Barking BR plus bus*). *Tel*: 01-590 1507. *Open*: Mon to Fri 9.30am to 4.30pm. Specialist suppliers all makes showers. Installations/repairs.

Max Pike's Bathroom Shop 4 Eccleston Street, SW1W 9LN. (*2 mins Victoria tube/BR*). *Tel*: 01-730 7216. *Open*: Mon to Fri 10am to 6pm. Max Pike is a pioneer and a celebrity in the bathroom world. Showroom reflects innovative/dedicated approach to bathroom fittings. Many exclusive designs, traditional/modern. Planning, colour schemes, layout/design. Free deliveries London area.

Taps & Tiles 127/129 Lower Marsh, Waterloo SE1 7AE. (*5 mins Waterloo tube/BR*). *Tel*: 01-261 9646/928 6125. *Open*: Mon to Sat 9.30am to 5.30pm.

Large displays (many working) of up-market products/traditional/modern styles. Colour schemes/plan/install. Also kitchens.

Outer Ring

ABC Exclusive Bathrooms Centre 8 Farr Avenue, Barking, Essex. (*15 mins Barking BR; parking outside*). *Tel*: 01-594 8265. *Open*: Mon to Sat 9am to 6pm. One of only four shops in country to offer Exclusive Bathrooms' exotic bathroom design. Owners are working plumbers who know their stuff. Sanitaryware can be matched to any colour: even loos and bidets. Plan/install.

The Bath House 25 High Street, Purley, Surrey. (*2 mins Purley BR*). *Tel*: 01-668 0600. *Open*: Mon to Sat 9am to 6pm. Up-to-date exclusive bathrooms, tiles, accessories from UK/abroad. Design/plan/install.
Also at: 145 High Street, Epsom, Surrey. *Tel*: 03727 42748.

The Bathroom Centre 194/196 High Road, Woodford Green, Essex 1G8 9EF. *Tel*: 01-504 1765. *Open*: Mon to Sat 9am to 6pm. Thirty roomsettings over 3 floors; exclusive ranges; all leading European makes. Plan/install. Complete service, including free coffee!

Bird Baths 13 Hainault Street, Ilford, Essex IG1 4EN. (*5 mins Ilford BR;*

opposite bus depot and multi-storey car park). *Tel*: 01-478 8213. *Open*: Mon to Sat 9am to 5pm. Family builders' merchants revamped into attractive bathroom specialist. Friendly, personal service. Styles from traditional Victorian to avant-garde continental. Tiles, accessories. Many exclusive items.

Original Bathrooms 143/145 Kew Road, Richmond, Surrey TW9 1PN. (*15 mins Richmond tube/BR*). *Tel*: 01-940 7554. *Open*: Mon to Sat 9am to 5.30pm. Very much family firm: current management are fifth generation! Up-market trendsetting displays. Many designs from Italy. Exclusive products. Plan/advise.

Walton Bathrooms The Hersham Centre, The Green, Molesey Road, Walton-on-Thames, Surrey KT12 4HL. *Tel*: 0932 224784. *Open*: Mon to Sat 9am to 5.30pm. Plan/install. Over 25 quality bathrooms on display. Members of Federation of Master Builders. Colour brochures.

Home Counties/S.East

The Bathroom Shop 4 Chapel Street, Guildford, Surrey GU1 3UH. *Tel*: 0483 573434. *Open*: Tues to Sat 9am to 5.30pm. Personal service, good prices, wide range traditional/modern styles.
Also at: Unit 3, Wykham Estate, Moorside Road, Winall, Winchester SO23 7RX. (*Own car park*). *Tel*: 0962 62554. *Open*: Mon to Sat 10am to 6pm.
And at: 37 Queen Street, Maidenhead, Berks SL6 1NB. *Tel*: 0628 32622. *Open*: Tues to Sat 9am to 5.30pm.

Bathroom Visions 12 Duke Street, Princes Risborough, Bucks HP17 0AT. (*Park at rear*). *Tel*: 08444 2028. *Open*: Tues to Fri 10am to 5pm. Sat 9am to 4pm. Mon by appointment. Trademark is elegant vintage van. Emphasis on traditional displays. Lots of choice, enthusiastic personal service.

Corniche Bathrooms 17/19 Elmshott Lane, Cippenham, Slough, Berks SL1 5QS. (*M4 Junction 7; park at rear*).

Tel: 06286 66668. *Open*: Mon to Fri 9am to 5.30pm. Sat 9.30am to 5.30pm. Co-ordinated bathroom roomsettings, up-market merchandise, modern/traditional styles. Knowledgeable staff, friendly service. Plan/install. Licensed credit broker: home improvement loans, instant credit.

County Bathrooms Oxford Tile House, Sandy Lane West, Littlemore, Oxon OX4 5LB. (*Ring Road South; park on site*). *Tel*: 0865 775642. *Open* (both branches): Mon to Sat 8.30am to 5.30pm. Planning. Personal service. Large stocks, lots of choice. Working displays. Thousands of tiles.
Also at: Northbridge Road, Berkhampstead, Herts HP4 1EH. (*Industrial estate, A41 London Road*). *Tel*: 04428 76244.

The following stores have installed Ideal-Standard's new Solutions concept. Find good displays of latest products, backed by specialist planning services.

London Postal Districts

BJ Brown See **Home Improvement Specialists**.

Home Counties/S.East

Atlantis Bathooms & Kitchens 69/71 Bower Street, Bedford MK40 3RB. *Tel*: 0234 214113.

Bathroom Centre 1 Hotspur Top Lane, Beaconsfield, Bucks. *Tel*: 04946 75665.

Cyril Ridgeon & Son Tenison Road, Cambridge CB1 2DS. *Tel*: 0223 61177.

B & K Furnishing Market Road, Tunbridge Wells, Kent TN1 2SY. *Tel*: 0982 23528.

Gammon & Smith Bedford Road, Petersfield, Hants GU32 3LW. *Tel*: 0730 62233.

Imperial Bathrooms 440 St Leonards Road, Windsor, Berks. *Tel*: 0753 850240.

Leaneys of Lancing 45/49 Penhill

Road, Lancing West Sussex BN15 8HA. *Tel*: 0903 752475.

West End Interiors Coggeshall, Essex. *Tel*: 0376 62733.

2/SANITARYWARE

Buy baths, basins, WCs, bidets etc from specialists, above, or from DIY Superstores, Home Improvements Specialists, or suppliers listed below.

London Postal Districts

Aston Matthews 143/147 Essex Road, Islington, N1. (*10 mins Highbury/Islington tube*). *Tel*: 01-226 7220/01-226 3657. *Open*: Mon to Fri 8.30am to 5pm. Sat 9.30am to 2pm. Established in Islington in 1823. Knowledgeable, enthusiastic, energetic staff. Large stocks, prompt deliveries. Excellent reputation. Wide-ranging often exclusive designs. And low prices.

Bargains!

Bathrooms & Showers 186 Upper Richmond Road West, East Sheen SW14 8AN. *Tel*: 01-878 5906. *Open*: Mon to Sat 8.30am to 5pm. Cheapest anywhere claim for suites/shower units. Supply/install.

Bargains!

Bathrooms Direct 764a Fulham Road, SW6 5SA. (*5 mins Putney Bridge tube*). *Tel*: 01-736 3081. *Open*: Mon to Fri 9am to 5pm. Cheapest (they claim) for main brands. Also French imported styles.

Bargains!

Bathroom Discount Centre 297 Munster Road, SW6 6BW. (*West Brompton/Parsons Green tubes*). *Tel*: 01-381 4222. *Open*: Mon to Fri 8.30am to 5.30pm. Sat 9am to 5pm. Sun 9am to 4pm. Rather shabby showroom but wonderful prices for major brands: around 30% off. Ideal-Standard, Armitage Shanks, Twyfords. Orders take around 2 to 3 days; deliveries mostly free.

Riverside Plumbers Merchants/ Bathroom Centre 180/188 Mile End Road, E1 4LS. (*7 mins Stepney Green* tube). Tel: 01-790 1323. Open: Mon to Fri 8am to 6pm. Sat 8am to 1pm. Late night Thurs 8pm. Keen prices quality sanitaryware: most leading makes. Full service for bathrooms: plan/supply/install (to include tiling, electrics, plastering etc). Phone for special seasonal offers.

Bargains!

West One Bathrooms 60 Queenstown Road, SW8 3RY. (5 mins Clapham Common tube; parking outside shop). Tel: 01-720 9333/6 Open: Mon to Sat 8.30am to 5.30pm. Sharp prices, friendly service. Displays feature British top brands, plus imported exclusive suites from Italy, Germany and France (Porcelain de Paris). Quick, often free, deliveries. Plumbing/DIY counter at back.

Outer Ring

Simply Bathrooms 5 Centreway, Ilford, Essex. (Off High Road). Tel: 01-514 8788. Open: Mon to Sat 9am to 6pm. Early closing Tues and Wed 5.30pm. Sun 10am to 4pm. Gigantic showroom, around 160 bathroom suites. Top makes: Armitage, Stelrad Doulton, Twyfords, et al. Showers, accessories, tiles.
Also at: 2 Bensham Lane, Croydon, Surrey. Tel: 01-689 4334. Open: Mon to Fri 8.30am to 5.30pm. Late night Tues & Thurs 8pm. Sat 8.30am to 5pm. Sun 10am to 4pm.
And at: 467-491 Northolt Road, South Harrow, Middx. Tel: 01-864 9534. Open: Mon to Fri 8am to 6.30pm. Sat 9am to 5pm. Plus Allia centres inside Courts Mammoth Superstores at Southend, Staples Corner, Milton Keynes, Bristol.

Home Counties/S.East

Simply Bathrooms 1341/7 London Road, Leigh-on-Sea, Essex. Tel: 0702 77517. Open: Mon to Sat 9am to 6pm. See Outer Ring above.

3/PERIOD BATHROOMS

Shop here for old-style elegance when restoring older homes, or for adding atmosphere to modern properties. Many bathroom specialists listed above also stock period-style ranges. For genuine fittings, comb **Architectural Salvage** merchants, but check with a plumber that your ideas are feasible!

London Postal Districts

Pipe Dreams 2 Hinde Street, W1M 5RH. (8 mins Bond Street tube) Tel: 01-486 1084. Open (all branches): Mon to Fri 9.30am to 5.30pm. Sat 10am to 5pm. Bathroom specialist; inspirational roomsettings. From trad. to modern, from taps to furniture. Design/plan. Fittings handpainted or stencilled to match furnishings.
Also at: 103 Regents Park Road, NW1 8UR. (5 mins Chalk Farm tube). Tel: 01-586 9856.
And at: 72 Gloucester Road, SW7 4QT. (5 mins Gloucester Road tube). Tel: 01-225 3978.
And at: 27 Wimbledon High Street, SW19 5BY. (10 mins Wimbledon tube/BR). Tel: 01-944 1550.

Sitting Pretty 131 Dawes Road, SW6 7EA. (5 mins Fulham Broadway tube). Tel: 01-381 0049. Open: Mon to Fri 10am to 5pm. Sat 11am to 3pm. In at the beginning of trad. bathroom revivals, SP is still tops (bottoms?) for wooden loo seats. Repro Victorian/Deco sanitaryware; roll-top cast-iron baths.

Traditional Bathroom Warehouse 92 Carnwath Road, Fulham, SW6 3HW. (10 mins Parsons Green tube). Tel: 01-736 1503. Open (both branches): Mon to Sat 9.30am to 6.30pm. Sun 10am to 4pm. Old-style sanitaryware, taps, accessories. Keen prices. Bath panels, tiles, whirlpools, etched bath screens. Delightful vanity units like old-style washstands. Deliveries, installations, custom-building.
Also at: 270/271 The Colonnade, Waterloo Station, Waterloo Road, SE1 8SF. Tel: 01-928 7982.

Home Counties/S.East

Pipe Dreams 11 Chequer Street, St Albans, Herts AL1 3YJ. (5 mins Abbey BR). Tel: 0727 37687. Open: Mon to Sat 9.30am to 5.30pm. See London Postal Districts above.

Pretty Bathrooms 103 West Street, Farnham, Surrey GU9 7EN. Tel: 0252 720611. Open: Mon to Sat 9.30am to 4.30pm. Closed all day Wed. Traditional/period bathroom specialists. Handpainted vanity units. Design/install.

Worth a Trip

The Deco Bathroom The Old School, Alderminster, near Stratford-upon-Avon, Warwicks. Tel: 0789 87616. Open: Sat 10am to 6pm. Sun by appointment. Original Edwardian/30s rolltop baths, bidets, loos, suites. Brass/chrome fittings.

David Woods Antiques The Stores, Skenfrith, Abergavenny, Gwent. (10m from Ross-on-Wye). Tel: 060084 201. Open: by appointment only. Genuine Victorian/Edwardian bathroom fittings: "no reproductions". Polaroid sent after phone consultations.

4/WHIRLPOOLS & SPECIAL EFFECTS

Whirlpools, massage showers, steam cabinets, saunas: all are part of the modern luxury bathing environment. At specialists listed you can try before you buy.

London Postal Districts

Arnull of London 13/14 Queen Street, W1X 7PL. (5 mins Green Park tube). Tel: 01-499 3231. Open: Mon to Fri 9.30am to 5.30pm. Sat 11am to 2pm. Up-market bathroom showroom; French/Italian sanitaryware, exclusive tiles. Working displays Jacuzzis/steam showers.

Bathroom Discount Centre See 2/Sanitaryware above. Powerjet Whirlpools for any bath, old/new: whether steel/cast iron/plastic. Complete systems include: pumps, jets, suction, air control, on/off switch, electronic control box, ELCB, Luxury options: Jacuzzi jets; low

5 / Accessories

water level safety cut-out; in-line heater; chrome/gold fittings. Fitted within 2/3 days.

British Bathroom Centre See **1/Specialists** above. W1: see the "Environmental Bath": computers control whirlpool, sauna, shower, sunlamps, and rain effects. Own-make whirlpools; working showers, and steam room. Try these out by arrangement.

The Jacuzzi Centre 157 Sloane Street, SW1 9BT. (*5 mins Sloane Square tube*). *Tel*: 01730 5835. All Jacuzzi bath models, with exclusive sanitaryware, taps, tiles, furniture, mirrors. 18 Jacuzzi baths; steam shower enclosures with side body jets. Book in for a Jacuzzi test drive! Personal service. Design/install.
Many firms listed under **1/Specialists** and **3/Period Bathrooms** above have working showroom models.

Max Pike's Bathroom Shop See **1/Specialists** above. A wide variety of luxury working airbaths, showers plus "environmental" enclosure.

Pipe Dreams See **3/Period Bathrooms** above.
W1: try out a Majestic steam room; see Rainbow whirlpools, and various working showers.
NW1: working steam/shower unit, whirlpools.
SW7: try out a steam room; see working showers.
SW19: try out a steam room; working Jacuzzi, and airjet system; various showers.
St Albans: try out a steam room; working Rainbow Jacuzzi and various showers.

Taps & Tiles See **1/Specialists** above. Try out a sauna or a steam shower. See working showers/Jacuzzi.

Outer Ring

Original Bathrooms See **1/Specialists** above. 2 working Jacuzzis, 2 showers, steam baths.

Walton Bathrooms See **1/Specialists** above. Working showers (5 different heads); Hydrospar whirlpool.

Home Counties/S.East

Bathroom Visions See **1/Specialists** above. Working air bath; Force 10 Performance showers; Nordic saunas/steam baths.

Corniche Bathrooms See **1/Specialists** above. 3 working Jacuzzis, 3 whirlpools, 2 spa baths, 2 pumped showers, 2 steam showers, and a hot tub you can try!

5/ACCESSORIES

Many bathroom specialists above also offer attractive bathroom accessories, notably **Pipe Dreams** *and* **Smallbone**. *Firms listed under* **Doors 3/Door Furniture** *sell bathroom accessories in brass.* **Tile Specialists** *may sell china accessories to match tile ranges.*

London Postal Districts

The Bathroom Shop John Lewis of Hungerford, Liberty. See **Department Stores**. Emphasis on furnishings/furniture rather than bleak fittings. Welcome back to the linen cupboard with lacey fretwork panels; sycamore/pine/oak. Slatted teak bath "mats" never get soggy. Pine bathroom tables, chairs, mirror frames. Freestanding towel rails.

Danico Brass See **Doors 2/Door Furniture**. Elegant brass taps, and tap/shower handsets. Towel rings/rails.

Diametric Modern Furniture See **Furniture 1/General**. Bathroom accessories (mirrors, glass shelves, etc) supported on floor to ceiling pole.

Ikea See **Furnishing Stores/DIY Superstores**. Dax cabinets/shelves for neat storage solutions: fitted look/unfitted price. Pine wall bars, slot-on fittings: hooks/towel rails/soap dish/toilet roll holder. Chunky rounded accessories in white moulded plastic. White plastic floor decking.

The Kite Store 69 Neal Street, Covent Garden WC2H 9PJ. (*5 mins Leicester Square tube*). *Tel*: 01-836 1666. *Open* (both branches): Mon to Fri 10am to 6pm. Sat 10.30am to 5pm. Polyurethane-coated ripstop nylon by the metre, makes good shower curtains. Colours include black, white, pink, orange and purple, plus primaries. *Also at*: 3 Marlborough Court, W1V 1PJ. *Tel*: 01-734 4320.

Riverside Plumbers Merchants See **2/Sanitaryware** above. Shower doors/enclosures made-to-measure, any size. Colour surrounds in silver, white or gold.

Sellar Bros See **Doors 2/Door Furniture**. Ritzy gold-plated dolphins stoically support shell soap dishes, towels rails, toilet roll holders etc.

A Touch of Brass See **Doors 2/Door Furniture**. Brass taps/shower mixers/accessories; modern/period. Stove lacquer finishes to order.

Mail Order

Beds Etc. 25 High Street, Southampton, Hants SO1 0DF. *Tel*: 0703 330513. *Open to personal callers*: Mon to Sat 9.30am to 5.30pm. Late night Mon 7.30pm. Victorian-style solid beech towel rails, flat-packed self-assembly. Antique pine waxed finish, or unfinished to stain/paint. Large shop (3 floors), all types beds/sofabeds, keen prices. National deliveries.

JAB Services 23 Oakwood, Partridge Green, Horsham, Sussex RH13 8JG. Sae for details. Corded bathroom lightpulls in range of colours, with tassel ends, or ceramic/wood/brass decorative knobs.

Hethecraft Pine Furniture Old Station Yard, Metheringham, Lincoln LN4 3HD. *Tel*: 0526 21926. Victorian towel racks in choice of woods or painted.

Si-Fast 206 Stafford Street, Walsall, West Midlands WS2 8DW. *Tel*: 0922 22523. Brochure. *Open personal callers*: Mon to Fri 9am to 5pm. Sat: 9am to 12.30pm. Victorian-style ceiling-suspended cast-iron drying rack.

6/RESTORATION/RENOVATION

Ideas for putting beauty back into your bathroom without full-scale replacement.

All Districts

The Bath Re-enamelling Company Main Road, Worleston, Nantwich, Cheshire CW5 5BN. *Tel*: 0270 626554. Offers genuine re-enamelling as opposed to older epoxy resin processes. Four applications, then coating is left for three days to cure. Teams cover whole country. Ring/write for details.

Renubath 248 Lillie Road, SW6 7QA. *Tel*: 01-381 8337/8. Established over 20 years. Trained operator, nationwide service. Repair/resurface metal baths, guaranteed for 12 months. Chipped enamel repairs.

Chemical cleaning for tiles/porcelain.

London Postal Districts

ABC Exclusive See **Bathrooms 1/Specialists**. Colour matching service for all sanitaryware.

HM James & Son 736 Romford Road, Manor Park, E12. *Tel*: 01-553 1521. Can supply major makes out-of-date sanitaryware for additions/replacements.

Thermo-Glaze 7 Lawn Terrace, Blackheath SE3 9LJ. *Tel*: 01-318 5042. In situ re-enamelling; white or 900 colours! Leaflet.

Outer Ring

AEA Edwards 85/89 Field End Road, Pinner, Middx HA5 1QG. (*5 mins Eastcote tube*). *Tel*: 01-868 6419. *Open*: Mon to Sat 8.30am to 5.30pm. Early closing Wed 1pm. Builders'

merchants supplying out-of-date bathroom colours.

Home Counties/S.East

Bath Renovations (Essex) 89 Water Lane, Purfleet, Essex RM16 1GX. No showroom: by appointment. *Tel*: 0708 868155; or (mobile) 0836 215235. Cast-iron and steel baths resurfaced; all sanitaryware chemically cleaned. Twelve years' experience, one-man business: mainly East London/Essex/Kent, but will travel further. Ring or write.

Mail Order

Bathroom Ceramics Beansheaf, Kirby Misperton, Malton, Yorks YO17 0UF. *Tel*: 065 386 437. White sanitaryware reglazed to match discontinued colours: same make (where possible) as original range.

CHILDREN'S ROOMS

Children! Delinquent or docile, lively or listless, bright or bored, they all need their own space – and so do you, so make theirs as nice as possible!

*Modern furnishings are a happy way to welcome a new baby. Later on, kids stay more eagerly in their own rooms if surroundings suit. Shop also at **Interior Design** stores, **DIY Superstores**, and at shops for **Decorating Materials**, plus **Furnishing Stores**. Many of the bed manufacturers listed in **Bedrooms** make sturdy bunks. equipment, bunk beds. Watch out for collections such as Animal Krackers and collections from Paper Moon. Wallcoverings featuring Disney cartoon coverings are widely available.*

London Postal Districts

Baby B's 779/781 Fulham Road, Fulham SW6 5HA. (*2 mins Parsons Green tube*). *Tel*: 01-731 7348. *Open*: Mon to Fri 9.30am to 5.30pm. Sat 10am to 5pm. "The most civilised place to shop for a baby in London." Advice from experienced staff. For 0 to 5 years with clothing from top end British market.

Bargains!

Babycare 74 High Street, Acton, W3. (*15 mins Acton Town tube; opposite Town Hall*). *Tel*: 01-993 8542. *Open*: Mon to Fri 9.30am to 5.30pm. Early closing Wed 1pm. Sat 9.30am to 6pm. Discount prices for leading makes of cots, prams, pushchairs, high chairs. Everything for babies/toddlers, from the premature to 4 years old, including clothes and toys.

Cartoon Carpet Company See **Accessories 8/Rugs**. Favourite cartoon characters cavort across quality Axminster rugs.

Children's World Unit 3, Angel Road, Edmonton, N18 3HD. (*Seven Sisters tube plus bus; 5 mins Angel Road BR*). *Tel*: 01-807 5518. *Open* (all branches): Mon to Fri 10am to 8pm. Sat 9am to 6pm. Wide selections all types baby/children's equipment, including good choice safety products. *Also at*: 317 Cricklewood Broadway, NW2 6PH. (*Kilburn Park tube plus bus*). *Tel*: 01-208 1088. *Open*: Mon to Fri 10am to 8pm. Sat 9am to 6pm.

Dragons 23 Walton Street, SW3 2HX. (*10 mins South Kensington tubes*). *Tel*: 01-589 3795/589 0548. *Open*: Mon to Fri 9.30am to 5.30pm. Sat 10.30am to 4.30pm. Rosie Fisher started making charming handpainted children's furniture 10 years ago, because there were no suitable designs for her own children. Now range includes: chests, tables, miniature chairs with rush seats (names to order), toy chests, etc. Also scaled-down upholstery for nurseries. Beatrix Potter fabrics/papers plus filmy voiles. Catalogue £2.50.

Moriarti's See **Bedrooms 3/Pine Beds**. Sturdy bunk beds in pine or hardwoods.

Mothercare Nearest branch/general enquiries. *Tel*: 0923 33577. *Open*: Mon to Sat (all branches; late nights vary) Mon to Fri 9.30am to 5.30pm. Sat 9am to 5.30am. Star store: 174/176 Oxford Street, W1 9DJ. (*5 mins Oxford Circus tube*). *Tel*: 01-580 1688. Late night Thurs 7pm. Attractive cribs/cots. Own brand linens in brights/pastels. Lamps/shades. Children's co-ordinates: vinyl/ready-made curtains/cot drapes/frieze plus accessories. Shopping service: orders assembled for later collection. Mother-and-baby rooms at larger branches. Mail order services. Catalogue 45p.
Also at: 461 Oxford Street, W1R 1DB. (*5 mins Bond Street tube*). *Tel*: 01-629 6621.
Also at: 145/147 Brompton Road, SW3 1QP (*5 mins Knightsbridge tube*). *Tel*: 01-584 1397.
Also at: Brent Cross Shopping Centre, NW4 3FD (*5 mins Brent Cross tube*). *Tel*: 01-202 5377.
Also at: Wood Green, 38/40 High Road, Wood Green N22 6BX. (*10 mins Wood Green tube*)). *Tel*: 01-888 6920.
And at: Brixton SW9. *Tel*: 01-733 1494.
And at: Clapham SW11. *Tel*: 01-228 0391.
And at: Ealing Broadway W5. *Tel*: 01-597 6181.
And at: Ealing West W13. *Tel*: 01-567 7067.
And at: East Ham E6. *Tel*: 01-472 4948.

And at: Edmonton N18. *Tel*: 01-803 9408.

And at: Eltham SE9. *Tel*: 01-859 7957.

And at: Fulham SW6. *Tel*: 01-381 6387.

And at: Hammersmith W6. *Tel*: 01-741 0514

And at: Holloway N7. *Tel*: 01-607 0915.

And at: Kensington W8. *Tel*: 01-937 9781.

And at: Kilburn NW6. *Tel*: 01-328 6466.

And at: Lewisham SE13. *Tel*: 01-852 2167.

And at: Peckham SE15. *Tel*: 01-358 0093.

And at: Stratford East. *Tel*: 01-534 5714.

And at: Tooting SW17. *Tel*: 01-672 3947.

And at: Tottenham Court Road, W1. *Tel*: 01-636 0192.

And at: Victoria Street, SW1. *Tel*: 01-828 0499.

And at: Walthamstow E17. *Tel*: 01-521 2535.

And at: Wandsworth SW18. *Tel*: 01-874 2699.

And at: Wood Green N22. *Tel*: 01-888 6920.

And at: Woolwich SE18. *Tel*: 01-854 3540.

The Nursery 103 Bishops Road, SW6 7AX. (*5 mins Parsons Green tube*). *Tel*: 01-731 6637. *Open*: Mon to Sat 10am to 6pm. Handpainted furniture in traditional designs. Antique children's furniture; exclusive children's enamelware. Toyboxes. China old/new. Silver christening presents, prints. Lace-edged cot linens, patchwork/paisley quilts.

The Nursery Window 83 Walton Street, SW3 2HX. (*10 mins Sloane Square tube*). *Tel*: 01-581 3358. *Open*: Mon to Sat 10am to 5.30pm. Exclusive co-ordinates; patterns range from chic tartans to rabbits/teddies. Fabrics, friezes, papers with accessories made to match.

Paper Moon 53 Fairfax Road, NW6 1EN. (*10 mins Finchley Road/Swiss Cottage tubes*). *Tel*: 01-624 1198. *Open*: Mon to Fri 9.30am to 5.30am. Sat 10am to 5pm. Wide selection

stylish children's wallpaper/fabrics/borders. Soft furnishings made to measure.

Peking Hippo See Hippo Hall (ex-Pimlico Road) now shares happily with Chinese porcelain. Children's co-ordinated fabrics/wallpapers/borders. Rainbows, animals, targets, aeroplanes . . . even embracing hippos, aptly called Hippo Love. Alphabet letters entwined with decorative animals adhere magnetically to a background board: instantly assemble personal gift/wall decoration . . . or stick on fridge.

Bargains!

Pillowtalk See **Bedrooms 12/Bed Linen**. Good stocks/keen prices duvet/pillowcase sets featuring comic cuts: Beano/Dandy. Also Postman Pat, Paddington, Thomas The Tank Engine. Plus BMX, Snooker, Calculator, American Football, Ghost Busters. Teenagers can curl up with Marilyn Monroe/James Dean. More extensive co-ordinates are Jungle Krazy, Teddytime, Zoo, Kids Kapers. Bed linens, ready-made curtains, fabrics by the metre. Also lampshades/waste bins, made-up specially.

Rockinghorse Bennet Court, 1 Bellevue Road, SW17 7EG. (*1 min Wandsworth Common BR*). *Tel*: 01-7672313. *Open*: Mon to Sat 10am to 6pm. Children's furniture handmade in own Cheshire factory and handpainted to order. Rush-seated chairs/hairbrushes take 2/3 weeks. Larger items around 3/5 weeks. Names/birthdates etc. Choose colours/patterns from sample boards. Bright strong colours. Favourite design is primary blue rocking chair with soldier legs: they're standing to attention, handcarved. Other designs include tumbling clowns, teddies, bows, garlands.

Swallows & Amazons 40 Webbs Road, Battersea, SW11 6SF. (*10 mins Clapham South BR*). *Tel*: 01-228 6909. *Open*: Mon to Fri 10am to 5pm. Sat 10am to 1pm. Sellers and buyers of "good-as-new" children's clothes/toys/equipment.

Peter de Wit 21 Greenwich Church

Street, Greenwich Village, SE10 9BJ. (*Centre Greenwich; 2 mins Cutty Sark*). *Tel*: 01-305 0048. *Open*: Mon to Fri 2pm to 5pm (but phone first). Sat & Sun 10.30am to 7pm. Tiny shop: exclusive handpainted toys/furniture. Special designs/colours to order.

Outer Ring

Children's World Trafalgar Way, Croydon CR9 4PB. *Tel*: 01-760 0484. See London Postal Districts above.

Home Counties/S.East

Children's World Vastern Court, Caversham Road, Reading RG1 8BA. *Tel*: 0734 503340. See London Postal Districts above.

Mail Order

Leap-Frog Children's Furniture Design House, Rank Xerox Business Park, Mitcheldean, Glos GL17 0SN. *Tel*: 0594 543077. Colour brochure. Handpainted teddy bears frolic across cream-painted cribs, chests, tables, chairs and so. Or choose authentic Alison Uttley Little Grey Rabbit woodland scenes. Four-posters and desks for older children.

Newcombe Marketing Freepost, Dronfield, Yorks S18 6LZ. *Tel*: 0246 416306. Brochure. Stackerjack plastic stacking storage boxes; 3 sizes, 5 colours, delivered flat. Lids available. Combine with System 80 lightweight aluminium shelving.

Poppy 44 High Street, Yarm, Cleveland. *Tel*: 0642 790000. Fabrics, wallpapers, borders especially for kids. Clowns, bears, moons, and the alphabet run riot. Primaries/pastels. Colour catalogue.

Ulike UK 24 Lambourn Road, SW4 0LY. *Tel*: 01-627 5244. Wire storage cubes for toys/general clutter. Red/black/white.

INTERIOR DESIGN

The whole of this book is relevant to interior design in its broadest sense. But in particular, look also at **Soft Furnishings** and **Decorating Materials**, where co-ordinates specialists are listed. Virtually every High Street now sports its own interior design specialist store: my selections appear below.

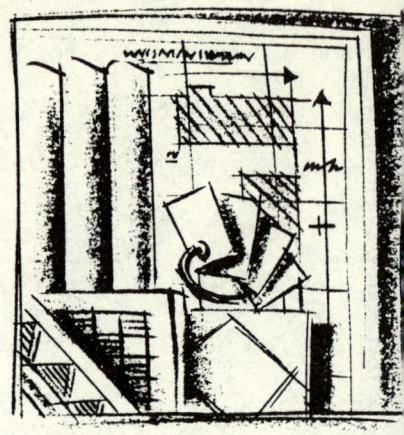

"Fashion magazines for the home and Interior Design Exhibitions have increased over the last few years but still the public in the UK drag far behind their Continental cousins in the amount that they spend on the furnishing of their homes. In Germany, Holland and Denmark for example they spend two, three, four times the amount we spend in this country. Why are the public so slow to react? If they took the trouble to seek out those shops and stores which offer excellent in depth services, they would be able to raise the standard of decor in their homes. Whether it be advice on a single purchase or a complete scheme for a whole house down to the last rug or ashtray, help is available. Discount and Special Offers abound but services fail to gain respect or the priority that they deserve. Genuine services won't be at cut prices but will give excellent value for money and a real investment for the future." **Hugh Joscelyne, JP**, *chairman, Clement Joscelyne Ltd.*

London Postal Districts

Armstrong Cummins 10 Fauconberg Road, Chiswick, W4 3JY. (*8 mins Chiswick Park/Gunnersbury tubes*). *Tel*: 01-747 8193. *Open*: Tues to Sat 10am to 5.30pm. Fabrics, wallpapers, carpets, rugs, cushions, paintings, antiques, accessories. Curtain-making, upholstery, special paint finishes.

Robina Cayzer 62/64 Pimlico Road, SW1W 8LS. (*10 mins Sloane Square*). *Tel*: 01-730 9136. *Open*: Mon to Fri 10am to 6pm. Sat 10am to 2pm. Attractive corner shop with team of 3 designers providing full interior design/soft furnishings service.

The Charles Hammond Shop 253 Fulham Road, SW3 6HY. (*10 mins South Kensington tube*). *Tel*: 01-376 5599. *Open*: Mon to Fri 9.30am to 5.30pm. Sat 10am to 4pm. Own chintzes, linens, handmade upholstery, plus extensive samples. Expert staff, 2 floors inspirational displays. Exclusive accessories/gifts, elegant classic handpainted furniture.

Clifton Interiors 10 Bristol Gardens, Little Venice, W9 2JG. (*3 mins Warwick Avenue tube*). *Tel*: 01-289 0902. *Open*: Mon to Fri 9.30am to 5.30pm. Sat by appointment. Down-to-earth but decorative approach; free initial consultation. Lots of samples plus ideas "library". Browsers welcome.

Colour Counsellors 3 Dovedale Studios, 465 Battersea Park Road, SW11 4LR. *Tel*: 01-978 5023. *Open*: strictly by appointment. Showcase for products of British Design Group. Also headquarters for network of "colour counsellors" who bring furnishing samples arranged in 8 colour groups: red, blue, green, yellow, purple, brown, orange and neutrals. Full interior design/soft furnishings service. Counsellors for the London area:
Virginia Bredin, SW6. *Tel*: 01-731 3848.
Carol Hearne, NW3. *Tel*: 01-435 2409.
Susan Wauchope, SW1 & SW4. *Tel*: 01-720 8253.
Karen Allyson-Green, SW18. *Tel*: 01-870 3006.

Cullis & Co 16 Horsely Down Lane, SE11LN (*5 mins London Bridge tube*). *Tel*: 01-407 4286. *Open*: Mon to Sat 10am to 6pm. Converted Victorian warehouse; vaulted brickwork, glass wall: striking setting for their metal furniture with verdigris finish. Top designer fabrics.

Crown Enterprises See **Ceilings 1/Mouldings**. Ferri Smith (Dip SIAD) offers full range of interior design services backed up by husband Jack's specialist knowledge of decorative plaster restorations/installations.

Design Affair Tir-Na-Nog, 6 Springbridge Road, W5 2AA. (*2 mins Ealing Broadway tube/BR*). *Tel*: 01-579 3688/3228. *Open*: Mon to Sat 9.30am to 5.30pm. Split-level showroom, 3000 sq ft. Upstairs, 5 roomsettings. Downstairs, library of samples/ideas. Full interior design/soft furnishings service.

Elizabeth Eaton 25a Basil Street, SW3 1BB. (*Back of Harrods*). *Tel*: 01-589

0118/9. *Open*: Mon to Fri 9am to 5.30pm. Large displays fabrics/wall-coverings. Furniture, lamps, antiques. French terracotta tiles. Full design services, including architectural advice.

Ellice Interiors Unit G6, Butler's Wharf Business Centre, 45 Curlew Street, Butler's Wharf, SE1 2ND. (*Near Tower Hill tube*). *Tel*: 01-403 7224. *Open*: Mon to Fri 10am to 5pm. Sat by appointment. Personal service from owner. Extensive samples. Making-up services. Paintings/prints of riverside London. Antique pine. Dried flower arrangements.

Homebase See **DIY Superstores**. Branches of Sainsbury's Homebase provide colour schemes for £5 a room. Fill in their form with details of your room size, existing furnishings, preferences etc., and back comes your scheme – with a £2 voucher to spend on paint!

Ideas Unlimited 10 Russell Hill Parade, Russell Hill Road, Purley, Surrey CR2 2LE. *Tel*: 01-645 9762. *Open*: Mon to Sat 10am to 5.30pm. Early closing Wed 1.30pm. Selections co-ordinated furnishings; full interior design /soft furnishings service.

Interpretations 308 Worple Road, Raynes Park, SW20 8QU. (*3 mins Raynes Park BR*). *Tel*: 01-879 0103. *Open*: Mon to Sat 9.30am to 5.30pm. Large bright showroom, with 3 connecting rooms. Full range of samples, fabrics, wallcoverings, carpets. Sofas, sofabeds; occasional furniture, mirrors. Personal, friendly service. Curtain-making, quilting, cushions, loose covers, upholstery, carpet fitting.

Interior Lines 87 Hammersmith Grove, W6 0NQ. (*10 mins Hammersmith tube*). *Tel*: 01-741 2403/4. *Open*: Tues to Sat 10am to 5pm. International selections fabric/wallcoverings, modern and traditional. Full interior design/soft furnishings service.

Mr Jones 175/179 Muswell Hill Broadway, Muswell Hill N10 3RS. (*About a mile from Highgate tube and*

134 bus). *Tel*: 01-444 6066. *Open*: Mon to Sat 9.30am to 5pm. Personal/dedicated service from experienced proprietor. Samples, making-up services.

The Little House 629 Watford Way, Mill Hill, NW7 3JN. (*15 mins Mill Hill BR*). *Tel*: 01-906 3117. *Open*: Mon to Fri 9am to 5pm. Sat 10am to 4pm. Closed Thurs. Pink-and-white doll's house for adults with latest samples, interior design and soft furnishing service.

McNeil & Cole 25 Battersea High Street, SW11 3JF. (*Junction of Church Road*). *Tel*: 01-223 9174. *Open*: Mon to Sat 10am to 5.30pm. Young company, young directors. Distinctive style, mixing old with new. Full interior design/soft furnishings services. Frames/mirrors covered with fabric to match curtains etc.

Nova Interiors 168 Regents Park Road, NW1 1XN. (*5 mins Chalk Farm tube*). *Tel*: 01-586 2001/586 7772. *Open*: Mon to Fri 10am to 6pm. Knowledgeable/friendly service; extensive samples in owners' shop/studio.

Pullingers 224/226 York Road, Battersea, SW11 3SD. (*Clapham Junction BR*). *Tel*: 01-924 2400. *Open*: Mon to Sat 10am to 6pm. 2,500 sq ft in old joinery factory recently transformed into showrooms with 11 roomsettings. Modern Ligne Roset French furniture; painted French rattan; hand-painted china from Thomas Goode; marble accessories; handmade dried flower arrangements. Fabrics/wallcoverings. Full interior design service.

Schemes 56 Princedale Road, W11 4NL. (*5 mins Holland Park tube*). *Tel*: 01-727 3775/1148. *Open*: Mon to Fri 9.30am to 6pm. Closed lunch 1 to 2pm. Small showroom full of samples. Fabrics, papers, carpets, ceramic tiles, borders. Own linen union prints have complementary small glazed tiles. Full interior design service.

The Study 55 Endell Street, WC2H 9AJ. (*5 mins Covent Garden tube*). *Tel*: 01-240 5844. *Open*: Mon to Fri 10am to 6pm. Sat 11am to 5pm. Small-

lish shop. Full interior design service with lots of samples. Awesomely original interior treatments, combining aesthetic avant-garde with professional panache.

The Upstairs Shop 33 Elystan Street, SW3. (*10 mins South Kensington tube*). *Tel*: 01-581 9959. *Open*: Mon to Fri 9.30am to 5.30pm. Sat by appointment. Exclusive mainly floral English Country House designs for fabrics, papers, and pretty accessories: cushions, tiles, bed linens, lampshades. *Mail order*.

Outer Ring

Alexi Church 11/13 High Street, Camberley, Surrey GU15 3RB. (*4 mins Camberley BR; opposite multi-storey car park*). *Tel*: 0276 66104. *Open*: Mon 9.30am to 5.30pm. Tues to Sat 9am to 5.30pm. Experienced advice from showhouse designer. Lots of samples. Full soft-furnishings service. Handpainted furniture; upholstery. Accessories: plaster buildings, lamps, china, cushions and pictures.

Cobham Interiors 52 High Street, Cobham, Surrey KT11 3EF. (*Cobham BR*). *Tel*: 0932 64767. *Open*: Mon to Fri 9am to 5.30pm. Sat 10am to 5.30pm. Wed 9am to 7pm. Fabrics, wallcoverings, furniture. Complete interior-design/soft-furnishing service.

Colour Counsellors See London Postal Districts above.
Sheila Garcia, Upminster. *Tel*: 04022 23517.
Pauline Shubrook, Woodford Green. *Tel*: 01-505 6876.

Fabrika of Teddington 6 & 8 Church Road, Teddington, Middx TW11 8PB. (*6 mins Teddington BR*). *Tel*: 01-943 2685. *Open*: Tues to Fri 9.30am to 5.30pm. Sat 9.30am to 4pm. Full interior design services, with soft furnishings workroom on premises.

Fazeh Interior Design The Warren, 33 King's Road, Brentwood, Essex CM14 4DW. (*Set back in yard, off Brentwood High Street*). *Tel*: 0277 213308. *Open*: Mon to Sat 10am to

Interior Design

5pm. Closed Thurs. Expert advice in shop from owner, with masses of samples. Home visits (chargeable).

Ideas Unlimited 10 Russell Hill Parade, Russell Hill Road, Purley, Surrey CR2 2LE. *Tel*: 01-645 9762. *Open*: Mon to Sat 10am to 5.30pm. Early closing Wed. Personal, enthusiastic design advice, full making-up services.

Home Counties/S.East

Bewl Interiors The Hall, Turners Green, Wadhurst, East Sussex TN5 6TU. (*6m South Tunbridge Wells*). *Tel*: 089 288 2028. *Open*: Tues to Fri 9.30am to 5pm. Closed lunch 1 to 2.15pm. Sat 9.30am to 12 noon. Peaceful, welcoming atmosphere conducive for browsing amidst plentiful samples from top makes. Wallpapers, fabrics, sofas, chairs, lamps and carpets.

Colour Counsellors See London Postal Districts above.
Troward Anderson, Guildford. *Tel*: 0483 60317.
Sara Allday, Banbury. *Tel*: 0295 811473.
Margo Brown, Winchester. *Tel*: 0962 55779.
Anne Butterworth, Cholesbury. *Tel*: 024 029 700.
Angie Crichton-Stuart, Charlbury. *Tel*: 0608 810976.
Chris Escritt, Bedford. *Tel*: 0234 713642.
Francesca Evans, Woking. *Tel*: 04862 71759.
Lisa Eyre, Surbiton. *Tel*: 01-397 0294.
Mary Ewing, Redhill. *Tel*: 0737 224393.
June Galczynski, Newbury. *Tel*: 0635 47691.
Vanse Gethin, Maidstone. *Tel*: 0622 743339.
Diana Harvey, Ham Street. *Tel*: 023 373 2796.
Lucienne Greig, Thames Ditton. *Tel*: 01-398 2661.
Joyce Hecks, St Albans. *Tel*: 0727 69540.
Wendy Meirion-Williams, Henley. *Tel*: 0491 574162.
Mills & Penny, Reigate. *Tel*: 07372 41489.
Rosemary Palmes, Wormley. *Tel*: 042879 2340.
Jane Sadler, Long Crendon. *Tel*: 0844 201692.
Kathryn Turner, Polegate. *Tel*: 032 12 5058.
Elaine Tyler, Royston. *Tel*: 0763 84744.
Jane Wessely, Winkfield Row. *Tel*: 0344 886301.

Cornucopia Interiors 40 Downing Street, Farnham, Surrey GU9 7PH. (*Central Farnham, park behind showroom*). *Tel*: 0252 716020. *Open*: Mon to Sat 9.30am to 5pm. Three inter-linked-showrooms: 1,000 sq ft. Co-ordinated collections, top brand furniture. Cushions, rugs, exclusive Italian accessories. Soft furnishings service. Expert advice.

The Decorating Workshop 7 Upper Brook Street, Winchester, Hants SO23 8AL. (*3 mins car parks*). *Tel*: 0962 841604. *Open*: Mon to Sat 9.30am to 5.30pm. Experienced designer; latest ranges, beautiful accessories. Handmade curtains, upholstery. Cabinet-making, special paint finishes. Period restoration/refurbishment.

Decorum 1 Steward House, Sydenham Road, Guildford, Surrey GU1 3SR. *Tel*: 0483 37077. *Open*: Mon to Sat 9.30am to 5.30pm. Fine furniture/furnishings, keen prices. Prompt professional curtain-making. Carpets, custom-made upholstery. Reupholstery, loose covers, quilting.

The Design Studio 39 High Street, Reigate, Surrey RH2 9AE. (*10 mins Reigate BR*). *Tel*: 0737 248228. *Open*: Mon to Fri 9am to 5.30pm. Sat 9.30am to 5pm. Half-day Wed. Owners specialise in period interiors. Full interior design products/services.

Designers Fountain 20 Heritage Close, High Street, St Albans, Herts AL3 4EB. (*Secluded shopping precinct off High Street, next to Abbey, opposite car park*). *Tel*: 0727 33390. *Open*: Mon to Sat 10am to 5pm. Personal attention from owner. Lots of samples; soft furnishings service.

Ellis Designs 12 High Street, Sunninghill, Berks SL5 9NE. *Tel*: 0990 291185. *Open*: Mon to Fri 9am to 5pm, Sat 10am to 1pm. Friendly expert advice. "No project too small or too large." Good samples/displays. Quick service for all soft furnishings.

John Hall Interiors 598 Western Road, Tring, Herts HP23 4BB. (*2m Tring BR*). *Tel*: 044282 6966. *Open*: Mon to Sat 9am to 5.30pm. Personal service/advice from owner. Mrs Hall runs workroom: all soft furnishings. Competitive prices.

Wendy Harris 69 Western Road, Palmeira Square, Hove, East Sussex BN3 2NB. (*10 mins Hove BR*). *Tel*: 0273 736365/204325. *Open*: Mon to Sat 9.30am to 5.30pm. Ground floor: fabrics/trimmings from all top names. Lower floor: Wallpaper samples/carpets. Full interior design/soft furnishings services.

Interiors of Ascot 35 High Street, Ascot, Berks SL5 7HG. (*Centre of Ascot, 100yds from race course*). *Tel*: 0890 28688. *Open*: Mon to Fri 9am to 5.30pm. Sat 9am to 1pm. Extensive ranges fabric/wallcoveringss; inspring displays. Friendly advice/professional schemes. Full interior design service. Comprehensive stocks/product library: furniture, lights, carpets, braids, gifts.

Langley Classic Interiors 286 High Street, Langley, Slough Berks SL3 8HF. (*5 mins M4 Junction 5, M25 Junction 15; 3 mins Langley BR; free parking*). *Tel*: 0753 42117/47899. *Open*: Mon to Sat 9.30am to 5.30pm. Over 2,000 sq ft bright spacious showrooms, newly designed to luxurious West End standards. Furniture, fitted bedrooms, designer carpets, fabrics/wallcoverings/ornaments, all top makes. Soft furnishings displays/service; interior design service.

Libra Interiors Northlands Farm, Oakwood, Chichester, West Sussex PO19 3PY. (*2m Chichester centre*) *Tel*: 0243 527055. *Open*: by appointment only. Personal service from experienced owner/designer. Showroom in converted barn: lots of samples, undivided attention.

Merrow Interiors 117 Collingwood Crescent, Boxgrove Park, Guildford, Surrey GU1 2PF. (*30 mins Guildford BR*). *Tel*: 0483 506244. *Open*: Mon to Sat 9am to 5pm. Experienced personal advice from carpet expert and soft furnishings specialist.

Mister Smith Interiors 1/3 The Parade, Croft Road, Crowborough, East Sussex TN6 1DR. (*Facing Waitrose, free car park*). *Tel*: 0892 664152. *Open*: Tues to Sat 9am to 5.30pm. Closed lunch 1 to 2pm. Interior design service/samples. Handmade soft furnishings, own workroom. Furniture, carpets, lamps, pictures.

Northover Interiors 82 High Street, Reigate, Surrey RH2 9AP. (*10 mins Reigate BR; Priory Car Park*). *Tel*: 0737 242236. *Open*: by appointment only. Personal service from experienced owner.

Paraphernalia 26/27 High Street, Fareham, Hants PO16 7AE. (*1½m Fareham BR*). *Tel*: 0329 281314. *Open*: Mon to Sat 9am to 5pm. Old-fashioned building crammed with up-to-date samples/stock backed by old-fashioned service from partners. Lighting a speciality: table lamps from all over. Lampshades to order/various fabrics.

Private Lives The Old Parsonage, Church Street, Crondall, Nr Farnham, Surrey GU10 5QQ. *Tel*: 0526 850527. *Open*: Mon to Fri 9.30am to 5pm, Sat to 1pm. Full decorator service from renovated barn packed with impressive samples and displays. Sophisticated soft furnishing ideas backed by making-up/installation services. Special paint finishes, fabric coverings for walls and ceilings.

Suttons Furnishings 59 High Street, East Grinstead, West Sussex RH19 3DD. (*Opposite Dorset Arms*). *Tel*: 0342 321695. *Open* (both branches): Mon to Sat 9.30am to 5pm. Family firm; huge range of samples. Trading for 40 years, in workrooms.
Also at: 6 Regent Arcade, East Street, Brighton BN1 1HR. *Tel*: 0273 723728.

Trestles 34 Minster Street, Reading, Berks RG1 2JB. *Tel*: 0734 597609. *Open*: Tues to Sat 9.30am to 5.30pm. Late night Thurs 7pm. Design advice, lots of samples. Own upholstery at keen prices.

Worth a Trip

Michael Bracken Fabrics & Furniture The Green, Warborough, Near Wallingford, South Oxon OX9 8DR. *Tel*: 086732 8354. *Open*: Mon to Fri 9.30am to 4.30pm. Sat 9.30am to 12.30pm. Or by appointment. Designer-maker of furniture in beautiful woods, with extensive fabric/wallpaper samples. Free design advice in showroom; full making-up service.

Pullingers High Street, Bishops Waltham, Southampton, Hants SO3 1AA. (*Local buses to Bishops Waltham; car parks nearby*). *Tel*: 04893 4546. *Open*: Mon to Fri 9am to 5.30pm. Full interior design service, showrooms. Top floor is called French Revolution. Extensive displays Ligne Roset sofas, convertibles.

CEILINGS

On top floors, remember that what goes above the ceiling is perhaps even more important than what goes below. Lofts should have at least 4in of insulation to keep fuel bills down and rooms cosy.

1/MOULDINGS & RESTORATION

*Firms abound to help restore ceilings to former glories. Many will copy mouldings and install them in your home. You can also add a rose or cornice to a modern room. Adding mouldings (ceiling rose, cornice etc) can improve a bleak featureless room. Many shops sell lightweight easy-to-fix versions (e.g. **DIY Superstores, Interior Design** Specialists). Ready-made plaster mouldings are also available. Restoring existing mouldings is trickier but specialists listed below can help with home service.*

London Postal Districts

Architectural Castings 59 The Arches, New King's Road, SW6. (*Putney Bridge tube*). *Tel*: 01-731 7172. *Open*: by appointment. Restorations in plaster, concrete and reconstituted stone.

Decorative Interiors 1010 Harrow Road, Kensal Green, NW10. (*Kensal Green tube*). *Tel*: 01-969 5000. *Open*: Mon to Fri 9am to 5.30pm. Sat 9am to 1pm. Plaster mouldings showroom. Install/restore.

Hodkins & Jones 23 Rathbone Place, W1. (*3 mins Tottenham Court Road tube*). *Tel*: 01-636 2617. *Open*: Mon to Fri 9.30am to 5.30pm. Showroom for

large Sheffield-based company. Catalogue. Installations.

Outer Ring

Alan Cardash 10 Station Parade, Whitchurch Lane, Canons Park, Edgware. (*Canons Park tube*). *Tel*: 01-951 3895. *Open*: Mon to Fri 8am to 5pm. Large showroom with helpful displays of numerous mouldings.

Essex Ornate Interiors 444 Beacontree Avenue, Dagenham, Essex RM8. (*Chadwell Heath BR*). *Tel*: 01-597 5562. *Open*: Mon to Sat 8am to 5.30pm. Showroom for plaster moulding displays. Catalogue. Installations.

G Jackson & Sons Unit 19, Mitcham Industrial Estate, Streatham Road, Croydon CR4 2AJ. (*Tooting BR*). *Tel*: 01-640 8611/648 4343. *Open*: Mon to Fri 8.30am to 4.45 pm. Impeccable pedigree: founded 1780 by Brothers Adam. Some 18th-century moulds still exist. Varied stocks. Install/restore.

The following firms also supply/fix plaster mouldings.

London Postal Districts

H & F Badcock Unit 9, 57 Sandgate Street, Old Kent Road, SE15 1LE. *Tel*: 01-639 0304.

Butcher Plastering Specialists 8 Fitzroy Road, Primrose Hill NW1 8TX. *Tel*: 01-722 9771.

Crown Enterprises 350 Cricklewood Lane, NW2 2HQ. *Tel*: 01-458 7478.

Decorative Plasterwork 46 Havil Street, SE5 7RS. *Tel*: 01-701 6713.

Hat Interiors (Veronese) Interior House, Linton Road, Crouch End N8 8SL. *Tel*: 01-348 4461.

London Fine Art Plaster 7/9 Audrey Street, E2. (*5 mins Bethnal Green/ Liverpool Street tubes*). *Tel*: 01-739 3594. *Open*: Mon to Fri 8am to 5pm. Sat 8am to 12.30pm.

JD McDonough 347 New King's Road, SW6 4RJ. *Tel*: 01-736 5146.

Michael F O'Reilly 46 Cumbrian Gardens, NW2 1EF. *Tel*: 01-458 2736.

A&A Plastering 68 Upper Richmond Road, SW15 2RP. *Tel*: 01-874 0145.

Riverside Mouldings Unit 18, Riverside Industrial Estate, Riverway, SE10. *Tel*: 01-853 4201.

Thomas & Wilson 454 Fulham Road, SW6 1BY. *Tel*: 01-381 116l.

Outer Ring

Clark & Fenn Unit 19, Mitcham Industrial Estate, Streatham Road, Mitcham, Surrey CR4 2AJ. *Tel*: 01-648 4343.

Hatcher Plastering Company 52 Lime Grove, Eastcote, Pinner, Middx. *Tel*: 01-868 6919.

GC Mouldings 10 West End Lane, Barnet, Herts EN5 2SA. (*7 mins High Barnet tube; own car park*). *Tel*: 01-449 2247. *Open*: Mon to Fri 8am to 4.30pm. Sat 8am to 12 noon. Workshop for fibrous plaster mouldings. Supply/fix. Repairs, commissions.

MW Mouldings Co Coppen Road, Dagenham, Essex. *Tel*: 01-593 5048.

Ornamental Design Plastering Co Unit 2, Johnson's Ind. Est., Off Silverdale Close, Hayes Middx. *Tel*: 01-573 3129.

Home Counties/S.East

Ron Chinery 264 Great Cambridge Road, Cheshunt, Waltham Cross, Herts. *Tel*: 0992 30157.

Georgian Design Associates Goodwood Parade, Courtlands Drive, Watford, Herts WD1 3HZ. *Tel*: 0923 673010.

RJ Young 15 Station Road East, Ash Vale, Aldershot, Hampshire GU12 5LT. *Tel*: 0252 542789.

Mail Order

Rainford House of Elegance Wentworth Street, Birdwell, Barnsley S70 5UN (*M1 Junction 36*). *Tel*: 0226 350360. Ornamental plaster mouldings: fireplaces, niches, cornices, wall panels, coving. Nationwide delivery service and installations.

Or available from: **Traditional Interiors**, 16/18 Lower Kings Road, Berkhamsted, Herts HP4 2AE. *Tel*: 0442 865501.

2/TIMBERS & BEAMS

Add a touch of olde England! Where to shop for timbers, old or fake. Explore also firms listed in **Architectural Salvage,** *for the real thing.*

London Postal Districts

WH Newson See **Home Improvement Specialists**. Timber beams distressed/stained by hand for effective aged look. Box versions can conceal an rsj. Matching wall panelling, mouldings, corbels, shelving, plate racks, architraves, skirtings, chair rails.

Outer Ring

Petit Roque See **Heating 2/Fireplaces**. Softwood beams distressed for traditional Tudor look. Real oak sometimes available.

Home Counties/S.East

Roy Blackman Associates See **Walls 4/Panelling**. Finely-crafted reproduction exposed oak beams. Lightweight, durable. Colour brochure.

Douglas P. Smith 3 Ivel Close, Barton-le-Clay, Beds MK45 4NT. *Tel*: 0582 881613. By appointment. Reproduction "olde worlde" beams. Architectural joinery to order, 50m radius workshop.

Mail Order

Aristocast Bold Street, Sheffield S9

3TW. *Tel*: 0742 561156. Reproduction oak beams. Design service. Colour brochure. Nationwide deliveries own transport.

Worth a Trip

Colin Baker, Timber Merchant Crown Hill, Halberton, Tiverton, Devon EX16 7AY. (*Near Halberton Village*). *Tel*: 0884 820152/821007. *Open*: by appointment ("any reasonable time"). Half an acre of beams and planks mainly in English oak at very reasonable prices. Nationwide delivery service. Cut to size. Phone for advice/quote.

3/TENTED CEILINGS

A tented ceiling has draped fabric billowing from centre to walls. This treatment hides anything unpleasant above, including layers of insulation for a cosy room. But it's a dust trap and fire hazard. Keep fabric well away from light/heat sources. Cut-price fabrics keep costs down: see **Soft Furnishings 1/Fabrics**. *Most firms listed in* **Interior Design,** *and some in* **Soft Furnishings 3/Made-to-measure** *can tackle tented ceilings.*

Home Counties/S.East

Ian Denney *Tel*: 0904 38112. Fabric-lining specialist. Works in London/SE at country prices. High ceilings can take full tented treatment; for low ceilings, fabric is stretched/pleated.

Private Lives See **Interior Design**. Lining rooms with fabric is a speciality; crowning glory is full-blown tented ceiling, with decorative lighting pendant as centrepiece.

WALLS

Probably the biggest single area in your homes, walls have lots of potential. For wallcoverings, paints, stencils, see **Decorating Materials**, which also lists specialists for co-ordinated collections. See also **Tiles**. And finish off with pictures/prints from **Accessories**.

1/FABRIC LINING

Walls covered with fabric, pleated or stretched tight, are expensive and difficult to clean. If fabric is suspended from expanded wires top and bottom, or poles, it can be taken down for cleaning. However this treatment conceals really bad wall surfaces and/or insulation for a cosy room. For firms that carry out "soft lining", see Interior Design and Soft Furnishings.

2/TAPESTRIES & HANGINGS

In medieval times, tapestries were essential for insulation, and of course they were decorative, too. Revive a forgotten charm from shops below. Or stitch your own: suppliers are suggested in Accessories 5/Needlepoint & Embroidery.

London Postal Districts

Belinda Coote Tapestries 29 Holland Street, Kensington W8 4NA. (*2 mins Kensington High Street tube*). *Tel*: 01-937 3924. *Open*: Mon to Sat 10am to 6pm. Tapestry wall hangings, tapestry fabrics, tapestry borders, handpainted furniture and wooden firescreens; small gifts.

Joanna Booth See **Antiques 3/Art Galleries & Services**. Antique tapestries/textiles collected by enthusiastic owner of this delightful shop.

Sarah Collins See **Soft Furnishings 8/Designer Fabrics**. Handpainted brightly-coloured cotton/silk wall hangings in captivating often amusing domestic designs.

Outer Ring

Flemish Tapestries 105 North Road, Kew, Richmond, Surrey TW9 4HN. (*Directly behind Kew Gardens tube/ BR*). *Tel*: 01-878 8182. *Open*: Mon to Sat 9am to 7pm. Sun by appointment. British outlet for Belgian tapestry manufacturer. Large stock of tapestries for wallhangings, cushions, furniture coverings, tablecloths. Home visits. Tapestry hanging.

Home Counties/S.East

Rosemary Atkinson Winchester Design Workshops, Park Avenue, Winchester, Hants SO23 8DL. *Tel*: 0962 842500 Ext 137. *Open*: by appointment. Striking/sophisticated silk wall hangings woven to commission. Rich colour effects. Bold geometric designs.

Liza Collins 79A Leigham Court Drive, Leigh-on-Sea, Essex SS9 1PT. *Tel*: (evenings) 01-517 6449. *Open*: by appointment. Handwoven tapestries, one-off pieces and commissions.

Hines of Oxford Weavers Barn, Windmill Road, Headington, Oxford OX3 7DE. *Tel*: 0865 741144. *Open*: by appointment, Mon to Fri 9am to 5pm. Closed lunch 1 to 2pm. Closed Sat & Sun. Tapestry/wall hangings, importers from 10 continental weavers. Reproductions from medieval times to 18th century woven in wool/cotton/artificial silk. 100s of panels always in stock, from small to large, including handweave. Full colour catalogue. Travelling representatives may visit your area: ring for details.

Thursley Textile Designs 1 Moushill Lane, Milford, Godalming, Surrey. (*A3 from London*). *Tel*: 04868 24769. *Open*: Mon to Sat 10am to 5.30pm. Handwoven tapestries from designer workshop. Furnishings, toys, clothes. Exhibitions/courses.

Worth a Trip

Stuart Interiors See **Furniture 4/Classics & Reproduction**. Antique/copies 16th/17th-century period tapestries.

3/WOODEN MOULDINGS

Once ripped untimely from all period properties, restoration is now the order of the day for skirtingboards, picture and dado rails. Many firms make to order, and will copy your patterns. Specialised joinery firms are also being listed under **Staircases 1/Wooden**. Mouldings memo: add detail to plain skirtings with scotia or quadrant beadings pinned along top edge. Fit dado rail at waist height with co-ordinating papers/paint above/below (cuts tall walls down to size). Rescue the once-despised picture rail and suspend paintings/prints in fine frames with parallel fine brass/chrome chains fixed one at each corner.

All Districts

Magnet See **DIY Superstores**. Magnamoulding packs of hardwood/softwood architrave/skirting. For plaster mouldings, see **Ceilings 1/Mouldings & Restoration**.

London Postal Districts

WH Newson See **Home Improvement Specialists**. Extensive stocks softwood/hardwood mouldings; instructions for fixing in catalogue. Victorian/Edwardian patterns. Copies to order.

Tempus Stet See **Lighting 2/Traditional**. Decorator classical reproduction carvings/decorations in moulded quality resins, variety of finishes. Frit and flower garlands, swag and drops, cherub circular plaques.

WR & A Hide See **Staircases 1/Wooden**. Made-to-measure skirtings, architraves, mouldings.

Home Counties/S.East

WH Newson See **Home Improvement Specialists**. Wide choice of standard traditional mouldings plus made-to-measure.

RGS Joinery Paldre, Rucklers Lane, Kings Langley, Hemel Hempstead, Herts. (*1m from A41*). *Tel*: 0442 61394. *Open*: Mon to Sat 8.30am to 6pm. Mouldings, skirtings, coving etc. in unusual shapes, sizes to order. Also traditional staircases. Installations.

4/PANELLING

*Panelling is the perfect panacea for ugly pipework/electrics: but leave removeable sections for maintenance access. In addition to wood, panelling can be plastic (to simulate white-painted planking or dark aged timbers), or fretted hardboard. In addition to listings below, see **Interior Design** businesses who can usually help with bespoke joinery.*

All Districts

In Situ See **Services 19/Building Services**. In-home stripping service for wood panelling, with bleaching/liming option. Popular for thirties-style houses.

Magnet See **DIY Superstores**. Magnalux. Choice of 7 grooved real wood veneers on 4mm ply panels for quick, easy fixing. Magnaplank panelling packs of kiln-dried tongued and grooved boards in hemlock, knotty pine, Douglas fir, hardwood (mahogany coloured stain), and whitewood (suitable for staining/painting). Magnadeck panels have a printed woodgrain finish.

Wickes See **DIY Superstores**. Panelling packs. Classic knotty pine vee-jointed boards. Also double Italian vee-jointed: has decorative extra groove. Boards appear narrower, more elegant. Rich red hardwood vee-joints boards machined from Philippine mahogany. White pvc vee-jointed panels: use imaginatively for sophisticated bathroom schemes.

London Postal Districts

Roger Board Designs 273 Putney Bridge Road, SW15 2PT. (*5 mins Putney Bridge tube; Putney BR*). *Tel*: 01-946 5251. *Open*: by appointment. Traditional well-established joinery company. Panelled rooms using only antique timber. Built-in fitments including bookcases/cupboards.

The National Trust Blewcoat School Gift Shop 23 Caxton Street, SW1H 9AX. (*2 mins St James's Park tube*).

Tel: 01-222 2877. *Open*: Mon to Fri 10am to 5.30pm. Late night Thurs 7pm. Print Room Borders. Decorative swags, ribbons, bows, braids. Inspired by Preint Room at Blickling Hall, Norfolk. Use to frame pictures/prints stuck directly on wall. Highlight architectural features.

WH Newson See **Home Improvement Specialists**. Alexander panelling: solid pine framework, with decorative veneer ponels for made to measure traditional look at stock prices. Varnish for natural look, or stain dark. Finish at top with matching plate shelf. Also realistic simulated brick panels, red/white, hand-grouted mortar effects. Pinboards, notice boards. Fretted hardboard panels: 5 highly-decorative designs.

Bargains!

TMW Timber & Builders Merchants 19/20 Latona Road, Peckham, SE15 6RX. *Tel*: 01-358 0076. *Open*: Mon to Fri 8am to 5.30pm. Sat 8am to 2.30pm. Closed 12.30 to 1.30pm. Timber/boards at discount prices (architraves, skirting, pinecladding) plus doors and other building materials.

Wansdown Joinery See **Staircases 1/Wooden**. Traditional panelled rooms.

Woodstock See **Kitchens 5/Luxury Bespoke Kitchens**. Custom-made panelling in pitch pine or limed oak.

Outer Ring

Dove Bell Enfield Works, Jeffreys Road, Enfield, Middx EN3 7UB. *Tel*: 01-805 1548. *Open*: by appointment. Made-to-measure service for panelled rooms.

Roy Blackman Associates 150/152 High Road, Chadwell Heath, Essex RM6 6NT. (*5 mins Chadwell Heath BR*). *Tel*: 01-599 5247. *Open*: Mon to Fri 9am to 5.30pm. Sat 10am to 5pm. Simulated oak linenfold/Jacobean wall panelling. Decorative plate-rack, carved friezes, cornices. Lightweight, durable, convincing: unless you touch them! Colour brochure.

The National Trust 14 High Street, Windsor, Berks SL4 1LD. (*Windsor BR*). *Tel*: 0753 850433. *Open*: Mon to Sat 9.30am to 5.30pm.
And at: Syon Park, Park Road, Brentford, Middx. *Tel*: 01-569 7397. *Open*: 7 days. Winter 10am to 5pm. Later in summer. See London Postal Districts above.

Oakwood Joinery Orchard Works, Church Lane, Wallington, Surrey SM6 7ND. *Tel*: 01-773 2141. Made-to-measure joinery; oak furniture and fittings.

Home Counties/S. East

Peter H Blomfield Willow Wood, Bit Lane, Luggershall, Near Aylesbury, Bucks HP18 9NZ. *Tel*: 0844 238278. Fitted panelled libraries in English/foreign woods. Custom-made furniture.

JJ Bunker & Sons 73 Common Road, Chandlers Ford, Eastleigh, Hants SO5 1HE. *Tel*: 0703 268176. Specialists in replacement and restoration joinery.

Samuel Elliott & Sons Gosbrook Road, Caversham, Reading, Berks. *Tel*: 0734 476622. Made-to-measure joinery. Fitting service.

James Longley & Co East Park, Crawley, West Sussex RH10 6AP. *Tel*: 0293 561212. Made-to-measure panelling/woodcarving. Fitting service.

Private Lives See **Interior Design**. Bespoke joinery. Panelled rooms/wall-to-wall bookcases highest standards.

Symm & Co Osney Mead, Oxford, OX2 0EQ. *Tel*: 0865 249567. Hardwood panelling/carving/made-to-measure joinery. Fitting service. Experts in conservation/restoration.

Wallis Broadmead Works, Hart Street, Maidstone, Kent ME16 8RE. *Tel*: 0622 690960. Made-to-measure panelling/joinery/fitting service.

5/MURALS & SPECIAL EFFECTS

*The past decade has seen an amazing resurgence for older types of painted wall decorations such as special paint effects, murals and trompe l'oeil. Stippling and sponging you could tackle yourself. Dulux sell kits through **DIY Superstores**. But murals and the fancy bits of eye deception need outside assistance.*

London Postal Districts

John Oliver See **Decorating Materials 1/Paints & Papers** Wide selection Gibbs & Dodd instant stick-on trompe l'oeil classical motifs. Greek pillars with Corinthian/Ionic capitals. Balustrades/niches. Also Ornaments stick-on trompe l'oeil decorator motifs: pretty bows/cherubs/cording/tassels etc. Japanese/Chinese silk-screened wall panels for mural effects in panels, or line a whole room.

The Mosaic Studio See **Accessories 3/Mirrors**. Artist Yehudit (Judy) Morrell creates murals from glass fragments.

*Thanks to the proficiency of our art schools, and an abundance of natural talent, a growing number of artists can paint trompe l'oeil/murals. Telephone to discuss requirements. Visits with photos/ideas by arrangement. Some artists can paint in their studio onto wall panels that can go with you if you move. Others work directly onto the wall. Providing you are seriously interested, and the commission is worthwhile, most are prepared to travel. Many firms listed under **Interior Design** can arrange commissions. Artists come and go as the inspiration ebbs and flows: check out the current Michelangelos in the small ads at the back of the ultra-glossy home interior magazines. The list below provides telephone contacts directly with artists for London/Home Counties/S.East.*

Michael Alford 127 Trentham Street, SW18 5DH. *Tel*: 01-870 2487. Own design murals: figurative, classical, vistas, trompe l'oeil. Murals on movable panels, complete rooms and ceilings. In oil and/or tempera on pre-prepared surfaces.

Bella Designs *Tel*: 01-672 1676. Decorative Murals, trompe l'oeil, restoration and gilding. Also widest range of paint finishes.

Brushstrokes *Tel*: 01-737 6876. Interior design partnership run by two design graduates, will undertake murals and specialist paint finishes, also large total concept projects including own sculptures/glasswork etc.

Nigel Crawley *Tel*: 01-733 1276. Murals, trompe l'oeil, dragging, rag rolling, sponging, stippling, marbling, faux bois, lacquer and stencilling. Restoration of painted and gilded furniture.

Colin Failes *Tel*: 01-272 2093. Trompe l'oeil mural and fresco interiors.

Fiona Latta *Tel*: 01-585 3035. 14 years in decorative painting. Also special firescreens, painted beds, bedheads, waste paper baskets to match fabric designs. Also painted window blinds. Specialises in delicate life-like flower designs. Oil-based/acrylic/water-based paint as appropriate. Murals on panels to move, or entire rooms including atmospheric clouds on sky ceilings, arcadian vistas, jungles. Lighting suggestions to enhance atmosphere. Also external murals using masonry paints.

Sheena Magill *Tel*: 01-607 6561. Any size mural, from 1 metre to complete rooms including ceilings, with own pictorial designs, trompe l'oeil, vistas and skies. Oil based paints on pre-prepared walls. Children's designs for nurseries in bright acrylic colours.

Jane Margrave *Tel*: 01-586 3341. Murals and painted decorations on various surfaces in acrylic/oil-based paint. Trompe l'oeil effects, own designs, period effects. Whole rooms and ceilings and movable panels.

Alice Mason Interiors *Tel*: 01-274 3379. BA Hons in fine art. Murals and special paint finishes: marbling, rag rolling, stippling, sponging, graining, all colour washing.

Plowden & Plowden Interior Decorators 4 Rylett Road, W12 9NL. *Tel*: 01-749 4811.

Christian Potter *Tel*: 01-741 9842. Wall specialist paint finishes and wall stencils. Also stencil/painting original or your own designs onto wood floors.

Rendering Services *Tel*: 01-674 1328/ 985 4974. Paint finishes "from the sublime to the ridiculous".

Michaela Sanderson E17. *Tel*: 01-531 6065.

Lincoln Seligman W6. *Tel*: 01-748 4670.

Verona Stencilling *Tel*: 0444 811267 (Balcombe, West Sussex). Own designs various styles, commissioned designs.

FLOORS

We rarely consider things we walk over, pavements, colleagues, spouses . . . floors! Often hidden under carpets or rugs, floors lack attention until it's too late. Have a good look right now before you put your foot in it.

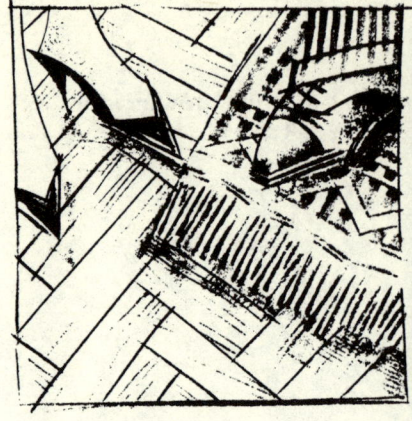

1/WOOD

Firms specialising in wood floors usually offer services for stripping/renovating older wood surfaces.

London Postal Districts

Campbell Marson (Alliance Flooring) Unit 34, Wimbledon Business Centre, Riverside Road, SW17 OBA. (*Behind Wimbledon Stadium*). *Tel*: 01-879 0672. *Open*: Mon to Fri 9.30am to 5pm. Sat 9.30am to 12.30pm. Hardwood flooring: parquet panels, blocks, strips, boards (some ready-sanded/sealed). Installations.

Hardwood Flooring Co Unit 2A, West Hampstead Trading Centre, Blackburn Road, West Hampstead NW6 1RZ. *Tel*: 01-328 8481. *Open*: Mon to Fri 8.30am to 5.30pm. Supply/lay all types hardwood floor new/reclaimed.

Tudor Flooring Co 2 Avenue Parade, Ridge Avenue, Winchmore Hill N21. *Tel*: 01-360 4242. *Open*: Mon to Fri: 9am to 5pm. Sat 10am to 5pm. Repair/restore wood floors. Supply/install parquet, wood strip etc. Amtico, cork, carpets.

Outer Ring

Patey & Sons 110 Stafford Road, Wallington, Surrey SM6 9AY. (*10 mins Wallington BR*). *Tel*: 01-647 8163. *Open*: Mon to Fri 8am to 5pm. Sanding/sealing, parquet renovations. New hardwood floors.

Mail Order

Heritage Woodcraft *Tel*: 0827 714761. *Fax*: 0827 715792. All types hardwood floor manufactured/supplied nationwide. Blocks, strips, overlays, mosaics, panels, sports and dance floors. Exclusive custom-made designs.

Woodstock Hardwoods Ponsharden, Falmouth, Cornwall TR10 8AB. *Tel*: 0326 76555. Specialist supplier all hardwood floors, nationwide deliveries. Easy-lay tongued-and-grooved strips. 20 varieties hardwood machined to any size for restorations/replacements.

2/VINYL, LINO, CORK

So-called hard floors are attractive enough to bring into soft living/dining situations. Vinyls are stocked by many carpet retailers (see below), and at **Furnishing Stores/Department Stores**, *but a specialist widens the scope.* **DIY Superstores** *have budget ranges of vinyl, cork and wood.*

All Districts

Laura Ashley Home See **Furnishing Stores**. At Last! Decorator designs for mass-market vinyls. Printed self-adhesive tiles in charming patterns.

London Postal Districts

The Cork Shop 185 Fulham Palace Road, W6 8QX. (*10 mins Hammersmith tube*). *Tel*: 01-386 9197. *Open*: Mon to Fri 10am to 7pm. Cork floor/wall tiles; cork gifts. Exclusive imports from Portugal: largest cork producer in world. Large range designs/patterns.

Bargains!

The Direct Bargain Centre See **Decorating Materials 1/Paints & Papers**. Changing stock often includes floor coverings e.g. cork/vinyl tiles/carpets.

First Floor 174 Wandsworth Bridge Road, SW6 2UQ. (*15 mins Fulham Broadway/Parsons Green tubes*). *Tel*: 01-736 1123. *Open* (both branches): Mon to Fri 9am to 5.30pm. Sat 10am to 2pm. Up-market individual designs for linoleum/vinyl. Inlays/borders. Also rubber, cork, wood. Bordered carpets, special rugs.
Also at: 244 York Road, SW11 2SJ. (*20 mins Clapham Junction BR*). *Tel*: 01-924 2145.

Graham Floorings 20 Queen's Parade, Friern Barnet Road, N11

3DA. (*15 mins Arnos Grove tube*). *Tel*: 01-361 0983. *Open*: Mon to Fri 8.30am to 5pm. Sat 9am to 4pm. Vinyl sheet/tiles. Cork tiles, wood/parquet, carpets. Accessories, screeds, adhesives. Expert advice, 35 years' experience. Installations.

Mail Order

Northern Cork Supplies Lily Street Mills, Milnrow, Rochdale, OL16 3NQ. *Tel*: 0706 38160. Cork/wood specialists. Warehouse prices. Personal callers welcome. Nationwide deliveries. Samples 50p.

Siesta Cork Tiles 127 Cherry Orchard Road, Croydon, Surrey CR0 6BE. *Tel*: 01-680 1250. Leaflets (two 2nd class stamps). Acrylic-sealed/pvc-surfaced cork tiles. Thicker tiles for insulation/pinboards.
Also at: **Allfloors** (shop), 307 Brighton Road, Croydon, Surrey CR2 6EQ. (*A23. 10 mins Croydon Bus Garage*). *Tel*: 01-688 6968. *Open*: Mon to Fri 8.30am to 5.30pm. Sat 8.30am to 5pm.

3/CARPETS

Carpets must combine a soft surface with hard wear: a problem. Solve it by taking specialist advice, and buying the best you can afford, even if you have to wait for your furniture. Check out grading schemes and fibre qualities. Never put down carpet until all building, plumbing and electrical work is completed.

London Postal Districts

Afia Carpets 60 Baker Street, W1M 1DJ. (*5 mins Baker Street tube*). *Tel*: 01-935 0414/2982. *Open*: Mon to Fri 9.30am to 5.30pm. Sat by appointment. David & Judy Afia are carpet experts. Design/custom-make fine quality fitted carpets, variety of textures. Exclusive range of needlepoint rugs. Brochure.

Brentford Carpet Tiles 2 A/B Stile Hall Parade, Chiswick High Road, W4. (*10 mins Gunnersbury tube*). *Tel*: 01-995 7617. *Open*: Mon to Fri 9am to 5pm. Early closing Thurs 1pm. Large range domestic/industrial carpet tiles, plus seconds at reduced prices.

Bargains!

Budget Carpets 390 Wharf Road, Camberwell SE17. (*5 mins Elephant & Castle tube*). *Tel*: 01-701 4460. *Open* (all branches): Mon to Sat 9am to 5.30pm. Room-sized remnants, low prices plus many cut-price ranges. Free measuring, same day deliveries. Cut-price fitting. Vinyls also.
Also at: Murphy's Yard, 30 Power Street, Woolwich, SE18. (*3 mins Woolwich BR*). *Tel*: 01-855 7359.
And at: Unit 93/97, Bargain Centre, Rye Lane, Peckham SE15. (*3 mins Peckham BR*). *Tel*: 01-639 5329. Closed Thurs.

Capitol Carpets 98/100 Northcote Road, Battersea, SW11. (*10 mins Clapham Junction BR*). *Tel*: 01-228 7167. *Open*: Mon to Sat 9am to 5.30pm. Supply/fit all major makes carpets/hard floors. Member of Metro group: competitive prices.
Also at: 2a The Broadway, Catford, SE6. *Tel*: 01-690 3811.
And at: 437/439 Upper Richmond Road West, East Sheen, SW14. *Tel*: 01-878 2051.

Carpet Carpets 7/11 Minerva Road, NW10 6HJ. *Tel*: 01-965 7471/Freephone 100. Four mobile van showrooms can bring 2000 carpet samples at convenient time: day, evening/weekends. Expert fitting.

Carpet Tile Centres 227 Woodhouse Road, Finchley N12. (*50 yds Barnet Town Hall*). *Tel*: 01-361 1261. *Open*: Mon to Sat 9am to 5pm. Sat closed lunch 12.30 to 2pm. Comprehensive stock carpet tiles, including Heuga at cheapest prices.
Also at: 150 Pinner Road, Harrow. *Tel*: 01-863 9551. *Open*: Mon to Fri 9am to 11am only.

Decorum Carpets 23 Pavilion Road, SW1. (*5 mins Knightsbridge tube*). *Tel*: 01-235 0104. *Open*: Mon to Sat 9am to 5.30pm. Huge choice plain carpets/borders/runners: 48-hour delivery.

Ealing Carpet Centre 1st floor, John Saunders Dept. Store, 69/79 The Broadway, Ealing, W5. *Tel*: 01-840 4017/567 3434. *Open*: Mon to Wed 9.30am to 6pm. Thurs 9.30am to 7pm. Fri 9am to 6pm. Sat 9am to 6pm. Large range carpets, competitive prices. Free fitting.

Bargains!

Also at: Hanger Lane Carpets Warehouse, 11 Ashbourne Parade, Hanger Lane, Ealing, W5 3QS. *Tel*: 01-997 1834/6955. *Open*: Mon to Sat 9am to 5.30pm. Vast range. Free fittings. No rugs.

Bargains!

Europa International Europa House, Meford Way, Penge SE20 8RA. (*near Sainsbury's Homebase*). *Tel*: 01-676 0064. *Open*: Mon to Fri 9am to 5pm. Sat 9.30am to 5pm. Ex-exhibition carpets. Carpet your house for £100! (they say).

Bargains!

Falcon Carpet Tiles 278 Upper Richmond Road, Putney SW15. (*10 mins East Putney BR*). *Tel*: 01-788 9075. *Open*: Mon to Sat 9.30am to 5.30pm. Ex-contract industrial carpet tiles.

John Lewis, Peter Jones & other stores in John Lewis Partnership. See **Department Stores**.
Plain carpets, all qualities, clearly displayed according to colour; super value Jonelle cord. Jonelle stock carpets laid within 14 days.

Marlows Carpets 67 East Hill, Wandsworth SW18 2QE. *Tel*: 01-871 1169. *Open*: Mon to Sat 8.30am to 6pm. Supply/fit carpets and vinyls, including Amtico. Carpet-/upholstery-/curtain-cleaning service.

Bargains!

S & M Myers 100/106 Mackenzie Road, N7 8RG. (*5 mins Caledonian Road tube*). *Tel*: 01-609 0091. *Open*: Mon Wed Fri 10am to 5.30pm. Sat 9.30am to 2pm. Remarkably cheap plain quality carpets sold off the roll.

Bargains!

Posners Carpet Centre 9 Westbourne Grove, W2. (*10 mins Bays-*

water tube). *Tel*: 01-229 4304. *Open* (both branches): Mon to Sat 9am to 5.30pm. Carpet oddments, seconds. Perfect ranges at keen prices.
Also at: 10 Graycoat Place, SW1. (*10 mins St James's tube*). *Tel*: 01-222 0186.

Bargains!

Resista Carpets 255 New King's Road, Fulham SW6. (*10 mins Parsons Green tube*). *Tel*: 01- 731 2588. *Open* (all branches except Sheen): Mon to Sat 9am to 5.30pm. Large stocks plain colour quality carpets. Twists, loops, velvets, plains, patterns, Axminster, Wilton, tufted. Also sheet vinyls, Amtico, woodblocks. Plan/fit 48 hours from stock. Expert advice. Free samples. Half-price carpet remnants.
Also at: 148 Wandsworth Bridge Road, Fulham SW6. (*10 mins Parsons Green tube*) *Tel*: 01-731 3368.
And at: 584 Fulham Road, SW6. (*10 mins Parsons Green tube*). *Tel*: 01-736 7551.
And at: 182 Upper Richmond Road West, East Sheen SW14. *Tel*: 01-876 2089. Early closing Weds 1pm.
And at: 410/412 Chiswick High Road, W4. (*5 mins Chiswick Park tube*). *Tel*: 01-994 9181.

Outer Ring

Capitol Carpets 34 Beddington Lane, Croydon. *Tel*: 01-688 6209. *Open*: Mon to Fri 8am to 5pm. Sat 9am to 5pm. See London Postal Districts above.

Bargains!

Carpet Town Unit 1, Great Western Industrial Park, Armstrong Way,

Norwood Green, Middx. (*Off Windmill Lane, close to Ealing Hospital*). *Tel*: 01-571 9333. *Open*: Mon to Fri 10am to 8pm. Sat 9.30am to 5.30pm. Sun 10am to 5pm. Huge variety, low prices. Lots of remnants/ends of ranges. West London's largest carpet superstore, they claim. Measure/estimate within 24 hours. Fitted from stock within 72 hours.

Home Call Carpets *Tel*: 01-998 8532/ 01-367 8575 (24 hours). Appointments any day, virtually any time. Mobile showroom (van) brings samples. Carpets usually fitted 48 hours. Free estimates. Discount prices.

4/MATTINGS

Not necessarily cheap these days, mattings can be chic, and blend well with natural materials such as wood and terracotta. For suppliers see 3/Carpets above and Furnishing Stores, Department Stores.

London Postal Districts

Eatons 16 Manetta Street, W1V 5LB. (*3 mins Tottenham Court Road tube*). *Tel*: 01-437 9391. *Open*: Mon to Fri 9.30pm to 5pm. Sat 11am to 5pm. Panels 3 by 6ft of Chinese palm mattings/Philippine reed matting. Also wall panels of split bamboo/rattan.

Habitat See **Furnishing Stores**. Low cost rough-textured coir matting by the metre, or in tiles.

Mail Order

Crucial Trading PO Box 689, W2 4BX. *Tel*: 0588 7666. Seagrass and sisal floorcoverings in wide widths. Free samples. Measuring/fitting service nationwide. Boucle sisal in attractive cream/honey shades. Twill weave in natural stripes/colour flecks. Herringbone in natural/flecked colours. Can be laid like fitted carpets; with/without underlay. Also sisal mats/runners.

5/MARBLE, STONE & SLATE

See also **Tiles 3/Marble**.

London Postal Districts

Castelnau Tiles See **Tiles 1/Specialists**. Natural stone slabs, slates and marbles.

Ceramic World See **Tiles 1/Specialists**. Granite and marble wall/flooring tiles a speciality.

Worlds End Tiles See **Tiles 1/Specialists**. Good selections marble floor/wall tiles in spacious settings.

Home Counties/S.East

Patrick Fireplaces See **Heating 2/Fireplaces**. *Old-established family stonemasons are specialists in marble floors, with impressive showrooms.*

WINDOWS

Windows make or mar the exterior of your home. Far too many modern designs are, quite frankly, horrible. Take your time, don't be pushed into it – or out of it!

1/REPLACEMENTS

Window firms are legion: the double-glazing cowboy is a national joke. Nevertheless, new windows can add substantially to comfort and exterior appearance, but rarely to market value. Materials offered include uPVC (plastic in white, brown, or even woodgrain); aluminium usually in white; or softwood or hardwood. Take time to investigate; don't be pressured. Membership of The Glass and Glazing Federation is reassuring. See **Help!** *for address. For credit agreement rights, also see* **Help!** *Many large firms operate nationally. Below is a selection of smaller firms. For made-to-measure replacement windows in hardwoods, consult specialised joinery firms listed under* **Staircases 1/Wooden** *and* **Walls 4/Panelling**.

All Districts

Wickes See **DIY Superstores**. Made-to-measure window frames in pine, Philippine mahogany, mahogany traditional sliding sash, aluminium, uPVC. Sealed double glazing units. Ready assembled, delivered.

Home Counties/S.East

Architectural & Display Woodwork Valley Road, Hughenden, High Wycombe, Bucks HP14 4LG. *Tel*: 024024 2551. Made-to-measure join-ery/fitting service.

Roy Debenham Unit 6, Shelf House, Industrial Estate, Newfarm Road, Alresford, Hants SO24 9QE. *Tel*: 096 273 3503. Made-to-measure windows/bespoke joinery/fitting service.

Elphick Joinery 77 Mill Road, Hailsham, East Sussex BN27 2HU. *Tel*: 0323 840471. Made-to-measure windows/bespoke joinery/fitting service.

Lifestyle Window & Door Centres 4 Elm Parade, St. Nicholas Avenue, Elm Park, Hornchurch, Essex RM12 4RH. (*2 mins Elm Park tube; car park opposite*). *Tel*: 04024 76655 (24 hrs). *Open*: Mon to Sat 9am to 5pm. Bright, busy well-stocked showroom for doors/windows. Aluminium, uPVC, hardwood. Oddments sold off cheaply. Speciality: DIY supplies; advice on fixing from staff surveyor. *Mail order*; own finance schemes. Please telephone for addresses of other branches Essex/East London.

The Original Box Sash Window Company Freepost 28, Windsor, Berks SL4 1BR. *Tel*: dial 100, ask for Freefone Box Sash. *Showroom open*: Mon to Fri 9am to 5.30pm. Or by arrangement. Showroom: 279 Lillie Road, SW6 (*10 mins West Brompton tube*). *Tel*: 01-381 1226. *Open*: Mon to Sat 10am to 6pm (phone first). Brochure. Replacement traditional box sash windows: pine with hardwood sills. Single glass or double-glazed. Finishes: natural wood, long-lasting stain/seal, or painted. Colour brochure.

Pandora Glaze 41/45 Lind Road, Sutton, Surrey. (Factory and showroom) *Tel*: 01-643 0727. *Open*: Mon to Fri 9am to 5.30pm. Sat 9am to 1pm. Make and install Georgian-style and leaded-light double-glazed replacement windows/doors. Hardwood surrounds or colour-matched maintenance-free outer frames. Guarantee. Colour brochure. Established 21 years.
Also at: 342 High Street, Dorking, Surrey.

Sarek Joinery Castle Hedingham, Halstead, Essex CO9 3EP. *Tel*: 0787 60808. Made-to-measure/fitting service.

Mail Order

Barco Joinery 59 King Street, Darlaston, West Mid WS10 8DE. *Tel*: 021 526 7409 (24 hours). *Office open*: Mon to Fri 9am to 5pm. Closed lunch 1 to 1.30pm. Early closing Fri 4pm. Sat 9am to 1pm. Small family business (established 15 years), nationwide de-liveries. Standard/made-to-measure joinery, windows/doors/frames at trade prices: claim 50% savings. Fit yourself or employ local builder. Fax requirements on 021 568 6005, and receive answer "in about half-an-hour".

Thomas Rhodes & Son See **Staircases 1/Wooden**. Made-to-measure windows in traditional styles including sash for old/listed properties.

2/STAINED & DECORATIVE GLASS

Sunlight streaming through coloured glass is as beautiful today as ever, a permanent and individual enhancement for your home, outside and in. Numerous firms can restore older windows, or make you new panels.

London Postal Districts

Acanthus 143 Northfields Avenue. W13 9QR. (*5 mins Northfields tube*). *Tel*: 01-840 3700. *Open*: by appointment. Enthusiastic youthful and energetic partnership for all stained glass design. Repairs/restorations. Much in demand locally to recreate Victorian/Edwardian splendours.

Leo Amery Stained Glass 110/116 Kingsgate Road, NW6 2JG. (*West Hampstead tube*). *Tel*: 01-624 3240. *Open*: by appointment. Modern/abstract style (often incorporating antique glass fragments). Windows, and panels which are lit behind to hang on a wall. Hefty design fee is deducted from final fee, if commission progresses. Installations.

Artful Glass, 106 Brune Street Workshops, Brune Street, E1. (*Aldgate East tube; Liverpool Street tube/BR*). *Tel*: 01-247 9777/01-519 3957. *Open*: Mon to Fri 9am to 6pm. Wide range of designs for stained glass panels/windows are created with glass-like coloured resin layers, a Japanese technique. Cheaper than stained glass, and also suitable for decorative and security glazing.

Ray Bradley 3 Orchard Studios, Brook Green, W6 7BU. *Tel*: 01-602 1840. *Open*: appointment only. Stained glass and variations of the medium for all situations on any scale, including some restoration of good period glass. Also decorative work on sheet glass with sand-blast engraving, acid etching, enamelling, guilding and silvering. Work in this country and abroad, in private collections and the V&A Museum, London. Slides of work in situ can be seen on the Crafts Council selective index, 12 Waterloo Place, London.

Susan M Cook The Stained Glass Studio, Unit 117, 31 Clerkenwell Close, EC1R 0AT. *Tel*: 01-608 1503. *Open*: 10am to 7pm (appointment only). Design/make/install stained glass windows/panels/screens. Traditional/modern/restoration. Commissions. Small design fee with estimate.

The Glasshouse 11 Lettice Street, SW6 4EH. (*10 mins Parsons Green tube*). *Tel*: 01-736 3113. *Open*: Mon to Fri 10am to 6pm. Sat by appointment. Stained glass panels designed/made/installed to order. Individual attention. See Caroline Benyon's samples in workshop office. Brochure.

Goddard & Gibbs 41/49 Kingsland Road, E2 6AD. (*Old Street tube*). *Tel*: 01-739 6563. *Open*: Mon to Fri 9am to 5pm. The biggest/oldest name in British stained glass, established in 1868, and creator of windows for prestigious commissions . . . Houses of Parliament, St Paul's Cathedral, no less. But private clients are welcome with a promise of close attention.

Kawala's Glass Studio 30c Camden Lock, Camden High Street, NW1. (*5 mins Camden tube*). *Tel*: 01-482 4847. *Open*: Sat 11am to 6pm. Sun 11am to 6pm. Innovative stained glass designs/techniques for windows, doors, screens etc. Studio/factory: Unit 54, Metropolitan Workshop, Enfield Road, N1 5AZ. *Tel*: 01-241 0932/609 5407.

Lead & Light 15 Camden Lock, NW1 8AP. (*5 mins Camden tube*). *Tel*: 01-485 4568. *Open*: Mon to Fri 10am to 5pm. Sat to Sun 11am to 5pm. Workshop for leaded window designs, with coloured glass sheets on display. Supplies for DIY. Also lighting.

Matthew Lloyd Stained Glass Studios 63 Amberley Road, Palmers Green N13 4BH. *Tel*: 01-886 0213. *Open*: by appointment.

Maria McClafferty Design 11 Hillside Road, SW2. *Tel*: 01-671 6782. *Open*: by appointment. Designs/makes stained and/or etched panels for doors, windows, doors, screens, skylights etc. Reproductions/original designs. Install/repair/restore.

Stoney Parsons 203 Southgate Road, N1 3LD. (*15 mins Highbury & Islington tube; Angel tube plus bus*). *Tel*: 01-354 0892. *Open*: by appointment only. From her home studio, Stoney creates windows/panels in coloured glass and sympathetic to surroundings (mainly hand-blown). Modern designs veering towards abstract. Favourite themes: landscapes, flowers. Installations.

James Preece Stained Glass 11 Portobello Green, 281 Portobello Road, W10 5TD. *Tel*: 01-968 8807. *Open*: Mon to Sat 9.30am to 6pm. Original modern window designs with panels of mouth-blown glass.

Prisms Stained Glass Design 34 Boundary Road, NW8 0HG. (*5 mins Swiss Cottage tube; 1 min South Hampstead BR*). *Tel*: 01-624 5812. *Open*: by appointment. Using traditional leading and Tiffany techniques, Beverly Bryon creates windows/skylights/door panels/mirrors in modern designs. Commissions undertaken.

Shades of Light Unit 40, Wimbledon Stadium Studios, Riverside Road, SW17 0BA. (*20 mins Earlsfield BR/Tooting Broadway tube*). *Tel*: 01-946 9101. *Open*: Mon to Fri 8.30am to 5pm. Commissions/repairs for stained glass/lead lights. Lavish colour brochure.

SW82 Designs 38A Darwin Road, W5. *Tel*: 01-569 8220. By appointment. Designer/craftsmen for stained/etched glass. Your ideas, or their standard/original designs. Installations/restorations.

Caroline Swash 88 Woodwarde Road SE22 8UT. (*North Dulwich BR*). *Tel*: 01-693 6574. *Open*: by appointment.

Glassmaking runs in the family: Caroline, well-known as a glass artist, is the 3rd generation. Repairs/restorations can be arranged.

Home Counties/S.East

Amersham Joinery 97 Farnham Road, Slough SL1 4UN. *Tel*: 0753 824242. *Open*: Mon to Fri 9am to 5.30pm. Sat 9am to 1pm. Windows made-to-measure in stained glass/genuine leaded lights. All other bespoke joinery, plus standard windows/doors.

Contemporary Stained Glass Art 28 Westfield Road, West Green, Crawley, West Sussex RH11 7BT. *Tel*: 0293 36188. *Open*: 28 Westfield Road, West Green, Crawley, West Sussex. *Tel*: 0293 36188. *Open*: by appointment. Christine Kirby creates modern stained glass panels/windows. Commissions.

Glass Studio 31 Tunfield Road, Hoddesdon, Herts EN11 9LQ. *Tel*: 0992 460665. *Open*: by appointment. Stained glass commissions.

The Glassery 83 East Barnet Road, New Barnet, Herts. (*3 mins New Barnet BR; adjacent car park*). *Tel*: 01-449 7971. *Open*: Mon to Fri 8am to 5.30pm. Sat 8am to 5pm. Stained glass, any design. Handmade reproduction bullions. Leaded lights, real/imitation. Tabletops/mirrors cut and polished to shape. In stock, clear, coloured, patterned glass, mirrors, double-glazing systems, antique/cathedral glass.

Tudor Leaded Light Co Rembrant House, Whippenell Road, Watford WD1 7WD. *Tel*: 0923 36932. Measure/make/fit genuine leaded lights with stained glass inserts. No job too large or too small, they say. Repairs. Colour brochure.

3/SHUTTERS, AWNINGS & GRILLES

More of a continental/American habit, *shutters are well worth consideration. A durable way to furnish windows, they also insulate and provide security. Awnings shade and protect furnishings from the fading effects of sunlight, and keep rooms/patios cool on hot days. Fixed inside the room, shutters replace curtains and are ideal for bays. Well-chosen exterior shutters can improve your home's outside even when folded back, and guard your windows against intruders when closed.*

Continental Awnings Unit 21, Headley Park 10, Headley Road East, Woodley, Berks RG5 4SW. (*M4 Junction 10*). *Tel*: 0734 699655 (24 hours ansaphone). *Open·* (showroom): Mon to Fri 9am to 5.30pm. Patio awnings/exterior Dutch blinds made-to-measure. Wide choice colours/designs. Manual or electric push-button operation. Aluminium frames; rot proof fabrics. Three-year guarantee. In-home service for samples/measure/fit. Exterior window roller shutters, made-to-measure. Foils burglars, conserves energy, reduces condensation, absorbs noise. Made from aluminium filled with foam (for maximum insulation/protection) or from pvc. Installations.

Godington Forge Godington, Bicester, Oxon OX6 9AF. *Tel*: 08697 423. Home visits London area by appointment. Richard List is the blacksmith who specialises in security. A fine tracery of metalwork for window/door grilles, inside or out.

Homeguard Shutters 44/6 Crouch Street, Colchester CO3 3HH. *Tel*: 0206 42711. Authorised distributors. Berks: 0734 883874. Sussex: 0903 754605. Exterior roll-up shutters in aluminium with foam core for insulation. Controlled from inside. Add insulation/security.

House of Shutters 19 Carnwath Road, Fulham SW6 3HR. (*15 mins Fulham Broadway tube; car park*). *Tel*: 01-731 6036 (24 hrs)/01-736 8787. *Open*: Mon to Fri 9am to 5.30pm. Sat 10am to 4pm. Pine shutters with adjustable slats to varnish or paint. 88 sizes, all trimmable. Ex-stock with hardware for DIY installation. Home

visits with samples, advice. Installer recommendations. Brochure/measuring guide. *Mail order*.

Pine Unlimited See **Kitchens 5/Luxury Bespoke Kitchens**. English panelled wood shutters; designs based on book published 1780. Fold back into box, out of view. Substantially add to security: acceptable to insurance companies. Made-to-measure.

The following firms make up wooden replacement windows.

Mail Order

American Shutters 72 Station Road, SW13 0LS. *Tel*: 01-876 5905. Exclusive USA designs in wood stains/colours. Arched tops to order. Adjustable louvres in choice of slat widths. Also traditional solid panel designs. Colour brochures.

The London Shutter Co St Martins Stables, Windsor Road, Ascot, Berks. *Tel*: 0990 28385. See displays in The Traditional Bathroom Warehouse (**Bathrooms 3/Period Bathrooms**). Shutters up to 84in high with wide/narrow adjustable louvres. Any colour/stain. Complete in-home service: design/supply/install.

Plantation Shutters 93 Antrobus Road, Chiswick W4 5NW. *Tel*: 01-994 2886. Kate and Peter Evans pioneer the louvre shutter trend, founding their business 7 years ago. Their American shutters come in standard sizes, or made-to-order. Expert fitter available. Viewing by appointment.

The Traditional Shutter Co Avilan, Carroll Crescent, South Ascot SL5 9EH. *Tel*: 0990 23647. Exterior shutters/window boxes with traditional heart-shaped cut-outs. Made-to-measure, sold direct complete with decorative hinges.

JC & R Wood (Metalcraft) 303 Hull Road, Anlaby Common, Hull HU4 7RZ. *Tel*: 0482 51915 (24 hours). DIY tools/metal supplies for window grilles, fancy/plain. Joins are riveted; no welding needed.

DOORS

Estate agents say that a house sale can be made or broken by the front door. Make sure yours creates the right impression. More importantly, ensure **Security** to keep burglars at bay.

1/FRONT & INTERIOR

*For genuine old doors, hunt through the yards of **Architectural Salvage** merchants. See **Walls 4/Panelling** and **Staircases 1/Wooden** for firms specialising in bespoke joinery, many of whom can make special sizes/designs of doors, and may be able to install.*

London Postal Districts

Cotswood Door Specialists 5 Hampden Way, Southgate, N14 5DJ. (*10 mins Southgate tube*). *Tel*: 01-368 1664/9635. *Open*: Mon to Sat 9am to 5.30pm. Supply fine-finish, install wide range domestic doors: external, internal, matching garage doors. Design advice. Door furniture/security fittings.

Door Stop Unit 6/7 Hanover West Industrial Estate, 161 Acton Lane, NW10 7PB. (*200 yds from Central Middx Hospital*). *Tel*: 01-965 6006. *Open*: Mon to Fri 8am to 5.30pm. Sat 9am to 12 noon. Unique range hardwood doors: mahogany/oak. Locks/door furniture. Experienced advice.

Just Doors 126 West Green Road, Tottenham N15 5AA. (*5 mins Seven Sisters tube*). *Tel*: 01-800 3118. *Open*: Mon to Sat 8.30am to 5.30pm. New doors, in stock or to order.

The London Door Company 165 St John's Hill, SW11 1TQ. (*5 mins Clapham Junction BR*). *Tel*: 01-223 7243. *Open*: Mon to Sat 9.30am to 5.30pm. Comprehensive supply/fit service for exterior/interior doors made to high standards in own workshops. Decorative glazing in etched/bevelled/brilliant cut/stained glass. Door furniture. Security products.

WH Newson *See* **Home Improvement Specialists**. Doors are a speciality; free catalogue tells you how to fix them. Wood folding doors for dividing rooms. Bi-folds: louvred/panelled. Made-to-measure: bi-folds; mirrored (silver/bronze); panelled.

Peco of Hampton 72 Station Road, Hampton, Middx TW12 2BT. (*Hampton BR*). *Tel*: 01-979 8310. *Open*: Mon to Sat 9am to 5.15pm. Closed lunch 1 to 2pm. Renovated (own workshops) period doors: Victorian, Edwardian, Deco. Lacquered/stained finishes, plus special paint effects: dragging, stippling, marbling.

Victorian Pine 298 Brockley Road, Brockley, SE4 2RA. (*Brockley BR*). *Tel*: 01-691 7162/639 7226 (evening, phone first). *Open*: Mon to Sat 9am to 6pm. Sun 10am to 2pm (phone first). Traditional stripped pine architectural fittings/doors. Also stripping service for huge range of items, including woodwork and metal.

Mail Order

Barco See **Windows 1/Replacements**. Standard doors in wide choice of hardwoods, including attractive panelled designs and stable doors. Also good choice of models with feature glazing. Direct-from-factory prices are claimed to save 50%. Made-to-measure service. Nationwide deliveries.

Grandisson Doors The Old Hall, West Hill Road, West Hill, Ottery St Mary, Devon EX11 1TP. *Tel*: 040 481 2876/5400. Colour brochure. Exclusive unique range hand-carved by Spanish craftsmen in mahogany, oak, rosewood. Designs range from simple Victoria with long oval cutout for glazing, to intricate Balmoral where 8 panels each feature elaborate acanthus leaf design.

Outer Ring

Classic Doors 294 Uxbridge Road, Hatch End, Pinner, Middx HA5 4HR. (*5 mins Hatch End BR*). *Tel*: 01-428 0155. *Open*: Mon to Fri 9am to 5pm. Sat 9am to 3pm. On display, standard hardwood doors. Made-to-measure/fitting.

Cotswood 63a Park Road, Kingston Hill, Kingston-upon-Thames, Surrey KT2 6DE. (*8 mins Norbiton BR*). *Tel*: 01-546 3621. *Open*: Mon to Fri 9am to 5.30pm. Sat 9am to 1pm. Hardwood doors. Made-to-measure/fitting service.

Bargains!

Toddoors 22/24 Mandeville Road, Northolt UB5 5BL. (*3 mins Northolt tube*). *Tel*: 01-845 2493. *Open*: Mon to Sat 8.30am to 5.30pm. Door seconds: exterior/internal, small blemishes. Also new doors. Installations.

2/DOOR FURNITURE

A strange term that covers knobs, handles, knockers, letter boxes and the like: the important finishing touches to offset your doors . . . windows, too.

London Postal Districts

A&H Brass 201/203 Edgware Road, Paddington W2 1ES. (*10 mins Edgware Road tube*). *Tel*: 01-402 3981. *Open*: Mon to Sat 9am to 6pm. Locks/ handles, various finishes: brass, bronze, copper, pewter, antiqued, shiny modern. Commissions. Restorations. Key cutting. Engraving. 24-hour locksmith service. Catalogue £1.50. *Mail order.*

Barry Bros See **Security.** Architectural ironmonger. Fittings for doors/ windows: brass, chrome, antique, iron and mercury.

JD Beardmore 3/4 Percy Street, W1P 0EJ. (*5 mins Tottenham Court Road tube*). *Tel*: 01-637 7041. *Open*: Mon to Fri 8.45am to 5.15pm. Sat 9am to 12.30pm. Established well before brass knobs became trendy! Courteous, knowledgeable service. Large range, from tiny brass handles/knobs to wrought iron rings for gates. Copying service. Key cutting.

Brass Tacks 50/54 Clerkenwell Road, EC1M 5PS. (*Barbican tube*) *Tel*: 01-250 1971. *Open*: Mon to Fri 9am to 5.30pm. Make/sell brass door/window furniture, locks, hinges, bathroom accessories, electrical fittings etc.

Comyn Ching 19 Shelton Street, Covent Garden, WC2H 9JN. (*5 mins Covent Garden/Leicester Square tubes*). *Tel*: 01-379 3026. *Open*: Mon to Fri 9am to 5.30pm. Trading since 1723! – arguably Britain's leading architectural ironmonger. Trade prices. Wide variety door/window fittings. Cheap aluminium to brass/antique-style black iron. Locks, hinges, sliding door gear etc. Catalogue. Engraving.
Also at: 110 Golden Lane, EC1Y 0SS. (*Barbican/Old Street tubes*). *Tel*: 01-253 8414. *Open*: Mon to Fri 8.30am to 5.30pm.

FW Collins 14 Earlham Street, WC2H 9LN. (*5 mins Leicester Square tube*). *Tel*: 01-836 3964. *Open*: Mon to Fri 8.30am to 5.30pm. Sat 8.30am to 1pm. Trading over 150 years: a Mr Collins is still in charge. All kinds ironmongery crammed into tiny shop. Key cutting.

Danico Brass 31/33 Winchester Road, NW3. (*Swiss Cottage tube*). *Tel*: 01-586 7398. *Open*: Mon to Fri 9.30am to 6pm. Late night Thurs 8pm. Excellent displays, comprehensive brass range. Trading nearly 10 years. Door, window, and electrical fittings, bathroom accessories.

Knobs & Knockers 385 King's Road, Chelsea SW10 0LR. (*Sloane Square tube plus bus*). *Tel*: 01-352 5693. *Open*: Mon to Sat 10am to 5.30pm. Conrad Monk pioneered mass-market brass fittings around 20 years ago. Now there are 70 stores nationwide! Brass door/window furniture, hearthware, occasional furniture, bathroom accessories, gifts. Catalogue 95p refundable orders over £10.
Stores in Greater London: Chiswick; Notting Hill Gate; Bromley; Kingston; Watford; Fenwicks/Brent Cross; Debenhams/Oxford Street, Croydon, Harrow, Romford, Staines; DH Evans/Oxford Street; Harrison Gibson/Ilford; Army & Navy/ Victoria.
All enquiries: *Tel*: 01-289 4764.

Locks & Handles 8 Exhibition Road, SW7. (*5 mins South Kensington tube*). *Tel*: 01-584 6800. *Open*: Mon to Fri 9am to 5pm. Sat 9am to 3.30pm. Good displays/stocks authentic period brass door/window furniture.

A Touch of Brass 123 Kensington Church Street, W8. (*10 mins Notting Hill Gate tube*). *Tel*: 01-221 9256. *Open* (all branches): Mon to Fri 9am to 5pm. Sat 10am to 5pm. Good displays/stocks door/window fittings.
Also at: 210 Fulham Road, West Brompton SW10. (*Putney Bridge tube*). *Tel*: 01-351 2255.
And at: 61 Fulham High Street, SW6. *Tel*: 01-731 6100.

Sellar Bros 5/9 Beadon Road, W6. (*5 mins Hammersmith tube*). *Tel*: 01-748 7162. *Open* (all branches): Mon to Sat 9am to 5.45pm. Courteous, knowledgeable counter service. Excellent clear displays. Hooks, handles, knobs, catches: not only brass, but wood, porcelain, glass, Perspex, even gold plate.
Also at: 59 The Mall, W5. (*5 mins Ealing Broadway tube*). *Tel*: 01-567 6117.
And at: 27b The Quadrant, Richmond, Surrey TW9. (*2 mins Richmond tube/BR*). *Tel*: 01-948 1504.

Yannedis 25/27 Theobalds Road, Holborn WC1. (*10 mins Holborn tube*). *Tel*: 01-242 7106. *Open* (both branches): Mon to Fri 8.30am to 5pm. Trade prices, comprehensive stock. Traditional brass, modern stainless steel, colour-coated aluminium. Catalogue. Lock installation.
Also at: 27 Payne Road, EC3. (*Bromley-by-Bow tube*). *Tel*: 01-981 0031.

Mail Order

Devon Cottage Pottery Stokeinteignhead, Devon TQ12 4QS. Sae for brochure. Decorative ceramic house plaques made to your design.

Erme Wood Forge See **Heating 4/Fireside Accessories.** Handwrought gates with delicate iron tracery. Standard patterns adapted/made-to-measure.

House of Brass 122 North Sherwood Street, Nottingham NG1 4EF. *Tel*: 0602 475430. Solid brass door/window fittings. Also switches, sockets, dimmers, taps and mixers. Brass beds, headboards.

House Name Plate Co The Business

Centre, 23 Northenden Road, Sale, Cheshire M33 2DH. *Tel*: 061 962 5879. All types supplied: aluminium, solid brass, engraved wood/stone, ceramic, handpainted designs. Brochure.

JAB Services 23 Oakwood, Partridge Green, Horsham, Sussex RH1 8JG. House signs in ceramic, slate or elm. Mail order only. Free brochures.

Petdoors Freepost, Market Harborough, Leics LE16 7BR. *Tel*: 0858 33591. Leaflet. Swing-flap exits for cats/dogs in 4 sizes.

Signs of the Times Tebworth, Leighton Buzzard, Beds LU7 9QD. *Tel*: 05255 4185. Oval or domed handpainted house signs based on 19th-century floral designs. Weather/corrosion-proof. Brochure (sae).

Tebworth Letter Boxes Tebworth, Leighton-Buzzard, Beds LU7 9QD.

Tel: 05255 4185. Attractive painted wooden letter-boxes with locks. Brochure/sae.

True Value 95 High Street, Orpington, Kent BR6 0LF. (*5 mins Orpington BR*). *Tel*: 0689 73886. *Open*: Mon to Sat 9.15am to 5.30pm. Catalogue. Georgian/Victorian-style solid brass door furniture, lion knockers, hooks; brass-plated cabinet fittings, locks and bolts, solid brass bathroom accessories.

STAIRCASES

Things that trip you up tend to be ignored or kicked aside. You can't, I hope, actually kick away your staircase, but you will, yes admit it, you will ignore it. Why? For safety, access, and underspace storage it's very important, so give it a thought.

1/WOODEN

*Traditional wooden staircases are vulnerable to wear and tear: traditional joinery shops will put them to rights. All will make-to-measure, and many stock standard staircase components. For the handy DIY person, **DIY Superstores** and **Home Improvement Specialists** meet the vogue for restoration with good selections of old-style stairway components.*

All Districts

Magnet See **Home Improvement Specialists**. Sweeping staircase or straight runs mahogany/Parana pine. Spiral staircase kits. Free instore computer design service for staircase planning: by appointment with staircase designers.

London Postal Districts

Clissold Joinery 69 Green Lanes, Stoke Newington N16 9BU. *Tel*: 01-226 4872.

Goodwood Systems 20 Tanners Hill, SE8 4PJ. *Tel*: 01-691 4311. Standard/made-to-measure/fitting.

WR & A Hide 161 Dalling Road, Hammersmith W6 OES. (*5 mins Ravenscourt Park tube*). *Tel*: 01-743 2589. *Open*: Mon to Fri 7am to 4.30pm. Closed lunch 12.45 to 1.30pm. Made-to-measure staircases, doors, windows.

EA Higginson & Co 1 Carlisle Road, Queensbury NW9 0HD. (*15 mins Burnt Oak tube*). *Tel*: 01-200 4848. *Open*: Mon to Fri 9am to 5.30pm. Sat by appointment. In stock: staircase components, keen prices. Replacements to order.

Mullen & Lumsden 39 East Smithfield, E1 9AP. *Tel*: 01-481 8261. Standard/made-to-measure.

The Loft Shop See **Services 18/Building Services**. Everything for loft access from ladders to attractive timber spirals/straight runs. Expert advice/information sheets on regulations/fitting etc.

Wansdown Joinery Works 327 & 339 Lillie Road, Fulham Cross SW6 7NR. (*20 mins Fulham Broadway tube*). *Tel*: 01-385 0351. *Open*: Mon to Thurs 8am to 5.30pm. Fri 8am to 4.30pm. Period staircases/ panelled rooms.

The following firms also make staircases to order.

Space Age Stairways 16/22 Martello Street, London Fields, E8 3PE. *Tel*: 01-249 3631.

Stairwell Cambridge Works, 2 Bedford Road, East Finchley, N2 9DA. *Tel*: 01-883 7885.

Outer Ring

EJ Bushell 453 Sunleigh Road, Wembley, Middx. *Tel*: 01-900 2905.

EJ Hearns Specialised Joinery 1a St Mark's Road, Teddington, Middx TW11 9DE. *Tel*: 01-977 0032.

Kier London (Constr.) Abridge Depot, Ongar Road, Abridge, Romford, Essex RM4 1UR. *Tel*: 037881 2666. Standard/made-to-measure/fitting.

R Mansell Roman House, 13/27 Grant Road, Croydon, Surrey CR9 6BU. *Tel*: 01-654 8191. Made-to-measure; fitting service.

Sandiford Son & Bannister Fairlight Works, 153 Croydon Road, Caterham, Surrey CR3 6PF. *Tel*: 0882 43545. Standard/made-to-measure.

Home Counties/S.East

Ampthill Joinery Flitwick Ind. Estate, Malden Road, Flitwick, Bedford MK45 5BS. *Tel*: 0525 716603.

Ashby & Horner Joinery 795 London Road, West Thurrock, Grays, Essex. *Tel*: 0708 866841. Make/fit.

Bespoke Britannia Joinery (Extend a Home), Unit 32, Industrial Estates, Leagrane Road, Luton, Beds LU8

1SD. *Tel*: 0582 400707. Standard/made-to-measure/fitting.

Cane End Joinery Rowsham Road, Bierton, Aylesbury, Bucks HP22 5DZ. *Tel*: 0296 88207.

Cox Brothers Builders (Kent) 80/82 Peel Street, Maidstone, Kent ME14 2SP. *Tel*: 0622 64255. Standard/made-to-measure/fitting.

Crockett & Eaton Charfleets Road, Charfleets Estate, Canvey, Island, Essex. *Tel*: 0268 696480. Standard/made-to-measure/fitting. Extensions/refurbishments.

DCS Joinery The Station, Bagmore Lane, Herriard, Basingstoke, Hants RG25 2PY. *Tel*: 025683 414. Standard/made-to-measure.

JA Elliott 133 Stansted Road, Bishops Stortford, Herts CM23 2AN. *Tel*: 0279 755962.

Ethringtons Joinery & Carpentry Unit 4, Miltons Yard, Petworth Road, Godalming, Surrey GU8 5LM. *Tel*: 042879 4217.

Hunkins & Frewin 14/22 Middleton Road, Banbury, Oxon. *Tel*: 0295 51931. Standard/made-to-measure/fitting.

Input Joinery Enham Arch, Newbury Road, SP10 4DU. *Tel*: 0264 55858. Standard/made-to-measure.

Lafford & Leavey Arrowhead Road, Theale, Reading RG7 4AZ. *Tel*: 0734 303333.

William Newman Unit No 6, Jubilee End, Sation Road, Lawford, Essex CO11 1UR. *Tel*: 0206 396280.

Nuthall Joinery Hanworth Trading Est., Hanworth Lane, Chertsey, Surrey. *Tel*: 09228 62520. Standard/made-to-measure.

Singleton Joinery Park Bottom, Arundel, West Sussex BN18 0AA. *Tel*: 0903 882380.

TF Smith (Newland) Joinery Works 150 Newland, Witney, Oxon OX8 6JH. *Tel*: 0993 702740. Standard/made-to-measure/fitting.

Sunningdale Joineries The Mill, Church Road, Bagshot, Surrey GU19 5EQ. *Tel*: 0276 76222. Made-to-measure joinery/fitting service.

Mail Order

Thomas Rhodes & Son Whitworth Yard, Red Lane, Rochdale, Lancs OL12 9DB. *Tel*: Tel: 0706 46704/39866. *Freephone*: 0800 269743. Wooden staircases made to measure/design in softwood/Parana pine/mahogany. Spindles, newel posts, handrails always in stock. Also all windows including tilt sliding sash, leaded lights. Specialists in preservation order listed building commissions. Catalogue £1.50.

2/SPIRAL

The archetypal solution to space problems, spirals can also be supremely decorative. Shop from a specialist who will inform on important building regulations.

All Districts

Safety Stairways Unit 45, Owen Road Industrial Estate, Owen Road, Willenhall, West Mid WV13 2PX. *Tel*: 021 526 3133. *Night number*: 0922 477722. Britain's largest maker of cast iron staircases. 60 models, wide variety of designs, over 20 years experience. Nationwide installation network, or cash and carry direct from factory.

London Postal Districts

Albion Design 12 Flitcroft Street, WC2H 8DJ. (*2 mins Tottenham Court Road tube*). *Tel*: 01-379 7359/836 0151. *Open*: Mon to Fri 9am to 5.30pm. Cast iron/steel/wood spiral/straight staircases. Catalogues.

R Bleasdale 301 Caledonian Road, Islington N1 1DW. (*Caledonian Road tube*). *Tel*: 01-609 0934. *Open* (both branches): Mon to Fri 10am to 5.30pm. Sat by appointment. Showroom: 125 King's Cross Road, St Pancras, WC1. (*King's Cross tube*). *Tel*: 01-833 4174. Reproduction Victorian cast-iron spiral staircases. Catalogues.

Higginson Staircases Unit 1, Carlisle Road, NW9 OHD. (*10 mins Edgware Road tube*). *Tel*: 01-200 4848. *Open*: Mon to Fri 9am to 5.30pm. Or by appointment. Elegant range of wood/metal spiral staircases; choice of colour/wood finishes.

Kensington Traders Unit 11, Mulberry Business Centre, Quebec Way, SE16 1AA. (*Behind Daily Mail building*). *Tel*: 01-232 1746. *Open*: Mon to Fri 9am to 5.15pm. Spiral stairs; wrought iron balusters.

FURNITURE

If you have rather old and unco-ordinated pieces you'll certainly be English. Living indoors most of the year our furniture does get more of a pounding than that fancy continental stuff, but can we be just a little more adventurous . . . ?

1/GENERAL

Before shopping, always measure spaces carefully, and take tape with you to check sizes in shops. Remember to allow space to use furniture comfortably: dining chairs must pull in and out, drawers and doors must open, and so on.

London Postal Districts

Adeptus 235 Finchley Road, NW3 6LS. (*2 mins Finchley Road tube*). *Tel*: 01-794 6154. *Open*: Mon to Sat 9.30am to 5.30pm. Upholstery/flip-over convertibles in combustion modified high resilient foam; in stock/to order, 200 fabrics, 7/10 days. Cottons, velvets, tweeds, patterns. Made in own Luton factory. Sleek modern shapes for tables/desks/chairs in glossy lacquers; in stock/to order (8 weeks). Danish shelving system.

Astrohome 47/49 Neal Street, WC2H 9PJ. (*3 mins Covent Garden tube*). *Tel*: 01-379 0555. *Open*: Mon to Sat 10am to 6pm. Exclusive contemporary British/foreign furniture/furnishings. Famous for "high tech" furniture/accessories. Pleasant atmosphere, good displays. Affordable. Constantly updated merchandise. Chunky style-bible catalogue £1.50 plus £1 p&p. *Mail order.*

Authentics 42 Shelton Street, WC2H 9HZ. (*3 mins Covent Garden tube*). *Tel*: 01-240 9845. *Open*: Mon to Sat 10.30am to 6pm. Terry Jonas has created a spacious, elegant setting for 20th-century classics, plus newest designs from leading international designers/architects. Also lighting, ceramics, glassware, desk/office accessories. Tableware, mirrors, photo/picture frames, and more. Unique service: will hunt worldwide/import all possible products. A model of how a general furniture shop could be.

Beau Regard 662 Old Kent Road, SE15 1JF. (*Elephant & Castle tube*). *Tel*: 01- 639 4220. *Open*: Mon to Sat 10am to 6pm. Closed Wed. Late night Thurs 7pm. Sun 1pm to 4pm. Practical modern furniture, tailored to requirements. Futons, rugs, pottery, shelving.

Bargains!

Direct Bargain Centre See **Decorating Materials 1/Paper & Paint.** Furniture/beds at low prices usually available.

Estia See **Living & Diningrooms 3/Sofabeds.** Ingenious designs using metal tube in black, white, green, red or yellow. Tables, desks, shelving, trollies etc. Affordable prices.

The Futon Company See **Bedrooms 11/Futons.** Elegant minimal matt black lounging furniture.

Gagliardi Design 509 King's Road, Chelsea, SW10 0TX. (*Earls Court tube plus Hopper bus to Chelsea Harbour*). *Tel*: 01-352 3663. *Open*: Mon to Sat 10am to 6pm. Long-established family firm selling own make Italian modern/traditional furniture direct to public. Dining/sitting/bedrooms. Good quality, wide choice, reasonable prices, personal service.

Bargains!

Charles Hall & Co Magdelen House, 136/148 Tooley Street, SE1 2TU. (*5 mins London Bridge tube/BR*). *Tel*: 01-403 0249. *Open*: Mon to Fri 9.30am to 5.30pm. Sat 9.30am to 12 noon. Salvaged furniture. Damaged carpets/rugs. Furniture repairs on premises.

Ligne Roset 132 Shaftesbury Avenue, W1N 7DN. (*5 mins Leicester Square tube*). *Tel*: 01-434 2071. *Open*: Mon to Sat 10am to 7pm. Ligne Roset of France hosts one of our largest showcases for European modern interiors, also storage systems for homes and offices. Beds, desks, lights, dining furniture, occasional tables. Ceramics, accessories. Interior design advice. Colour brochure £1.25.

Maison 917/919 Fulham Road, SW6 5HU. *Tel*: 01-736 3121. *Open*: Mon to Sat 9.30am to 6pm. Wide selections modern living/dining/bedroom furniture from Britain, Italy, Spain. Wood, lacquers, glass. Also modern lighting/

Furniture

accessories. Table/cookware.

New Venture Furniture 15/17 Colindale Avenue, NW9 5DR. (*5 mins Colindale tube*). *Tel*: 01-205 7547. *Open*: Mon to Fri 9am to 7pm. Sat 9am to 6pm. Sun 9am to 5pm. 14,000 sq ft of well-known brands. They promise same-day deliveries. Beds/livingroom furniture, keen prices.

The Treske Shop 5 Barmouth Road, SW18 2DT. (*Vauxhall tube plus bus*). *Tel*: 01-874 0050. *Open*: Tues to Sat 11am to 6.30pm. See *Mail Order* below.

Home Counties/S.East

Charles Hall & Company 13 West Street, Reigate, Surrey. See London Postal Districts above.

Ligne Roset 57 Western Road, Hove, Sussex BN3 1JD. *Tel*: 0273 722929. *Open*: Mon to Sat 9.30am to 5.30pm. Early closing Wed 1.30pm. See London Postal Districts above.

Mail Order

Treske Station Works, Thirsk, North Yorkshire YO7 4NY. *Tel*: 0845 22770. Excellent informative catalogue. Furniture in homegrown hardwoods (oak, ash, beech) commissioned from many famous designers. Beautiful simple shapes that will never date; customers can often dictate details. Small private family firm catering for every room. Everything guaranteed; maintenance service. Visitors welcome.

2/PINE & COUNTRY

Pine furniture lasts and doesn't date. But new pieces will go darker. Stripped pine is usually Victorian and was probably once painted. Pine made from old wood is romantic but new pine with an antiqued finish mostly looks the same. Colour stains include an attractive burgundy shade; some ranges are painted.

London Postal Districts

Adams Antiques See **Antiques 2/Furnishing Antiques**. Fine reproduction dressers etc. as well as antiques.

Chest of Drawers 281 Upper Street, Islington N1 2TZ. (*7 mins Highbury/Islington tube*). *Tel*:01-359 5909. *Open*: 7 days 10am to 6pm. Antique/repro pine/country furniture. Farmhouse, refectory, wake, square leg, oval, round, gateleg, dropleaf tables. Irish, Welsh Lancs, Lincs dressers. Can make to any size; plan chests a speciality.

Chiswick Country Pine 158 Chiswick High Road, W4 1PR. (*5 mins Turnham Green tube*). *Tel*: 01-747 0734. *Open*: Mon to Sat 10am to 6pm. Sun 12 noon to 5pm. Varied stock pine furniture; special sizes, details, finishes to order.

Danta Pine 88 The Broadway, Mill Hill Circus, NW7. (*5 mins Mill Hill Broadway BR; Mill Hill East tube, plus bus*). *Tel*: 01-959 4292. *Open*: Mon to Sat 9.30am to 5pm. Half-day Thurs 1pm. Well-made solid pine furniture from own Luton workshops. Unfinished, varnished, or antiqued. Special sizes to order (4 to 6 weeks). Budget bedroom range. Price lists/drawings.

Geranium 121 Upper Street, N1 1QP. (*5 mins Angel/Highbury Islington tubes*). *Tel*: 01-359 4281. *Open*: Mon to Fri 10am to 5.30pm. Sat 10am to 6pm. Bright little shop with country-style mix of old/new pine. Tables/beds: special sizes to order.

Icor Interiors 195 Upper Richmond Road, Putney, SW15 6SA. (*4 mins East Putney tube*). *Tel*: 01-788 0982. *Open*: Mon to Sat 10am to 5.30pm. Closed Thurs. Reliable direct-selling workshop. Simple chunky shapes in solid pine, natural or 20 wood stains. Shelving, bookcases, chests, wardrobes, desks, sideboards, wall units. From stock (many showroom models are reduced) or within 14 days – even special sizes/colours. Futon sofabeds: pine or black lacquer, easily converted with-

out futon removal. Catalogue/price list. *Mail order*.

Jasco Antiques 134 Upper Richmond Road, Putney SW15. (*5 mins East Putney tube*). *Tel*: 01-789 0060. *Open*: 7 days 9am to 5pm. Antique/reproduction pine. Old/new wood refectory/farmhouse tables. Bedroom furniture. Bookcases made to measure.

John Lewis of Hungerford See **Kitchens 5/Luxury Bespoke Kitchens**. Living room furniture, dressers and so on in distinctively different designs.

Pine Grove 186 Wandsworth Bridge Road, Fulham, SW6. (*15 mins Putney Bridge tube*). *Tel*: 01-731 7673/736 5802. *Open*: 7 days 10am to 6pm. Sturdy pine furniture from 20 small country workshops. Good stock, or will make to order. Reasonable prices.

Pine Interiors 49 Montpelier Vale, SE3 O27. (*3 mins Blackheath BR*). *Tel*: 01-318 0477. *Open*: Mon to Sat 10am to 6pm. Late nights Tues & Fri 8pm. Good choice reproduction furniture for living/bedrooms. Three main makes: Ducal, Younger, Lovelace. Brochures.

The Pine Market 3/4 Varley Parade, Edgware Road, Colindale NW9 6RR. (*5 mins Colindale tube*). *Tel*: 01-205 5150. *Open*: Mon to Sat 10am to 6pm. Sun 12 noon to 4pm. Large shop: vast selection pine furniture, from spice racks to fitted wardrobes. Quick deliveries: sometimes same day. *Also at*: 150 West End Lane, NW6. *Tel*: 01- 624 6628.

Sophisto-Cat 192 Wandsworth Bridge Road, SW6 2UF. (*Fulham Broadway plus bus, or 15 mins Parsons Green tubes*). *Tel*: 01-731 2221. *Open*: Mon to Fri 10am to 6pm. Sat 10am to 5pm. Explore 3 adjoining shops filled with traditional repro pine furniture, some in old wood. Furniture in old wood made to order, including wardrobes and chests.

This & That 50/51 Chalk Farm Road, NW1 8AN. (*5 mins Chalk Farm tube*). *Tel*: 01-267 5433. *Open*: Tues to Sun

10.30am to 6pm. Mix of old and new pine; bedrooms, living rooms, kitchens. Bookcases made to order. *Also at*: 256/258 Chiswick High Road, Chiswick W4 1PD. (*7 mins Turnham Green tube*). *Tel*: 01-995 4403. *Open*: Tues to Sat 10.30am to 6pm. Sun 12am to 5pm.

Village Collection Nearest branch/general enquiries: PO Box 2, Freshwater, Isle of Wight B39 0AJ. *Tel*: 0983 754968. Mail order colour catalogue £1.50 from shops; £2 (inc. p&p) from address above. Extensive range craftmen's traditional/country solid pine furniture for home/office. Many branches also have restored furniture. Mirrors/prints/lighting. Pleasant helpful service. *Open* (all branches unless stated otherwise): Mon to Sat 9.30am to 6pm. Sun 10am to 6pm. Major branches: 19 Chalk Farm Road, NW1. (*3 mins Camden Town tube*). *Tel*: 01-485 4034. Large showrooms on 4 floors; busy Camden atmosphere. Good selections restored furniture.
Also at: 1 Pembridge Villas, W2 4XA. (*5 mins Notting Hill Tube*). *Tel*: 01-221 7044. *Open*: Mon to Sat 9.30am to 6pm. Sun 10am to 6pm. Good selections restored pine in stock.
And at: 162 Wandsworth Bridge Road, SW6. (*Corner of Maiden Road, 20 mins Fulham Broadway tube*). *Tel*: 01-736 2753. Large selection on 3 floors, interesting restored furniture.
And at: 195 Upper Richmond Road West, SW14. (*15 mins Mortlake BR; or Richmond tube plus bus*). *Tel*: 01-876 4053. *Open*: Mon to Sat 9.30am to 6pm. Sun 10am to 6pm. Friendly helpful shop. 2 floors, good range of solid pine furniture. Mirrors, prints, lightnings. Good range restored furniture always in stock.

Vogue Pine Superstore, 12 Springbridge Road, Ealing Broadway, W5 2AA. (*5 mins Ealing Broadway tube*). *Tel*: 01-579 4414. *Open* (all branches): Mon to Sat 9am to 5.30pm. Sun 10am to 4pm. 4,500 sq ft modern/traditional pine furniture from top makes. Ducal/Jaycee/Craftsman/Orchard/Harvest. Plus their own Vogue Collection. Livingrooms/bedrooms/kitchens. Discounted prices. Art gallery/1 hour

picture framing. Exclusive sofabeds. *Also at*: The Pine Shop, 167 Uxbridge Road, Hanwell W7 3TH. (*Next to clock tower*). *Tel*: 01-840 5303. Displays over 2 floors. Specialist bedding centre.

Outer Ring

The Pine Factory 32 Church Street, Twickenham, Middx. (*10 mins Twickenham BR*). *Tel*: 01-744 1382. *Open*: please phone (times vary). Manufacturers' showroom. Solid pine chests, Welsh dressers, dressing tables, corner units etc. Keen prices.
Also at: 226 Harlesden High Street, NW10 4TD. (*5 mins Willesden Junction BR*). *Tel*: 01-961 1004. *Open*: Thurs to Sun 10am to 4pm.
And at: Little Clanfield, Clanfield, Oxon OX8 2RX. (*A420 from Oxford*). *Tel*: 036 781 529. *Open*: Sat & Sun 10am to 4pm. Or by appointment. Old barn houses pine furniture displays.

Pine Productions 12/16 Whytecliffe Road, Purley, Surrey CR2 2AU. (*Next to Purley BR*). *Tel*: 01-660 2690. *Open*: Mon to Thurs 9am to 5.30pm. Fri to 7pm. Closed Sat. Pine furniture (bedroom, diningroom, kitchen) with workshop behind for fitted kitchens in pine and oak. Immediate delivery.

The Pine Workshop Swan Island, 1 Strawberry Vale, Twickenham TW1 4RX. (*10 mins Strawberry Hill BR*). *Tel*: 01-891 6436. *Open*: Mon to Sat 10am to 6pm. Sun viewing 11am to 5pm. All furniture made to order: new pine, or reclaimed seasoned timbers. Takes around 4 weeks. Browse around in 15,000 sq ft showroom, then specify your own style/size/finish. (No stock). Upholstery service.

Village Collection Old Greys Brewery Yard, 5 The Maltings, Springfield Road, Chelmsford, Essex. (*10 mins Chelmsford BR*). *Tel*: 0245 266865. *Open*: Mon to Sat 9.30am to 6pm. Sun 10am to 6pm. Handy central location; 3 floors, good stocks, friendly staff. See London Postal Districts above.
And at: 93 South Street, Romford. (*2 mins Romford BR, multi-storey parking by BR*). *Tel*: 0708 23111. *Open*:

Mon to Sat 9.30am to 6pm. Sun 10am to 6pm. Friendly shop; 2 floors of solid pine furniture. See London Postal Districts above.

Vogue Pine Andrews Parade, off Prestwick Road/Brookdene Avenue, South Oxhey, Watford WD1 6AD. (*Carpenters Park BR*). *Tel*: 01-428 5042. See London Postal Districts above.

Home Counties/S.East

Danta Pine 96 Leagrave Road, Luton, Beds. *Tel*: 0582 36236.
Also at: 17 High Street, Hemel Hempstead. *Tel*: 0442 214040. See London Postal Districts above.

The Pine Market 222 St Albans Road, Watford. *Tel*: 0923 229626. See London Postal Districts above.

Sussex Windsors Dormers Farmhouse, Windmill Hill, Herstmonceaux, Hailsham, East Sussex BN27 4RY. *Tel*: 0323 832388. In a village workshop, Barry and Mary Murphy handmake 11 designs of traditional country chair. Seats: wide plank elm cut to shape. Arms, bows, stetchers: local young ash, steam-bent. Hardwood commissions. Brochure 20p. *Mail order*.

Village Collection 51 High Street, Tunbridge Wells, Kent. (*10 mins Tunbridge Wells BR; Safeways car park*). *Open*: Mon to Sat 9.30am to 6pm. Sun 10am to 6pm. Recently refurbished; friendly atmosphere. Three floors, good selection old restored pine. See London Postal Districts above.
Also at: 38/40 High Street, Guildford, Surrey. (*10 mins BR; Sainsbury's car park*). *Tel*: 0483 67005. *Open*: Mon to Sat 9.30am to 6pm. Sun 10am to 6pm). Large 2-floor showroom. Good selection solid pine furniture.
And at: 15 Chequer Street, St Albans, Herts. (*5 mins St Albans BR; central NCP car park*). *Tel*: 0727 41599. *Open*: Mon to Sat 9.30am to 6pm. Sun 10am to 6pm. Solid pine furniture in a period setting. Good selections restored furniture.
And at: 122 Thornycroft Industrial Estate, Worting Road, Basingstoke,

Furniture

Hants. (*Just off Worting Road; 10 mins Basingstoke BR*). *Tel*: 0256 842702. Large showroom; extensive solid pine furniture. Mirrors/prints/lighting. Next to warehouse: vast range, some slight seconds available at reduced prices. Local deliveries.
And at: 94 Western Road, Brighton, East Sussex. (*Next to Debenhams; 15 mins Brighton BR*). *Tel*: 0273 26493. *Open*: Mon to Sat 9.30am to 6pm. Sun 10am to 6pm. Three floors; good selections.
And at: (Star Store) 42/3 Peascod Street, Windsor. (*1m Riverside BR; ½m Eton & Windsor BR*). *Tel*: 0753 855730. *Open*: Mon to Sat 9.30am to 6pm. Sun 10am to 6pm. Main showroom; 2 floors; extensive selections. Mirrors/prints. Also restored furniture.

3/SCANDINAVIAN

The simple shapes pioneered by the Scandinavian countries in the fifties and sixties have a classic and enduring appeal. Quality is usually good, with lots of solid wood. NB Teak only needs an occasional oiling.

London Postal Districts

Danish Guild 25 Leegate Centre, Burnt Ash Road, Lee SE12 8SS. *Tel*: 01-318 9111. *Open*: Mon to Fri 9am to 5.30pm. Sat 9am to 6pm. Sun (viewing) 10am to 4pm. New 9,000 sq ft showroom over 2 floors with comprehensive selection good quality Danish/European living/dining furniture; British upholstery. Franchises: Feniche Italia, selling marble dining/occasional tables; and Leegate Beds, for specialist advice on beds/headboards. Personal service. Yearly colour catalogue.

Scandinavian World 72-94 Park Road, Crouch End, N8 8JP. (*Finsbury Park tube, plus bus; W7 stops outside*). *Tel*: 01-348 1854. *Open*: Mon to Sat 10am to 5pm. Sun 10am to 2pm. Classic undating Danish designs. Over 70 displays/2 floors. UK outlet (6 years) for Dyrlund manufacturer of quality furniture in teak/rosewood. Living/diningrooms. Lights. Leather reclin-

ers. Beautifully constructed and finished, to stand the test of time. Free colour brochure.

Wharfside Furniture 66 Buttesland Street, N1 6BY. (*10 mins Old Street tube*). *Tel*: 01-253 3206. *Open*: Mon to Thurs 9am to 5pm. Fri 9am to 1pm. Sun 9am to 2pm. Rambling warehouse with vast selection dining/livingroom furniture, imported directly from Scandinavia at very good prices.

Outer Ring

Danish Guild 47 Whitgift Centre, Croydon, Surrey CR10 1UQ. *Tel*: 01-680 2175. *Open*: Mon to Fri 9am to 5.30pm. Sat 9am to 6pm. 4,000 sq ft of showspace. See London Postal District above.

Home Counties/S.East

Danish Interiors 34 Molesey Road, Hersham, Walton-on-Thames, Surrey. (*Hersham BR plus bus*). *Tel*: 0932 231344. *Open*: Mon to Fri 10am to 7pm. Sat 9am to 6pm. Quality living/dining/storage furniture direct from Denmark in rosewood/teak/natural oak. Also grey/black lacquer finishes. Deliveries within 8 weeks.

Mail Order

Distinctive Designs 6 Sweetcroft Lane, Hillingdon, Middx UB10 9LD. *Tel*: 0895 30280. Brochure (large sae). Evergreen designs: some 25-year-old models are still in production. Classic Finnish solid pine tables, chairs, drawing boards. Sizes compact to Jumbo (table for 12 people unextended!). Attractive self-assembly Swedish solid pine: bunk beds, storage, seating, etc, ideal for young people.

Worth a Trip

Chancery Antiques 8/10 Barrington Street, Tiverton, Devon. (*M5 to Tiverton Link Road*). *Tel*: 0884 252416. *Open*: Mon to Sat 9am to 5pm. Closed Thurs. Stripped pine/country furniture imported direct from Scandinavia. 150 Danish antiques arrive weekly. Wardrobes, chests, farmhouse tables, desks, cup-

boards. Beautifully handfinished. Weekly deliveries London/SE.

4/ CLASSICS & REPRODUCTION

Quality reproductions cost a fraction of their antique counterparts. Reproduction furniture at top end of the market is not cheap, but has investment value. Cheaper reproductions (readily available from warehouses) often with extensive veneers on chipboard is widespread. Furniture of this type will not have the same potential value. And "antique-style" cabinets for TVS/hi-fis lose 18th-century credibility! Also likely to appreciate: quality copies of already-classic modern furniture designed around 50 to 60 years ago.

London Postal Districts

Antique Designs 277 Lillie Road, SW6 7PN. (*10 mins Fulham Broadway tube*). *Tel*: 01-385 0127. *Open*: Mon to Fri 10.30am to 6pm. Sat 10.30am to 2.30pm. Decorative Italian reproduction furniture, Biedermeier and Empire. "Papa" Biedermeier was a cartoon character in the early 19th century. He gave his name (from "bieder", plain, and "Meier", a common German surname) to the solid simple furniture style that originated in Vienna 1815/1830. Reproductions suit new or old schemes. Lighter hardwoods (cherry, maple, walnut) with fruitwood/ebony ornamentation. Owner Simon Pugh (one-time Christie's furniture "runner") discovered Italian craftsmen making this style 2 years ago. Also Art Deco, Georgian, Colonial Indian and Dutch Colonial.

Atrium 22/24 St Giles High Street, WC2. (*2 mins Tottenham Court Road tube*). *Tel*: 01-379 7288. *Open*: Mon to Fri 9.30am to 6pm. Sat by appointment. Spacious well-arranged modern designs, highlighted by own French halogen lighting range. Le Corbusier Petit Confort/Chaise Longue designed in France, 1928. A little later, Gerrit Rietveld emulated Mondrian with The Red and Blue chair; sharp sloping uncomfortable angles have sculptural impact. Also desks/tables with sharp, modern styling, Italian/French/German.

Authentics See **1/General** above. In stock: Le Corbusier chaise longue in steel/black leather plus club chair/matching coffee table. Famous Marcel Breuer Wassily (1925) named after Wassily Kandinsky, and made for his Bauhaus home: black strip of leather for seat/sides/back intersect in different planes around the tubular chromed steel frame. Two ultra-elegant Mies van der Rohe cantilevers: the MR, with sweeping chromed curves and one-piece seat/back of woven cane; and the Brno (1930). Probably best known is the M van der R Barcelona with scimitar curved chromed frame and buttoned black leather seat/back cushions, designed for the Barcelona International Exhibition of 1929. The brief from the German Government Pavilion was to design a chair fit to receive a king!

English Period Interiors 6 Fulham High Street, SW6 3LQ. (*5 mins Fulham Broadway tube*). *Tel*: 01-736 9088. *Open*: Tues to Sat 10am to 6pm. Specialists for fine 17th and 18th-century style furniture made by hand/traditional methods of Gostins of Liverpool. Over 250 designs in oak, walnut, mahogany, many with exquisite marquetry embellishments. Handcarved mirrors, Japanese/classical lamps, paintings, antiques, decorative objects.

Freud 198 Shaftesbury Avenue, WC2 8JL. (*10 mins Covent Garden tube*). *Tel*: 01-831 1071. *Open*: Mon to Fri 10am to 6pm. Sat 11am to 6pm. At last (after exorbitant Italian copies): the striking geometric designs of Glasgow architect Charles Rennie Mackintosh at affordable prices. Immaculate reproductions, made in England. Leaflets.

Graham & Green See **Accessories 10/General**. Reproduction Lloyd Lloom furniture.

Mahogany & Yew 154/156 Upper Richmond Road West, East Sheen, London SW14 8AG. (*Richmond*

tube/*BR plus bus*). *Tel*: 01-876 3886. *Open*: Mon to Sat 10am to 6pm. Sun 11am to 4pm (1st in month only). Desks, bureaux, occasional tables, bookcases, TV/video cabinets, stereo units, sideboards, chests in 18th century styles. Dining chairs in 14 designs, Regency drum edge and standard dining tables from 6ft upwards.

Parsons Green Reproductions 151 Lower Richmond Road, Putney, SW15 1EZ. (*20 mins Putney Bridge tube*). *Tel*: 01-788 3197/3616. *Open*: Mon to Sat 9.30am to 5.30pm. Late night Wed 8pm. Six large showrooms quality reproductions mahogany/yew. Mostly ex-stock. Catalogues.

Treske See **1/General** above. Modern British classics in solid wood from the past 15 years, by Dinah Casson/Robert Heritage.

Viaduct See **11/Designer Furniture** below. Classics by Le Corbusier and Mies van der Rohe.

Sasha Waddell 22 North End Parade, W14 0SJ. (*5 mins West Kensington tube*). *Tel*: 01-603 0474. *Open*: Mon to Sat 10am to 6pm. Exclusive designs inspired by turn-of-century Swedish artist, Carl Larsson. Oak/ash/painted finishes. Elegant, well-proportioned, similar to arts/crafts movement styles. cot-sofa, tables, chairs, plate rack etc.

Youngs Reproduction Furniture 570/574 Commercial Road, Stepney E14 7JD. (*Next to Limehouse Dockland Light Railway*). *Tel*: 01-790 4474/4691. *Open*: Mon to Sat 9.30am to 6.30pm. Closed all day Thurs. Sun 10am to 2pm. Mahogany veneers with some yew. Large selection, warehouse cash-and-carry prices. Storage for TV/video/hi-fi. Also diningroom ranges, nests of coffee tables, corner cabinets, library bookcases.

Outer Ring

Brights of Nettlebed Kingston House, Nettlebed, near Henley-on-Thames RG9 5DD. (*4m Henley BR, plus coach*). *Tel*: 0491 641115. *Open*: Tues to Sat 9am to 5.30pm. Probably

largest collection reproduction furniture under one roof in UK, if not Europe: 6,000 sq ft of handmade 17th/18th-century styles. Oak/walnut/mahogany/yew from 40 cabinet makers, including own Exeter workshops. Immediate deliveries, or to order: 10 to 12 weeks. Tailor-made upholstery. Furniture on approval. *Also at*: Topsham, Berkeley, Wimborne.

5/LEATHER

Today's upholstery leathers are soft and supple, in furnishing fashion colours that go right through the thickness of the hide. It's the one upholstery covering that doesn't noticeably deteriorate with age.

London Postal Districts

Italeather Sealand House, North Circular Road, Stonebridge Park, NW10 7JS. (*15 mins Stonebridge Park tube, adjacent Grand Union Canal*). *Tel*: 01-965 5717. *Open*: Mon to Sat 10am to 7pm. Sun viewing. Imported direct from Italy, over 100 modern and classic quality leather designs.

Kingdom of Leather Unit 3, Gallions Road, Charlton, SE7 7SA. *Tel*: 01-305 0101. *Open*: Mon to Sun 10am to 6pm. See Home Counties/S.East below.

World of Leather North Circular Road, NW10 7SX. (*10 mins Hanger Lane tube*). *Tel*: 01-961 4949. *Open*: Mon to Fri 10am to 7pm. Sat 10am to 6pm. Huge choice modern leather sofas/chairs in fashion colours. *Also at*: 156 Tottenham Court Road, W1P 9LJ. (*2 mins Warren Street tube*). *Tel*: 01-388 6084. *Open*: Mon to Sat 9.30am to 5.30pm. Late night Thurs 7.30pm. Sun 10am to 5pm. *And at*: Morden Road, Merton SW19 3BL. (*10 mins South Wimbledon tube*). *Tel*: 01-542 1571. *Open*: Mon to Fri 10am to 7pm. Sat 10am to 5pm. *And at*: Clifton's Roundabout, Sidcup Road, SE9 5LT. (*Eltham BR plus bus*). *Tel*: 01-850 6483. *Open*: Mon 10am to 8pm. Tues to Sat 10am to 6pm. Sun 10am to 5pm.

Furniture

Outer Ring

Bargains!

Just Leather Wembley Retail Park, Wembley Hill Road, Wembley, Middx. (*Wembley Park tube, near Stadium*). Tel: 01-903 6503. Open (all branches): Every day 10am to 5.30pm. UK's largest leather upholstery supplier (they claim): mainly imported leather suites. Changing promotions/ good credit offers.
Also at: Croydon Suite Centre, Ladyline Unit, Royal Oak Shopping Centre, 16/17 Brighton Road, Purley, Croydon CR2 2BG. (*A23*). Tel: 01-660 2998.

World of Leather Lakeside Retail Park, West Thurrock, Essex RM16 1NN. (*Off M25, Grays BR plus bus. Free parking*). Tel: 0708 863865. Open: Mon to Sat 10am to 6pm. Late nights Thurs & Fri 8pm. Sun 10am to 5pm.
And at: 643 Eastern Avenue, Ilford, Essex IG2 6BW. (*5 mins Newbury Park tube; free parking*). Tel: 01-554 6721. Open: Mon to Sat 10am to 6pm. Late night Mon 8pm. Sun 10am to 5pm. See London Postal Districts above.

Home Counties/S.East

Just Leather Maynard Road, Wincheap Industrial Estate, Canterbury CT1 3RH. (*5 mins Canterbury East BR*). Tel: 0227 472672. Open (all branches): 7 days 10am to 5.30pm. See Outer Ring above.
Also at: Boulevard 25, Theobald Street, Borehamwood, Herts WD6 4PR. (*New shopping precinct behind High Street*). Tel: 01-207 5099.
And at: Unit 1, Farleigh Hill, Tovil, Maidstone, Kent ME15 6RG. *Tel*: 0622 687702.
And at: Lakeside Retail Park, Unit 5, 726 London Road, West Thurrock, Essex RM16 1HH. (*Grays BR*). *Tel*: 0708 863710.

Kingdom of Leather Western Avenue, Tunnel Estate, Grays, West Thurrock, Essex. (*Grays BR; plus bus to retail park*). *Tel*: 0708 864162. Open: Mon to Sun 10am to 6pm.

15,000 sq ft of fine leather upholstery from Italy. Largest collection of leather under one roof, they tell me. Over 100 designs/many colours/7 grades of leather. High quality, good value. About 6 weeks delivery; special designs to order.

World of Leather Jubilee Square, London Road, Reading, Berks RG1 2TA. (*10 mins Reading BR; free parking*). Tel: 0734 861481. Open: Mon to Sat 10am to 6pm. Late night Thurs 8pm. Sun 10am to 5pm.

Mail Order

Thomas Lloyd Abergorki Estate, Treorchy, Mid Glam, CP42 6DL. Colour brochure/leather samples. Traditional heavily-buttoned chesterfields, club chairs etc in rich old-style colours. Also pastel shades/modern styles.

6/CANE

"Cane" describes various materials. Bamboo (now less popular) is hollow with decorative rings and knots. Cane (sometimes called rattan) is solid and its natural rings and blotches can be enhanced with clear lacquer. Peeled cane can be stained and lacquered, or lacquered in vast range of colours, though white is most usual. Woven willow or wicker is lightweight; often lacquered white. Cane quality varies according to method and country of manufacture. Buy from reputable supplier who can guide on durability: some designs like the famous Peacock chair (made from very fine cane) are predominantly decorative.

London Postal Districts

Cane & Abel Unit 29, Camden Lock, Chalk Farm Road, NW1. (*5 mins Camden Town/Chalk Farm tubes*). Tel: 0l-485 2350. Open: 7 days 10am to 5pm. Showroom/workshop with stock, plus special colours/sizes to order. Brochure. *Mail order*.

Cane Connection 57 Wimbledon Hill Road, SW19 7QW. (*2 mins Wimbledon tube/BR*). Tel:01-947 9152.

Open: Mon to Sat 9.30am to 5.30pm. Exclusive quality cane designs. White/ pastel bedroom sets; lounge suites from natural to rich dark stains.

Cane Creations 903 Fulham Road, SW6 5HU. (*10 mins Parsons Green/ Putney Bridge tubes*). Tel: 01-384 1130. *Open*: Mon to Sat 10am to 5pm. Late night Wed 7pm. Large stock from Spain: colours from natural to grey, white or black. Sofa sets with cushions covered to order; bedroom suites, nursery sets, rocking chairs, elephant-shaped tables. Mirrors. Brochure. *Mail order*.

Cane Designs 200 Blackstock Road, N5 1EN. (*7 mins Arsenal tube*). *Tel*: 01-704 9673. *Open*: Mon to Sat 10am to 6pm. Early closing Thurs 1pm. Special sizes/finishes made on premises. Also imported Chinese conservatory furniture.

The Cane Furniture Centre 1 & 10 Chingford Road, E17 4PW. (*5 to 10 mins Walthamstow Central tube*). Tel: 01-531 8369. *Open*: Mon to Fri 9.30am to 5.30pm. Sat 9am to 5.30pm. Two facing stores: vast selections for every room. Instant credit. Deliveries. Brochures. *Mail order*.

The Cane Store 207 Blackstock Road, N5 2LL. (*7 mins Arsenal tube*). *Tel*: 01-354 4210. *Open*: Mon to Sat 10am to 7pm. Materials for cane/basketwork, including recaning. Books, expert advice. Attractive panels of woven cane, split bamboo and reed screening; grass/straw Chinese mats. Cane/ rush repairs. Price lists (sae).

Chicane 40 Turnham Green Terrace, Chiswick W4 1QP. (*3 mins Turnham Green tube*). Tel: 01-995 1229. *Open*: Mon to Sat 9.30am to 6pm. Small shop conceals 2 floors of cane/willow/ basketware/gifts. Personal service.

Forecast Furniture 34 Avenue Road, NW8 6BU. (*5 mins St Johns Wood tube*). *Tel*: 01-722 8698. *Open*: by appointment. Imposing, flamboyant low glass tables, supported by dogs, gargoyles, etc. Colour leaflet.

Home Time 159/161 Green Lanes,

Palmers Green, N13 4SP. (*Wood Green or Arnos Grove tubes, plus bus*). *Tel*: 01-888 4220. *Open*: Mon to Sat 9.30am to 5.30pm. Makers/importers cane/basketware, sprayed white or to your colour choice. Stocks for immediate delivery.

Outer Ring

Cane & Things 55 King Street Parade, Cross Deep, Twickenham, Middx TW1 3SG. (*20 yds from corner of Kings Street and Cross Deep*). *Tel*: 01-892 7647. *Open*: Mon to Sat 10am to 5.30pm. Family business with large warehouse and quick deliveries of cane furniture. Accessories/gifts including pottery, beanbags, cushions; dried and silk flowers.
Also at: 7 Odeon Parade, Isleworth, Middx.
And at: 50 The Centre, Feltham, Middx.

Settings 4 Fife Road, Kingston-on-Thames KT1 1SZ. (*2 mins Kingston BR*). *Tel*: 01-549 2123. *Open*: Mon to Sat 9.30am to 5.30pm. Lots of pretty cane furniture with fabrics, cushions, lamps, vases. Worth a browse.

Trumps 9 The Hersham Centre, Hersham, Walton-on-Thames KT12 4HL. (*Junction 10 off M25, large free car park*). *Tel*: 0932 246951. *Open*: Mon to Sat 10am to 6pm. Rattan furniture that's definitely different. Stylish shapes by British designer Arthur Edwards. Dining/livingrooms. Upholstered in your fabric choice. Also artificial trees, plants, baskets, accessories. Good quality. Brochure. *Also at*: 57/59 Poole Road, Westbourne, Bournemouth BH4 9BA. *Tel*: 0202 763822.

Home Counties/S.East

Cane Direct New Town Garden Room, Burnt Mills Road, Basildon, Essex SS13 1DY. (*Off A127, few mins M25*). *Tel*: 0268 590779. *Open*: Mon to Sun 10am to 4pm. Closed Tues. Cane furniture/basketware for every room. Good prices: sold direct by importers. Choice of fabrics for cushion covers/curtains.

Jamco 179 Oxford Road, Reading, Berks RG1 7UZ. (*400 yds from Ramada Hotel*). *Tel*: 0734 575835. *Open*: Tues to Sat 9.30am to 5pm. Wicker furniture for conservatories, dining rooms, bedrooms. Affordable prices. Also mahogany traditional styles: occasional, dining room, drawing rooms. Brochures.

Settings Pump Corner, 4/6 South Street, Dorking, Surrey. (*20 mins Dorking BR*). *Tel*: 0306 885871. Open Mon to Sat 9.30am to 5.30pm. See Outer Ring above.

7/Glass & Marble

Smooth and hard, furniture from more unusual materials adds a sophisticated touch to any room.

London Postal Districts

Atrium. See **4/Classics & Reproduction** above. Coffee/dining/console tables in Marquinia Italian marble: black with whitish streaks. Glass tops reveal the beauty of the marble base.

Glass Distinction 196 New King's Road, SW6 4NF. (*3 mins Putney Bridge tube*). *Tel*: 01-731 3460. *Open*: Mon to Fri 9.30am to 5.30pm. Sat 10am to 1pm. Mark Elliot designs/makes inventive designs for dining, coffee, console tables. Also clocks, mirrors, shelving, bathroom accessories. Special sizes/shapes to order. Also Italian lacquered sideboards, chairs. Plus fibreboard pedestals/columns sprayed in lacquer, speckled or satin, any colour. Colour brochure.

Marble Interiors 1 Bathurst Street, Lancaster Gate, W2 2SD. (*Lancaster Gate tube*). *Tel*: 01-724 7890. *Open*: Mon to Fri 10am to 6pm. Sat 10am to 1pm. Elegant displays marble/granite furniture/flooring/tiles.

Quality Marble See **Tiles 3/Marble**. Table/desk tops cut to size in granite or superb choice of marble colours.

Townhouse Interiors 25g Lowndes Street, Belgravia SW1X 9JF. (*5 mins Knightsbridge tube*). *Tel*: 01-235

3180/9. *Open*: Mon to Fri 9.30am to 5.45pm. Sat 10am to 5pm. Closed Sat 1 to 2.30pm. Unusual furniture in clear Perspex acrylic sheet: largest collection in London. Imported Italian top makes including Fabian of Rome. Every size of table. Upholstered furniture. Interior design service.

8/PAINTED

The current fashion for painted finishes includes dragging, marbling, stippling and the like: ideal, in pastel shades, for bulky pieces to minimise size. Decoration can be painted freehand or stencilled. Why not try out your own skills on furniture that's second-hand?

London Postal Districts

Balfours 228 Merton Road, South Wimbledon, SW19 1EQ. (*5 mins South Wimbledon tube*). *Tel*: 01-543 7146. *Open*: Mon to Sat 10am to 6pm. Katie Winterbourne is a dab hand at stippling, dragging etc for ottomans, chests, coffee tables, bedside cabinets. Special effects to order. Also gifts/accessories: rugs, cushions, lampbases, baskets, dried flowers.

Dragons See **Children**. Specialists in handpainted furniture. Made by craftsmen in firm's own workshops, and decorated by Rosie Fisher's team of artists largely based in Sussex. Chests, bedside tables, storage boxes, etc. with stippled/marbled/sponged backgrounds for handpainted motifs.

Huston Designs on Furniture 7 Leopold Road, Wimbledon SW19 9ZZ. (*3 mins Wimbledon Park; 10 mins Wimbledon BR*). *Tel*: 01-947 3592/4. *Open*: Mon to Sat 10am to 5.30pm. Handpainted tables/chests etc. in stock, or to order. Signed by artist. Catalogue.

Robert & Colleen Bery Designs 157 St Johns Hill, SW11 1TQ. (*Clapham Junction BR*). *Tel*: 01-924 2197. *Open*: Mon to Sat 10am to 6pm. Exclusive handpainted chests, tables, bedheads by leading stencil artists.

Furniture

Worth a Trip

Chalon UK Old Hambridge Mill, Hambridge, near Langport, Somerset TA10 0BP. (*Taunton BR; customer collection service*). *Tel:* 0458 252374. *Open:* by appointment. Around 2,000 sq ft inter-linking showrooms in old mill. Traditional dressers, drawers etc. handmade from old pine; handpainted in old-look finishes.

Mail Order

Cranham House Rank Xerox Business Park, Mitcheldean, Glos GL17 0SN. *Tel:* 0594 543077. Colour brochure. Glass-fronted cabinets, linen/cutlery chests, pedestal tables, rolltop desks, four-poster beds/drapes, wardrobes: handpainted furniture. Mainly floral/leafy designs.

9/LUXURY

Glamour and glitz from large luxurious shapes and lavish materials: if this is what you yearn for, go shopping below.

London Postal Districts

Furniture Crafts Rays House, North Circular Road, Stonebridge Park, NW10 7XP. (*5 mins Hanger Lane tube*). *Open:* Mon to Sat 10am to 6pm. Sun 11am to 5pm. Unique, spectacular and glamorous furniture from many continental suppliers. Diningrooms, sitting rooms, bedrooms.

Maples 145 Tottenham Court Road, W1P 9LL. (*2 mins Warren Street tube*). *Tel:* 01-387 7000. *Open:* Mon to Sat 9am to 5.30pm. Ground floor: vast range of furniture. including luxurious Italian designs, leather suites, traditional English styles, and reproduction models. In the glamorous Mall, lower ground, bed/bedroom furniture, lighting and selections paintings/prints.

Roche Bobois 50 Baker Street, W1M 1DH. (*3 mins Baker Street tube*). *Tel:* 01-486 1614. *Open:* Mon to Sat 9.30am to 6pm. Makers/distributers exclusive upholstery/dining/occasional.

10/DESKS

London Postal Districts

Astrohome See **Furniture 1/General** above. Streamlined modern desks/office furniture.

Direct Desks Ground floor, 78/79 Lots Road, SW10. *Tel:* 01-352 4051. *Open:* Mon to Fri 10am to 6pm. Stylish modern desks/office furniture direct from own factories.

Estia See **Living & Diningrooms 3/Sofabeds**. Smart modern desks in tubular steel/melamine. Filing drawers, including trolleys. Plan chests.

Just Desks 20 Church Street, NW8 8EP. (*Close to M40 Westway, Edgware Road tube*). *Tel:* 01-723 7976. *Open:* Mon to Sat 9.30am to 6pm. Three floors of showrooms in 150-year-old building. Antique and repro desks, chairs, filing cabinets, writing tables, bookcases. Home computer desk with "wire management". Good quality, keen prices, quick deliveries. Commissions. Restoration. Releathering including DIY postal kit with full instructions.
Also at: 6 Erskine Road, NW3 3AJ. (*Chalk Farm tube*). *Tel:* 01-722 4902. *Open:* Mon to Sat 9am to 5pm. Large open showroom, 6,000 sq ft.

Bargains!

The cheapest desks are second-hand, and several shops specialise in used office equipment, which may include filing cabinets, plan chests and so on for that authentic high-tech touch!

Andrews Office Equipment 48 Shepherd's Bush Road, W6. (*5 mins Shepherd's Bush tube*). *Tel:* 01-602 6767. *Open:* Mon to Fri 9am to 5pm. Sat 9am to 2pm. Large selections new/used office furniture.

The Desk Depot 274 Queenstown Road, SW8. (*2 mins Queenstown Road/Battersea Park BRs*). *Tel:* 01-627 3897. *Open:* Mon to Sat 9am to 5.30pm. Sun by appointment. Reconditioned/reproduction desks. Filing cabinets/tables. Releathering service.

East London Office Equipment Centre Stirling Works, Canning Road, Abbey Lane Junction, Stratford E15. (*5 mins West Ham tube*). *Tel:* 01-534 4191. *Open:* Mon to Fri 8.30am to 5.30pm. Sat 10am to 1pm. Closed lunch 1 to 2pm. Huge second-hand stocks. Desks/filing cabinets/screens. Substantial discounts new furniture.

Langham Office Equipment Winchester Wharf, Clink Street, SE1 9DG. (*10 mins London Bridge tube*). *Tel:* 01-403 1555. *Open:* Mon to Fri 9am to 5pm. Over 10,000 sq ft new, used and reconditioned office furniture. Quality ex-hire executive desks/filing cabinets/swivel chairs. Plan chests. Drawing-boards.
Also at: 10 Fulham High Street, SW6 3LQ. (*5 mins Putney Bridge tube*). *Tel:* 01-736 6360/3624. *Open:* Mon to Fri 9am to 5pm.

Ron Harris Business Equipment Unit 3B, Juno Way, Elizabeth Industrial Estate, New Cross, SE14 5RW. (*20 mins New Cross Gate tube*). *Tel:* 01-469 2442. *Open:* Mon to Fri 9am to 5.30pm. Discount prices for office furniture.

Worth a Trip

David Burkinshaw Sugworth Farmhouse, Borde Hill Lane, Haywards Heath, Sussex RH16 1XP. (*1 mile Haywards Heath Station, 47 mins Victoria Station*). *Tel:* 0444 459747. *Open:* Mon to Sat 9am to 5pm (appointments advisable). Expert antique restorer works in 500-year-old farmhouse on around 20 genuine 18th/19th-century desks, all for sale. Excellent investments. Set of photos of current models, £4.

11/DESIGNER FURNITURE

Nick Allen Consultancy 29 Ifield Road, SW10 9AZ. *Tel:* 01-351 6626. *Open:* by appointment. The Studio Collection by Nick Allen has slender tubular lacquered steel frames with subtle curves and tapered legs to support table tops in colour-washed wood veneer or polished glass. Dining/console tables, coffee/side-tables, chairs, desks, dressing tables.

Atrium See **4/Classic & Reproduction** above. A showcase for the finest modern Italian designers: the classics of the future, alongside the classics of the past.

Andy Beauchamp 50 Brixton Road, SW9 6BT. *Tel*: 01-582 9972. *Open*: by appointment. Theatre set-builder makes furniture from 'junk' steel.

Cullis & Co See **Interior Design**. Exclusive range of metal and verdigris finish chairs, tables, lamps. Some in stock, or to order.

Jakki Dehn A-Z Studios, 3/5 Hardwidge Street, SE1 3SY. *Tel*: 01-378 0512. *Open*: by appointment: Furniture and accessories to commission.

Diametric Modern Furniture 18 Odhams Walk, Long Acre, Covent Garden WC2E 9SA. (*2 mins Covent Garden tube; entrance also from Neal Street, pedestrian walkway*). *Tel*: 01-240 7493. *Open*: Mon to Sat 10am to 6pm. Inventive, witty, minimalist shapes in metal and glass. Beds, shelving, dining tables and chairs.

Julienne Dolphin-Wilding 34 Cecil Rhodes House, Goldington Street, NW1 1UG. *Tel*: 01-380 0950. *Open*: by appointment. Gulliver's Chair. Carved wood reminiscent of charcoal or driftwood. Upholstery fabrics by Betty Vaughan-Richards. Rope upholstery inspired by traditional Celtic "suiochan" chair, indoor or garden use.

Nicholas Dyson Unit 2, Home Farm, Ardington, Wantage, Oxfordshire OX12 8PN. *Tel*: 0235 634311. *Open*: by appointment. Furniture designed/made to order for private/business clients.

Edge Furniture 18 Ashwin Street, Dalston E8. *Tel*: 01-249 8328. *Open*: by appointment. Suzanne Darling/Dawn Carter combine product design/fine art sculpture for limited

edition minimalist sculptural furniture.

FB Design David James Forrest, 14 Hazel Road, Four Marks, Alton, Hants GU34 5EY. *Tel*: 0420 64470 and 0962 733432. *Open*: by appointment, Furniture designers/makers. Skilled/imaginative. Furniture/fittings of lasting quality. Six years' experience in solid hardwood/veneers, fibreboard/laminates. Contemporary/traditional commissions.

The Furniture Workshop Unit D3 3/19 Victorian Grove, N16 4RS. (*15 mins Dalston Kingsland BR*). *Tel*: 01-249 9962. *Open*: by appointment. A small group of young designers combine innovation with quality manufacture. Nigel Worlidge has worked in English oak with cane and leather. Michael Whelan has created the witty/practical folding "Jousting Tent Wardrobe".

Luke Hughes 1 Stukeley Street, WC2B 5LQ. (*5 mins Holborn tube*). *Tel*: 01-404 5995. *Open*: Mon to Fri 9am to 6pm. Evenings and Sat by appointment. Designer-maker of natural oak classic modern furniture in deceptively simple styles. Personal service. Commissions.

Nigel Lofthouse The Old Church, Rishangles, Suffolk IP23 7JZ. *Tel*: 037 971 715. *Open*: by appointment. Functional art. Chairs, tables, lamps, mirrors, vases made from leather/wood/copper. Embellished in horn, bone, pewter, copper. Style is heavily decorative; grand proportions; rich, even decadent feel.

Derek Pearce Pieces 31 Appach Road, SW2 2LD. *Tel*: 01-674 2074. *Open*: by appointment. Well-crafted witty furniture but not for the faint hearted. Commissions welcomed. His Hippo Table is popular.

John Prestwood 14 Wellington Court, Spencers Wood, Reading RG7 1BN. *Tel*: 0734 882236. *Open*: by appointment. Beautiful furniture made to individual requirements. A bespoke service for design, sizes, timbers and finishes. Lovely to use

and touch, functional and long-lasting.

Quark Designs Workshop 30, Royal Victoria Patriotic Building, Trinity Road, SW18 3SX. *Tel*: 01-870 8056. *Open*: by appointment. Imaginative design/materials for one-off furniture commissions.

George Robertson Barden Mill Farm, Barden Road, Speldhurst, Kent TN3 0LH. *Tel*: 0860 821921. *Open*: by appointment. George Robertson designs/makes and paints furniture/decorative items. Murals, paint effects and other decorative work.

SCP 135/139 Curtain Road, EC2A 3BX. (*10 mins Old Street tube*). *Tel*: 01-739 1869. *Open*: Mon to Fri 9am to 6pm. Sat 10am to 5pm. Minimalist modern furniture in chrome, glass, wood. Chairs, tables, shelving, trolleys and so on. Copies of 30s classics. plus the very best of latest design. A visit is essential for lovers of modern style.

Soho Design 263 King's Road, SW3 5EL. (*10 mins Sloane Square tube*). *Tel*: 01-376 5855. *Open*: Mon to Sat 10am to 6pm. Late night Wed 7pm. Distinctive, individual, maybe even a little eccentric: new style English in sleek metal tube, black/dull green. Evocative details: chintzy prints, Gothic arches. Furniture/lighting/accessories: all designed by Peter Leonard. Catalogues free.
Also at: 1/5 Poland Street, W1. *Open*: Mon to Fri 10am to 6pm.

Something Wild 35 Winchester Road, NW3 3NR. (*5 mins Swiss Cottage tube; behind library*). *Tel*: 01-586 2251. *Open*: Mon to Sat 10.30am to 5.30pm. Late night Thurs 8pm. New shop, with furniture based on 1930s and 1950s. Black pedestal dining table, kidney-shaped dining chairs. Chaises longues. All to order, 4/6 weeks.

Viaduct Spring House, 10 Spring Place, NW5 3BH. *Tel*: 01-284 0156. *Open*: Mon to Fri 9.30am to 5.30pm. Showcase for innovative quality furniture designs. John Werner makes unusual tables/chairs/mirrors; metal

Furniture

frameworks combined with black/brown stained mdf. Nick Carey exploits intricate graining of South American lacewood for tabletops with cast aluminium curved legs; matching upholstered chairs. Toby Winteringham, craftsman par excellence: inlays of mother-of-pearl/ebony for tables/mirrors. John Coleman has fine reputation for beautifully veneered modern tables/mirrors; also new metal stacking chair.

DECORATING MATERIALS

Today's technologies have brought decorating within the scope of most amateurs, who, as a result, have become dab DIY hands. But it's not just skills that are important: as with other jobs, materials and tools also count. See below where to shop, and watch out for Bargains!

1/PAINTS & PAPERS

For spur-of-the-moment jobs, shops below can cope. If you can wait a few days, you can order from books at co-ordinates specialists (listed next) or in **Interior Design** *or* **Soft Furnishings** *shops. Paints and papers also abound at* **DIY Superstores***.*

London Postal Districts

Bargains!
Alexander Collins Homecare Centre 59/60 Stratford Centre, Stratford E15 1XF. (*Stratford tube/BR*). Tel: 01-534 0770. Open (both branches): Mon to Sat 9am to 5.30pm. Low prices for lesser-known paint brands. Also wallpapers/vinyls up to 30% off.
Also at: Alexander Collins Interior Design, 17 High Street, Wanstead E11 2AA. (*Wanstead or Snaresbrook tubes*). Tel: 01-989 9058. Wallcoverings/paint.

Bargains!
Bernard Allen Wallpapers 72 High Street, Walthamstow E17. (*Walthamstow Central tube/BR*). Tel: 01-509 1381. Open (all branches): Mon to Sat 9am to 5.45pm. Own-brand paints. Good wallpaper selections.
Also at: 74 East Street, SE17. (*Elephant & Castle tube*). Tel: 01-703 9629.

Also at: 29 High Street North, East Ham E6. (*East Ham tube; near town hall*). *Tel*: 01-471 9015.

JW Bollom 13/15 Theobalds Road, WC1 8SN. (*15 mins Holborn tube*). *Tel*: 01-242 0313. Open (all branches): Mon to Fri 8am to 5pm. Sat 8am to 12noon. Quality own-brand Bromel paints. Full range BS colours; specialist paints/varnishes. Tints/glazes for special paint effects.
And at: 314/316 Old Brompton Road, SW5. (*West Brompton tube*). *Tel*: 01-370 3252.

Bargains!
The Colour Centre 184 Seven Sisters Road, N7 7PX. (*Finsbury Park tube*). *Tel*: 01-272 3138. *Open*: Mon to Sat 8.15am to 5.30pm. Early closing Thurs 1pm. Paint at trade prices. Monthly special offers. Wallpaper discounts: from 10% for quality collections to 50% massmarket brands. 25% off Amtico vinyl flooring.
And at: 514 Holloway Road, N7 6JD. *Tel*: 01-272 4300. *Open*: as above.
Also at: 29a Offord Road, N1 1EA. (*Caledonian Road tube*). *Tel*: 01-609 1164. *Open*: Mon to Sat 8.15am to 5.30pm.

Bargains!
Cut Price Paints 148 High Road, East Finchley N2 9ED. *Tel*: 01-883 9522/ 2419. *Open*: Mon to Fri 8.10am to 5.30pm. Sat 8.30am to 5.30pm. All makes at discounts: "never under-

sold"! Nationwide deliveries.

Bargains!
Daves DIY 296 Firs Lane, Palmers Green N13. *Tel*: 01-807 3539. *Open*: Mon to Sat 9am to 6pm. Early closing Thurs 1pm. Low price wallcoverings. Anaglyptas (from stock): 50% off. Wallpapers 30% off, 24 hour delivery.

Bargains!
Direct Bargain Centre 69/79 Mile End Road, Stepney E1 4TT. (*2 mins Stepney Green tube*). *Tel*: 01-790 1094. *Open*: Mon to Fri 8am to 5pm. Late night Thurs 8pm. Early closing Fri 3.30pm. Closed Sat. Sun 10am to 4pm. "Great bargains for your home": their catchy radio jingle sums up constantly-changing stock. Decorating materials usually include: paint, wallcoverings, ceramic tiles.

Bargains!
Discount Decorating 157/159 Rye Lane, Peckham SE15 4TL. (*Peckham Rye BR*). *Tel*: 01-732 3986. *Open*: Mon to Sat 9am to 5.30pm. Discounts: paint, wallpapers, ceramic tiles.

Featherstones Interior Designers 13 The High Parade, Streatham High Road, SW16 1EX. *Tel*: 01-769 1044/5. *Open*: Tues to Sat 9am to 5.30pm. Large (2,000sq ft) up-market shop. Stock wallpapers displayed on screens. Full sample service. Sanderson and Brolac paints mixed to order. Family firm trading for over 30 years ago. Friendly atmosphere. Experienced on-the-spot colour/design advice.

Bargains!

Hoe Street Bargain Stores 78 Hoe Street, Walthamstow E17 4PG. (*10 mins Walthamstow Central tube/BR*). *Tel*: 01-520 7075. *Open*: Mon to Sat 9am to 5.30pm. Early closing Thurs 1pm. Large stock wallpapers half-price or less, from this old-established shop. Good value paint/decorating equipment.

Bargains!

Leslux 148 High Road, East Finchley N2 9ED. (*4 mins East Finchley tube*). *Tel*: 01-883 9522. *Open*: Mon to Sat 8.10am to 5.30pm. Wallpapers 40% off. 50% box 12 rolls. Paints up to 50% off. Cut-price floor/ceramic tiles including Cork-o-Plast/Amtico.

Leyland 424 Edgware Road, W2 1EG. (*10 mins Edgware tube*). *Tel*: 01-723 8048. *Open*: Mon to Sat 7.15am to 6pm. Own-brand paints, good colours. Wallpaper discounts. Cut-price Bosch power tools.

Bargains!

Lomax Wallpapers & Paints 283/285 New North Road, Islington N1 7AA. (*10 mins Essex Road tube*). *Tel*: 01-226 1516. *Open*: Mon to Sat 8.30am to 5.30pm. Good paint prices: Leyland, ICI, Carsons. Large shop: 2500 wallpapers in stock, some discounted up to 50%. Enormous pattern book bar. Free paste on all wallpaper sales over 1 roll. Money refunded on unused rolls. Friendly, knowlegeable DIY advice.

John Oliver 33 Pembridge Road, W11 3HG. (*2 mins Notting Hill Gate tube*). *Tel*: 01-221 6466/727 3735. *Open*: Mon to Sat 9.30am to 5.30pm. The man and his shop have stayed engagingly the same for a quarter century. Products have changed but not dramatically. John Oliver is one of the great innovators that brought interior colour and design to London in the Swinging Sixties. Inimitable hand-/machine-printed wallpapers; metallic foils. Paints in all colours/finishes. Any colour in 7/10 days. Hand trimming service for wallpapers.

Palmers 114a Chiswick High Road, W4 2ED. (*3 mins Turnham Green tube*). *Tel*: 01-994 6569. *Open*: Mon to Sat 8am to 5.30pm. Trade prices: major paint brands. All BS colours Dulux trade paints.

Papers & Paints 4 Park Walk, SW10 0AD. (*15 mins Gloucester Road tube*). *Tel*: 01-352 8626. *Open*: Mon to Fri 8am to 6pm. Family business, trading over 30 years. Specialist colour mixers for paints: any colour, with your unique match kept on file. Historic shades for period properties. Sanderson paint stockists. Varnishes, glazes, brushes, tools, pigments, books for special paint effects.

JW Percival 150 Bethnal Green Road, E2 6DG. (*10 mins Bethnal Green/Liverpool Street tubes*). *Tel*: 01-739 4494. *Open*: Mon to Fri 7am to 5pm. Sat 8am to 12 noon. Trade prices, major paint brands. Wallpapers ex stock, or to order (takes 48 hours).

Peter Topp Wallcoverings 343 Fulham Palace Road, SW6 6TD. (*10 mins Putney Bridge tube*). *Tel*: 01-736 4821. *Open*: Mon to Fri 9.30am to 5.30pm. Sat 9.30am to 1pm. Old-established wallcoverings specialists; bright comfortable showrooms. Heaps of samples/display panels, all top makes. Fabrics/soft furnishings to order. Trimming service for wallpapers.

Simpsons Paints 354 Edgware Road, W2 1EB. (*2 mins Edgware Road tube*). *Tel*: 01-723 3762. *Open*: Mon to Sat 8.30am to 5.30pm. Huge selection paints, wallpapers, decorative mouldings, ceiling roses. Radiator covers made to measure. Or buy decorative panels to make your own. Most items in stock, or within 24 hrs.

RV Tass 368 Richmond Road, Twickenham TW1 12DX. (*10 mins Richmond tube/BR*). *Tel*: 01-892 3643. *Open*: Mon to Fri 7am to 5.30pm. Sat 9am to 5.30pm. Paint/papers good prices; DIY advice from professional decorator.

Bargains!

G Thornfield 321 Gray's Inn Road, WC1. (*Opposite Kings Cross tube*).

Tel: 01-837 2996. *Open*: Mon to Sat 7.15am to 2pm. Wallpapers up to 50% off; 10% off co-ordinating fabrics. Super value ends of ranges. Experienced advice: family firm trading over 35 years.

Wallpaper Warehouses 32/34 Willesden Lane, NW6. (*5 mins Kilburn tube*). *Tel*: 01-328 0487. *Open* (all branches): Mon to Sat 8am to 5.30pm. Large stocks paints, papers, vinyls. New Dulux Colour Dimensions paint mixing system. Wall/floor ceramic tiles.

Outer Ring

Bargains!

Daves DIY 4 Enfield Road, Enfield, Middx. (*Opposite Jolly Farmers*). *Tel*: 01-363 1680. *Open*: Mon to Sat 9am to 5pm. Early closing Wed 1pm. See London Postal Districts above.

John T Keeps & Sons Croydon Road, Beckenham, Kent BR3 4BL. (*Elmers End BR*). *Tel*: 01-658 7723/4. See London Postal Districts above.

Wallpaper Warehouses 142/144 Kenton Road, Harrow, Middx. (*5 mins Kenton BR*). *Tel*: 01-907 3020. *Also at*: 714/722 London Road, Hounslow, Middx. (*3 mins Hounslow East tube*). *Tel*: 01-577 5592. See London Postal Districts above.

Mail Order

A Taste of America (Mailbox) See **Accessories 8/Rugs.** Old Village low sheen oil-based paints with natural pigments for authentic American Colonial "muddy", dulled colours e.g. Bayberry green, Williamsburg blue. Also American Colonial colours for stencil paints in bottles or sprays (ideal for floor designs) plus ranges based on English cottage and French Provençal styles.

2/CO-ORDINATED COLLECTIONS

Taking the agony out of mix and match, this is where you'll find the real goers.

London Postal Districts

Laura Ashley Decorator Collection 71/73 Lower Sloane Street, SW1W 8DA. (*5 mins Sloane Square tube*). *Tel*: 01-730 1771. *Open*: Mon to Fri 9.30am to 6pm. Laura Ashley mainstream merchandise, sold so successfully through own shops/Homebase boutiques, is epitome of country cottage style with recent decorator innovations. Find here more dramatic decorator collections of papers/paints/fabrics. Curtains/upholstery/design services.

Nina Campbell 9 Walton Streeet, SW3 2JD. (*7 mins South Kensington/Knightsbridge tubes*). *Tel*: 01-225 1011. *Open*: Mon to Fri 9.30am to 5.30pm. Sat 10am to 4pm. Cotton/linen fabric/papers. Co-ordinating rugs/bed linens/accessories. Interior design service.

Jane Churchill 135 Sloane Street, SW1. (*5 mins Sloane Square tube*). *Tel*: 01-730 6379. *Open*: Mon to Fri 9.30am to 5.30pm. Essentially English look for fabrics, papers, borders, furniture, rugs, lamps, bed linens.

Cole & Son 18 Mortimer Street, W1A 4BU. (*10 mins Oxford Circus/Goodge Street tubes*). *Tel*: 01-580 1066. *Open*: Mon to Fri 9am to 5pm. Traditional collections English/French handprints/fabrics/borders, plus decorator paint colours.

Colefax and Fowler 39 Brook Street, W1Y 2JE. (*5 mins Bond Street tube*). *Tel*: 01-493 2231. *Open*: Mon to Fri 9.30am to 5.30pm. Closed lunch 1 to 2pm. Archetypal English country house co-ordinates recreated from original designs.
Also at: 110 Fulham Road, SW3 6Rl. (*7 mins South Kensington tube*). *Tel*: 01-244 7427. *Open*: Mon to Fri 9.30am to 5.30pm. Sat 10am to 4pm.
And at: 149 Ebury Street, SW1W 9QN. (*5 mins Knightsbridge tube*). *Tel*: 01-730 9847. *Open*: Mon to Fri: 9.30am to 5.30pm.

Danielle 148 Walton Street, SW3 2JJ.

(*10 mins South Kensington/Knightsbridge tubes*). *Tel*: 01-584 4242/1900. *Open*: Mon to Fri 10am to 5pm. Closed lunch 1 to 2pm. Hand-printed silks, moirés, cottons; plain cottons. To order in client's own colours. Wallpapers, tiles, bed linens. Interior design.

Designers Guild 271 & 277 King's Road, SW3 5EN. (*12 mins Sloane Square tube*). *Tel*: 01-351 5775. *Open*: Mon to Sat 9.30am to 5.30pm. Wed 10am to 5.30pm. Superb fabrics/papers in jewel shades. Stripes, checks, florals. Don't miss. 277 concentrates on fabrics/papers. 271 is furniture, ceramics, lighting.

Anna French 343 King's Road, Chelsea SW3 5ES. (*Sloane Square tube plus bus*). *Tel*: 01-351 1126. *Open*: Mon to Fri 9.30am to 5pm. Sat 10am to 4pm. Modern prints/papers/borders. Traditional lace collections made on original Victorian looms. Also furniture/accessories. Catalogue (mail order) £3.50.

Hill & Knowles 133 Kew Road, Richmond, Surrey TW9 2PN. (*10 mins Richmond tube/BR*). *Tel*: 01-948 4010. *Open*: Mon to Sat 9.30am to 5.30pm. Some of the prettiest co-ordinated collections of wallpapers/fabrics/borders on the market, including their well-known stencil and rag-roll designs.

Osborne & Little 304 King's Road, SW3 5UH. (*15 mins Sloane Square tube*). *Tel*: 01-352 1456. *Open*: Mon to Fri 9.30am to 5.30pm. Sat 10am to 5.30pm. Recently extended. 7,000 sq ft: fabric/paper screens upstairs, roomsettings downstairs. Upholstery, lampshades, quilts, cushions from stock or to order in choice of fabrics. Peter Osborne and his brother-in-law Tony Little were in the van of London's 1960s style renaissance. Today, they are as up-to-date as ever. Interior design/soft furnishings service.

Sanderson 52 Berners Street, W1P 3AD. (*10 mins Oxford Circus tube*). *Tel*: 01-636 7800. *Open*: Mon to Fri 9.30am to 5.30pm. Sat 9am to 5.30pm.

Inimitable world-famous co-ordinated collections, including William Morris hand-blocks. Fabrics, papers/vinyls, borders, bed linens. Two large floors fabrics, wallcoverings, carpets, accessories, cabinet/upholstered furniture. Paint mixed on the spot. Ten fully-furnished roomsets. Knowledgeable staff, excellent service. Coffee shop.

Sue Stowell 813 Fulham Road, SW6 5HG. (*7 mins Fulham Broadway tube*). *Tel*: 01-731 2050. *Open*: Mon to Fri 9.30am to 5.30pm. Sat 10am to 4pm. Sue Stowell, relative newcomer, brings inspired originality – witness her Classic Collection, with cut-out rose border, and Empire with flamboyant symbols of Greece and Rome.

Outer Ring

Jane Churchill 21 The Market Place, Kingston-upon-Thames, Surrey KT1 1JP. (*7 mins Kingston BR*). *Tel*: 01-549 6292. *Open*: Mon to Fri 9.30am to 5.30pm. See London Postal Districts above.

K and K Designs Unit 8, Cranbourne Ind. Est., Potters Bar, Herts EN6 3JN. *Tel*: 0707 49300. *Open*: Mon to Fri 9am to 5.30pm. Original fresh collections vinyls/papers, borders, fabrics, including popular miniprints, and more fabrics.

Home Counties/S.East

Laura Ashley Decorator 26 Little Clarendon Street, Oxford OX1 2HU. *Tel*: 0865 52477. See London Postal Districts above.

Jane Churchill 13/14 Christopher Place, St Albans, Herts AL3 5DQ. *Tel*: 0727 60293. See London Postal Districts above.

Mail Order

Hugh Ehrman See **Accessories 6/Needlepoint & Embroidery.** Wallpapers by Kaffe Fassett, famous for brilliant colour work in tapestry and knitting.

3/STENCILS

The stencil craze is at its peak. Try your hand with the help of suppliers below.

All Districts

Laura Ashley Home See **Furnishing Stores**. Traditional brass stencils; matchpot paints co-ordinate with LA furnishings.

London Postal Districts

The Carolyn Warrender Stencil Store 91/93 Lower Sloane Street, SW1W 8DA. (*5 mins Sloane Square tube*). *Tel*: 01-730 0728. *Open*: Mon to Fri 10am to 5.30pm, Sat 10am to 1pm. Founder Carolyn Warrender initiated then fostered the British stencil craze. Unique shop for enthusiasts. Stencils from baby bunnies to Greek Keys; brushes, paints for various surfaces (including fabric and china). Advice/tuition. Stencils cut to order. Stencilling service. Colour catalogue, £1.35 (inc. p & p). *Mail order.*

Paperchase 213 Tottenham Court Road, W1P 9AF. (*5 mins Tottenham Court Road tube*). *Tel*: 01-580 8496. *Open*: Mon to Sat 9.30am to 6pm. Late night Thurs 7pm. First store way back to promote stencils, which are now the current craze. Main stock is out-of-ordinary cards, stationery, decorations, paper tableware. Selective stencil range includes Painted Garden Stencil Books on 4 garden themes, each with stencils/instructions. Also good stocks American Dover books with cut-and-use stencils plus pre-cut designs; themes include Christmas, Early American, Folk Art, American Indian, Teddy Bears.
Also at: 167 Fulham Road, SW3 6SN. *Tel*: 01-589 7839.
Also at: 199/201 Oxford Street, W1R 1AH. *Tel*: 01-437 2476.
And at: Waterloo Station, SE1; Victoria Street, SW1; Queensway W2; Ealing W5; Cheapside EC2; Haymarket SW1; Kingston-on-Thames; Bromley; Reading; Winchester; Guildford; Epsom; Mail order service from Tottenham Court Road.

Mail Order

Antonia Spowers Designs Unit 3, Ransome's Dock, 35/37 Parkgate Road, SW11 4NP. *Tel*: 01-622 3630. Selections subtle stencil motifs/borders drawn from variety of traditional/ethnic sources. Brochures.

4/PERIOD PAPERS

*Some decorating shops cater specifically for period authenticity. Good decorating shops (see **Interior Design**) stock pattern books with authentic period papers/fabrics. Look out for sample sets from GP & J Baker (Chinese Collection, Victorian Exuberance); Monkwell (An Edwardian Portfolio: scenic friezes with co-ordinating papers/fabrics); Design Archives (18th/19th-century designs from Courtauld archives printed on cotton, linen union, silk, glazed chintz).*

Colefax & Fowler See **2/Co-ordinated Collections** above. Unrivalled for chintzes in the grand English Country house tradition.

Cole & Son See **2/Co-ordinated Collections** above. Papers/fabrics reproduced from their extensive archives.

Habitat See **Furnishing Stores**. Co-ordinating papers/fabrics faithfully based on originals in the V&A; subdued and pretty small scale prints.

The Charles Hammond Shop See **Interior Design**. Rich subtle colourings for Charles Hammond's own fabrics taken from 81-year old company archives.

Paper Moon See **Children's Rooms**. Classics Collection from archives of Henry Ford Museum and Greenfield Village, in Dearborn, Michigan.

Sanderson See **2/Co-ordinated Collections** above. Guardian of William Morris's inestimable legacy of pattern. Faithful, original handblocks. Also smaller scale collection to suit cramped rooms.

London Postal Districts

Watts of Westminster 7 Tufton Street, SW1P 3QE. (*5 mins Westminster/St James's tubes*). *Tel*: 01-222 9863/01-233 0424. *Open*: Mon to Fri 9am to 5pm. Founded in 1874. Unbroken family links with designs of George Frederick Bodley, and Gilbert Scott the Younger. Richly coloured/patterned, these are produced to order. Also available: stock collections of paper/fabrics. Linen fabrics in original Watts' designs; plain grained papers in over 50 shades. Wallpaper specials of any kind.

Zoffany 63 South Audley Street, W1Y 5BF. (*5 mins Bond Street tube*). *Tel*: 01-629 9262. *Open*: Mon to Fri 9am to 5.30pm. Designs based on 18th/19th-century originals, many with huge bold pattern repeats; co-ordinating chintzes.

Outer Ring

Hamilton Weston 18 St Mary's Grove, Richmond, Surrey TW9 1UY. (*10 mins Richmond tube/BR*). *Tel*: 01-940 4850. *Open*: Mon to Fri 9.30am to 6pm. Sat 10am to 1pm. 18th/19th-century document wallpapers taken from London townhouses. Also books, lists of craftsmen, fabrics/paints for restored interiors.

Worth a Trip

Alexander Beauchamp Griffin Mill, Thrupp, near Stroud, Gloucester GL5 2AZ. *Tel*: 0453 884537. Cloaked by a ''deliberately anonymous name'' Karen Beauchamp collects/presents patterns from the past. The Archibald Knox Collection; fabrics/papers 1897 by leading Liberty light of Arts & Craft Movement. 17th-Century Collection: designs *c*.1680 from Bourne Hall Museum, Ewell. Also Hampton Court; late 18th/early 19th-century designs. Dado & Border delights: High Victorian, Art Nouveau, Art Deco, Thirties. Any colourways to special order. Hand-brushed backgrounds available. Also from many shops listed under **Interior Design**.

SOFT FURNISHINGS

Many of the merchants listed below can offer as skilled decor advice as *Interior Design* specialists (who also provide soft furnishings services). Home Service may well be part of the deal, with a visit to advise/measure, and a return to hang curtains, fit blinds and so on. But as always check whether this is free.

1/FABRICS

*It's getting more and more difficult to buy fabrics from stock: **Interior Design** shops sell mainly to order, but fabrics come within 3 days. Always measure for projects very carefully, and allow for seams, turnings and pattern repeats.*

London Postal Districts

Alexander Furnishings 51/61 Wigmore Street, W1H 9LF. (*Corner Wigmore Street and Marylebone Lane*). *Tel*: 01-935 2624/7806/8664/1678. *Open*: Mon to Fri 9am to 6pm. Sat 9am to 1pm. Late night Thurs 7pm. Six interconnecting shops: huge choice of ex-stock curtain/upholstery fabrics. Keenest prices (many discounted). Co-ordinated collections, including wallpapers. Tracks, poles, cushions, trimmings, nets. Sofas, sofabeds. Trading for 35 years. Personal service, friendly atmosphere. Free advice/samples. Curtains: measure, make, fit and hang. Made-to-measure blinds. Loose covers/reupholstery. Bedcovers, headboards, quilting to order.

Bruno Galetti 72 Haverstock Hill, NW3 2BE. *Tel*: 01-267 6936. *Open*: Mon to Fri 8.30am to 5pm. Fabric/wallpaper sample library; track/pole samples. Blinds/trimmings. Curtain/upholstery workshops; personal reliable service.

John Lewis, & other stores in **John Lewis Partnership** See **Department Stores**. Own studio/printers/weavers for Jonelle furnishing fabrics. Outstanding designs/colours, quality, price. Traditional and modern. Curtaining/upholstery/loose cover fabrics, with some matching wallcoverings. Mostly in stock. Coloured and insulated curtain linings. Jonelle Duracolour fabrics will be replaced if they fade.

McNeil & Cole See **Interior Design**. French chintz/cotton satin sold by the metre at very good prices.

Nice Irma's See **Ethnic**. Wonderful imported furnishing fabrics for curtains/upholstery, all natural fibres. Wide selections ikats, cut lace, textured plains, cotton embroidered with wool Kashmiri crewel-work.

Bargains!

Corcoran & May 161 Lower Richmond Road, SW15. (*15 mins Putney Bridge tube*). *Tel*: 01-788 9556. *Open*: Mon to Sat 10am to 6pm. Closed lunch 1 to 2 pm. Seconds in top make furnishing fabrics. Curtains/blinds made to measure.

Felt & Hessian Shop 34 Greville Street, EC1 8TD. (*5 mins Farringdon tube*). *Tel*: 01-836 7521. *Open*: Mon to Fri 10am to 2pm. (but check as times vary). 70 shades of felt 72in wide: ideal for wide curtains (not washable). 3

qualities. Also dyed hessians. Plus suede and leather effect fabrics, moirés etc.

Jason D'Souza Designs 38 Graham Street, Islington N1 8JX. (*5 mins Angel tube*). *Tel*: 01-253 9294. *Open*: Mon to Fri 9.30am to 5.30 (phone first). Ritzy up-market hand-prints on moirés, silks, voiles, many with rich metallic lustres.

Jerry's 2 Loampit Vale, SE13 7TA. (*2 mins Lewisham BR*). *Tel*: 01-852 7251. *Open*: Mon to Sat 9am to 5.30pm. Furnishing fabrics, tracks, linens, haberdashery. Helpful service. Curtain-making/hanging.

Liberty Prints 340a King's Road, SW3 5UR. *Tel*: 01-352 6581. *Open*: Mon to Sat 9.30am to 5.30pm. Late night Weds 6.30pm. A chance to explore at leisure beautiful curtain/upholstery fabrics from famous parent store in Regent Street (see **Department Stores**).

Ian Mankin 109 Regents Park Road, Primrose Hill, NW1 8UR. (*5 mins Chalk Farm tube*). *Tel*: 01-722 0997. *Open*: Tues to Fri 10am to 5.30pm. Sat 10am to 4pm. No synthetics: natural fibres only. Cotton, raw silk. Jacquards, unbleached calico, tickings, gingham, muslin, scrim, plus own exclusive weaves. Reasonable prices. Cream weave samples: 1. Ticking samples: 2. Telephone orders: next

1 / Fabrics

day deliveries by Interlink. Cash/cheques only.

Mistakes 654B Fulham Road, SW6 5PY. (*5 mins Parsons Green tube*). *Tel*: 01-736 2108. *Open*: Mon to Sat 10.30am to 5pm. Subtitled The Interior Designers Sale Shop, bargains here are definitely up-market. This is where misplaced orders, showflat furnishings, and surplus stock come to live at reduced prices. Made-up soft furnishings, lengths of fabric, furniture etc. at reduced prices.

Reputation 186 Kensington Park Road, W11 2ES. (*7 mins Ladbroke Grove tube*). *Tel*: 01-221 7641. *Open*: Mon to Sat 10am to 6pm. Exclusive and original changing designs from partners/owners printed on to cotton. Special colourways to order. Curtain-making.

Russell & Chapple 23 Monmouth Street, WC2H 9DE. (*5 mins Leicester Square/Covent Garden tubes*). *Tel*: 01-836 7521. *Open*: Mon to Fri 8.30am to 5pm. Cramped, busy shop catering for theatrical trade. Three qualities natural hessian, 72 in wide. 14 shades dyed hessian (warning: it tends to fade). Fire-retardant gauzes for filmy drapes; butter muslin; cotton duck, calico, linens. Samples/price list.

Souleiado 171 Fulham Road, SW3 6JW. (*5 mins South Kensington tube*). *Tel*: 01-589 6180. *Open*: Mon to Fri 9.30am to 5pm. Sat 10am to 5pm. For South of France sunshine, immense yourself in authentic Provençal cottons printed from original traditional woodblocks. Cut lengths, or made-up accessories.

Bargains!

Spoils 157 Munster Road, SW6 6DA. (*5 mins Parsons Green tube*). *Tel*: 01-736 4088. *Open*: Mon to Fri 10am to 6pm. Sat 10am to 4pm. Manufacturers' reject furnishing fabrics at much reduced prices for near perfect stock. Also own lines of pretty stencil-style fabrics/wallpapers, with matching crockery/tiles.

Woodward (Hampstead) 20 Heath Street, NW3 6TE. (*10 mins Hampstead tube*). *Tel*: 01-435 8876. *Open*: Mon to Sat 9am to 5.30pm. Curtain/upholstery fabric specialist. Curtains made, tracks fitted. Reupholstery; upholstery made to order. Wallcoverings/paint.

Outer Ring

Addingtons Furnishing Shop 448 Ewell Road, Tolworth, Surbiton. (*A3, just off Kingston-by-pass*). *Tel*: 01-399 1032/1445. *Open*: Mon to Fri 9.30am to 5pm. Sat 9am to 5pm. Early closing Wed 2pm. Browse peacefully amidst fabrics for curtains and covers, wallpapers and carpets. Making-up service for curtains and loose covers; reupholstery; carpet-laying.

APK Interiors 90 Queens Road, Twickenham, Middx TW1 4ET. (*5 mins Twickenham BR*). *Tel*: 01-744 1515/892 1206. *Open*: Mon to Fri 9am to 5pm. Soft furnishings/interior design. Home hints/advice.

Hammond Furnishings 1 Hadley Parade, High Street, Barnet, Herts EN5 5SX. (*10 mins High Barnet tube*). *Tel*: 01-441 4424. *Open*: Mon to Sat 9am to 5pm. Early closing Thurs 1pm. They reckon on "one of best fabric selections in Hertfordshire". Friendly family business; well-trained staff. DIY advice or full making-up service, including fitting curtain rods/tracks.

E. T. Horne 3 Kings Court, 141 Uxbridge Road, Hampton Hill, Middx TW12 1BJ. (*2m Hampton BR*). *Tel*: 01-979 2744. *Open*: Mon to Thurs 9am to 5.30pm. Fri until 5pm. Closed lunch 1 to 2pm. Sat until 12.45pm. Established for 35 years, shop is crammed with samples for fabrics to order (no stock). Curtain-making, loose covers. Blinds, bedspreads, reupholstery.

Materialistic Curtain Studio, 60 Hampton Road, Twickenham TW2 5QB. (*5 mins Strawberry Hill BR*). *Tel*: 01-898 2212. *Open*: Mon to Sat 9.30 to 5.30pm. Closed Wed. Evenings by appointment. Around 100 rolls of furnishing fabrics, with masses more to order. Plus all tapes, tracks, etc. for DIY. Or they can fit tracks, make curtains etc. at well below West End prices. Samples, advice. Furniture.

Home Counties/S.East

Bargains!

Catherine Russell 8 Connaught Avenue, Frinton-on-Sea, Essex CO13 9PW. (*10 mins Frinton BR*). *Tel*: 0255 674759. *Open*: Mon to Sat 9am to 5.30pm. Early closing Wed 1pm. Large, well-stocked shop. Sanderson fabrics: slight seconds at substantially reduced prices. Fabrics for DIY curtains can be cut with matching pattern repeats. Or have curtains made-to-measure on premises.

Mail Order

A number of firms can supply cut-price designer fabrics by mail order. When you've found the fabric you want, telephone the numbers below for quotes on discounted prices, with nationwide deliveries. Understandably, interior design/furnishing shops do not like the way these companies trade. A specialist shop/department may take a lot of trouble to help you with colour/style advice, estimating, and hints for making-up. It's not fair to take your trade elsewhere, and you have to ask yourself if the money you save is really worth the trouble. On the whole, making-up services are more satisfactory if a firm helps choose/supplies the fabric, so that its choice can be taken into account for the overall style. Telephone with exact fabric details (maker, design number/name, colourway, quantities) and compare quotes:

Elizabeth Ann Interiors *Tel*: 08242 3804 (Ruthin, Wales).

Jenny Clark Fabrics *Tel*: 09662 4686 (Windermere). Making-up service for lined/interlined curtains. Will make up your own fabrics, too.

Carrie Ann Fabrics *Tel*: 0243 543919 (Chichester). Fabrics/papers.

Finman fabrics *Tel*: 02357 60223 (Wantage). Up to 40% discounts; making-up service.

Sue Foster Fabrics *Tel*: 0243 378831 (Emsworth, Hants). Branded curtain/loose cover fabrics.

Just Fabrics *Tel*: 0392 51967. Nationwide delivery.

2/LACE & NETS

Net curtains are a furnishing cliché: fashion them in your own image from the shops below. Successful nets must be generously full: at least three times the width of the window.

All Districts

Laura Ashley Home See **Furnishing Retailers**. Good selections cotton lace/voile white/ivory made on 19th-century looms.

London Postal Districts

Michelle 435 Kingsbury Road, NW9 9DU. (*4 mins Kingsbury tube*). *Tel*: 01-204 8710. *Open*: Mon to Sat 9am to 6pm. Selections voiles/nets, plus top name fabrics. Handmade blinds, drapes, pelmets, swags/tails.

Anna French See **Decorating Materials 2/Co-ordinated Collections** Wonderful cotton lace from original Victorian looms.

John Lewis See **Department Stores**. Good net selections including cotton macramé.

Zebra 58 Mill Lane, NW6 1NJ. (*10 mins West Hampstead tube*). *Tel*: 01-435 3108. *Open*: Mon to Sat 10am to 6pm. Traditional cotton lace curtains. White/cream, many woven on original looms. Panels or by the metre. Stiffening service for making into lacey blinds.

Mail Order

Haddow, Aird, & Crerar 76 Brown Street, Newmilns, Ayrshire, Scotland KA16 9AF. *Tel*: 0560 21219. Brochures £1. Flat panels/window drapes high-quality cotton lace to traditional patterns using looms established in 1881.

3/MADE-TO-MEASURE

*Soft furnishings to fit your home are an affordable luxury. Explore all styles of curtains, blinds, cushions, bedcovers and so on. Firms listed under **Decorating Materials 2/Coordinated collections** also offer made-to-measure soft furnishings services.*

London Postal Districts

Andrews & Baxter 191 West End Lane, West Hampstead NW6 2LJ. (*1 min West Hampstead tube*). *Tel*: 01-372 6990. *Open*: Mon to Sat 9.30am to 5.30pm. All soft furnishings (plus wallpapers, carpets, upholstery). Small friendly shop, masses of samples. Prices "budget to luxury". Advise, measure, estimate anywhere in London.

Pam Ballard Furnishings 9 Bedford Corner, The Avenue, Chiswick W4 1HA. (*3 mins Turnham Green tube*). *Tel*: 01-995 4465. *Open*: Mon to Fri by appointment. Wide selections fabrics. Full personal professional soft-furnishings service.

Bradleys 184 Kentish Town Road, NW5 2AE. (*10 mins from Kentish Town tube*). *Tel*: 01-485 0029. *Open*: Mon to Sat 9am to 6pm. Curtain-making/track-fitting; free estimates.

Cedar Interiors 68 Pembroke Road, Kensington W8 6NX. *Tel*: 01-602 8388. *Open*: Mon to Fri 9.30am to 5.30pm. All curtains, blinds, pelmets, swags and tails etc made-to-measure. Mrs Audrey Dean has been trading for over 10 years. Decorating/joinery. Headboards/bedspreads. Modern/traditional furniture. Linens/carpets.

Curtain Dream 19 Broadway, West Ealing W13 9DA. (*Ealing Broadway/Northfields tubes plus bus*). *Tel*: 01-567 4818. *Open*: Mon to Sat 9.30am to 5.30pm. Wed closing 4pm. Beautifully-arranged shop; fabrics, wallcoverings, carpets, sofas, linens. Full soft furnishing service. Part of franchise-operation. (Head office: *Tel*: 0274 728719.)

Curtain Contracts 47 Church Road, NW4. (*15 mins Hendon tube*). *Tel*: 01-203 3772. *Open*: Mon to Fri 9.30am to 4.30pm. Trading for 30 years. Specialist makers curtains, bedspreads, blinds, headboards, tracks (including electric/remote control).

Elite Curtains Rookery Way, The Hyde, West Hendon NW9 6QG. (*10 mins Colindale/Hendon Central tubes*). *Tel*: 01-205 0061. *Open*: Mon to Fri 8am to 5pm. Curtain-making; nets, shears, handsewn headings and pelmets. Made-to-measure festoons, Austrian, Roman blinds. Tracks installed. Curtains cleaned. Repairs/adaptations.

Highstyle *Tel*: 01-328 9044 for appointment. Handfinished soft furnishings from North London workshop. Home visits with samples/advice. Tracks/poles supplied/fitted. All types blinds.

Interiors 454 Chiswick High Road, W4 5TT. (*5 mins Chiswick Park tube*). *Tel*: 01-994 0073. *Open*: Mon to Fri 8.30am to 6pm. Late night Thurs 8pm. Sat 9am to 6pm. Spacious (over 3,000 sq ft) airy showroom; lots of samples/curtain styles. Advice/measuring. Track fitting. Hang/dress/steam curtains Own workrooms for all soft furnishings. Curtain cleaning: take down/rehang. Upholstered headboard, screens, ottomans. 5000 paint colours ex stock: Crown, Dulux, Sanderson.

John Lewis, Peter Jones & other stores in **John Lewis Partnership**. See **Department Stores**, London Postal Districts & Home Counties/S.East. Professional making-up for curtains, pelmets, loose covers. By hand or machine. Blinds, continental quilt covers, tablecloths to order.

Mr Nicholas Curtain Service 442 Church Lane, Kingsbury NW9 8AB. (*10 mins Kingsbury tube*). *Tel*: daytime 01-205 7996; evenings 01-205 0415. *Open*: Mon to Fri 9am to 5pm. Work/showroom supplies wide range of fabrics. Tracks etc fitted. Curtains made by hand and hung in your home: plus swags/tails, pelmets, pinch pleats, blinds. Advise, measure, estimate.

Penbrice Interiors The Studios, 165 Lanark Road, W9 1NZ. (*2 mins Maida Vale tube*). *Tel*: 01-328 3546. *Open*: Mon to Fri 9am to 5.30pm. Closed lunch 1-2pm. Sat by appt. Personal/ enthusiastic service from Mrs Penny Dixon. Showroom filled with soft furnishing inspirations: to order and on time. Reupholstery.

Pickwick Papers & Fabrics 6 Nelson Road, Greenwich SE10 9JB. (*10 mins Greenwich BR*). *Tel*: 01-858 1205. *Open*: Mon to Sat 9.30am to 5.30pm. Early closing Thurs 3.30pm. Well-established. Well-trained staff who supervise orders in on-site workrooms. Numerous fabric/paper pattern books.

Rooms *Tel*: 01-622 2420. By appointment. Home visits. Advice/estimates. All soft furnishings. Takes from 1 week to 6 months, depending on project!

Royston Locke Curtains 19 Market Place, Hampstead Garden Suburb NW11 6JY. *Tel*: 01-455 7977. *Open*: Mon to Fri 9am to 6pm. Curtains designed/made/fitted. Also blinds. pelmets, bedcovers, bed-drapes. Fabrics, trimmings, poles.

Studio 101 Interiors 44E Newlands Park, Sydenham SE16 5NF. (*3 mins Penge East/Sydenham Hill BRs*). *Tel*: 01-676 8822. *Open*: Mon to Fri 9.30am to 5pm. Early closing Wed & Sat 1pm. Small friendly shop; soft furnishing workroom on premises. Samples all leading makes. Advise/ measure/fit/hang.

Outer Ring

Cascade 11 Western Parade, Great North Road, Barnet, Herts EN5 1AD. (*10 mins High Barnet tube*). *Tel*: 01-449 9638. *Open*: Mon to Fri 9.30am to 5pm, Sat 10am to 4pm. Pretty welcoming shop; personal friendly service. Lots of samples fabrics/wallcoverings. On premises workroom for curtains, pelmets, blinds, quilts, loose covers, upholstery.

Curtain Dream 19 Castle Street, Kingston-upon-Thames, Surrey KT1 1ST. *Tel*: 01-547 1107. *Also at*: 56 High Street, Ruislip, Middx HA4 7AA. *Tel*: 0895 679188. See London Postal Districts above.

RA Defries 279 Preston Road, Harrow HA3 0PS. (*1 min Preston Road BR, adjacent public car park*). *Tel*: 01-904 7691. *Open*: Mon to Sat 8.30am to 5.30pm (Wed 4.30pm). Family firm, trading for 25 years. Vast fabric stocks, from budget to luxury. Personal advice. Samples (evenings/ weekends). Curtains, festoons, roller and Venetian blinds, tracks and rods, nets, wallpapers, matching bed linens, upholstery etc. Speedy service for London & Home Counties: often within 2 weeks.

Ideas Unlimited 10 Russell Hill Parade, Russell Hill Road, Purley CR2 2LE. *Tel*: 01-645 9762. *Open*: Mon to Sat 10am to 5.30pm. Early closing Wed 1.30pm. Or by appointment. Complete made-to-measure soft furnishing service, including curtains, upholstery, carpet laying. Interior design; redecoration. Lampshades made to measure in customers own fabric.

Home Counties/S.East

Curtain Dream 10 Park Street, Luton, Beds LU1 3EP. *Tel*: 0582 453474. *Also at*: 32 London Road, St Albans, Herts AL1 1NG. *Tel*: 0727 59401. *And at*: 24 High Street, Woking, Surrey GU21 1BW. *Tel*: 04862 29901.

Curtain Concerns 219 Leigh Road, Leighpon-Sea, Essex SS9 1JA. (*1m Leigh-on-Sea BR*). *Tel*: 0702 715520. *Open*: Mon to Sat 9.30am to 5.30pm. Handmade curtains, reupholstery. Pelmets, blinds, bedspreads. Lampshades, tablecloths, loose covers. Fitting; interior design advice, home visits.

Mail Order

Coward Designs Church Street, Windemere, Cumbria. *Tel*: 09662 4686. Small workshop makes up all soft furnishings. Curtains, lined or interlined, tailored to your measurements/styles. Pelmets, accessories. Supply your fabric, or buy theirs.

Darnadelle Cobden Mill, Gower Street, Farnworth, Bolton BL4 7YZ. *Tel*: 0204 794534. Free brochures/ colour samples. Cotton velvet made-to-measure curtains handfinished with mitred corners. Fully-lined with polycotton, or thermal-coated polycotton for greater insulation. Co-ordinating cushion covers, tie-backs, pelmets and fabric by the yard. Plain satin also available.

Draperite Ltd Metroplex, Unit 120, Broadway, Salford, Manchester M5 2UW. *Tel*: 061-848 9922. Brochures/ samples. Made-to-measure lined cotton velvet curtains at factory prices. Also silk-look Dupion, and cheaper velours. Orders take 14 days.

Lyn-Plan 43 Imperial Way, Croydon, Surrey CR9 4LP. *Tel*: 01-680 4750 (24 hours). Individually tailored covers for most well-known brands of British modern upholstery: including Ercol, Minty, G-Plan, Parker Knoll, Cintique. Write with make/model number for free fabric samples/ details.

4/TRIMMINGS

*Today's more ornate furnishing styles can be enhanced with braids, tassels, fringes, borders. Find trimmings at **Interior Design** shops and **Department Stores** or shop for them at the shops below which can advise on the most effective use.*

London Postal Districts

Colefax & Fowler See **Decorating Materials 2/Co-ordinated Collections.** Wool trimmings from stock, 16 colours. Fan/fringe edgings; bullions; small tie-backs; large tassell tie-backs; button tufts; ropes.

Designers Guild See **Decorating Materials 2/Co-ordinated Collections.** Cotton braids/fringes; brilliant colours to co-ordinate with DG razzle-dazzle fabrics. For upholstery/cushions.

Distinctive Trimmings 17d Kensington Church Street, W8 4LF. (*5 mins Kensington High Street tube*). *Tel*: 01-937 6174. *Open*: Mon to Fri 9.30am to 5.30pm. Sat 9.30am to 1pm. Around 25 years ago, it was difficult to add stylish trims to DIY curtains or upholstery. DT was a much-needed plug to fill that gap. All cords, braids, borders, fringing and so on for curtains, upholstery, lampshades, cushions. Special colours dyed to order. Made-to-measure curtain tiebacks and staircase ropes.

John Lewis, Peter Jones & other stores in the **John Lewis Partnership.** See **Department Stores**, London Postal Districts & Home Counties/S.East. Jonelle trimmings in 9 colours: braids, tassles, fringes, gimp, ruche, cords. Also brass tie-backs, coronets for sweeping drapes at head of bed. Plus many other selections.

Osborne & Little See **Decorating Materials 2/Coordinate Collections.** Style pundits O&L recently added a sumptious trimmings range to their comprehensive furnishing merchandise.

5/BLINDS

Often a neater window solution than curtains, blinds can also be made to measure, see 3/Made-to-measure above.

London Postal Districts

Apollo Around 100 showrooms nationwide. *Tel*: 01-739 0035 for your nearest. All types of blinds, louvre, Austrian, Venetian, roller, festoons. Good showroom displays or ask for home visit.

Eatons See **Floors 4/Mattings.** The original suppliers for cane stick roll-up blinds, standard sizes, or made-to-measure. Samples sae.

Flamingo Blinds and Curtains 2 Chaseville Park Parade, Winchmore

Hill N21 1PG. (*15 mins Oakwood tube*). *Tel*: 01-360 1359. *Open*: Mon to Fri 9am to 5.15pm. Sat 9.30am to 4.45pm. Blinds/curtains custom-made, fitted. Good range of fabrics/wallpapers. Own factory for canopies/awnings, and vertical blinds.

Rainbow Blinds 339 Regents Park Road, Finchley N3 1DP. (*2 mins Finchley Central tube*). *Tel*: 01-346 1679. *Open*: Mon to Fri 9.30am to 5.15pm. Sat 10am to 2pm. All blind types: roller, Venetian, vertical, pleated, conservatory, exterior, and so on. Prices from budget to luxury. Experienced, friendly advice. Can make up your own fabric; handpainting service. Telephone quotes, or within 24 hrs. Complementary nets, cushions, bedcovers, headboards.

Shades 2B Chingford Road, Bell Corner, Walthamstow E17 4PJ. (*Blackhorse Road tube plus bus*). *Tel*: 01-527 3991. *Open*: Mon to Sat 9.30am to 5.30pm. All window coverings except curtains! Roller (including lace), Venetian (including wood), vertical, festoon, Roman, Austrian, cane blinds, pelmets.

Outer Ring

Blinds From Us 62 Cullington Close, Harrow, Middx HA3 8LY. *Tel*: 01-907 5729. Venetian, vertical, roller, festoon blinds. Measuring/fitting. Blind cleaning. Curtains made to measure. Tracks/poles fitted or repaired. London area.

Express Blinds 15/17 Church Street, Staines, Middx TW18 4EN. (*Hatton Cross tube, Staines BR*). *Tel*: 0784 463320. *Open*: Mon to Sat 9am to 5.30pm. All types exterior/interior window blinds made to measure. Wallcoverings, fabrics by the metre, curtains made to measure. Advice, measuring. Brochures.

Home Counties/S.East

Flamingo Blinds Factory showroom, Unit 6, Garden Court Business Centre, Tewin Road, Welwyn Garden City, Herts. *Tel*: 0707 331055. See London Postal Districts above.

Mail Order

Sunvene 7 Greenhays Lane, Manchester M15 6NQ. *Tel*: 061 226 4636. Colour brochure, slat and fabric samples. Venetian blinds, stove-enamelled slats, 3 widths. Six colours in same blind at no extra cost. Bottom rail locks for extra security. Plus rollers/verticals.

Dainty Designs 68 Church Road, Tiptree, Colchester, Essex CO5 0HB. *Tel*: 0621 819194. *Open to personal callers*: Mon to Sat 9am to 5pm. Early closing Wed 1pm. Free catalogue. Broderie anglaise/chintz Austrian blind specialists. Also co-ordinating frilled curtains, lampshades, cushions, wastepaper bins, dressing table sets. Full soft-furnishings/linens service from shop.

6/TABLES & CLOTHS

Using fabric that co-ordinates with or matches the complete room scheme, dressing tables and bedside tables made from humble chipboard can be covered to look a million dollars.

Home Counties/S.East

The Dormy House Stirling Park, East Portway Industrial Estate, Andover, Hampshire SP10 3TZ. (*M3 plus A303; brochure has directions*). *Tel*: 0264 65808. *Open*: Mon to Fri 9am to 5.30pm. Sat 9am to 1.30pm. Huge selection slot-together chipboard tables with instructions for making tablecloths or drapes (limited range of cloths available ready-made). Round, square, oblong, oval, semi-circular; various heights. Glass tops. Also headboards, screens, mirrors, stools.

Mail Order

Belinda Bell Union Road, Smallburgh, Norwich, Norfolk NR12 9NH. *Tel*: 069260 384 (24 hours). Details/pattern samples. Designer chipboard tables, self-assembly: no tools. Cloths and overcloths, co-ordinating cushions.

Lynwood Unit 4, Brunel Craft Centre, Wribbenhall, Bewdley, Worcs DY12 1BS. *Tel*: 0299 402342/ 0562 740571. Round chipboard tables; good choice of polycotton floor length cloths. Lace top cloths; Nottingham lace 36 in and 50 in squares, white/cream.

Trade Fit 73 Kensington Road, Southport PR9 0RT. *Tel*: 0704 31094. Round tables/stools/dressing-tables in chipboard designs that slot together. Free pattern instructions for round table cloths. Special sizes to order.

Wedgeberry 11 Church Road, Brewood, Stafford. Sae for details. Round chipboard tables/breakfast tables. Full length fitted cloths in 6 colours, with optional lace trim.

7/READY-MADES & TRACKS

Curtain track used to be so ugly you had to hide it with a pelmet. New smart tracks/poles are too good-looking to cover up. See good displays at Department Stores, in particular Selfridges and John Lewis. Buy curtain poles off the peg from DIY Superstores. Interior Design shops will explain your track options, arrange to have it fitted, and make the curtains, too. Many shops listed in Soft Furnishings stock track, and some have a fitting service, with or without curtain making. Ideas for slightly more unusual tracks are sketched below.

London Postal Districts

John Lewis See **Department Stores.** Splendid selections wood/brass poles; all curtain accessories: tie-backs, coronas, tassells.

Tempus Stet See **Lighting 2/Traditional.** Splendid curtain finials from moulded resins in various finishes. Every possible pineapple, plus elegant laurel leaves. Also tie-backs (including splendid gold lion head on black circular frame) and coronas.

The Study See **Interior Design.** Poles

that bridge the gap between hardware and art. Gilded spears to stand guard vertically over your drapes; or hang fabric from hand-gilded arrows.

Uglows 26/30 Station Road, Chingford E4 7BE. (*10 mins Chingford BR*). *Tel*: 01-529 0011. *Open*: Mon to Sat 9am to 5.30pm. Early closing Thurs 1pm. Every conceivable type of track/pole. These are the experts, trading since 1910, but with a brand new shop. Special tracks for valances, Austrian blinds, festoons, soft furnishings. Specialists, with own workrooms. The Kirsch Contour machine can bend brass pole round bays. For other stockists of this innovatory equipment *Tel* the distributors (Antiference): 0296 82511.

Mail Order

Baypole McComb Developments PO Box 179, Orpington, Kent. Wood-finished curtain pole/wooden rings/brass fittings. Made to fit bays. Direct from manufacturers.

Ready-made curtains satisfy the urge for instant decor: but couldn't you wait just a little longer for what you really want?

All Districts

Allied Carpets Good choice sizes/patterns; cotton velvets.

British Home Stores See **Chain Stores.** Stylish selections with co-ordinating ranges of linens, china, and other home accessories.

Marks & Spencer Attractive designs; co-ordinated ranges.

The John Lewis Partnership See **Department Stores.** Jonelle ready-mades and leading brands; deep pinch pleat headings.

Wickes See **DIY Superstores.** Yes, now you can get ready-made soft furnishing at what was once a builders' merchant.

8/DESIGNER FABRICS

Britain's Art Colleges are the best in the world. It shows in stunning fabrics, some printed by hand; others by machine in designer patterns and small runs. See selections below. Many fabrics featured in Decorating Materials 2/Co-ordinated Collections also fall in the designer category.

Hilary Barry 26 Rotherwick Road, NW11 7DA. *Tel*: 01-458 4599. *Open*: by appointment. Hand painted fabrics to commission for individually designed interiors and soft furnishings. Colour fast/washable. "My clients want something unique, not mass-produced."

Marie-Helene Bradley 20 Ashley Road, N19 3AE. *Tel*: 01-272 6539 or 01-923 0063. *Open*: by appointment. Screen-printed fabrics: ethnic motifs, abstract patterns, traditional styles. Made to measure curtains, shower curtains, blinds, bed covers, lengths of fabric to order.

Sarah Chester Designs 55 Beaumont Road, W4 5AL. *Tel*: 01-995 8025. *Open*: by appointment. Handpainted silks and printed textiles; fabrics for fashion and interiors, also bed heads, screens, cushions, hair accessories, earrings, scarves, ties, bow ties, cummerbunds and cufflinks.

Rebecca Cole 39 Alexandra Grove, N4 2LQ. *Tel*: 01-800 7086. *Open*: by appointment. Rich colours/textures for modern interpretations of botanical drawings. Printed and commissioned fabrics/furnishings.

Sarah Collins Home Farm, Delaport, Lamer Lane, Wheathampstead, Herts AL4 8RQ. (*A1/Junction 4*). *Tel*: 058 283 3483. *Open*: by arrangement. Closed Tues & Fri. Wonderful domestic designs (cats, flowers etc.) in bright colours influenced by childrens' paintings and ethnic sources. Handprints onto cottons/silks. Sarah uses bold simplistic designs to cover antique/traditional furniture. Also fabric by the metre, cushions, tableware. Mail order service for T-shirts, scarves (fashion items). Brochure available on request.

Custom Designed Prints 60 Wheatlands, Heston, Hounslow, Middx TW5 0SA. *Tel*: 01-570 3828. *Open*: by appointment. Irene Browning designs/prints on natural fibres; curtains, cushions, wall panels, place mats, table cloths.

De Winter 60b Wansey Street, SE17 1JP. *Tel*: 01-703 6271. *Open*: by appointment. Textile designers Nicola Thwaite/Tracy Corker can carry out commissions from cushions to furniture.

Jay Edwards 5 Holly Road, E11 2PF. *Tel*: 01-989 5110. *Open*: by appointment. Wide range of handwoven one-off furnishings on 60in wide 4-shaft floor loom, wonderful glowing colours, often dyed specifically to achieve a particular effect.

Veronica Gould 45/46 Charlotte Road, EC2 3PD. *Tel*: 01-729 0772. *Open*: by appointment. Handpainted cushions, wallhangings, screens.

Yumiko Inagaki 56 Ayres, SE1 1EU. *Tel*: 01-403 1216. *Open*: by appointment. Ikat and natural-dyed woven textiles.

Anthony Jones 45 Lowden Road, SE24 0BJ. *Tel*: 01-326 1480. *Open*: by appointment. Printed furnishing fabrics is bold, large scale modern designs. Bold motifs. Special colours to order. All cotton, 48in wide.

London Cloth Company 1 Eatwick House, Park St, Camberley, Surrey GU15 3NU. *Tel*: 0276 681433. *Open*: by appointment. Contact: Toby Jennings, Fleur Parkinson. Handblock/screen-printed silks and cottons for interiors, including printed silk net.

Shelagh Morgan-Tipp & Eddie Yap

132 Busbridge Lane, Godalming, Surrey GU7 1QJ. *Tel*: 04868 25145. *Open*: by appointment. Painted batik fabrics.

Tempera Fabrics Howfield Lane, Chartham, Canterbury, Kent CT4 7HQ. *Tel*: 0227 457894. *Open*: by appointment. Art-school trained husband-and-wife team design/handprint contemporary fabrics for interior furnishings. Monochromes or brights; cubist/Byzantine/linocut influences. Cottons/linens/soft matt pvc; 54in wide, many with bold borders. Special colours to order.

Timney Fowler 388 King's Road, SW3 5UZ (*12 mins Sloane Square tube*). *Tel*: 01-351 6562. *Open*: Mon to Sat 9.30am to 6pm. The ultimate black-and-white fabrics, with baroque classic motifs. Contrasted with new printed crushed furnishing velvets.

TILES

As the pace of home improvements hots up to bring back the materials used by the Romans two thousand years ago, so demand grows for tiles for newly-improved kitchens/bathrooms. Shop also at **Bathroom/Kitchen Specialists**, and at **Home Improvement Specialists** and **DIY Superstores**.

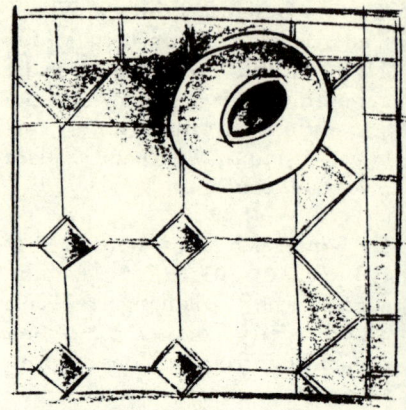

1/SPECIALISTS

Tile specialists have good displays, backed up by stocks. Obtain professional advice on planning and laying/maintaining.

London Postal Districts

Laura Ashley See **Decorating Materials 2/Co-ordinated Collections** and **Furnishing Stores**. Good choice of tiles integrated with wallcovering/fabrics/borders collections.

Capital Ceramics Priors House, Beaumont Road, E13. (*Plaistow tube*). *Tel*: 01-472 4321. *Open*: Mon to Sat 9am to 5.30pm. 3,000 tile types. Sophisticated imports from Italy/France/Holland/Germany. Supply all top kitchen/bathroom showrooms; opened own showrooms 2 years ago. Pastels/brights/lustres/budget. Marble effects: half price of the real thing!

Castelnau Tiles 175 Church Road, Barnes SW13 9HR. (*Hammersmith tube plus bus, opposite Red Lion*). *Tel*: 01-741 2452/748 2452. *Open*: Mon to Sat 8.30am to 5.30pm. Friendly service from efficient tile specialists. Brochure. *Mail order*.

Ceramic World 4 The Green, Winchmore Hill, N21 1AJ. (*2 mins Winchmore Hill tube*). *Tel*: 01-886 1320. *Open*: Mon to Sat 9am to 5pm. In-

spirational displays of over 4,000 tiles from all over. Personal, friendly service.Planning/estimating/designing/fixing. Granite/marble. Handmade murals to order in 1 week.

The Criterion Tile Shop 196 Wandsworth Bridge Road, SW6 2UF. (*15 mins Parsons Green tube; own parking*). *Tel*: 01-736 9610. *Open*: Mon to Sat 9.30am to 5.30pm. Wide range including handmade/handpainted/terracottas.

Danielle See **Decorating Materials 2/Co-ordinated Collections**. Tiles to match own ranges wallcoverings/fabrics/borders/bedlinens: ideal for the en suite bathroom.

Ealing Tile Centre 7 The Pavement, Popes Lane, Ealing W5. (*10 mins South Ealing tube*). *Tel*: 01-840 3501. *Open*: Mon 8am to 7.30pm. Tues to Fri 8am to 5.30pm. Sat 9am to 4pm. Over 200 continental ceramic tiles. Fixing service, design studio for commissions.

Just Tiles 46/48 Willesden Lane, NW6 7ST. (*Kilburn tube*). *Tel*: 01-328 6161. *Open* (both branches): Mon to Sat 8am to 5.30pm. Good choice tiles in stock: trade prices: "you can't beat us on price"!
Also at: 134a King Street, Hammersmith W6 9JG. (*5 mins Hammersmith tube*). *Tel*: 01-741 5396.

Langley London The Tile Centre, 161/167 Borough High Street, SE1 1HU. (*5 mins London Bridge tube/BR*). *Tel*: 01-407 4444. *Open*: Mon to Fri 9am to 5.15pm. Importers of exclusive decorative tiles for kitchens/bathrooms. Design service for mosaics.

London Ceramics 171 Kingston Road, Teddington, Middx TW11 9JP. (*10 mins Teddington BR*). *Tel*: 01-977 0427. *Tel*: 943 3819. *Open*: Mon to Sat 9am to 5.30pm. Sun 10am to 4pm. Early closing Wed 1pm. Imported Spanish/Italian tiles. Studio service for hand/screen prints to order. Design service. Slate/terracotta/marble.

Rye Tiles 12 Connaught Street, W2 2AS. (*5 mins Marble Arch*). *Tel*: 01-723 7278. *Open*: Mon to Fri 9.30am to 5pm. Closed 1pm to 2.15pm. London showroom for Sussex-based makers. Charming designs for walls/floors, including handpainted birds, flowers etc made to order.

Star Ceramics Unit 19, The Talina Centre, 23A Bagleys Lane, SW6 2BW. (*5 mins Fulham Broadway tube*). *Tel*: 01-731 3108. *Open*: Mon to Fri 9am to 6pm. Imported terracottas/stone/marble/handmades. Mostly ex-stock. Design/install.

Tiles, Tiles, Tiles 168 Old Brompton Road, SW5. (*3 mins Gloucester Road tube*). *Tel*: 01-373 6890. *Open*: Mon to

Sat 9am to 5.30pm. Extensive/varied tile selections. Lots of samples on display; design/fixing service.

Tiles & Flooring 175 Muswell Hill Broadway, N10 3RS. (*Highgate tube plus bus*). *Tel*: 01-883 8879. *Open*: Mon to Sat 9.30am to 5pm. Extensive selections ceramic tiles. Attentive service.

Tile & Wall Finds 46 Enborne Road, Newbury, Berks. (*M4 from London; 10 mins Town Centre*). *Tel*: 0635 49779. *Open*: Mon to Sat 9am to 5.30pm. Over 2,000 tiles, from budget to exotic. Samples loan service. Professional tilers can be recommended. Grouts/adhesives/tools.

Tile Collection of West Hampstead 60 Fortune Green Road, NW6. (*10 mins West Hampstead tube*). *Tel*: 01-431 0900. *Open*: Mon to Sat 9.30am to 5pm. Specialise in Victorian reproductions, Moorish designs, handmades. Design service.

Tile Mart 107 Pimlico Road, SW1W 8PH. (*Next to Chelsea Barracks*). *Tel*: 01-730 7278. *Open*: Mon to Fri 9.30am to 5.30pm. Closed lunch 1pm to 2pm. Around 37 makes of tiles on swing panels. Rustic, handpainted or ultra-modern. Most in stock for quick delivery. Advice, samples, fixing. Light, spacious, friendly.
Also at: 151 Great Portland Street, W1N 5FB. *Tel*: 01-580 3814.

Tile With Style 270 Kentish Town Road, NW5 2AA. (*Adjacent Kentish Town tube*). *Tel*: 01-485 9455/01-267 6835. *Open*: Mon to Sat 9.30am to 5.30pm. Wide range imported wall/border tiles in good choice colours/designs. Or your designs/colours to order. Art Tiles Victorian reproductions: printed and plain majolica colours. Importers of handmade Chinese tiles/Spanish terracotta. Technical information/samples service.

Triangle Tile 207/209 Gipsy Road, West Norwood SE27 9QY. (*Gipsy Hill BR*). *Tel*: 01-761 3931. *Open*: Mon to Fri 8am to 4.45pm. Sat 8am to 12.15pm.

West London Tiles 15 Portobello Road, W11 3DA. (*5 mins Notting Hill Gate tube*). *Tel*: 01-221 0033/7280. *Open*: Mon to Fri 8.30am to 5pm. Sat 9am to 4pm. Late night Thurs 8pm. Display over 4000 tiles, mostly available 24 hours. Courteous willing service. Help plan/estimate. Cutters for hire.
Also at: 119 Northfields Avenue, W13 9QR. (*5 mins Northfields tube*). *Tel*: 01-567 1640/2930. *Open*: Mon to Fri 8.30am to 5pm. Sat 9am to 4pm.

World's End Tiles British Rail Yard, Silverthorne Road, Battersea SW8 3HE. (*5 mins Queenstown Road BR*). *Tel*: 01-720 8358. *Open*: Mon to Fri 8.30am to 5pm. Closed lunch 1 to 2pm. Sat 8.30am to 1pm. Zingy designs for wall/floor ceramic tiles; well displayed on large panels and in settings. One of largest selections in London, they claim. Speedy deliveries: all tiles are made in London. Special colours to order. Traditional patterns and marbles also feature.
Also at: 9 Langton Street, World's End, Chelsea SW10 0JL. *Tel*: 01-351 0279.

Outer Ring

DR Betts (Ceramics) The Barn, Church Road, Noak Hill, Romford, Essex. *Tel*: 04023 81349/ 0708 47106. *Open*: Mon to Sat 9.30am to 4pm. Or ring for appointment. Selections British/continental wall/floor tiles, including borders/marble effects. Adhesives, grout, trim. Supply only, or supply/fix.

Color 1 412 Richmond Road, Twickenham, Middx. (*5 mins Richmond tube/BR*). *Tel*: 01-891 0691. *Open*: Mon to Fri 9.30am to 6pm. Sat 9.30am to 5.30pm. Over 2,000 floor/wall tiles on display. Ceramic, terracotta, marble, slate. Handmade ranges, Victorian reproductions. Also decorative plaster mouldings. Wallpapers/fabrics. Tile fixing.

Bargains!

Decor Tiles 1/3 Euston Avenue, Watford WD1 8LZ. (*15 mins Watford tube*). *Tel*: 0923 248531. *Open*: Mon to Sat 9am to 5.30pm. Large selections

at discount prices. Also carpet/vinyl/cork tiles.

Interior Ceramics 3 York Street, Twickenham, Middx TW1 3JZ. (*10 mins Twickenham BR*). *Tel*: 01-892 9002. *Open*: Mon to Fri 9.30am to 5.30pm. Sat 10am to 5pm. Selections ceramics wall/floor tiles. Marble, terracotta, Victorian reproductions, handpainting.

Tilebase 141 Stanley Road, Teddington, Middx TW11 8UF. (*Main road, South of Teddington High Street*). *Tel*: 01-943 0251. *Open*: Mon to Fri 8.30am to 5.30pm. Sat 9am to 5pm. Looks small but has extensive stocks of ceramic wall/floor tiles. Specialist selections and advice. Tile planning, cutting and fixing.

Home Counties/S.East

Tilebase Bagshot Road, Bracknell, Berks RG12 3SE. (*Bracknell by-pass*). *Tel*: 0344 420585. *Open*: Mon to Fri 8.30am to 6pm. Sat 9am to 5pm. Sun 10am to 4pm. Largest tile store in the South, they say. Vast selections, unusual designs. Tile planning, cutting, fixing.
Also at: Wich House, Bone Lane, Newbury, Berks RG14 5SH. *Tel*: 0635 45356. *Open*: Mon to Fri 9am to 5pm. Sat 9am to 12 noon.
And at: Unit 2, Abingdon Distributions Centre, 12 Eyston Way, Abingdon, Oxon OX14 1TR. *Tel*: 0235 33939. *Open*: Mon to Fri 8am to 5.30pm. Sat 9am to 5pm. Sun 10.30am to 4.30pm.
And at: Lafford Leavey, Arrowhead Road, Theale, Reading, Berks RG7 4AZ. *Tel*: 0734 303485. *Open*: Mon to Fri 8am to 5pm. Sat 8am to 12 noon.

2/TERRACOTTA & QUARRIES

The fashion for solid wood kitchens has brought a revival for imported terracottas and home grown tough quarries in the rich reds, browns, and buffs of natural clays. Many of these tiles are also suitable for conservatories and patios, but always check for frost resistance if for outdoor use. Some tiles need sealing when laid: check with supplier. Specialist laying is usually advisable.

London Postal Districts

Castelnau Tiles See **Tiles 1/Specialists** above. Handmade terracotta floor tiles from Spain.

Ceramic Tile Design See **Tiles 4/Handpainted & Designer** below. Terracotta specialists.

Bargains!

Decor Tiles See **Tiles 1/Specialists** above. Large stocks quarries, discounted prices. Brown/red/sand/non-slip from stock.

Elizabeth Eaton See **Interior Design.** Own range of mellow terracottas: handmade clay floor tiles in wide choice of shapes.

Fired Earth 102 Portland Road, W11 4LX. (*10 mins Holland Park tube*). *Tel*: 01-221 4825. *Open* (all branches): Mon to Fri 9.30am to 5.30pm. Sat 10am to 4pm. Handmade floor/wall tiles from all over the world, including 200-year-old tiles from French chateaux. Design/technical help. Brochures.
Also at: 37/41 Battersea High Street, SW11 3JF. *Tel*: 01-924 2272.

Bargains!

Leslux See **Decorating Materials 1/Paints & Papers.** Discounted prices for quarries.

Paris Ceramics 543 Battersea Park Road, SW11 3BL. (*10 mins Clapham Junction BR*). *Tel*: 01-228 5785. *Open*: Mon to Fri 10am to 5.30pm, by appointment. Antique floor tiles, brought from grand houses in France: an historic patina, but pretty pricey! Newly introduced: reproduction ranges from Spain. Some in stock, others to order. Design/install.

Bargains!

The Reject Tile Shop 178 Wandsworth Bridge Road, SW6 2UQ. (*15 mins Parsons Green tube*). *Tel*: 01-731 3795. *Open*: Mon to Fri 9.30am to 5.30pm. Sat 9.30am to 5pm. Around

80% is seconds, from British makers, including much from Marlborough. Good selections plain colours mainly 6in square, but also other sizes including 8 by 6in. Also seconds in quarries, plus marble and flooring grade ceramics at good prices.

Bargains!

Tile Clearing House Ace Corner, North Circular Road, NW10 7UD. (*5 mins Hanger Lane tube*). *Tel*: 01-965 8062. *Open*: Mon to Fri 9am to 6pm. Sun 10am to 4pm. Good selections floor/wall tiles at budget prices, especially Spanish up to 16in square. Also quarries/terracotta/marble.

Bargains!

Tile Warehouse See **1/Specialists** above. Budget-priced quarries.

Tile With Style See **1/Specialists** above. Spanish terracottas.

Home Counties/S.East

Acorn Ceramic Tiles B7 Marabout Industrial Estate, Dorchester, Dorset DT1 1ST. *Tel*: 0305 60185. *Showroom open*: Mon to Fri 9am to 5pm. Closed lunch 1 to 2pm. Leaflets. 20 terracottas from Spain; handmade, hand-pressed or machine-made; various sizes/shapes.

Fired Earth Twyford Mill, Oxford Road, Adderbury, Oxon OX17 3HP. *Tel*: 0295 812088. See London Postal Districts above.

Tile and Wall Finds 46 Enborne Road, Newbury, Berks. (*South side of Newbury*). *Tel*: 0635 49779. *Open*: Mon to Fri 9am to 5.30pm. Closed lunch 1 to 2.30 pm. Sat 9am to 5.30pm. Wide selection terracottas. Nationwide deliveries. *Mail order.*

Mail Order

The York Handmade Brick Co Forest Lane, Alne, N Yorks YO6 2LU. *Tel*: 03473 8881. Colour brochure. Traditional terracotta floor tiles of Vale of York clay. Natural orange/pink: touches of whites, yellows, browns, reds. Sizes 8 by 8in, and 8 by 12in, 3/4in thick. Profes-

sional fixing/sealing recommended. Direct deliveries nationwide.

3/MARBLE

The charm of natural materials is infinite: each tile is unique, with subtle variations in surface colouring and texture. In most cases professional fixing is advisable. See also **Floors 5/Marble, Stone & Slate**.

London Postal Districts

Castelnau Tiles See **Tiles 1/Specialists** above. Natural stone slabs, slates and marbles.

Ceramic World See **1/Specialists** above. Granite and marble wall/flooring tiles a speciality.

Marble & Granite Trading See **Kitchens 6/Worktops.** Wall/floor tiles in 2 sizes, from Greece, Italy, Portugal, Spain. Colours span delicate white Calacatta Oro to rich black drama of Nero Marquina.

Paris Ceramics See **2/Terracotta & Quarries**.

Quality Marble Unit 1, Fountayne House, Fountayne Road, Tottenham N15 4QL. (*5 mins Seven Sisters tube*). *Tel*: 01-808 1110. *Open*: Mon to Fri 8am to 5.30pm. Sat 8.30am to 4pm. Polished marble tiles for walls and floors. Also granite/terrazzo. Fixing service.

Star Ceramics See **1/Specialists** above. Good selections stone and marble tiles.

Worlds End Tiles See **1/Specialists** above. Good selections marble wall/floor tiles in spacious settings.

Zarka Marble See **Kitchens 6/Worktops.** Marble specialists. Supply/install.

Outer Ring

Art Marbles, Stone and Mosaic Co Dawson Road, Kingston-upon-Thames, Surrey KT1 3AX. *Tel*: 01-546

2023/3240. *Open*: Mon to Fri 9am to 5pm. Closed 1 to 2pm. Marble craftsmen: trading for over 50 years. Their installations have included The London Hilton and The Geological Museum. Complete service: design/manufacture/install marble/granite/slate. Plus technical advice. Can supply/process marble "for almost any use". Specialise in large projects, where stone is used for cladding, flooring, sills, jambs, copings and stair treads; but can also supply and fix marble for paving, vanity-unit tops, bathroom wall linings, paving and fireplaces. Around 90 samples on view at Building Centre, 26 Store Street, WC1. Colour brochure/small samples available.

4/HANDPAINTED & DESIGNER

Order tiles to a special design for complete exclusivity.

Sally Anderson Tiles Parndon Mill, Harlow, Essex CM20 2HP. *Tel*: 0279 20982. Wide choice of mural options from combinations of clever tile designs. Classic/trompe l'oeil styles. 4/6 weeks delivery. Samples at good specialist tile shops.

Art on Tiles Unit 230, Wandsworth Workshops, 86/96 Garratt Lane, SW18 4DJ. *Tel*: 01-871 3965. *Open*: by appointment. Handpainted hand glazed tiles in traditional/modern styles. Originals/copies/reproductions. From single tiles to repeat patterns and complicated borders. Panels, murals.

The Aztec Tile Company 50 Patshull Road, Kentish Town NW5 2LD. (*5 mins Kentish Town tube*). *Tel*: 01-485 0016. *Open*: by appointment. Handpainted Mexican tiles; patterns, plains, borders. Brochures. *Mail order.*

Ceramic Tile Design 56 Dawes Road, Fulham SW6 7TT. (*3 mins Fulham Broadway tube*). *Tel*: 01-381 1455. *Open*: Mon to Fri 9am to 5.30pm. Late night Tues 7pm. Sat 9.30am to 5pm. Unusual handpainted imported wall tiles. Antique reproductions. Tile murals; trompe l'oeil. Terracotta a speciality.

Decoramic Designer Tiles Unit 15, Northpoint, Enterprise Close, Medway City Estate, Rochester, Kent ME2 4LY. *Tel*: 0634 710083. *Open*: By appointment. Handpainted tiles; any colours, your design or theirs. Single tile or whole wall. Leaflet.

Elon Tiles 8 Clarendon Cross, Holland Park W11 4AP. (*5 mins Holland Park*). *Tel*: 01-727 0884. *Open*: Mon to Fri 10am to 5.30pm. Sat 10am to 1pm. Stunning hand-decorated tiles from Mexico and France. Naïve motifs in rich colours that never go out of fashion: add flair to bottom-budget kitchens. Flower tiles from Provence and stencilled tiles from Normandy. Colour catalogue £1 inc. p&p.

Eleanor Greeves 12 Newton Grove, Bedford Park W4 1LB. (*5 mins Turnham Green tube*). *Tel*: 01-994 6523. *Open*: strictly by appointment. Wall tiles in delightful graceful repeating foliage patterns reminiscent of the Arts and Crafts Movement. Hand-printed/fired in small studio at bottom of inspirational lovely garden; 10 standard colours, or any colour to order; around 30 exclusive designs.

Richard Henriques 25 Sumner Workshops, 80 Sumner Road, SE15 6LA. *Tel*: 01-708 5904. *Open*: by appointment. Hand-decorated ceramic wall tiles, exclusively designed in colourful underglazes or striking enamels and precious metal lustres for murals, furniture, mirror surrounds, architectural inserts, kitchens, bathrooms. Commissions.

Lambeth Tiles Unit 12/14, Pensbury Street, SW8 4TJ. (*Lambeth tube/BR*). *Tel*: 01-720 4511. *Open*: Mon to Fri 9am to 5.30pm. Handpainted/screen painted tiles in tradition of English 18th-century Delftware. Blue and white single designs, or panels.

Pazuki Prints 2 Beverley Gardens, SW13 0LZ. *Tel*: 01-878 8504. *Open*: by appointment. Splash out on Fish/Ships bathroom tiles. Also boldly original/colourful printed fabrics.

Reptile 494 Archway Road, Highgate N6 4NA. *Tel*: 01-341 4908. *Open*: by appointment. Original handpainted tiles and ceramics, predominately in majolica, traditional Persian/European designs. Ships, flowers, animals, birds, fish.

Joanna Veevers 8A Peacock Yard, Iliffe Street, SE17 3LH. *Tel*: 01-701 3302. *Open*: by appointment. Tiles, porcelain friezes.

HEATING

Now that three-quarters of all homes have central heating installed, shopping for heating will mainly be replacement or repair. Even so, you think about the heating for all your home. Do you want radiators everywhere? Do you want some electric fan convectors to give rapid heat-up? Do you want solid fuel or fuel-effect fires for extra heating and visual effect?

It will not normally be worth changing fuels to save money, but you might want to change for convenience – from solid fuel to gas, for example. But think carefully before you do: modern "Coalflow" boilers have automatic de-ashing and stoking and require very little attention. Details of Coalflow are available from the nearest office of the Solid Fuel Advisory Service.

Gas needs no storage space and the system is easy to control. Where gas is not available or not connected, oil is at the moment cheaper than gas. It offers the same advantages of control, but you do need a large storage tank outside. Electricity is the other main choice. Clean and simple to use in the home, it can be economical if the home is well insulated and today's storage heaters are more attractive and easier to control than their predecessors.

When installing, replacing or upgrading a central heating system, don't forget the provision of hot water. With "wet" central heating systems (that is, those with water heated by a boiler going to radiators or convector heaters), there should be a separate circuit going to a hot water cylinder.

Many existing systems will have a "gravity" circuit for providing the hot water. This works on the principle that hot water is lighter than cold, thus causing the water to circulate around the circuit. But it can take a long time for the water to heat up and it will get very hot unless there is some kind of thermostatic control fitted. A well-designed central heating system is "fully-pumped", that is circulation in both the radiator circuit and the hot water circuit is by the pump and motorised valves are fitted to send the water to whichever circuit needs the heat (a cylinder thermostat will need to be fitted to the hot water cylinder).

For hot water heating in the summer, (or all year round if the home has electric heating), an immersion heater can be fitted to the hot water cylinder. The house should be converted to Economy 7 (a free service offered by Electricity Boards) and a timer control fitted to take advantage of the cheap-rate electricity available at night for hot water heating.

For all systems be certain to have an adequate control mechanism.

1/BOILERS & RADIATORS

When buying a new or replacement boiler, there are several choices you have to make.

Floorstanding or wall-mounted? All solid-fuel boilers and most oil boilers are floor-standing, but many gas (and LPG) boilers are available for mounting on the wall which will take up less space and, if you choose the right model, can blend in well with, say, kitchen cupboards.

Natural or balanced flue? Many gas boilers and some oil boilers are available with a balanced flue – that is, a two-part duct which allows in the fresh air needed for the boiler to work and allows the gases produced to escape.

A natural flue – or chimney – is needed for solid fuel boilers and most floor-standing oil and gas boilers. Provision has to be made separately for fresh air.

New types of boiler. There are three important new types of gas boiler. A fan-assisted boiler can be mounted away from its balanced flue terminal (which means it does not have to be on an outside wall); a condensing boiler has a second heat exchanger and is more efficient (and more expensive) than a normal boiler; a combination (or "combi") boiler provides instantaneous hot water as well as radiator heating. Although the supply of water is always available, flow rates are slower than with a conventional hot water cylinger, so the bath will take a little longer to fill.

When choosing ordinary radiators, remember that many different sizes are available and that you can have different heat outputs for the same size depending on whether the radiator is single or double panel and whether it has added "fins" on one or both panels.

But steel radiators are not the only choice available. You can get traditional cast-iron column radiators, "hitech" radiators in a variety of designs, skirting radiators to avoid taking up wall space plus a variety of convectors, including floor-mounted ones and "kickspace" heaters which fit into the plinth below kitchen units or in the risers of stairs.

The heat output of boilers and radiators will be given either in Btu/hr or in kW. As a rough guide, a three-bedroomed house needs a boiler of around 45,000 Btu/hr (13 kW) and a normal size living room needs a radiator of around 10,000 Btu/hr (3 kW).

London Postal Districts

Bisque 244 Belsize Road, NW6 4BT. (*5 mins Kilburn Park tube*). *Tel*: 01-328 2225. *Open*: Mon to Fri 9am to 5.30pm. Closed lunch 1 to 2pm. Sat 10am to 1pm. Huge choice of radiators sizes, colours and styles (from old-fashioned pillar to ultra-modern sculptural wall-hung panels, long and low or tall and thin). Brochures.

Diamond Merchants 43/45 Acre Lane, SW2 5TN. (*10 mins Brixton tube/BR*). *Tel*: 01-274 6624/5. *Open*: Mon to Fri 8am to 5.30pm. Sat 8am to 4pm. Plumbing/heating supplies. Small, independent, service conscious. Combination boiler specialists. *Also at*: 371 Lewisham High Street, SE23. *Tel*: 01-690 8445.

WH Newson See **Home Improvement Specialists.** Diamond-fretted DIY radiator covers with moulded shelf.

Bargains!

Priority Plumbing Supplies 175 Uxbridge Road, W12. (*10 mins Shepherd's Bush tube*). *Tel*: 01-740 5952. *Open* (both branches): Mon to Fri 8am to 6pm. Sat 8am to 4pm. Discount prices for large range boilers/radiators/copper tube. Press steel baths/lagged cylinders. Watch out for "bargain buys": sometimes bottle of Scotch is thrown in! Services: radiator angling/curving; white/gold plating. *Also at*: 86 Askew Road, W12. *Tel*: 01-749 2966.

The Radiator Cover Company Rear of 105 East Hill, SW18 2QB. *Tel*: 01-871 0722. *Open*: by appointment. Custom-made/installed covers. Fronts: brass/lattice/Screenlite.

Shelves: mdf/marble. Colour brochure.

Rainbow Fairweather Unit 14, The Talina Centre, Bagleys Lane, SW6. (*20 mins Fulham Broadway tube*). *Tel*: 01-736 1258. *Open*: Mon to Fri 9.30pm to 5pm. Tailor-made Cover Charm radiator covers. Natural or coloured woods and metal grilles. Colour brochure.

Outer Ring

Bargains!

Ashford Heating Supplies 193 London Road (A30), Staines, Middx TW18 4HR. *Tel*: 0784 59432/4. *Open*: Mon to Fri 8am to 12 noon. Large stocks top heating brands; substantial discounts. Potterton, Glow Worm, Baxi, Vaillant boilers. Radiators and controls.

Bargains!

Circuit Heating 1 Westbourne Parade, Uxbridge Road, Hillingdon, Middx. *Tel*: 01-573 2261/8869. *Open*: Mon to Fri 8am to 6pm. Sat 8am to 12 noon. Discount plumbing/heating merchants. Gas boiler specialists. Radiators/fan convectors. Showers/sanitaryware, multi-point water heaters. Programmers/heating controls.

RB Classics (London) Unit C14, Charles House, Bridge Road, Southall, Middx UB2 4BD. *Tel*: 01-843 9120 (24 hours). Radiator covers. Satin white surrounds, brass or white grilles. Designed and fitted by craftsmen. Also strong elegant bookcases.

Home Counties/S.East

Design-A-Rad 122 Milton Road, Bedford Place, Southampton, Hants SO1 2HW. *Tel*: 0703 221883. By appointment. Radiators: any size/style/colour. Designers' consultations: London/SE. Leaflet.

2/FIREPLACES

The past 20 years have seen a major revival for The Great British Fireplace. The firms below will help you take

part. Make sure installers are properly trained and experienced: mistakes could be very dangerous. See also **Architectural Salvage**.

London Postal Districts

Acquisitions 269 Camden High Street, NW1 7BX. (*3 mins Camden Town tube*). *Tel*: 01-485 4955. *Open*: Mon to Sat 9.30am to 5.30pm. Sun (Nov to Feb) 11am to 5pm. Specialists in Victorian cast-iron antique fireplaces. Plus reproductions taken from originals (available also from 150 stockists nationwide). Victorian reproduction tiles. Log/coal gas fires. Brochure £1.50 (refundable).

The Antique Fireplace Warehouse 194/196 Battersea Park Road, SW11 4ND. (*5 mins Queenstown Road/Battersea Park BR*). *Tel*: 01-627 1410. *Open*: Mon to Sat 9am to 6pm. Original antique English fireplaces: they say they have largest stock in London, with 1600 sq ft display space, 4000 sq ft warehousing. Marble, pine, cast-iron fireplaces, plus gas coal-effect fires. Expert period advice; experienced fitters. Brochures.

The Cast Iron Fireplace Company 103 East Hill, Wandsworth, SW18 2QB. (*3 mins Wandsworth Town BR/15 mins East Putney tube*). *Tel*: 01-870 1630/4284. *Open*: Mon to Sat 9am to 5.30pm. Sun 10am to 3.30pm. Antique (over 200) and repro fireplaces/accessories: designs date back to 1830. Cast iron, pine, marble. Overmantle mirrors. Antique/hand-screen repro tiles for insets/hearths. Renovations, re-polishing, casting. Gas coal/log fires. Installations. Brochure £1 (refundable).
Also at: 3/4 Fromow Corner, Wellesley Road, Chiswick W4 4HA. *Tel*: 01-994 9303.
And at: 167 Lower Richmond Road, Mortlake, Surrey SW14 7HX. *Tel*: 01-876 1281.
Foundry works: 1 Franciscan Road, Tooting SW17. *Tel*: 01-767 3438.

Chimney Pieces 227 Westbourne Grove, W11. (*7 mins Notting Hill Gate tube*). *Tel*: 01-727 0102. *Open*: Mon to Sat 10am to 5.30pm. Small, friendly individual service. Original or high-quality repro fire surrounds. Regency, Victorian, French marble, modern. Antique stone/marble. Unique accessories. Brochures/price lists/installation leaflet.

Elegance 570 Romford Road, Manor Park E12 5AS. (*2 mins Manor Park BR*). *Tel*: 01-553 1066. *Open*: Mon to Sat 10am to 5pm. Late night Mon 8pm. Ornate classical plaster fire surrounds, also cornices and ceiling decorations and wall panels at very keen prices. Fitting service.

Firecraft 188 Northfield Avenue, Ealing W13 9SJ. (*7 mins Northfields tube*). *Tel*: 01-840 4077. *Open*: Mon to Sat 9am to 5pm. Sun (winter) 12 noon to 4pm. Original Victorian and cast-iron fireplaces, pine and mahogany mantels, coal-effect gas fires. Model marble works for surrounds, hearths etc. at keen prices. Gas coal-effect fires. Fenders/fireguards. Installations. Brochures.

The Fire Place 257 High Street, Eltham SE9 1TY. (*5 mins New Eltham BR*). *Tel*: 01-850 4887. *Open*: Mon to Sat 9am to 5pm. Victorian/Edwardian original fireplaces plus handmade marble reproductions. Log/coal gas fires. Service/advice. Installations. own fitters. Brochures.
Also at: 1 Burnt Ash Hill, Lee SE12. *Tel*: 01-857 2229.

Fireplace Designers 157c Great Portland Street, W1N 5FB. (*5 mins Great Portland Street tube*). *Tel*: 01-580 9893. *Open*: Mon to Fri 9.30am to 5.30pm. Sat 9.30am to 4pm. Hand-carved and handfinished traditional mantelpieces, classical firegrates.

Hallidays Carved Pine Mantelpieces 28 Beauchamp Place, SW3 1NJ. (*10 mins Knightsbridge tube*). *Tel*: 01-589 5534. *Open*: Mon to Fri 10am to 6pm. Carved pine mantelpieces. See Home Counties/S.East below.

Huxley and Davies 70 Mountgrove Road, Highbury N5 2LT. (*Arsenal/ Finsbury Park tubes*). *Tel*: 01-359 8179. *Open*: Mon to Sat 9am to 6pm. Sun 10am to 2pm. Other times by appointment. Mainly antique fireplaces (no reproductions) but also stained glass, leaded lights, bathroom fittings, etc. 5,000 sq ft of showroom, workshops, warehouse. Restorations, installations. Search service.

Ideal Fireplaces 300 Upper Richmond Road West, East Sheen SW14. (*10 mins Mortlake BR*). *Tel*: 01-878 7887. *Open*: Mon to Sat 9.30am to 5.30pm. Antique marble, pine, cast-iron and mahogany fireplaces. Modern designs. Woodburning stoves. Advice. *Also at*: 62 South Parade, Chiswick W4. (*5 mins Turnham Green tube*). *Tel*: 01-994 2981. *Open*: Mon to Sat 10am to 6pm. Late night Thurs 8pm.

Jonathan Murray Fireplaces 358 Upper Richmond Road West, East Sheen SW14 7JT. (*Richmond tube/BR plus bus*). *Tel*: 01-876 7934. *Open*: Tues to Sat 10am to 6pm. Antique and quality reproduction fireplaces in English marble and antique pine. Expert advice & installations.

La Belle Cheminee 81/85 Albany Street, NW1 4BT. (*3 mins Great Portland Street tube*). *Tel*: 01-486 7486. *Open*: Mon to Fri 10am to 5pm. Sat 10am to 1pm. Showroom filled with unique decorator designs by Robert Hamilton, great fireplace innovator. See the Obelisk, and the Deco Arc de Triomphe. Exotic materials: lapis lazuli/gold/smoked glass/stainless steel … it's more like a jewellers. Marble/fossil stone. Free standing metal designs; Provençal timber beams. Plus semi-assembled kits from leading European manufacturers. Also cash-and-carry warehouse.

Old Flames 22 Battersea Rise, SW11 1EE. (*5 mins Clapham Junction BR, parking opposite*). *Tel*: 01-228 7594. *Open*: Mon to Sat 9.30am to 5.30pm. Everything for marble, cast-iron and pine mantels. Shotblasting, cleaning, welding, taking out, installing. Gas log/coal fires fitted. Friendly advice.

Picketts of Camberwell 164 Camberwell Road, SE5 0EE. (*7 mins Elephant & Castle tube*). *Tel*: 01-701 7040. *Open*: Mon to Fri 8.30am to 5.30pm. Sat 8.30am to 4.30pm. Experienced fireplace builders to your own ideas and sizes. Free technical/design service. Agents for Kohlangas and Jet-master.

Realistic Fires 135 Kingston Road, Wimbledon SW19 1LT. (*10 mins Wimbledon tube/BR*). *Tel*: 01-543 2170. *Open*: Mon to Sat 9.30am to 5.30pm. Antique cast-iron/modern fireplaces. Installations.
Also at: 89 Battersea Rise, SW11. *Tel*: 01-924 2610.
And at: 1563/5 London Road, Norbury SW16 4AD. *Tel*: 01-679 8233.

Thornhill Galleries rear 78 Deodar Road, Putney SW15 2NJ. (*5 mins East Putney tube*). *Tel*: 01-874 2101/5669. *Open*: Mon to Fri 8.30am to 5pm. Sat 9am to 12 noon. Family firm. English/ French period chimney pieces. Period panelling, architectural items.
Also at: 76 New King's Road, Fulham SW6 4LT. (*8 mins Parsons Green tube*). *Tel*: 01-736 5830. *Open*: Mon to Fri 10am to 5pm. Sat 9am to 2.30pm.

Outer Ring

Galleon Claygate 216/230 Red Lion Road, Tolworth, Surbiton, Surrey KT6 7RB. (*Tolworth/Surbiton BR, own car park*). *Tel*: 01-397 3456. *Open*: Mon to Fri 9am to 5pm. Sat 9am to 12 noon. One of largest fireplace manufacturers in the country (they claim). Extensive showrooms; around 80 fireplaces. Ceramic, stone, slate, marble; 5 types of briquette. Installations within 50m radius. Colour brochure.

Marble Hill Fireplaces 70-72 Richmond Road, Twickenham, Middx TW1 3BE. (*5 mins Twickenham BR*). *Tel*: 01-892 1488. *Open*: Mon to Sat 10am to 5.30pm. Expert, personal service. Quality fireplaces handcrafted in own workshops. Waxed pine, or white mantels. Adam-style firebaskets for open fires or log/coal-effect gas fires. Also electric fires and mahogany or oak mantelpieces. Large selection antique French marble mantels. Old-style fenders (made-to-measure service on 3 designs); fire irons, fire screens, tile surrounds. Over 30 colours marble slips and hearths. 16-

page colour brochure.

Petit Roque 5a New Road, Croxley Green, Rickmansworth, Herts WD3 3EJ. (*Rickmansworth/Croxley tubes*). *Tel*: 0923 779291/720968. *Open*: Mon to Fri 9am to 5.30pm. Sat 9am to 4pm. Late night Fri to 8pm. Extensive showrooms, established over 25 years. Particularly caters for DIY enthusiasts. Exclusive fireplace designs, each with installation instructions. Individual design and installation within 50m radius. Also marble, panelling, beams and fireplace accessories.

M A Pope (Fireplaces) 14 Western Parade, Great North Road, Barnet, Herts EN5 1AD. (*5 mins High Barnet tube*). *Tel*: 01-449 5893. *Open*: Mon to Sat 10am to 5.30pm. Closed Thurs. Established 28 years. Large displays own fireplace designs, made in workshops on premises. Marble, mahogany, pine, briquettes. Hole-in-the-wall kits. Helpful colour leaflet.

Home Counties/S.East

Hallidays Carved Pine Mantelpieces The Old College, Dorchester-on-Thames, Oxon OX9 8HL. (*Off A423*). *Tel*: 0865 340028. *Open*: Mon to Fri 9am to 5.15pm. Sat 10am to 5pm. Period showroom for pine mantelpieces carved on the premises in traditional Georgian styles. Marble slips, infills, hearths. Grates, accessories.

Worth a Trip

Patrick Fireplaces Guildford Road, Farnham, Surrey GU9 9QA. (*Just off A31, Guildford to Winchester Road*). *Tel*: 0252 722345. *Open*: Mon to Fri 8.30am to 5.30pm. Sat 9am to 12 noon. Family stonemasons firm trading in area over 150 years. Fireplace showroom. Almost 100 marbles/granites; samples supplied. Also granite worktops/floors and marble bathrooms.

3/STOVES

A stove is an enclosed heater burning solid fuel, either coal or wood. In smokeless zones, you will need to use special smokeless fuel, known as "open fire", which will give enough flame to keep the fire alive and interesting.

For woodburning stoves (and "multifuel" stoves), you need wood which is well seasoned, which means having sufficient storage space to keep it for at least a year. As haulage is a considerable proportion of the costs of wood for fuel-burning, it helps keep costs down if you can have a lot delivered at once – say ten tons or more.

Stoves themselves can vary from the traditional "box" stove, popular in Scandinavian countries (the cylinder stove has always been more popular here), to the glass-fronted stove which can either be free-standing or partially inset into a fireplace. These will usually provide convected heat as well as radiant heat.

Many stoves can be fitted with a backboiler to provide heating for radiators or to provide hot water heating (or, sometimes, both). All will need a proper chimney, though there are various methods for providing a chimney in homes not fitted with one and some types of stove come with their own chimney.

One kind of stove enjoying a revival is the cooker/stove, such as the Aga. These days, this type of stove is available powered by gas, oil or even electricity as well as the more traditional solid fuel.

London Postal Districts

Gallery La Cornue 60 Westbourne Grove, W2 5SH. (*10 mins Queensway tube*). *Tel*: 01-229 7681. *Open*: Mon to Fri 9am to 5pm. New showroom; luxury French exclusive stoves based on traditional kitchen range. Handbuilt to order, incorporating client's choice of features. Much favoured by top chefs for saucemaking, so I am told. Installations.

The London Stove Centre 49 Chiltern Street, W1M 1HQ. (*3 mins Baker Street tube*). *Tel*: 01-486 5168. *Open*: Tues to Fri 9.30am to 5.30pm. Sat 9.30am to 4pm. Around 25 stoves on display, to burn solid fuel/gas. From Britain, America, France, Belgium, Sweden, Denmark. Vermont Intrepid installed and working; downstairs a working Rayburn. No installations.

Outer Ring

Cranleigh Heating Supplies Littlemead Industrial Estate, Cranleigh, Surrey GU6 8ND. *Tel*: 0483 271897. *Open*: Mon to Fri 8am to 5.30pm. Closed lunch 1 to 2pm. Sat 9am to 12 noon. Discount prices Rayburn cookers. Central heating/plumbing supplies. Boilers/flues, radiators. Sanitaryware/showers.

Home Counties/S.East

The Stove Shop The Street, Hatfield, Peveral, Chelmsford, Essex CM3 2DY. (*Just off A12; 10 mins Chelmsford BR*). *Open*: Mon to Fri 9am to 6pm. Sat 10am to 5.30pm. Sun 11am to 4pm. Woodburning stove specialist John Opie has purpose-built premises for Coalbrookdale/Rayburn stoves/fires/cookers/Proheat/Anki flue pipes/chimneys/liners. Stove/fireplace accessories from flue cleaning equipment to brassware/ceramics.

Mail Order

Chase Heating & Plumbing Merchants Pickersleigh Road, Malvern, Worcs. *Tel*: 06845 68898/66410. Nationwide deliveries. Solid-/multifuel stoves/cookers. Discounts radiators/controls/boilers.

The Hot Spot 53/55 High Street, Uttoxeter, Staffs ST14 7JQ. *Tel*: 0889 565411. Robust wood-burning stoves at low prices. Plain no-nonsense designs, 6 sizes. Popular for homes, caravans, boats, workshops.

The Graham Wright Stove Company 303 Bolton Road, Edgworth, Bolton BL7 0AW. *Tel*: 0204 852076 (24 hours). Nationwide deliveries/discount prices leading makes/models multi-fuel stoves in cast iron/steel. Around half are British, half imported from Europe. Can suggest installers.

Worth a Trip

Country Cookers 5 Sherford Street, Bromyard, Hereford. *Tel*: 0885 483633. *Open*: Mon to Fri 9am to 5pm. Closed lunch 1 to 2pm. Sat 9.30am to 4.30pm. Rebuilt/reconditioned Agas/Rayburn cookers: good savings. Also own designs new wood burning stoves. Nationwide deliveries.

4/FIRESIDE ACCESSORIES

Keep your fire burning smoothly and add style to your hearth. Most specialists (see 2/Fireplaces above) offer a good choice of coal buckets, firescreens, tongs and so on. A hunt among Architectural Salvage shops is profitable. Handmade items are often offered by craft shops (see Antiques 5/Craft Shops & Galleries.

London Postal Districts

La Belle Cheminee See **2/Fireplaces** above. Firebaskets, firegrates. Tinted glass firescreens. Leather fenders. Tools; mesh spark curtains.

Townsend See **Architectural Salvage.** Abbey Road shop sells wide range antique/reproduction fire-side accessories. Grates, fenders, fire-dogs, fire-tool sets, screens.

Home Counties/S.East

Fires and Things Abingdon (*Tel*: 0235 32560); Cheltenham (*Tel*: 0242 226266); Tunbridge Wells (*Tel*: 0892 43029); Dorking (*Tel*: 0306 883201); Winchester (*Tel*: 0962 840320). Group of shops displaying fireplaces, stoves, grates and fenders.

Mail Order

Erme Wood Forge Woodlands, Ivybridge, Devon PL21 9HF. *Tel*: 0752 892343. *Open to personal callers*: Mon to Fri 9am to 5pm. Delightful fire irons, choice of handles. Elegant fire screens. Made-to-measure fire baskets, dogs. Excellent leaflet includes history of the British grate!

Luscombe Bellows Luscombe Farm, Buckfastleigh, South Devon TQ11 0JD. Fine handmade bellows in elm, oak or beech. Bellow/restoration.

Mail order catalogue.

5/LOG & COAL-EFFECT GAS FIRES

If you want the effect of a coal or log fire, but not the dirt and effort, you can get a range of fuel-effect fires powered by electricity or gas.

Electric fuel-effect fires rely on a flickering light to achieve the fuel effect so are not totally realistic. However, they are easy to install and to control. Some come fitted with thermostats; some even have a remote control so you can turn them on and off without leaving the comfort of your armchair. Electric fuel-effect fires have radiant heating elements which can be turned off leaving just the fuel effect.

Some gas fuel-effect fires also use a flickering light to achieve the fuel effect (the heat comes from radiant gas elements) but most have real flames passing through imitation coal or logs. Inset living-flame gas fires fit into an existing fireplace; versions are also available which fit into a basket in a larger fireplace. Some living-flame gas fires are enclosed behind glass doors and have a high efficiency heat exchanger which will also give convected heat through a grille at the top of the fire. A recent type (the Derwent Free-flue) has a condensing heat exchanger and can be installed without a flue, needing only a 28mm horizontal plastic pipe to get rid of the combustion gases.

London Postal Districts

La Belle Cheminee See **2/Fireplaces** above. Robert Hamilton introduced coal-/log-effect gas fires into Britain in 1974. See them burning now complete with pine cones (true or false?). Plus colour crystals for multi-coloured flames; twigs for real-life aromatic incense; woodland moss-effect embers; flame gas lighters.

Gas Coal Fires 50 Honor Oak Park, Forest Hill SE23 1DY. (*2 mins Honor Oak BR*). *Tel*: 01-291 1748/690 2353. *Open*: Mon to Sat 10am to 5pm. Early

closing Wed 1pm. Dedicated personal service from experienced gas fitter and wife. Coal-effect gas fires a speciality. Victorian/marble fireplaces. Customers journey from all over.

The Gas Log Fire Centre 232 Fulham Road, SW10 9NB. ((*15 mins Gloucester Road tube*). *Tel*: 01-352 2560/ 351 5298. *Open*: Mon to Sat 9.30am to 5.30pm. Working displays of log/coal effect gas fires.

Real Flame 80 New King's Road, SW6 4LT. (*8 mins Parsons Green tube*). *Tel*: 01-731 3056/2704. *Open* (all branches): Mon to Sat 9.30am to 5.30pm. Largest manufacturer in Europe (they claim) of decorative log-/coal-effect gas fires. Fireplace designers. Installers: into your existing grate or choose from their extensive range. Qualified builders and fitters. Courteous painstaking personal service. New: decorative gas fire that needs no chimney.
Also at: Balham (*Tel*: 01-767 7811/ 7812); Finchley Road (*Tel*: 01-455 9473); Sydenham (*Tel*: 01-659 5899).

Outer Ring

Blazes 122 High Street, Epsom, Surrey KT19 8BJ. *Tel*: 03727 22305. *And at*: 1186 Uxbridge Road, Hayes End, Middx. *Tel*: 01-561 8450. See Home Counties/S.East below.

Real Flame 29 Widmore Road, Bromley, Kent BR1 1RW. *Tel*: 01-290 1548. *Open*: Mon to Sat 9.30am to 5.30pm. See London Postal Districts above.

Home Counties/S.East

Blazes 111 High Street, Slough, Berks SL1 1DH. *Tel*: 0753 70656. *Open*: Mon to Fri 10am to 5.30pm. Sat 9am to 6pm. Or by appointment. Specialist in gas log-/coal-effect fires; wide choice decorative fire surrounds. Good selection fireside accessories.
Also at: Canterbury, Epsom, Hayes, West Thurrock. *Tel* (nearest branch): 0753 70656.

LIGHTING

Lighting possibilities are legion: visit a specialist and explore the mysteries of new low-voltage energy-saving slim-line fittings with daylight halogen bulbs. Always plan lighting changes before you decorate so that wiring is unobtrusive.

1/GENERAL

A whole range of fittings is available from the stores below, which can offer specialist advice.

London Postal Districts

After Dark Lighting 229 Kensington High Street, W8 6SA. (*5 mins Kensington High Street tube*). *Tel*: 01-937 6314. *Open* (both branches): Mon to Fri 10am to 7pm. Sat 9.30am to 6pm. Modern, traditional, classic fittings arranged in groups: bedroom, living-room, garden, kitchen, bathroom, hi-tech. Friendly, helpful staff. Design advice. Lampshades to order in your fabric.
Also at: 402 North End Road, SW6. (*5 mins Fulham Broadway tube*). *Tel*: 01-381 8987.

BhS See **Chain Stores**. Buy nothing until you've seen what's on offer at BhS. Their stylish selections, modern and trad, remain unrivalled for the price.

John Cullen Lighting 1 Woodfall Court, Smith Street, SW3 4EJ. (*15 mins Sloane Square tube*). *Tel*: 01-730 8585. *Open*: Mon to Fri 9.30am to 5,30pm. Sat 10am to 1.30pm. Emphasis here is on lighting design. Displays show light distribution of various fittings: up-lighters, down-lighters, spots, tracks etc., plus potential of new-style low voltage halogen lighting. Elegant modern fittings. Middle to upper price brackets. Lighting designer.

Home-Lights 98 Berwick Street, W1V 3PP. (*10 mins Piccadilly Circus*). *Tel*: 01-437 3443. *Open*: Mon to Fri 10am to 6pm. Sat 10am to 5pm. Traditional/modern lighting; statues, busts, columns, mirrors. Lampshades made to order.
Also at: Umaka Lampshade Co, 5A Walkers Court, Brewer Street, W1R 3FQ. *Tel*: 01-437 5193.

Lightstyle 94 Tottenham Court Road, W1P 9HE. (*5 mins Tottenham Court Road tube*). *Tel*: 01-637 4858/ 5084. *Open*: Mon to Sat 9.30am to 6pm. Retail outlet for The Lighting Workshop. Latest technology at affordable prices. Expert advice. Modern mirrors/clocks.

London Lighting Company 135 Fulham Road, SW3. (*5 mins South Kensington tube*). *Tel*: 01-589 3612. *Open*: Mon to Sat 9.30am to 6pm. Large modern showroom, with high quality Italian/English fittings. Expert advice. Today's sophisticated bathroom showrooms have working models of sybaritic equipment; in some, you can even try before you buy!

Menos 225/227 High Street, Acton W3 9BY. (*15 mins Acton Town tube*). *Tel*: 01-993 7013. *Open*: Mon to Thurs 9.30am to 6pm. Fri 9.30am to 7pm. Sat 9.30am to 6.30pm. Sun 10.30am to 5pm. Large showroom selling from stock. Modern/traditional designs. Crystal chandeliers; brass, spots, wall lights, table and floor lamps. Friendly advice.

Millet Lighting 197/201 Baker Street, NW1 6UY. (*5 mins Baker Street tube*). *Tel*: 01-935 7851. *Open*: Mon to Fri 9am to 6pm. Sat 9am to 5.30pm. Vast selections traditional/modern exclusive light fittings from all over the world. Catalogue.

Private Lives See **Interior Design**. Decorator lighting demonstrated in beautiful converted barn. Low voltage halogen for minimal elegance. Ceramic bases/handmade silk shades, any style. Glass/marble column lamps. Handpainted bases. Hall lanterns. Wall sconces.

Quip 243 Westbourne Grove, W11 2SE. (*5 mins Notting Hill Gate tube*). *Tel*: 01-727 5377. *Open*: Tues 2.30 to 6pm. Wed to Sat 10am to 6pm. Architectural lighting consultants, with stylish indoor/outdoor light fittings in stock/to order.

Ryness 37 Goodge Street, W1. (*3 mins Goodge Street tube*). *Tel*: 01-636 9681. *Open* (all branches): Mon to Sat 9am to 6pm. Over 3000 electrical lines for DIY enthusiast/electrical contractor. Light fittings: interior, exterior, gar-

den. Tracks, spots, down-lighters, recessed etc. Cables, 1500 light bulbs, sockets, switches, telephones, small appliances. Ceiling fittings turned on for demonstrations. Expert, friendly approach has led to rapid recent expansion.
Also at: 326 Edgware Road, W2. *Tel*: 01-723 5376.
And at: 54 Fleet Street, EC4. *Tel*: 01-353 0575.
And at: 67 Camden High Street, NW1. *Tel*: 01-387 4594.
And at: 84 Victoria Street, SW1. *Tel*: 01-828 8377.
And at: 211 Kensington High Street, W8. *Tel*: 01-937 9830.
And at: 103 King Street, Hammersmith W6. *Tel*: 01-741 4398.

Christopher Wray's Lighting Emporium See **2/Traditional** below. CW is best known for period lighting. But at massive new showrooms find modern fittings, including low voltage halogen track. Uplighters, downlighters, wall floods, pin spots. Bulb Boutique: every type of lamp. Cast iron 19th-century spiral leads to Lighting Laboratory: experiment with different lighting, using cut-away ceiling, chimney breast, and kitchen.

Outer Ring

Ryness 184 High Street, Sutton, Surrey. *Tel*: 01-643 8339. See London Postal Districts above.

2/TRADITIONAL

Fittings that echo Victorian/ Edwardian styles are gentle on the eye.

London Postal Districts

Ampersand 62 Park Road, NW1 4SH. (*5 mins Baker Street tube*). *Tel*: 01-262 5444. *Open*: Mon to Fri 10am to 5pm. Sat 10am to 1pm. Antique/modern lamps. Fine silk and cord shades, handpainted to order. High-quality conversions.

Ann's Lighting 34a/b Kensington Church Street, W8 4HA. (*8 mins Kensington High Street tube*). *Tel*: 01-937 5033. *Open*: Mon to Fri 9am to 6pm.

Sat 9am to 5.30pm. Good range traditional lighting.

Bella Figura 154 Fulham Road, SW10 9PR. (*10 mins South Kensington tube*). *Tel*: 01-373 1250. *Open*: Mon to Fri 9.30am to 6pm. Sat 10am to 6pm. Classic fittings, lamps, shades. Copies Florentine 18th-century chandeliers/ wall lights; gilded or painted metal. Best lead crystal Italian chandeliers. Handmade silk, chintz/ cord lampshades; shades to order in clients' fabrics. Distinctive lampbases: ceramic, wood and Murano glass urns.

Dernier & Hamlyn 17 Lydden Road, Wandsworth SW18 4LT. (*15 mins Southfields tube*). *Tel*: 01-870 0011/2. *Open*: Mon to Fri 9am to 4.30pm. More than 200 styles repro light fittings 18th-/19th-centuries; 8 different finishes. Catalogue.

The End of Day Lighting Co 54 Parkway, NW1 7AH. (*2 mins Camden Town tube*). *Tel*: 01-485 6846. *Open*: Mon to Sat 9am to 5.30pm. Handmade copies of Victorian/ Edwardian/Deco styles. Brochures.

Jones (Lighting) 194 Westbourne Grove, W11 2RH. (*5 mins Notting Hill Gate tube*). *Tel*: 01-229 6866. *Open*: Mon to Sat 9.30am to 6pm. Largest selection in Europe, they claim, of original lighting 1860 to 1960.

The Lamp Gallery 355 New King's Road, Fulham SW6 4RJ. (*5 mins Putney Bridge/Parsons Green tubes*). *Tel*: 01-736 6188. *Open*: Mon to Sat 10am to 6pm. Authentic decorative lighting from around 1815 to 1950. Good displays, competitive prices.

Libra Designs See **Antiques 2/Furnishing Antiques**. Original art deco wall lights and pendants.

Tempus Stet Trinity Business Centre, 305/309 Rotherhithe Street, SE16 1EY. (*5 mins Rotherhithe tube; ample parking*). *Tel*: 01-231 0955. *Open*: strictly by appointment. "Let time stand still". Or roll gently backwards. Unique collection of decorator lighting moulded from resins into wonder-

ful wall-lights, chandeliers, lamp bases. Nine finishes: 3 burnished gilts; dull French grey, verdigris, and Chinese red; and 3 woods: limed oak and medium oak, and grained mahogany. Colour catalogue.

Turn on 116/118 Islington High Street, Camden Passage N1 8EG. (*5 mins Angel tube*). *Tel*: 01-359 7616. *Open*: Wed to Sat 10.30am to 5pm. Genuine antique lighting 1840 to 1940. Wall lamps, chandeliers, table/ standard lamps. Original shades, varying designs/colours. Fittings converted for North Sea Gas!

Christopher Wray's Lighting Emporium 600 King's Road, SW6 2DX. *Tel*: 01-736 8434. *Open*: Mon to Sat 10am to 6pm. Approaching 25 years ago, ex-actor Christopher Wray started the Victorian light fittings craze, and mopped up the market. Now he has the largest traditional lighting centre in the UK, and possibly in Europe. Opened early 1989: 10,000 sq ft of showrooms ablaze with 10,000 lit fittings. Bohemian/Georgian crystal chandeliers, sconces, pendants. Sconces in carved pickled pine. Downstairs (see the waterfall): ships' lanterns, blue-and-white Chinese vase lamps, simple shaded candle lamps, lights in pâte de verre art glass (including famous serpent lamp). Antique fittings, painstakingly restored by CW's full-time craftsmen. Antique oil/gas/early electric lights: all restored, cleaned, polished; brasswork rebrazed, broken/missing parts replaced; new parts may be made specially. 500 different types replacement shades from stock. Bulb Boutique: all bulb types plus spare parts for oil/gas lamps.

Home Counties/S.East

Royston Browne 31 Palmeira Square, Hove, East Sussex. *Tel*: 0273 774161. Specialists in antique lighting. Repairs/renovations.

Temple Lighting Stockwell House, 1 Stockwell Lane, Wavedon, Milton Keynes, Bucks MK17 8LS. *Tel*: 0908 583597. Lighting specialists for 18th/ early 19th-century interiors. Original shades; good selections Victorian oil lamps. Gas lamp conversions; early fittings can be rewired for safe modern electrical supply.

3/CHANDELIERS

Chandeliers are the antithesis of low voltage minimalist lighting: a glorious centrepoint for any room. Styles range from ornate period cut-glass to stark modern. All are heavy and must be fixed securely into a joist. Plan at outset for changing myriads of bulbs.

London Postal Districts

A&H Brass See **Doors 2/Door Furniture**. Brass/crystal chandeliers.

Bella Figura See **Lighting 2/Traditional** above.

Mrs ME Crick 166 Kensington Church Street, W8 4BN. (*3 mins Notting Hill Gate tube*). *Tel*: 01-229 1338. *Open*: Mon to Fri 9am to 5.30pm (appointments advisable). Chandeliers, wall-lights, candelabra.

Delomosne & Son 4 Campden Hill Road, W8 7DU. (*2 mins High Street Kensington tube*). *Tel*: 01-937 1804. *Open*: Mon to Fri 9.30am to 5.30pm. Antique English glass chandeliers, candelabra.

Hooper & Purchase 303/305 King's Road, SW3 5EP. (*12 mins Sloane Square tube*). *Tel*: 01-351 3985. *Open*: Mon to Fri 9.30am to 5.30pm. Evenings by appointment. English/continental antique 18th/early 19th-century chandeliers, wall-lights.

Kensington Lighting Company 59 Kensington Church Street, W8 4HA. (*7 mins Kensington High Street tube*). *Tel*: 01-938 2405. *Open*: Mon to Fri 9.30am to 6pm. Sat 9.30am to 5.30pm. Crystal/metal chandeliers, wall fittings, lampbases.

Period Brass Lights 9a Thurloe Place, Brompton Road, Knightsbridge SW7 2RZ. (*10 mins South Kensington/ Knightsbridge tubes*). *Tel*: 01-589 8305. *Open*: Mon to Fri 9.30am to

5.30pm. Sat 9.30am to 6pm. Glorious chandeliers/period lighting over 3 floors. Austrian glass drops reflect brilliant rainbows; Czech styles are duller and more gracious. Assemblies to your specifications. Expert fixing/ advice. Handmade period brass wall candle brackets can burn real candles or convincing imitations complete with fake wax drip. Repairs/restorations.

Outer Ring

Elite Lighting 18 Bromley Hill, Bromley, Kent BR1 4JX. (*A21; Bromley South BR*). *Tel*: 01-290 0371. *Open* Mon to Sat 9.30am to 5.30pm. Chandelier specialists. Importers/manufacturers. High quality/low prices. Vast stock for all rooms from domestic living rooms to banqueting halls. Matching wallbrackets. Commissions. Individual attention. *Mail order*.

4/TABLE LAMPS & SHADES

The traditional solution to living room/bedroom lighting, table lamps are still unmatched for atmosphere.

London Postal Districts

Ampersand 62 Park Road, NW1 4SH. (*5 mins Baker Street tube*). *Tel*: 01-262 5444. *Open*: Mon to Fri 10am to 5pm. Sat 10am to 1pm. Elegant displays of lampbases and shades. Variety of styles and prices. Friendly service, expert advice. Wide selection of silks. Shade specials to order; recovering of old shades. Lampbase conversions.

Bella Figura See **Lighting 2/Traditional** above.

Clare House 35 Elizabeth Street, SW1. (*10 mins Victoria tube/BR*). *Tel*: 01-730 8480. *Open*: Mon to Fri 9.30am to 6pm. Specialises in lamps and shades. Chinese vases, Italian columns, turned wood designs. All shades made to order.

Green & Stone See **Accessories 2/Frames** London Postal Districts.

Hand-marbled lampshades.

Audrey Scannell 14 Wilton Crescent, SW1X 8RN. *Tel*: 01-235 6237. *Open*: by appointment. Exclusive silk/ pleated decorator shades made to order. Old shades recovered. Selection lampbases including fabulous ceramic unicorn.

Philip Vian See **Antiques 6/Designer Ceramics**. In stock or to order ceramic fluted square column lamp bases in matt black, or crackle glazed in cream, or pastels.

Outer Ring

Ideas Unlimited See **Soft Furnishings 3/Made-to-measure**. Shades made to order in customers own fabric.

Mail Order

Silk Shades 33 Prentice Street, Lavenham, Suffolk CO10 9RD. *Tel*: 0787 247029. Silks: beautiful colours, patterned/plains/textured. Samples: £2 refundable.

Wiltshire Woodwork Leafield Trading Estate, Corsham, Wilts SN13 9UA. *Tel*: 0225 810344. Beautiful candlesticks, choice of woods/colours in 17th and 19th century designs. Also candlestick-style wooden lamps and new chunky column design. Marbled finishes. Colour brochures.

5/STAINED GLASS

Light behind stained glass fittings produces a magical glow. Firms listed in **Windows 2/Stained & Decorative Glass**. *can also make up light fittings.*

London Postal Districts

Lead & Light See **Windows 2/Stained & Decorative Glass**. Tiffany-style pendants, wall-lights and elegant up-lighters.

James Preece Unit 11 Portobello Road, W10 5TD. (*3 mins Ladbroke Grove tube*). *Tel*: 01-968 8807. *Open*: Mon to Sat 9.30am to 6pm. Selections

Lighting

stained glass lamps, including black and shades. Lamps, windows, screens to order.

Tiffany Art Studio 12E Bracknell Gardens, NW3 7EB. *Tel*: 01-794 7053. *Open*: strictly by appointment. Alexander Daszewski imports/sells direct at reasonable prices superb Tiffany/Art Nouveau reproduction lights by Edward Magdziarz. I have seen them meticulously crafted in Warsaw. Dragonflies, clematis, wisteria and other favourite Tiffany motifs. Over 100 different designs; made to order: special colours/designs (3 to 4 weeks). Choice of solid brass lamp bases cast by hand. Finish: high sheen, or antique patina. Colour catalogue.

Christopher Wray's Lighting Emporium. See **2/Traditional** above. Splendid reproduction Tiffany/stained glass table/pendant lamps. Louis Comfort Tiffany, son of the famous jeweller, a painter turned interior decorator, produced colourful imaginative art nouveau lamps around turn of the century. CW has impressive repertoire of original Tiffany designs. Intricate pieces of hand-made opalescent glass all match for continuity, and are banded together. Bases are individually bronzed, burnished, lacquered.

6/ELECTRICAL ACCESSORIES

Many firms listed under **Lighting 1/General** *above have good selections of switches, plugs, dimmers and so on, as do* **DIY Superstores** *and* **Home Improvement Specialists**. *For brass fittings see* **Doors 2/Door Furniture**.

London Postal Districts

Forbes & Lomax 40 Elsynge Road, SW18 2HN. *Tel*: 01-874 2635. Clear Perspex light switches with brass dolly rockers. Switches/sockets prepared for painting.

Christopher Wray See **2/Traditional** above.

Mail Order

House of Brass See **Doors 2/Door Furniture**. Solid brass switches, sockets, dimmers.

Woods Electrical Accessories Goodleigh House, Blackborough, Cullompton, Devon EX15 2JA. *Tel*: 0823 680774. Switches and sockets in six hardwoods.

7/AVANTE-GARDE

The avant-garde in lighting seems to go in hand with furniture: designers of the one often excel at the other, and shock-of-the-new shops often stock both. Suggestions to spark you off . . .

Atrium See **Furniture 4/Classics & Reproduction**. In the van with classy modern Italian styles.

Butler-Radice X Building, Wapping Wall, E1 9SS. *Tel*: 01-480 6564. *Open*: by appointment. Wall-mounted lamps in steel and glass. Aluminium track system with lamps strung from slender curves.

John Cullen See **1/General** above. John Cullen was a lighting designer par excellence and created fittings for designing with light, as so excellently demonstrated in the shop.

Diametric See **Furniture 11/Designer**. The slenderest halogen lamps you ever saw on etiolated stalks.

Formula 376 St John Street, EC1V 4NN. *Tel*: 01-837 1473 or 01-253 3693. *Open*: by appointment. Ryan Solomon/Maerisna Adnan design/produce lights, bowls, clocks patinated in a variety of colours.

Ligne Roset See **Furniture 1/General** Nouveau neon notions . . . strips of brilliant coloured tubes for impact rather than function. Plus variety of adventurous fittings.

Margaret O'Rourke 13 Quarry High Street, Headington, Oxford, OX3 8JT. *Tel*: 0865 68394. *Open*: by appointment. Fine high-fired porcelain lights, thrown on a potter's wheel for calm restful atmosphere.

SKK Shiu-Kay Kan 34 Lexington Street, W1R 3HR. (5 mins Piccadilly Circus). *Tel*: 01-434 4095. *Open*: Mon to Fri 10am to 6pm. Sat 11am to 5pm. Original modern fittings; lighting advice/consultancy.

ARCHITECTURAL SALVAGE

Anything remotely useful or ornamental from old buildings currently attracts dealers. AS includes timber beams, doors, panelling, stained glass, paving stones, bricks, fireplaces, slates, tiles, bathroom fittings and so on. But buy on demolition sites if possible (pay foreman cash). And ask permission before you raid builders' skips.

London Postal Districts

City Roofing 28 Aldermans Hill, Palmers Green N13 4PN. (*Next to Palmers Green tube*). *Tel*: 01-882 1905. *Open*: Mon to Fri 7.30am to 4.30pm. Sat 7.30am to 12 noon. Large stocks second-hand tiles/slates. Plus all roofing materials. Free deliveries.

Floyds 349-357 Ilderton Road, SE15 1NW. (*Corner of Old Kent Road; New Cross Gate/New Cross tubes*). *Tel*: 01-639 6991/635 8977. *Open*: Mon to Fri 8am to 5.30pm. Sat 8am to 1pm. Reclaimed yellow and mixed London stock bricks; old Welsh slates.

William Fry & Co Mitre Works, Neasden Goods Depot, Neasden Lane, NW10 2UG. (*2 mins Neasden tube*). *Tel*: 01-459 5141. *Open*: Mon to Fri 8am to 5pm. Closed lunch 12.30 to 1.30pm. Sat 8am to 12 noon. Second-hand RSJs for through lounges, extensions etc. Deliveries arranged.

Nick Gifford-Mead The Furniture Cave, 533 King's Road, SW10 0TZ. (*10 mins Fulham Broadway tube*). *Tel*: 01-352 6008. *Open*: Mon to Fri 9.30am to 5.30pm. Sat 10am to 2pm. High-quality fittings: glass, mirrors, old lights. Architectural woodwork (e.g. balusters) to order.

Hardwood Flooring Co See **Floors 1/Wood**. Reclaimed flooring/doors, planks 6 to 12in wide, 1in thick, kiln dried.

House of Steel 400 Caledonian Road, N1 1DN. (*Caledonian Road tube*). *Tel*: 01-607 5889. *Open*: Wed, Fri and Sat 10am to 4.30pm. Large warehouse, showrooms, workshops. Around 350 cast-iron fireplaces. Railings, gates, staircases, door knobs, etc. Also light-fittings, cast-iron and steel garden and interior furniture, fire accessories. Antiques, or copies.

Lazdan 218 Bow Common Lane, Bow Common E3. (*5 mins Mile End tube*). *Tel*: 01-981 4632. *Open*(both branches): Mon to Fri 8am to 5pm. Used bricks/slates in large quantities. *Also at*: 45 Holloway Road, N5. (*2 mins Holloway Road tube*). *Tel*: 607 0701.

London Architectural Salvage & Supply Co (LASSCO) St Michaels Church, Mark Street, off Paul Street, EC2A 4ER. (*10 mins Old Street tube*). *Tel*: 01-739 0448/9. *Open*: Mon to Sat 10am to 5pm. De-consecrated church/grounds provide unusual setting for vast stocks architectural salvage. Panelling, gates, fencing, chimney pieces, bathroom/kitchen fittings. Reclaimed wooden floorings/floorboards/beams. Flagstones, stonework, sculptures, garden furniture.

Pub Farm/Turnpin Contracts 161/165 Greenwich High Road, SE10 8JA. (*Greenwich BR*). *Tel*: 01-853 2658/5571. *Open*: Mon to Fri 8.30am to 6pm. Original Victorian/Edwardian architectural items, plus reproductions. Large warehouse with panelling, doors, seating, pews, benches, leaded lights, etchings, glass, lighting, mirrors, prints, signs. Installations/restorations by skilled craftsmen.

Reclaimed Building Material Supplies Railway Goods Works, Morden Road, Mitcham, Surrey. (*5 mins Morden tube; 1 min Mitcham BR*). *Tel*: 01-646 0467. *Open*: Mon to Fri 9am to 5.30pm. Sat 9am to 5pm. Second-hand building materials; "anything and everything for building a house". Doors, tiles, slates, bricks, timber, railings, fences etc.

Townsends 1 Church Street, NW8 8EE. (*10 mins Marylebone tube*). *Tel*: 01-724 3746. *Open* (all branches): Tues to Sat 10am to 6pm. Large stocks Victorian/antique tiles. Brass door furniture.
Also at: 81 Abbey Road, NW8 0AE. (*15 mins Swiss Cottage/Kilburn tubes*). *Tel*: 01-624 4756. Restored fireplaces: wood, cast iron, marble. Reproduction fire grates, firebacks, coal scuttles. Gas coal/log fires. Installations (London area).
And at: 36 New End Square, NW3 1LS. (*4 mins Hampstead tube*). *Tel*: 01-794 5706/7. 7,000 sq ft mirrors, glazed doors, panelling, handrails, garden furniture. Victorian/

Edwardian stained glass; rare brilliant-cut and bevelled pieces. Workshop restores/makes stained-glass windows, acid-etched security panels.

Whiteway & Waldron 305 Munster Road, SW6 6BJ. (*10 mins Barons Court tube*). *Tel*: 01-381 3195. *Open*: Mon to Fri 10am to 6pm. Sat 10am to 5pm. Ecclesiastical atmosphere. Stained glass, salvaged church furnishings, statuary. Victorian fireplaces, doors, spindles.

Home Counties/S.East

Brighton Architectural Salvage 33/4 Gloucester Road, Brighton, East Sussex BN1 4AQ. *Tel*: 0273 681656. *Open*: Mon to Fri 10am to 5.30pm. Sat 9.30am to 4.30pm. Specialities: fireplaces/stained glass. Over half stock is restored and ready to take away. Workshop makes Victorian-style pine surrounds. Full installation service.

Oxford Architectural Antiques The Old Depot, Nelson Street, Jericho, Oxford OX2 6BE. *Tel*: 0865 53310. *Open*: Mon to Sat 10am to 4pm. Closed Wed. Relatively new business; 3 directors are keen to help individual homeowners to renovate/restore period homes. Salvaged building materials, period fixtures/fittings. Bathroom fittings, doors, woodblock floors, fully restored fireplaces, Victorian and earlier. Installers recommended. Telephone enquiries welcomed.

Sussex Demolition Services Hoskins Road, Oxted, Surrey RH8 9HT. (*Oxted BR; ample parking*). *Tel*: 0883 715413. *Open*: Mon to Fri 8am to 5pm. Sat 8am to 4pm. Demolition/site clearance specialists offer good choice salvaged materials. Second-hand timber (hardwoods/softwoods); bricks; doors, stripped pine/painted (cheaper); tiles. Stair spindles. Rolled-steel joists (RSJs), paving slabs. Deliveries.

Mail Order

The York Hand Made Brick Co Forest Lane, Alne, North Yorkshire YO6 2LU. *Tel*: 03473 8881. Reclaimed bricks and clay roof pantiles. Deliver direct anywhere in country.

Worth a Trip

Architectural Antiques Savoy Showrooms, New Road, South Molton, Devon EX36 4BH. (*M4, M5, Junction 27*). *Tel*: 07695 3342/4167 (warehouse). *Open*: Mon to Sat 9am to 5pm. André Busak claims "best organised architectural salvage business in the country". He could be right. Telephone or Fax (07695 4363) an enquiry, and the computer checks the stock. Housed in an old cinema (6,000 sq ft), with warehouse nearby. Substantial constantly-changing stock from home/abroad. Fireplaces, tiles, bathroom fittings. Ironwork, marble, stone. Panelling, doors. Workshop restoration service.

Architectural Heritage Taddington Manor, Taddington, near Cutsdean, Cheltenham, Glos GL54 5RY. (*4m Broadway, 8m Stow-on-the-Wold*). *Open Easter to October*: Mon to Fri 9.30am to 5.30pm. *October to Easter*: Mon to Fri 9.30am to 5pm. *Tel*: 038 673 414. Chimneypieces, original/antique garden statuary, complete panelled rooms, oak/mahogany doors, stained glass, "bizarre decorative items".

Baileys Architectural Antiques The Engine Shed, Ashburton Industrial Estate, Ross-on-Wye, Herefordshire HR9 7BW. (*M40, turn off at Swindon; A40*). *Open*: Mon to Fri 9am to 5pm. Sat 10am to 5pm. Don't let the address put you off. A magnificent Brunel engine shed houses Mark and Sally Bailey's treasures, all beautifully restored, and there's a friendly welcome from manageress Sian Richards. Upstairs, a bathroom showroom for reproduction period fittings. Fireplaces, stained glass, doors. Staircases, panelling.

The Original Choice 1340 Stratford Road, Hall Green, Birmingham B28 9EH. (*M42, Junction 4 plus 6m drive*). *Tel*: 021-778 3821. *Open*: Mon, Thurs & Fri 11am to 6pm. Sat 10am to 6pm. Or by appointment. "We're strongest for fireplaces" says glass-restorer Pete Thorington. Ring first, and they'll check out stock. Plus well-restored stained glass, and other bits and pieces. Everything fully repaired/renovated, with full installation service by own employees. Restoration services for customers' items.

Solopark The Old Railway Station, Station Road, near Pampisford, Cambridge CB2 4HB. *Tel*: 0223 834663. *Open*: Mon to Thurs 8am to 5pm. Fri 8am to 4pm. Closed lunch 1 to 2pm. Sat 8am to 12 noon. One of largest suppliers in UK of reclaimed building materials; 6 acres storage/buildings. Up to 2.5 million reclaimed bricks, over 4,000 internal/external doors. Brick types include soft reds, handmades, Tudors etc. Roofing tiles/slates. Stripped pine, mahogany, teak timbers. staircases, window frames, RSJs. Oak, elm, chestnut rafters. York stone pavings/tiles. Search service: leave your phone number and they'll try and find what you want.

Walcot Reclamation 108 Walcot Street, Bath BA1 5BG. (*Bath centre; 10 mins Bath BR; car park*). *Tel*:0225 444404. *Open*: Mon to Fri 8.30am to 5.30pm. Sat 9am to 5pm. Fireplaces, statues, gates.
Also at: Unit 8A, Riverside Business Park, Lower Bristol Road, Bath. *Tel*: 0225 335532. *Open*: Mon to Fri 8.30am to 5pm. Sat 8am to 4pm. Chimneypieces, reclaimed timber/wood floorings.

ANTIQUES, FINE ART & CRAFT

Space is limited, and entries below are just a tiny taste of the vast riches that can be found for sale in London and the South East.

1/ GOOD AREAS

Antique shops flourish in London and the South East. Good areas to explore include the Fulham and King's Roads, Westbourne Grove/Portobello Roads, Camden Town, and Kensington Church Street. Go and goggle at the treasures on show in Bond Street. Antique markets give small traders an under-cover permanent base. Well worth browsing, and often surprisingly affordable.

Alfies Antique Market 13/25 Church Street, NW8 8DT. *Tel*: 01-723 6066. *Open*: Tues to Sat 10am to 6pm.

Antiquarius 135/141 King's Road, SW3. *Tel*:01-351 5353. *Open*: Mon to Sat 10am to 6pm.

Bond Street Antique Centre 124 New Bond Street, W1. *Open*: Mon to Fri 10am to 5.45 pm. Sat 10am to 4pm.

Bermondsey Antique Market Long Lane, SE1. *Tel*: 01-351 5353. *Open*: Fri 7am to 2pm.

Camden Antique/Collectors' Market Camden High Street, NW1. *Tel*: 01-351 5353.

Chenil Galleries 181/183 King's Road, SW3. *Tel*: 01-351 5353. *Open*: Mon to Sat 10am to 6pm.

Cutler Street Antique Market Goulston Street, E1. *Tel*: 01-351 5353. *Open*: Sun 7am to 2pm.

Grays Antique Market 58 Davies Street, W1Y 1LB. *Tel*: 01-629 7034. *Open*: Mon to Fri 10am to 6pm.

Grays in the Mews 1/7 Davies Mews, W1Y 1AR. *Tel*: 01-629 7034. *Open*: Mon to Fri 10am to 6pm.

2/ FURNISHING ANTIQUES

Do you desire deco or favour the fifties? London has furniture shops to help you.

London Postal Districts

Adams Antiques 47 Chalk Farm Road, NW1 8AJ. (*5 mins Chalk Farm tube*). *Tel*: 01-267 9241. *Open*: 7 days 10am to 6pm. Around 75% old pine, including magnificent dressers; rest is repro. Knowledgeable friendly staff.

David Martin-Taylor 56 Fulham High Street, SW6 3LQ. (*1 min Putney Bridge tube*). *Tel*: 01-731 4135. *Open*: Mon to Fri 9.30am to 6pm. Sat 10am to 4pm. Other times by appointment. Early American/English wicker furniture; 18th-century English/continental antiques.

The Furniture Cave 533 King's Road, SW10. (*Sloane Square tube plus bus*). *Tel*: 01-352 4229. *Open*: Mon to Sat 10am to 6pm. Late night Wed 7pm. One of largest collections antique furniture in London. 10 individual galleries: 17th to 19th-century English/continental furniture/furnishings, architectural salvage, garden ornaments, oriental furniture, paintings, Art Deco, antique pine.

The Furniture Store West Hampstead Trade Centre, Blackburn Road, NW6 1RZ. (*5 mins West Hampstead tube*). *Tel*: 01-328 2221. *Open*: 7 days 10am to 6pm. 10,000 sq ft of furniture, lighting, fittings. Gothic, Arts & Crafts, Art Nouveau, Art Deco, 1950s/60s. Bentwood, cane, Lloyd Loom.

Jazzy Art Deco 67 Camden Road, NW1 9DT. (*15 mins Camden tube; next to Camden BR*). *Tel*: 01-267 3342. *Open*: Tues to Sat 10am to 6pm. Sun 11am to 5pm. Over 1300 sq ft original fine art deco furniture (1920s/30s). Plus ceramics, glass, bronzes. Good investments/reasonable prices. Reupholstery, French polishing.

Libra Designs Unit 45, Alfies Antique Market, Church Street, Marylebone NW8. (*5 mins Edgware Road tube*). *Tel*: 01-402 1976. *Open*: Tues & Thurs 10.30am to 5pm. Fri & Sat 12 noon to 5pm. Closed Sun, Mon, Wed. Or by appointment. Marie Gottlieb scours the country for original art deco furniture. Substantial 3-piece suites with e.g. cloud- or shell-shaped backs. Original coverings; upholstery can be arranged with appropriate fabrics. Also wardrobes, cupboards, dressing tables, occasional furniture, much in burr walnut, with its distinctive swirly graining, or the flecked yellowy shades of birds eye maple. Distinctive details include brown/amber/cream handles in bakelite or chrome. 30s accessories, too. Glass by Lalique. China by Clarice Cliff. Search/find service.

Metropolis 3 D'Arblay Street, W1V 3FD. (*5 mins Oxford Circus tube*). *Tel*: 01-494 2531. *Open*: Mon to Fri 9.30am to 7pm. Sat 11am to 6pm. Original pieces of furniture, lamps, etc. from 1920s right through to the present. This small shop on two levels salvages the best of the 1960s and 1970s.

The Old Cinema 160 Chiswick High Road, Chiswick W4 1PR. (*5 mins Turnham Green tube*). *Tel*: 01-995 4166. *Open*: Mon to Sat 10am to 6pm. Sun 12am to 5pm. Lofty spacious premises built for cinema crowds before the advent of universal TV. Benefit today from large selection original upholstery/cabinets/chests/tables/chairs. Victorian/Edwardian/art nouveau. Reupholstery and furniture restoration can be arranged. Chargeable deliveries.

Old English Antiques 190 Westbourne Grove, W11. (*Off Portobello Road*). *Tel*: 01-727 2699. *Open*: Mon to Sat 9.30am to 6pm. Large shop on 2 levels with good selection of cherrywood/oak country furniture and Regency/Georgian mahogany. High quality. Expert advice. Instant availability.

Jill Saunders 46 White Hart Lane, SW13 0PZ. (*5 mins Barnes Bridge BR*). *Tel*: 01-878 0400. *Open*: Mon to Sat 9am to 5.30pm. Original Lloyd Loom furniture, cheaper than reproductions (see **Furniture 4/Classics & Reproduction**). Sofas, chairs, tables, linen baskets. Original covered steel framework woven with coiled paper strips.

Repairs with original materials. Authentic colours; or can be resprayed to any colour. Replacement cushions feather-filled/foam wrapped with Dacron wadding kept in stock; covers to order. Victorian/Edwardian sofas/chairs plus reproduction upholstery. Pleasant, efficient service from knowledgeable proprietor.

Outer Ring

Phelds 133/135 St Margaret's Road, East Twickenham, Middx TW1 1RG. (*Adjacent St Margaret's BR*). *Tel*: 01-892 1778. *Open*: Mon to Fri 9am to 5.30pm. Closed lunch 1pm to 2pm. Sat 9am to 5pm. Over 13,000 sq ft of antique, second-hand and repro furniture. Furniture conversions, restorations.

Rogers Antique Interiors 22 Ewell Road, Cheam Village, Surrey SM3 8BU. (*12m south of London, off A3*). *Tel*: 01-643 8466. *Open*: Mon to Sat 10am to 5.30pm. Closed Wed. Georgian, Victorian, Edwardian furniture in roomsettings to demonstrate decorative potential. Samples from all major paper/fabric ranges. Interior design, soft furnishings, valuations.

Worth a trip

Adams Antiques Houghton Road, St Ives, Huntingdon PE17 4RG. (*Huntingdon BR*). *Tel*: 0480 300455. *Open*: Mon to Fri 8.30am to 5pm. Sat 10am to 4.30pm or by appointment. Two vast warehouses, one for old pine, one for new. Restoration/finishing. Pine-stripping service.

Stuart Interiors Barrington Court, Ilminster, Somerset TA19 0NQ. (*Taunton BR; company will collect, M3 Junction 7*). *Tel*: 0460 40349. Magnificent National Trust lichen-encrusted Elizabethan manorhouse: most beautiful "shop" I have ever visited. Fabulous showcase for Tudor/Stuart furnishings. Green labels: antiques. Red labels: faithful loving reproductions. Complete design/furnishing service for early houses, or lovers of earlier English interiors. Particularly attractive: authentic-looking repro diningchairs, upholstered with authentic fabrics.

Also at: Seechem Manor, off Rowney Green Lane, Alvechurch, Worcs B48 7EL. (*Close to M42*). *Tel*: 021 445 2240. *Open*: Mon Wed Fri Sat 9am to 5.30pm. Please write/ring for appointment. Well-restored medieval hall house with 17th/18th-century adaptions. Period interiors by Stuart Interiors. Handmade furniture, antiques, fabrics, lighting. Tapestries, pottery, treen, brass, tiles.

3/ART GALLERIES

London's art galleries rival the museums in the beauty of their exhibits. Explore the cluster of galleries around Cork Street, W1. Below are just a few galleries of special interest for furnishing.

London Postal Districts

Avril Noble 2 Southampton Street, Strand, Covent Garden WC2E 7HA. (*5 mins Covent Garden tube*). *Tel*: 01-240 1970. *Open*: Mon to Sat 10am to 6pm. Antique maps/prints from all over, arranged by counties for Britain, by country for overseas. Help for first-time buyers, expertise for collectors.

Birch & Conran 40 Dean Street, Soho W1V 5AP. (*5 mins Piccadilly Circus tube*). *Tel*: 01-434 1246. *Open*: Mon to Fri 11am to 6pm. Sat by appointment. Contemporary avant-garde British art by emerging young artists.

Joanna Booth 247 King's Road, SW3. (*10 mins Sloane Square tube*). *Tel*: 01-352 8998. *Open*: Mon to Sat 10am to 6pm. Old master drawings. French antiquarian books in fine leather bindings. Antique silk ribbons/bows for suspending pictures. Cushions from early tapestries, silks trimmed with antique fringes/braid. Tapestries and textiles. 16th- and 17th-century woodcarvings, furniture.

Galerie Moderne 10 Halkin Arcade, Motcomb Street, SW1. (*5 mins Knightsbridge tube*). *Tel*: 01-245 6907. *Open*: Mon to Fri 10am to 6pm. Sat by appointment. Decorative arts 1890-1940. Specialises in beautiful art deco shapes of René Lalique (French, d.1945).

Hurlingham Gallery 297 New King's Road, SW6. (*5 mins Parsons Green tube*). *Tel*: 01-736 6911. *Open*: Mon to Fri 10am to 7.30pm. Sat 10am to 6.30pm. Contemporary artists, wide price range. Landscapes, city scenes. Picture restoration. Framing.

Incisioni Stands B006/7/8, Alfies Antique Market, 13/25 Church Street, NW8 8DT. (*5 mins Marylebone BR*). *Tel*: 01-706 2970. *Open*: Tues to Sat 10am to 6pm. Designs for interior and exterior decorative schemes depicted in prints, lithographs, watercolours. Original, unique: reasonable prices.

London Contemporary Art 132 Lots Road, Chelsea SW10 0RJ. *Tel*: 01-352 7694. *Open*: Mon to Fri 10am to 6pm. Sat 9am to 1pm. Publishers' original prints.Etchings/silkscreens/lithographs/monotypes.

Pigeonhole Gallery 13 Langton Street, SW10 0JL. *Tel*: 01-352 2677. *Open*: Mon to Fri 10am to 6pm. Closed 1 to 2pm. (Appointments preferred). Quality prints of famous historical artwork – architecturals by Piranesi, for example, and the great botanical engravings of Redouté Decorative mounting, framing. 90-page colour brochure, £5.

Porcelain & Pictures The Studio, Gastein Road, Fulham W6 8LT. (*10 mins Hammersmith tube*). *Tel*: 01-385 7512. *Open*: Mon to Sat 9.30am to 5.30pm. Reasonably-priced fine art. Watercolours, small oils, limited edition and reproduction prints, handcoloured engravings. High-quality picture framing. Porcelain restorations in own workshop.

Zella 9 2 Park Walk, Fulham Road, SW10 0AD. (*10 mins Sloane Square tube*). *Tel*: 01-351 0588. *Open*: 7 days 10am to 9pm. Large selections limited edition prints, etchings, lithographs. Framing. Pictures on approval.

4/CRAFT CENTRES & WORKSHOPS

All craft centres are **Worth a trip**: *you can visit several craftworkers under one roof, and explore shops, café/restaurants, children's amusements and so on. Many centres are in attractive old buildings, and beautiful countryside with nearby stately homes/castles often thrown in for good measure.*

London Postal Districts

Kingsgate Workshops 110/116 Kingsgate Road, NW6 2JG. (*5 mins West Hampstead tube*). *Tel*: 01-328 7878. *Open*: by appointment. 50 artists/craftsmen & women. Ceramics, sculpture, painting, stained glass, textiles, furniture, all under one roof.

The South Bank Craft Centre Hungerford Arches, Royal Festival Hall, SE1 8XX. (*5 mins Waterloo tube*). *Tel*: 01-928 0681. *Open*: Tues to Sun 12 noon to 8pm. Designer/craftsmen occupy 20 studio spaces, for metals, ceramics, glass etc. Shop stocks variety original craft work.

Home Counties/S.East

Viables Craft Centre Harrow Way, Basingstoke, Hants RG22 4BJ. (*M3 Junction 6; 20 mins Basingstoke BR*). *Tel*: 0256 473634. *Open*: Tues to Fri 1pm to 4pm. Sat & Sun 2 to 5pm. Old farm buildings. Framing, crackermaking, spinning, ceramic restorations, glassmaking, bronze casting/restoration, American patchwork, glass/metal engraving.

The Digswell Arts Trust Attimore Hall Barn Studios, The Ridgeway, Welwyn Garden City AL7 2AD. (*Between Shamrock Club and Attimore Hall pub*). *Tel*: 0707 334848. *Open*: 10am to 5pm every day. But telephone first. Weaver/designer, etcher/printmaker, painter/papermaker, sculptor (stone furnishings for garden and home), wood-turner, ceramicist.

Langston Priory Workshops Kingham, Oxon 0X7 6OP. (*Between Stow*

& *Chipping Norton on B4450*). *Tel*: 060871 645. *Open*: by appointment. Specialist paint finishes, stained glass and leaded lights (including repairs and terrariums). Wood-turning and carving, Cotswold chair making. Antiques, photograph restoration; picture framing. Built-in furniture commissions. Interesting shop.

Worth a Trip

The Cirencester Workshop Brewery Court, Cirencester, Glos. *Tel*: 0285 61566. *Open*: Mon to Sat 10am to 5.30pm (phone first). Contemporary arts/crafts centre in converted Victorian brewery (20 designer/makers). Gallery holds 8 shows a year; shop shows exciting new work selected by the Crafts Council. Coffee House/wholefood. Tuition/workshops.

Wroxham Barns Tunstead Road, Hoveton, Norwich NR12 8QU. *Tel*: 06053 3762. *Open*: every day April to Dec 10am to 6pm; Jan to March 10am to 5pm. China restorer, bookbinder, wood-turner, lace and quilt maker, and stained glass artists. Also dolls' houses and miniatures. Shop, tearooms, adventure playground in 10 acres of Norfolk parkland.

5/CRAFTS SHOPS & GALLERIES

The lure of the handmade is potent: for a modest sum, you own/use an artefact that is truly unique. Makers are currently very sensitive about the word "craft". Many feel that association with corn dollies and baskets detracts from the creative worth of individually-designed and made modern artefacts. Be that as it may. Some serious entrepreneurs now call their premises galleries rather than shops. And their wares are described as "applied arts."

London Postal Districts

Al-Bizarre Gallery 9 Jerdan Place, SW6 1GE. (*2 mins Fulham Broadway tube*). *Tel*: 01-385 0278. *Open*: Mon to Sat 10.30am to 6.30pm. Ceramics, textiles, tapestry, paintings, jewellery, prints. Wide price range. Relaxed atmosphere.

Amalgam Gallery 3 Barnes High Street, Barnes SW13. (*Barnes/Barnes Bridge BR*). *Tel*: 01-878 1279. *Open*: Tues to Sat 10am to 6pm. Closed lunch 1.30 to 2.30pm. Tim Boon stocks 3 rooms with paintings/prints out front, and pots/glassware at rear: mostly functional, some one-offs. Hand-thrown mugs, small jugs. Vases, platters, storage jars, casseroles.

Contemporary Applied Arts 43 Earlham Street, WC2H 9LD. (*Corner of Neal Street; 4 mins Covent Garden tube*). *Tel*: 01-836 6993. *Open*: Mon to Sat 10am to 5.30pm. Formerly the British Crafts Centre: but now "craft" has too low an image! – they say. Glass, woodware, ceramics, textiles etc. of highest quality: prices to match.

The Craft Council Shop Victoria & Albert Museum, South Kensington SW7 2RL. (*5 mins South Kensington tube*). *Tel*: 01-589 5070. *Open*: Mon to Sat 10am to 5.30pm. Sun 2.30pm to 5.30pm. Best of modern art/crafts at steepish prices.

Crucial 204 Kensington Park Road, W11 1NR. (*3 mins Ladbroke Grove tube*). *Tel*: 01-229 4866. *Open*: Mon to Sat 10am to 6pm. Past impression of harsh steel brutish artefacts is unjust, they say. Current offers: furniture richly crafted in curvaceous aerodynamic forms by Fred Beverton. Funky rock furniture for aging rollers from cut-up motor cars. Steel sculptures by John Mills: witness a cacti-structure 8ft high with metallic appearance softened by iridescent heat marks. Baroque fabrics by Ros Mortimer are not a little macabre. Yes, but is it art? Who cares. Essential viewing. *Also at*: 34/35 Dean Street, W1. *Tel*: 01-734 4686. Changing shows featuring 2 artists at a time.

The Glasshouse 65 Long Acre, WC2E 9JH. (*5 mins Covent Garden/Holborn tubes*). *Tel*: 01-836 9785. *Open*: Mon to Fri 10am to 6pm. Sat 11am to 5pm. In front: irresistible studio glass (bowls, vases, plates) but prices reflect workmanship/investment value. Behind: engrossing sight of their hot glass workshop.

JK Hill 151 Fulham Road, SW3 6SN. (*5 mins South Kensington tube*). *Tel*: 01-584 7529. *Open*: Mon to Sat 10.30am to 6.30pm. Janet Hill has created unpretentious yet professional shop for British studio ceramics. 150 potters (handbuilt or thrown) fill racks for easy browsing. Functional mugs, jugs, tableware, casseroles etc plus decorative pieces. *Mail order*.

Leigh Gallery 17 Leigh Street, WC1. (*5 mins Russell Square tube*). *Tel*: 01-242 5177. Pottery/glass by new/established artists; resident potter is Masutaro Murata.

Naturally British 13 New Row, Covent Garden WC2N 4LF. (*5 mins Covent Garden/Leicester Square tube*). *Tel*: 01-240 0551. *Open*: Mon to Sat 10.30am to 6.15pm. Ecologically sound bird tables and feeders – and bat boxes (nesting facilities for an endangered species)! The endearing theme here is handmade goods from the past to the present, but all made entirely in Great Britain. Stock ranges from antique furniture in pine/yew/oak/fruitwood to traditional clothes/Arran sweaters. Lots of small gift ideas: wooden spoons, egg cosies, firescreens, ceramic house name plaques, pin cushions and so on. Allow time for a good browse.

North Street Potters 24 North Street, SW4 0HB. (*7 mins Clapham Common tube*). *Tel*: 01-622 0681. *Open*: Tues to Sat 11am to 6.30pm. Women potters' workshop. Robust stoneware/tableware. Unusual shapes Colourful glazes. Reasonable prices.

Studio 18 80 Sumner Road, Peckham SE15. (*10 mins Peckham Rye BR; park outside*). *Tel*: 01-708 0864. *Open*: by appointment. Ceramic workshop welcomes visitors; artists sell direct. Philip Vian: vases and bowls in fantasy shapes, marvellous colours. Rob Turner: floral and marbled bone china tableware.

Westside Gallery 317 Upper Richmond Road West, East Sheen SW14 8QR. (*South Circular*). *Tel*: 01-878 6209. *Open*: Mon to Sat 9.30am to 5.30pm. New gallery with paintings, etchings, prints. Glass, wood, ceramics. Coffee bar.

Outer Ring

The Gowan Gallery 3 Bell Street, Sawbridgworth, Herts CM21 9AR. (*Large free car park*). *Tel*: 0279 600004. *Open*: Tues to Sat 10am to 6pm. Contemporary arts include ceramics, glass, wood, fine art, sculpture. Precious jewellery designed/made on the premises.

Heirlooms Upstairs at Fern Cottage, 28/30 High Street, Thames Ditton, Surrey KT7 0RY. *Tel*: 01-398 2856. *Open*: Mon to Sat 9.30am to 5.30pm. Glass, pottery, handpainted silk, collage, embroideries, cards.

The Old Bull Arts Centre 68 High Street, Barnet, Herts EN5 5SJ. (*High Barnet tube*). *Tel*: 01-449 0048. *Open*: Mon to Sat 9.30am to 5.30pm. Contemporary witty modern ceramics include tableware by Repeat Repeat, and splendid vases by Philip Vian. Jewellery, glass, toys, cards, prints.

Trading Place Art Galleries 11 New Road, Ware, Herts SG12 7BS. (*Car park opposite*). *Tel*: 0920 69620. *Open*: Fri & Sat 12.30 to 6pm. Sun 2 to 5pm. Or by appointment. Elegant/comprehensive/excellent selections British arts/crafts over 3 floors. Paintings/sculptures. One-off ceramics, tapestries, turned/carved wood.

Home Counties/S.East

Applebees Craft Centre & Gift Shop 2/4 Crown Street, Castle Hedingham, Essex CO9 3DB. *Tel*: 0787 62172. *Open*: by appointment. Closed Mon & Wed. Wood, textiles. Handmade cards, calligraphy. Weaving/tapestry supplies.

The Ashdown Gallery 70 Newtown High Street, Uckfield, Sussex TN22 5DE. (*A22 via Croydon/East Grinstead*). *Tel*: 0825 67180. *Open* (Feb to

Dec): Tues to Sat 10am to 5pm. Converted Victorian pub. Glass, ceramics, textiles, furniture in well-lit spacious displays.

Hugo Barclay 7 East Street, Brighton, East Sussex. *Tel:* 0273 21694. *Open:* Mon to Sat 10am to 5.30pm. Closed lunch 1 to 2pm. Functional/decorative pieces, individual and original. Mostly one-offs from one-person workshops. Ceramics, glass, wood, prints.

Broughton Crafts High Street, Stockbridge. *Tel:* 0264 810513. *Open:* Mon to Sat 9.30am to 5.30pm. Closed lunch 1 to 2pm. Best British work in 2 large rooms; mix of well known makers plus newer discoveries.

Calshot Crafts Centre Badminston Farm, Calshot Road, Fawley, Hants SO4 1BB. (*Follow signs from Fawley Power Station*). *Tel:* 0703 898846. *Open:* 7 days 10am to 5pm. Resident craftworkers with shop/gallery in beautiful landscaped grounds on edge of New Forest with seaside views. Rockinghorses, blacksmith, glass blower.

The Candover Gallery 22 West Street, New Alresford, Winchester, Hants SO24 9AE. (*M3 from London Junction 6*). *Tel:* 0962 733200. *Open:* Mon to Sat 9.30am to 5.30pm. Or by appointment. 200-year-old listed building, 2 floors. Pottery, studio glass, woodware, watercolours. Commissions.

The Craft Shop Southill Park Arts Centre, Bracknell, Berks RG12 4PA. (*Bracknell BR*). *Tel:* 0344 427272. *Open:* Mon to Sat 12 noon to 4pm & 7pm to 10.30pm. Sun 12 noon to 4pm. Decorative/functional ceramics, glass, wood bowls, small prints, framed pictures. Resident jeweller and ceramicist. November 1989: new expanded premises.

The Craft Shop Lamb Arcade, High Street, Wallingford, Oxon OX10 0BS. (*Just off High Street*). *Tel:* 0492 33800. *Open:* Mon to Fri 9.30am to 5.30pm. Sat 9.30am to 5.30pm. Wed 10am to 4pm. Anne Brooker stocks her shop in a converted Georgian Hotel with

varied selection British crafts. In same building: 15 antique shops, wine bar, coffee shop: a pleasant day out.

The Craftsman Gallery 8 High Street, Ditchling, East Sussex BN6 8TA. *Tel:* 07918 5246. *Open:* Mon to Sat 10am to 5pm. Closed lunch 1 to 2pm. Early closing Wed 1pm. Pottery workshop for thrown earthenware by Jill Pryke, including anniversary plates and named mugs. Other Sussex crafts: batik, copperware, wallhangings, weaving, wood.

Fenny Lodge Gallery Simpson Road, Fenny Stratford, Bletchley, Milton Keynes MK1 1BD. (*M1, Junction 13; Bletchley BR: taxi. Or come by canal from Little Venice, moor outside!*). *Tel:* 0908 642207. *Open:* Mon to Fri 9am to 5pm. Sat 9am to 4pm. Decorative/functional pottery, glass, patchwork, lamps, woodware. Wallhangings, rugs. etc.

Hitchcock's (formerly **Country Fare**) 11 East Street, New Alresford, Hants. (*East of Winchester*). *Tel:* 096 273 4762. *Open:* Mon to Sat 9.30am to 5pm. Closed lunch 1 to 2pm. British craftwork in glass, ceramics, treen, wooden toys, jewellery. Hand-painted/printed silks. Collectors' dolls house furniture.

Lannards Gallery Okehurst Lane, Billinghurst, W Sussex. (*1 hour from London; off A29, 25 mins from M25*). *Tel:* 040381 2692. *Open:* Wed to Sun 11am to 5pm. Octagonal pine-built country gallery. Sculpture, ceramics, glass. Paintings. Pottery Workshop; individual handthrown pieces. Licensed restaurant, afternoon teas. Jolly day out.

The Laurimore Gallery The Mews, 29 Swan Street, Boxford, Suffolk CO6 5NZ. (*M25, A12, A134, A1071 from London*). *Open:* by appointment. Victorian stables, coach house and kitchens now display ceramics, woodware, textiles, glass, calligraphy, and furniture, with many special exhibitions. Commissions.

The Minories 74 High Street, Colchester, Essex CO1 1UE. (*Opposite

castle, next to multi-storey car park*). *Tel:* 0206 577067. *Open:* Tues to Sat 10.30am to 5pm. Sun 2 to 6pm. New shop for design/craft work. Ceramics, wood, toys, knives.

Nexus 14 Broad Street, Brighton, Sussex BN2 1TJ. *Tel:* 0273 684480. *Open:* Tues to Sat 11am to 6pm. A Georgian window fronts Bebbe Klatt's uncluttered displays of original crafts; around half is from local workshops. Monthly exhibitions. Raku ceramics; hand-sponged bone china. Saltglazed jugs, turned wood boxes. Scent bottles, vases, wooden toys/games.

Terrace Gallery 7 Liverpool Terrace, Worthing, West Sussex BN11 1TA. (*50yds Montague Centre; 8 mins Worthing BR*). *Tel:* 0903 212926. *Open:* Tues to Fri 10.30am to 4.30pm. Sat 10.30am to 1pm. Closed Mon, Aug & Jan. Paintings, etchings, ceramics, studio glass, turned and carved wood, sculpture, textiles. Commissions.

Worth a Trip

Collection Gallery 13 The Southend, Ledbury, Hereford HR8 2EY. (*M4, M5, M50; or M4 and Severn Bridge*). *Tel:* 0531 4631. *Open:* Mon to Fri 9am to 5.30pm. Closed lunch 1 to 1.45pm. Longish drive from London but pretty gallery in half-timbered building is worth seeing. Refurbished with white-washed walls, mellow original flooring, unobtrusive hi-tech lighting. Glass, blown/etched. Carved/turned wood. Baskets, framed prints. Clocks, brass desk accessories. Saltglaze ceramics, handthrown pottery. Next door, The Shell House Gallery offers fine art, limited editions, and signed prints, plus bespoke framing service.

The Connoisseur Art Gallery 2 Victoria Street, Bourton-on-the-Water, Cotswolds, Cheltenham, Glos GL54 2BU. (*Near the Perfumery*). *Tel:* 0451 20154. *Open:* 7 days 10am to 6pm. Studio glass/ceramics. Pottery, sculpture, woodturning, textiles. Books, cards, prints, posters.

Yew Tree Gallery Green Lane, Little Witcombe, Gloucester. *Tel:* 0452

863516. *Open*: by appointment. Tapestries, rugs, paintings. Ceramics, metal/mosaic mirrors. Brochure/map.

6/DESIGNER CERAMICS

Halina Bayfield Ceramics 54 Ashwell St, Leighton Buzzard, Beds LU7 7BG. *Tel*: 0525 377996. *Open*: by appointment. Hand thrown ceramics, vividly decorated with bright fish, flora, fruit and abstract pattern. Cups and bowls, plates, platters. Slip-stencilled plates in sets. Commissions. One-off jugs, urns, vases.

Rachel Clark 25 Limehouse Cut, Colmans Court, Morris Road, London E14 6NQ. *Tel*: 01-987 8776. *Open*: by appointment. Platters, bowls and vases combine the functional and decorative.

Isobel Dennis Clockwork Studios 38 Southwell Road, SE5 9PG. *Tel*: 01-326 1880. *Open*: by appointment. Ceramic bowls.

Sheila Dobson Decorative Ceramics Priors Hatch Cottage, Priors Hatch Lane, Godalming, Surrey GU7 2RJ. *Tel*: 0483 810786. *Open*: by appointment. Decorative plates/bowls of individual design. Commissions.

John Dunn Beach Ceramics 168 The Arches, King's Road, Brighton, East Sussex BN1 1NB. *Tel*: 0273 725013. *Open*: by appointment. Large raku dishes.

Jill Fanshawe Kato 58 Beechfield Road, N4 1PE. *Tel*: 01-800 7101. *Open*: by appointment. Decorated stoneware.

Margaret Forde Pot Workshop Collins Street, Blackheath Village SE3 0BY. *Tel*: 01-852 4133 Studio, 01-858 5875 Home. *Open*: by appointment. Richly painted surfaces and fine line drawings for ceramics.

Robert Goldsmith Lower Neatham Mill, Holybourne, Alton, Hants GU34 4ET. *Tel*: 0420 87597. *Open*: by appointment.

Belen Gomez 41B Lyndhurst Grove, Peckham SE15 5AN. *Tel*: 01-708 3448. *Open*: by appointment. Painted ceramics.

Mary Knowland College Farm Little Minster, Minster Lovell, Oxford OX8 5RS. *Tel*: 0993 775480. *Open*: by appointment. The porcelain pieces/domestic pots decorated with sponged colours or stencilled white designs through black glaze. All work is once-fired.

Mike Levy The Illustrated Potter, 26 Camden Lock Place, Chalk Farm Road, NW1 8AF. *Tel*: 01-485 5116. *Open*: by appointment. Decorated domestic slipware.

Loudware 14c St Charles Square, W10 6EE. *Tel*: 01-969 5756. *Open*: by appointment. Painted ceramics.

Sophie MacCarthy 77A Lauriston Road, E9 7HA. *Tel*: 01-986 9585. *Open*: by appointment. Slip-painted earthenware.

Michaelson & Orient 318 Portobello Road, W10 5RU. (*5 mins Ladbroke Grove tube*). *Tel*: 01-969 4119. *Open*: Tues to Sat 10.30am to 5.30pm. Or by appointment. Maureen and Anatol are ardent pioneers for art status for the finest of British ceramics. They believe the work they stock should be considered on the same level sculpture. In addition to ceramics from established artists, they comb Degree shows to present the best of fresh-from-art-school talent.

Sue Mundy Ceramics 53 Anderson Ave, Earley, Reading, Berks RG6 1HD. *Tel*: 0734 65063. *Open*: by appointment. One-off sculptural vessels made by handbuilding techniques in stoneware.

Jane Staniland 401½ Workshops. See **4/Craft Centres & Workshops** above. Decorated ceramics.

Idonia Van Der Bijl 122 Columbia Road, E2. *Tel*: 01-387 0741 Studio, 01-729 7996 Shop. *Open*: Sun 8am to 2pm. From one-off to short run handmade ceramics, in Columbia Road's Flower Market.

Sarah Walton Keepers Selmeston, Polegate, East Sussex BN26 6UH. *Tel*: 0321 83517. *Open*: by appointment. Salt-glazed ceramics.

7/DESIGNER GLASS

Jonathan Andersson 23 Bow Street, Alton, Hants GU34 1NY. *Tel*: 0420 87155. *Open*: by appointment. Blown glass with electro-formed metals.

Sarah Broadhead 69 Riverdale, Wrecclesham, Farnham, Surrey GU10 4PJ. *Tel*: 0252 724395. *Open*: by appointment. Kiln-formed glass.

Michael Carman 41 Windmill Road, Brentford, Middx. *Tel*: 01-568 2543. *Open*: by appointment. Kiln-formed glass. Abstract designs with metal inclusions sandwiched between layers of glass, with fine glass rods and chips.

Chris Comins 19 Cedar Way, Camley Street, NW1 0PD. *Tel*: 01-388 9144. *Open*: by appointment. Blown glass.

Corrine Edwards 7 Portobello Green, 281 Portobello Road, London W10 5TZ. *Tel*: 01-969 8370. *Open*: by appointment. Hand applied designs in abstract patterns/textures using various processes: acid etching, enamels, transfers. Vases, bowls, plates, drinking glasses. Etched glass, tabletops, screens, windows, shelves. Shop/showroom with glassware, ceramics, papier mâché vases.

Fladgate Glass Studio Manor Farm Centre, Seale, Farnham, Surrey. (*Just off A31*). *Tel*: 02518 2101. *Open*: Tues to Sat 12 noon to 5pm. Sun 2 to 5pm. Ring first during winter. Studio glass: watch glassmaking take place.

Gail Gill 49 Arnold Road, N15 4JF. (*Bruce Grove BR*). *Tel*: 01-388 9144/01-808 2918. *Open*: by appointment. Glass-blowing commissions. Perfume bottles, vases, sculptures.

London Glassblowing Workshop 109 Rotherhithe Street, SE16 4NF. (5 mins *Rotherhithe* tube). *Tel*: 01-237 0394. *Open*: Mon to Fri 11am to 6pm. Sat and Sun by appointment. The London Glassblowing Workshop was established in 1976 by Peter Layton. It is housed in a refurbished shipwright's shed overlooking the River Thames, with a gallery/shop in adjacent building. Peter and fellow artists Carin von Drehle and Karen Lawrence free-blow innovative shapes in sumptuous colours and finishes. Each has an individual style. Bowls, vases, sculptures, ornaments. Decorative techniques include sand blasting, electro-forming and acid etching.

Anthony Stern 205 Avro House, Havelock Terrace, SW8 4AL. *Tel*: 01-622 9463. *Open*: by appointment. Studio glass.

8/MODERN METALWORK

Heather Burrell The Steel Studio, 206B Bedford Hill, Balham SW12 9HJ. *Tel*: 01-673 5492. *Open*: by appointment. Individual interior accessories in handcrafted steel. Tables, mirror frames, candlesticks, candelabras.

Paul Jobst 28 Tower Street, Alton, Hants GU34 1NV. *Tel*: 0420 87432. *Open*: by appointment. Unique ironwork using traditional blacksmithing skills combining other materials: paper/textiles/non ferrous metals. For special interiors.

Metal Art 151 Deptford Market, Deptford SE8. *Tel*: 01-469 2729. *Open*: by appointment. Kevin Boys deploys matt black finished steel into wandering curvaceous forms reminiscent of a Gaudi facade. Furniture, gates, grilles, candelabra.

Charles Normandale Wheely Down Forge, Warnford, near Winchester SO3 1LG. *Tel*: 073 086 300. Designer blacksmith for contemporary/modern architectural ironwork to commission.

Toby Russell 1 Arlington Cottage, Sutton Lane, W4 4HB. *Tel*: 01-995 0064. Working pewter into innovative sculptured configurations. Toby Russell creates candleholders, vases, twisted cups, boxes and dishes.

9/WOOD, PAPER & BASKETS

Julie Arkell 501 Hornsey Road, N19 3QH. *Tel*: 01-272 3709. *Open*: by appointment. Papier mâché vases, sculpture.

John Galloway 72 Vicars Hill, Ladywell, SE13 7JL. *Tel*: 01-690 3925. *Open*: by appointment. Individual dyed willow baskets using traditional techniques, for subtle or bold shapes.

Bert Marsh 43 Wolverstone Drive, Brighton, Sussex BN1 7FB. *Tel*: 0273 554587. *Open*: by appointment. Turned wooden vessels.

Paul Nicholls The Old Barn, Holwell, Burford, Oxfordshire OX8 4JS. *Tel*: 0993 822116. *Open*: by appointment. Decorated wooden clocks, boxes and toys.

Rod Wales Longbarn Workshop, Muddles Green, Chiddingly, East Sussex BN8 6HJ. *Tel*: 0825 872764. *Open*: by appointment. Desk accessories/furniture.

Louis Walpole 100 Fairfoot Road, E3 4EH. *Tel*: 01-515 6014. *Open*: by appointment. Baskets.

Ellie Yannas 36 Westbridge Road, SW11 3PW. *Tel*: 01-223 2422. *Open*: by appointment. Painted boxes and dolls' houses.

ETHNIC

From all over the world, decorative and/or functional goods pour into London. Why struggle with heavy baggage when you can buy ethnic souvenirs (and more) on your doorstep? Inspect current garnerings at addresses below.

London Postal Districts

Casa Catalan 15/16 Chalk Farm Road, NW1. (*10 mins Camden Town/Chalk Farm tubes*). *Tel*: 01-485 3975. *Open*: 7 days 10am to 6pm. Casa means home in Spanish, and decorative accessories which spill from this pretty shop onto pavement are imported from Spain/Portugal. Add a sunny Mediterranean touch to conservatories/patios with plain or fancy handmade terracotta vases, jardinières, pots/urns.

Casa Fina See **Accessories 10/General.** For a touch of Southern sun, dress your home with ornate Spanish ceramics in the prettiest of pastels.

Casa Pupo 56/60 Pimlico Road, SW1W 8LR. (*10 mins Sloane Square tube*). *Tel*: 01-730 7111. *Open*: Mon to Sat 9.30am to 6pm. Extensive rather rambling premises for the shop that first introduced Londoners to Mediterranean accessories over 20 years ago. Stock includes huge selections of Italian ceramics. Ornate lampbases, tableware. Display columns, picture frames, plant pots, ornaments in shiny glazes from white/pastels to vivid lime/fuschia/cobalt/lemon. Decorative wicker/cane furniture in white/pastels.

Coconut 7 Adelaide Road, Chalk Farm NW3 3QE. (*Opposite Chalk Farm tube*). *Tel*: 01-483 2060. *Open*:

Tues to Sun 11am to 7pm. Exclusive handmade furnishings from India/Bangladesh. Cotton, silk, wool dhurries in subtle pastels; exquisite raw silk quilted bedspreads/matching silk cushion covers; paintings/rosewood statues. Bedspreads, curtains, tablecloths, cushion covers in natural undyed handwoven cotton.

Eastern Accents 111 Walton Street, SW3 2HP. (*5 mins South Kensington tube*). *Tel*: 01-581 3702. *Open*: Mon to Sat 10.30am to 6pm. Painted furniture, new/antique, from Korea/China. Wedding boxes/double-layer storage chests. Unusual woods. Mother-of-pearl, inlays, brass/iron fittings. Also wide range decorative accessories: porcelain, fans, screens, carved boxes etc.

Filipina Store 5 Kensington Church Walk, W8 4NB. (*4 mins Kensington High Street tube; behind St Mary Abbot's Church*). *Tel*: 01-937 8332. *Open*: Mon to Fri 11.30am to 6pm. Sat 11.30am to 4.30pm. Handcrafts from the Philippines. Embroidered tablecloths, shell photo frames, mother-of-pearl butter dishes/knives, shell place mats/trays, salad bowls.

Ganesha 6 Park Walk, Fulham Road, SW10 0AD. (*15 mins South Kensington tube*). *Tel*: 01-352 8972. *Open*: 7 days 12 noon to 7pm. Ann and Marten Timmer pack their small shop with home accessories/gifts from Indone-

sia, Thailand, Nepal. Incense, oils, wood carvings, baskets, cookware, parasols, porcelain and more.

The Greek Shop 6 Newburgh Street, W1V 1LH. (*8 mins Oxford Street tube*). *Tel*: 01-437 1197. *Open*: Mon to Fri 10.30am to 6pm. Sat 11.30am to 5pm. Memories of Grecian holidays permeate this pleasant shop. Hand-decorated boldly-coloured ceramics very reasonably priced.

Inca 45 Elizabeth Street SW1W 9PP. (*5 mins Victoria tube/BR*). *Tel*: 01-730 7941. *Open*: Mon to Fri 10am to 6pm. Sat 10am to 2pm. Largely South-American fashion sweaters, but also colourful rugs, and accessories. See also Home Counties/S.East below.

Indiaworks Dove Walk, 107A Pimlico Road, SW1W 8PH, (*12 mins Sloane Square tube*). *Tel*: 01-730 2454. *Open*: Mon to Fri 10am to 6pm. Sat 10am to 5pm. Tucked away at the end of an intriguing alley off posh Pimlico Road find a spacious ex-warehouse filled with Eastern artefacts by Robin Guild, author of *The Finishing Touch*, best book written on the art of furnishing accessories. Selections have magic touch of the assured interior designer that he is: he works over the shop. Stock changes frequently, and includes unique oriental antiques/architectural salvage. Also ornate heavily carved mirrors; chairs exquisitely inlaid with mother-of-pearl.

Plus chests and cabinets by Sawasdee Trading.

Lotus and Frog 32 England's Lane, NW3 4UE. *Tel*: 01-586 3931. (*5 mins Belsize Park tube*). *Open*: Mon to Fri 9.30am to 5.30pm. Sat 10.30am to 5.30pm. Rosewood and inlaid black lacquer furniture. Coramandel and silk screens. Handpainted table lamps with Thai silk shades. Antique porcelain bowls. Vases and temple jars. Stone figurines.

Andrew Martin 11 Sheen Road, Richmond, Surrey. (*10 mins Richmond tube/BR*). *Tel*: 01-940 5432. *Open*: Tues to Sat 10am to 6pm. Good quality oriental accessories include dhurries/rugs, cushions, carvings, decorative mirrors, bedspreads.

Meuble Espanol 168 Upper Richmond Road, East Sheen SW14 8AW. (*Richmond tube plus bus*). *Tel*: 01-878 7775. *Open*: Mon to Sat 9am to 5.30pm. Heavily-carved antique-style dining/living room furniture in mahogany/yew, or stunning limed pine finish.

Morning Calm 86 Wandsworth Bridge Road, SW6. (*15 mins Parsons Green tube; park in side streets*). *Tel*: 01-736 5134. Classic Korean Lee Dynasty handcrafted furniture, mahogany finish, richly decorated with carvings and brass. Brass ornaments, lampbases, vases.

Neal Street East 5 Neal Street, WC2H 9PU. (*2 mins Covent Garden tube*). *Tel*: 01-240 0135. *Open*: Mon to Sat 10am to 7pm. Christina Smith, Covent Garden suprema with shops, restaurant and gallery, trail-blazed Oriental imports into Britain. Through countless buying trips to China (from 1972 on) she has lavishly stocked this shop (recently reorganised) with fashion, jewellery, accessories; plus affordable homeware/gifts. Explore the arcane calligraphy gallery and bold basement bazaar. Traditional Oriental paintings/prints; cookware/cookbooks. Multi-purpose baskets for many storage needs. Prettiest of artificial flowers, silk/feathers. Lengths of Japanese Kasuri/tie-dye fabric. Screens, lighting, leather, lacquer chests. Ornamental toys, kites, fans, parasols, puppets. Goods also from India, Burma, Thailand, Bali, Malaya.

Nice Irma's 46 Goodge Street, W1P 1FJ. (*5 mins Goodge Street tube*). *Tel*: 01-580 6921. *Open*: Mon to Fri 10am to 6pm. Late night Thurs 7pm. Sat 10am to 5pm. Dan and Della Hirsch have tirelessly imported Indian furnishings/accessories for 15 years. In the beginning, Dan carried back rugs from remote villages on his back! Bedspreads, rugs, china, cushion covers, brassware and more, much in decorator fashion colours.

Peking Hippo 47 Palliser Road, W14. (*Adjacent Barons Court tube*). *Tel*: 01-381 4837. *Open*: Tues to Fri 10am to 6pm. Close Sat 5pm. Large stocks high-quality reasonably priced porcelain from Chinese mainland. Predominantly larger decorative items: ginger jars, vases, tureens, fish bowls. Lamp conversions (very popular). Shades available. Elephant candlesticks. Chinese dogs. Sweet boxes: hearts/circular/rectangular.

The Russian Shop 278 Hi Holborn, WC1. (*5 mins Holborn/Chancery Lane tubes*). *Tel*: 01-405 3538. *Open*: Mon to Fri 9.30am to 6pm. Nesting Matrioshka wooden dolls are international celebrities. Explore other Eastern European delights: affordable craftmanship for carved soapstone, wooden boxes, lacquerwork, trays. Catalogue. *Mail order*.

Home Counties/S.East

Perusal Wessex Place, 127 High Street, Hungerford, Berks. (*Hungerford BR*). *Tel*: 0488 84002. *Open*: Mon to Sat 9am to 5pm.
Also at: **Latin Adventures** 15 East Street, Brighton, Sussex. *Tel*: 0273 23725. *Open*: telephone first.

Orientique 40 Oak End, Gerrards Cross, Bucks SL9 8BR. *Tel*: 0753 888361. *Open*: Mon to Sat 9.30am to 5.30pm. Late night Thurs 7pm. Large shop with selections Oriental furniture/decorative arts. Coffee tables, Korean chests, Chinese lacquer, screens, ceramics, lamps, conservatory furniture.

Mail Order

Oriental Imports Concorde House, Stewart Close, Eccleshill, Bradford BD2 2EE. *Tel*: 0274 633315. Colour leaflet. Richly exotic storage chests individually carved with Chinese designs. Some have camphor wood linings, others are inlaid with mother-of-pearl. Originally used as "bottom drawers" by Chinese brides. Personal callers welcome at warehouse.

Worth a Trip

Alain Rouveure Crossing Cottage Galleries, Todenham, near Moreton-in-Marsh, Gloucestershire GL56 9NU. *Tel*: 0608 50418. *Open*: Fri Sat 11am to 5.30pm. Sundays/other times by appointment. Rare Tibetan rugs and Himalayan folk art brought back by gallery owner.

ACCESSORIES

Accessories set the seal on a room, stamping it with your own personality. They are a marvellous corrective measure, adding touches of colour to bland schemes, and even concealing mistakes.

1/POSTERS & PRINTS

Prints are "real art" at a price you can afford. Inexpensive and colourful, use posters with panache.

London Postal Districts

The Antique Print Gallery 197 New King's Road, Fulham SW6 4SR. (*3 mins Parsons Green tube*). *Tel*: 01-731 7378. *Open*: Mon to Fri 9.30am to 5.30pm. Sat 10am to 1pm. Framed prints, reasonable prices. Mounts, framing 4/5 days.

Artbeat 703 Fulham Road, SW6 5UL. (*5 mins Parsons Green tube*). *Tel*: 01-736 0337. *Open*: Mon to Sat 10am to 6pm. Small shop crammed with unusual prints/posters plus frames. Framing service on premises.

Robert Douma 4 Henrietta Street, WC2. (*5 mins Covent Garden tube*). *Tel*: 01-836 0771. *Open*: Mon to Fri 10am to 6pm. Sat 10am to 5pm. Antique prints/charts/maps from all over the world.

Hugh Evelyn 357 New King's Road, Fulham SW6 4RJ. (*5 mins Parsons Green tube*). *Tel*: 01-731 6775. *Open*: Tues to Fri l0am to 6pm. Sat l0am to lpm. Or by appointment. Old prints, drawings, watercolours. Friendly atmosphere. Specialist framers: some

antique frames. Watercolour conservation; frame restoration. Valuations.

Flashbacks 6 Silver Place W1R 3LJ. (*5 mins Piccadilly Circus tube*). *Tel*: 01-437 8562. *Open*: Mon to Sat 10am to 7pm. Specialists in movie posters old and new.

Grosvenor Prints 28/32 Shelton Street, WC2. (*3 mins Covent Garden tube*). *Tel*: 01-836 1979. *Open*: Mon to Fri 10am to 6pm. Sat 10am to 1pm. Antiquarian prints, many several centuries old: dogs, portraits, maps, architecturals.

The Picture Man 184 Chiswick High Road, Chiswick W4 1RP. (*2 mins Turnham Green tube*). *Tel*: 01-995 6359. *Open*: Mon, Tues, Fri 9.30am to 5.30pm. Wed 9.30am to 7.30pm. Thurs 10am to 5.30pm. Sat 9.30am to 6pm. Limited edition prints/posters. Fine art cards. Framing, plus frame and picture restoration.

Picture World 220 Kilburn High Road, Kilburn NW6 4LJ. (*5 mins Kilburn tube; 2nd floor, above Crest Dry Cleaners*). *Tel*: 01-328 2787. *Open*: Mon to Sat 10am to 6pm. Prints at reasonable prices framed to order. Posters, fine art. Personal, friendly framing service for tapestries, oil paintings, mirrors, photos etc. Heatsealing, dry-mounting, decorated mounts. Phone for quote, collections, deliveries.

Pigeonhole Gallery 13 Langton Street, SW10 0JL. *Tel*: 01-352 2677. *Open*: Mon to Fri 10am to 6pm. Closed lunch 1 to 2pm. Appointments preferred. Reproductions of great botanical engravings of 18th/19th centuries by Redoute, Ehret, Thornton and others. Also full-sized Audubon "Brids of America" and birds by Lear and Gould. New portfolio of architecturals, by Piranesi and others. 90-page colour catalogue of complete range, £5. Decorative mounting/framing specialists, supplying prestigious interior designers.

The Postcard Gallery 56 Earlham Street, Covent Garden WC2H 9LA. (*3 mins Covent Garden tube, adjacent to Smiths' Galleries*). *Tel*: 01-379 4886. *Open*: Mon to Sat 11am to 6pm. Over 3,000 fine art cards from early Renaissance, through impressionism, cubism and surrealism to pop and contemporary. From publishers and museums all over.

The Poster Shop 1 Chalk Farm Road, Camden NW1. (*2 mins Chalk Farm tube*). *Tel*: 01-267 6985. *Open*: Mon to Fri 10am to 6pm. Sat & Sun 10.30am to 6.30pm. Instant take-away art. Over 1800 images from all over world; top 350 ready-framed. Rest framed 2 weeks maximum. Art/photographic reproductions. Advertising. Full colour catalogue, £4.95 plus £2.20 p&p. *Mail order*: *Tel*: 01-267 6985 *Also at*: 168 Fulham Road, Chelsea

SW10. (*7 mins South Kensington tube*). *Tel*: 01-373 7294. *Open*: Mon & Tues 10am to 6pm. Wed to Fri 10am to 7.30pm. Sat 10.30am to 6.30pm.
And at: 28 James Street, Covent Garden WC2. (*3 mins Covent Garden tube*). *Tel*: 01-240 2526. *Open*: Mon to Sat 10am to 6pm.
And at: 34 Great Marlborough Street, W1. (*5 mins Oxford Circus tube*). *Tel*: 01-434 0248. *Open*: Mon, Tues & Sat 10am to 6pm. Wed to Fri 10am to 7pm.
And at: 109 King's Road, Chelsea SW3. (*8 mins Sloane Square tube*). *Tel*: 01-376 5569. *Open*: Mon & Tues 10am to 6pm. Wed to Fri 10am to 7pm. Sat 10.30am to 7pm.

M R Sketches 303 Munster Road, Fulham SW6 7PR. (*10 mins Fulham Broadway tube*). *Tel*: 01-386 8975. *Open*: Mon to Sat 9.30am to 5.30pm. Closed Thurs. Traditional prints, exquisite mirrors, modern posters, prints. Frames: brass and silver, clips. Framed old prints of Fulham. Personal service. In-home framing advice service free for order of more than 10 pictures. Mount decorating, dry mounting, heat sealing. Oil stretching and restoration, gold stippling, marbling.

The Studio 1b Gastein Road, Fulham W6 8LT. (*10 mins Hammersmith tube*). *Tel*: 01-383 7512, *Open*: Mon to Sat 10am to 5pm. Limited edition prints, watercolours, oils, reproductions, ready-framed. Framing; hand-cut mounts: marbled, or with wash-lines. Porcelain restoration.

The Tate Gallery Shop Millbank, SW1P 4RG. (*5 mins Pimlico tube*). *Tel*: 01-821 5001. *Open*: Mon to Sat 10am to 5.30pm. Sun 2pm to 5.30pm. Marvellous selections of old master prints: impressionists, modern favourites. Allow plenty of time for browsing.

2/FRAMES

No picture is complete without a frame, but choosing the right one can be tricky. Shops listed can cope.

London Postal Districts

Fellowes & Saunderson 116 Blythe Road, Brook Green W14 OUH. (*Behind Olympia*). *Tel*: 01-603 7475/0577. *Open*: Tues to Fri 10am to 6pm. Sat 10am to 4pm. High-class bespoke framing. Unique frames/mounts. Handfinished frames: painted, stained, gilded. Picture restoration for oils, paper, frames. Prints, framed/unframed. Reliable, friendly expert service.

Fix-a-Frame 280 Old Brompton Road, SW5. (*10 mins Earls Court tube*). *Tel*: 01-370 4189. *Open*: Tues to Fri 11.30am to 8pm. Make instant frames, guided by experts. All materials plus help with mitres and mounts. Phone for session times. Last orders for DIY 1 hour before shop closes.
Also at: 47 Fairfax Road, NW6 4EL. (*Swiss Cottage/Finchley Road tubes*). *Tel*: 01-624 9026. *Open*: Tues to Sat 10am to 6.30pm.

Frame Express 1 Queens Road, Wimbledon SW19 8NG. *Tel*: 01-879 3366. *Open* (all branches): Mon to Sat 9am to 6pm. Speedy framing, while you wait. Good choice frames/mounts, trad. or mod. Clear sample displays with prices. Clip and photo frames, cards, posters.
Also at: 81 Baker Street, W1. *Tel*: 01-935 7794.
And at: 172 Queensway, Bayswater W2. *Tel*: 01-243 0219.
And at: 82 Charing Cross Road, WC2. *Tel*: 01-836 2948.
And at: 137 Strand, WC2. *Tel*: 01-497 2607.
And at: 266 Kensington High Street, W8. *Tel*: 01-602 2277.
And at: 111 Old Brompton Road, South Kensington SW7. *Tel*: 01-589 7635.
And at: 376 King's Road, Chelsea SW3. *Tel*: 01-351 5975.
And at: 658 Fulham Road, SW6. *Tel*: 01-731 2394.
And at: 1 Queens Road, Wimbledon, SW19. *Tel*: 01-947 7838.
And at: 845 High Road, North Finchley, N12. *Tel*: 01-445 2477.

Green & Stone 259 King's Road, Chelsea SW3 5EL. (*Sloane Square tube plus bus*). *Tel*: 01-352 0837. *Open*: Mon to Fri 9am to 5.30pm. Sat 9.30am to 6pm. Picture framing/restoration. Restoration materials for china, paper, paintings. Watercolour gallery. Antique writing materials: eg fountain pens. Hand-marbled books, boxes, albums, lampshades. Decorative paint finishes: glazes, brushes, stencils, books. Catalogue.

Harris Fine Art 712 High Road, North Finchley N12 9QD. (*10 mins Woodside Park*). *Tel*:01-445 2804/446 5579. *Open*: Mon to Sat 9am to 5.30pm. Thousands ready-made picture frames in stock. Or framing to order. Artists'/graphic materials. Prints gallery.

Ikea See **Furnishing Stores**. Remarkably wide selection instant frames, most supplied with squared mount; buy their cheap passe-partout knife and cut to size. Glass/clips; silver aluminium; white/black epoxy-lacquered metal frame, synthetic glass (good for posting); black plastic oval fres with glass. Also sophisticated strip picture lighting.

The Picture Factory 44/48 Birkbeck Road, North Finchley N12 8DZ. *Tel*: 01-446 3164. *Open*: Mon to Sat 9am to 6pm. Sunday 10am to 2pm. Not much like a factory. Converted stables with cobbled yard and ivy up walls. Established over 25 years. Skilled craftsmen; over 500 wood/metal mouldings. Speciality: rag-rolling, staining, gilding. Tapestries/embroideries stretched/framed. Ready-made frames. Picture restoration (to museum standards) for oils, watercolours, prints.

Outer Ring

Frame Express 12 High Street, Epsom. *Tel*: 03727 45861.
Also at: Griffin Centre, Market Place, Kingston. *Tel*: 01-549 8915.
And at: 224 High Street, Bromley. *Tel*: 01-466 5955.
And at: 44 High Street, Croydon. *Tel*: 01-681 3168.
See London Postal Districts above.

Masterframes 857 Honeypot Lane, Stanmore, Middx HA7 1AR. *Tel*: 01-952 2664. *Open*: Mon to Fri 9am to 6pm. Closed 1pm Thurs. Sat 9am to 5pm. Bespoke framing service, own workshop. Prints, watercolours, tapestry, embroidery, mirrors, etc. Own handfinished frames/decorated mounts. Speciality: frames with your own fabrics, wallpapers. Customers journey from all over.

Home Counties/S.East

Frame Express 9 Queen Street, Maidenhead. *Tel*: 0628 21732. See London Postal Districts above.

3/MIRRORS

Mirror, mirror on the wall . . . where did you come from?

London Postal Districts

The Dormy House See **Soft Furnishings 6/Tables & Cloths.** Pine or mahogany triple dressing table mirrors or elegant freestanding full-length chevals.

Fellowes & Saunderson See **2/Frames** above. Unusual mirror frames to order: your ideas or theirs.

House of Mirrors 597 King's Road, SW6 2EL. (*5 mins Fulham Broadway tube*). *Tel*: 01-736 5885. *Open*: Mon to Sat 9am to 6pm. Genuine 19th-century mirrors; restorations.

Linda McVeigh 170 Brick Lane, E1 6RU. *Tel*: 01-375 2961. *Open*: by appointment. Burnished pewter mirrors/picture frames; exotic designs. With Matthew Collins: distinctive furniture with decorative pewter-work panels.

The Mosaic Studio 43 Vallance Road, N22. (*Alexandra Palace BR; Bounds Green tube*). *Tel*: 01-889 0190. *Open*: by appointment. Yehudit (Judy) Morrell, born in Israel, creates glittering mosaic frames around bevelled geometric mirror shapes: diamonds, octagons, rectangles, squares. Glass from a centuries old firm in Italy is cut into tiny pieces and set onto a wooden frame. Commissions to suit your ideas/colour schemes take about 2 weeks. Some designs usually in stock. Mirrors come ready to hang.

Overmantels 66 Battersea Bridge Road, SW11 3AG. (*Sloane Square/ South Kensington tubes*). *Tel*: 01-223 8151. *Open*: Mon to Sat 9.30am to 5.30pm. Mirrors for chimney breasts. Traditional Victorian/Regency styles. Triptychs (three sections) are particularly impressive. Also upholstered fender stools in calico for covering or your choice of fabric. Advise, deliver, fit.
Also at: 3 Highgate High Street, N6 5JR. (*10 mins Hampstead/Archway tubes*). *Tel*: 01-348 8362. *Open*: Mon to Sat 9.30am to 5.30pm.

SW82 Designs See **Windows 2/Stained & Decorative Glass.** Spectacular decorated mirror panels, your design or theirs.

Through the Looking Glass 563 King's Road, SW6 2EB. (*10 mins Fulham Broadway tube*). *Tel*: 01-736 7799. Open (both branches): Mon to Sat 10am to 5.30pm. Antique mirrors: varied styles, shapes, sizes.
Also at: 137 Kensington Church Street, W8 7LP. (*2 mins Notting Hill Gate tube*). *Tel*: 01-221 4026.

T R Worthington 14 Alexander St, W2. *Tel*: 01-229 1418. *Open*: by appointment. Mirror frames, designed and carved in wood, painted with gesso and gilded. A traditional method for craftsmen throughout history, more often now practised in restoration/reproduction.

4/CUSHIONS

Cushions add comfort, style, colour: you really cannot have too many.

London Postal Districts

Bargains!

Alexander Furnishings See **Soft Furnishings 1/Fabrics.** Plain/patterned cushions made from their fabric remnants sold complete with pads for prices that really hit the bottom rock.

Claridge & Co 154 Wandsworth Bridge Road, SW6 2UH. (*15 mins Fulham Broadway tube*). *Tel*: 01-384 1265. *Open*: Mon to Sat 10am to 6pm. Cushion specialist. Antique needlepoint/kelim covers. New embroidery/applique. Plus stripes, checks, frills: Indian fabrics. Covers sold separately from pads. Most 15/18in square. Also quilts, bedcovers, throws.

Graham & Green See **Accessories 10/ General** below. Wonderful cushion selections include Kashmiri intricate crewel wool work, designed in Britain by Veronica Marsh; good range sizes/ designs. Also Ikat fabrics from India: characteristic blurred designs with plain weft through shaded warp. Square cushions from old kelims. And exquisite old cotton lace square pillowcases; Dutch/German with cushions to fill. Tapestry cushion kits.

Nice Irmas See **Ethnic.** Standard cushion sizes: 18/21/36 in square, made up in virtually all their exclusive fabrics, piped/zipped, in stock. Shiny glazed chintz; subtle ikats; textured natural cottons. Intricate Kashmiri embroidered crewel work. Plus exotics: rich brocades, and zari work, whch sparkles with multi-layers colours/metallic sequins/threads.

Sussex House Material Revivals 24 Narborough Street, SW6 3AR. *Tel*: 01-731 1057. Single-sided kelim cushions made from old rugs, backed with cotton/linen. Also available: larger carpet/ floor cushions & stools.

Mail Order

Anka Fabrics See **Bedrooms 7/Headboards.** A stylish cushion-making services (any shape or size) with co-ordinating accessories which include covered waste-bins (can be fringed and tasselled) and lampshades of any shape.

5/NEEDLEPOINT & EMBROIDERY

Needlepoint is therapeutic and can be done on handmade cushion covers, chairseats, firescreens, stools and the like.

London Postal Districts

Creativity Needlecrafts 45 New Oxford Street, WC1A 1BH. (*4 mins Tottenham Court Road/Holborn tubes*). Tel: 01-240 2945. *Open*: Mon to Sat 9.30am to 6pm. Late night Thurs 7pm. Substantial needlecraft specialists, aiming to take on where Needlewoman (RIP) left off. Tapestry, knitting, embroidery, rug-making, machine-knitting, haberdashery. *Mail order*.

Ehrman 21/22 Vicarage Gate, Kensington W8 4AA. (*8 mins High Street Kensington tube*). Tel: 01-937 5077. *Open*: Mon to Fri 9.30am to 5.15pm. Sat 10.30am to 4.30pm. Wonderful designer tapestry kits for cushions, including stunning effects from the celebrated Kaffe Fassett. His original wallpapers are now available. Colour catalogue. *Mail order*.

Glorafilia The Old Mill House, The Ridgeway, NW7 4EB. (*Mill Hill/ Edgware tubes plus bus*). Tel: 01-906 0212. *Open*: Mon to Fri 10am to 5pm. Sat 10am to 4pm. Exquisite samplers, cushion covers, tapestries, footstools, chair seats, pictures. Colour catalogue £1, refundable. *Mail order*.

Pearson School of Needlepoint 25 Kildare Terrace, W2 5JT. Tel: 01-727 9696. *Open*: by appointment. Tapestry kits for cushions, samplers, stools. Tuition available.

Home Counties/S.East

The following shops stock tapestry supplies.

In Stitches, Brentwood (*Tel*: 0277 230448); **Riverside Yarns**, Winchester (*Tel*: 0962 60238); **Craft Centre & Wool Shop**, Chipping Norton (*Tel*: 0608 2412). **Dorothy Leivers**, West Malling (*Tel*: 0732 849131); **Crown Needlework**, Hungerford (*Tel*: 0488 84011); **Yarns**, Halstead (*Tel*: 0787 472400); **Barbara of Windsor** (*Tel*: 0753 854151).

Coleshill Collection The Griffin, The Broadway, Old Amersham, Bucks HP7 0HP. (*Free parking opposite*). Tel: 0494 727700. *Open*: Mon to Sat 10am to 5pm. Unusual kits for cushions, stools (including long low fender versions), fireplace screens, pictures. Making up service. Colour catalogue. *Mail order*.

Mail Order

J & J Designs 57 Lonesome Lane, Reigate, Surrey RH2 7QT. Delightful Elizabeth-style samplers.

Elisabeth Bradley Designs 1 West End, Beaumaris, Anglesea, Gwynedd. Tel: 0248 811055. Unique Victorian-style kits featuring animals and birds. Use as cushions or sew together for rug.

Limited Edition Embroidery Kits 73 Badminton Road SW12 8BL. Tel: 01-673 0156. Catalogue £2 (refundable). Tapestry kits in limited editions.

Royal School of Needlework 5 King Street, WC2E 8HN. (*4 mins Covent Garden tube*). Tel: 01-240 3186. Tapestry kits, chair seats, rugs, cushions, pictures – all ready to sew. Stretching, mounting, cushion-making. Antique textile restoration. Colour catalogue £2.25 inc p&p.

6/FLOWERS & PLANTS

No longer naff . . . fake blooms can be obvious and fun, like blue tulips, or incredibly realistic. For fresh flowers and plants straight off city street, visit specialists below, who can also help with vases, dried flowers, and flower arrangements/accessories.

London Postal Districts

The Bonsai Shop 224 Middle Lane, Hornsey N8. (*15 mins Turnpike Lane tube*). Tel: 01-340 7200. *Open*: Tues to Sat 9.30am to 6pm. In stock: hundreds of Japanese/Chinese miniature trees (bonsai), varying ages/prices. Ceramic bonsai pots, trays; books, tools, accessories. Dedicated, enthusiastic owners demonstrate wiring, re-potting, branch/root pruning. Telephone advice. Holiday minding service! Brochure.

Clifton Nurseries 5 Clifton Villas, Warwick Ave, W9 2PH. Tel: 01-289 6851.

Conservatory 29/31 Montpelier Vale, SE3. Tel: 01-318 9134.

Felton & Sons 220/224 Brompton Road, SW3. Tel: 01-589 4433.

The Flower Shop Heal's Building, 196 Tottenham Court Road, W1. Tel: 01-636 1666.

The Flowersmith 34 Shelton Street, WC2. Tel: 01-240 6688.

General Trading Company See **10/ General** below.

Homebase See **DIY Superstores**.

Marks & Spencers See **Chain Stores**.

Moyses Stevens, 6 Bruton Street, W1. Tel: 01-493 8171.

Neal Sheet Shop See **Ethnic**.

Jane Packer Floral Design 56 James Street, W1. Tel: 01-493 8171.

Joan Palmer 31 Palmer Street, SW1. Tel: 01-222 4364.

Pulbrook & Gould 181 Sloane Street, SW1. Tel: 01-235 3920/3186.

The Silk Plant Company 164 Old Brompton Road, SW5 0BA. (*5 mins Gloucester Road tube*). Tel: 01-835 1500. *Open*: Mon to Sat 10am to 6pm. Realistic silk flowers. Plants and trees on natural stems, in choice of attractive pots. Special arrangements to order.
Also at: The Chelsea Gardener, 125 Sydney Street, SW3. (*5 mins Sloane*

7 / Columns & Cabinets

Square tube). Tel: 01-376 8080. *Open*: Mon to Sun 10.30am to 6pm.

Trumps See **Furniture 6/Cane**. Artificial trees.

7/COLUMNS & CABINETS

Columns for sculptures and trailing plants are standard decorators' accessories. Show off collections safely behind glass in special cabinets.

Caligari Cabinets 120 St Thomas's Road, N4 2QW, *Tel*: 01-354 4538. *Open*: by appointment. Will Milne (settled in London from USA in 1970) makes to order one-off cabinets/shelving in sculptured forms that frequently contrast flowing organic curves with stark geometry, using materials from coloured laminates to rough-cut slate and timber.

DKM Designs 1/5 Chance Street, E1 6JT. *Tel*: 01-388 2828/739 4253. *Open*: by appointment. From a small East London factory, Dek Messecar produces the China range of beautiful bow-fronted cabinets with curved doors, elegant upright glazed panels, bun feet. MDF/hardwoods. Finishes: satin black/red. Natural mahogany with cross-banding. Red/blue/green crackle over black.

Glass Distinction See **Furniture 7/Glass & Marble**. Handsome fibreboard display columns sprayed in lacquer, speckled or satin, any colour.

Libra Interiors See **Interior Design**. Handsome square fluted columns in mdf lacquered any colour/any finish.

Tempus Stet See **2/Traditional**. Definitive collection classical columns in cast resin/various finishes. Classic urns for classic ferns as a finishing touch.

Wiltshire Woodwork See **Lighting 4/Table Lamps & Shades** Wooden Doric columns in range of heights and colours. Also marbled finish. Special colours to order.

8/RUGS

Add flair to a floor that's seen better times, or has a humdrum budget aura. Use rugs to cushion wear, add softness to hard surfaces, or even to conceal stains and other imperfections.

London Postal Districts

Caroline Bosley 13 Princess Road, Regents Park NW1 8JR (*Close London Zoo, unresticted parking*). *Tel*: 01-722 7608. *Open*: By appointment. Small showroom/office. Caroline Bosley (Persian/oriental rug "broker") has been trading over 20 years. Takes clients by appointment to bonded carpet warehouses – about 10 mins by car. Handmade new/antique rugs at reasonable prices. Excellent value/investments. Expert advice.

Casa Pupo See **Ethnic**. Classic Spanish heavy woven wool rugs, with deep fringing. Circular, oval, square, rectangles. Wonderful vivid colour combinations, or woven to order any colours.

Duval Carpet Co Duval House, 1/2 Glebe Road, E8. (*Liverpool Street tube plus bus*). *Tel*: 01-249 9635. *Open*: Mon to Fri 9.30am to 5pm. Closed Sat. Sun 9.30am to 1.30pm. Three floors packed with thousands of beguiling rugs/carpets from Persia, Pakistan, China, Turkey, Afghanistan, Romania, Russia. Three-generation family business founded in 1927 by Mr Hajioff. Friendly atmosphere: "We take the mystique out of Orientals". They buy direct in order to sell at best prices. Take rugs on approval to check out colourschemes.

Ealing Carpet Centre See **Floors 3/Carpets**. Belgian, Wilton, Chinese-style rugs at very keen prices. From doormats to full room size. Twenty on show, several hundred in stock.

Daphne Graham 1 Elystan Street, SW3 3NT. (*10 mins South Kensington tube*). *Tel*: 01-584 8724. *Open*: Mon 2pm to 6pm. Tues to Fri 10am to 6pm. Sat 10am to 1pm. Fine antique kelims, and kelim-upholstered furniture. Also exclusive floral kelim-style flat-woven rugs in floral designs, made to 19th-century designs.

Graham & Green See **Accessories 10/General** below. Antonia Graham visits Turkey annually to buy kelims in variety of sizes; "attractive usable rugs rather than collectors' pieces". Turkey/Iran/Afghanistan.

Sally Hampson 45 Charlotte Road, EC2A 3PD. *Tel*: 01-739 4988. *Open*: by appointment. Woven rugs/blankets to commission.

Kelim & Nomadic Rug Gallery 5 Shepherds Walks, Hampstead NW3. (*5 mins Hampstead tube*). *Tel*: 01-435 8972/9739. *Open*: Tues to Sat 10.30am to 5.30pm. Del Blacker hunts down kelims from antique to merely second-hand. Kelim-covered cushions. Rug repairs/restorations on premises.

The Kelim Warehouse 28a Pickets Street, SW12 8QB. (*5 mins Clapham South BR*). *Tel*: 01-675 3122. *Open*: Mon to Sat 10am to 4pm. Flat woven kelims, old/new. Variety sizes, designs, colours from Turkey, Afghanistan, Yugoslavia, Persia.

Bargains!

Nice Irmas See **Ethnic**. Top value rag rugs from 2 by 3ft upwards in brights/pastels. Also Pokhran rugs. Simple heavyweight natural shades in wool/some cotton; cover large areas at surprisingly low cost.

Orientalist 74 & 78 Highgate Road, NW5 1PB. (*3 mins Kentish Town tube*). *Tel*: 01-482 0555. *Open*: Mon to Sat 10am to 5pm. Ground floor displays, workrooms above. Oriental handmade rugs, carpets, textiles, tapestries. Expert repair of all antique rugs and textiles.

Annie Sherburne Waterside Workshops, 99 Rotherhithe Street, SE16 4NF. *Tel*: 01-237 0017. *Open*: by appointment. Rugs, felt hangings.

Surface Solutions 4 Tress House, 3/7 Stamford Street, SE1 9NT. *Tel*: 01-401

2339. *Open*: by appointment. High quality tufted rugs and wall hangings.

Something Wild See **Furniture 1/General**. Zebra-striped wool rugs to order, 4/6 weeks.

Home Counties/S.East

Lucy Clegg 42 Cross Tree Road, Wicken, Milton Keynes, Bucks MK19 6BT. *Tel*: 0908 57318. *Open*: by appointment. Tufted rugs inspired by forms in nature.

Jason Collingwood 22 Gladstone Road, Colchester, Essex CO1 2EA. *Tel*: 0206 26241 and 0206 762010. *Open*: by appointment. Flatwoven reversible wool and linen rugs.

Christopher Legge Oriental Carpets 25 Oakthorpe Road, Summertown, Oxford OX2 7BD. *Tel*: 0865 57383. *Open*: Mon to Sat 9.30am to 5pm. 19th & early 20th-century Oriental carpets; new vegetable-dyed Turkish rugs. Expert advice. Cleaning/restoration.

Judy Ramov 2 Maldive Road, Popley, Basingstoke, Hants RG24 9AS. *Tel*: 0256 478262. *Open*: by appointment. Richly textured and decorative rugs, wall-hangings and throws from hand-dyed. Felted wool cotton and silk which is then embroidered. Commissions are welcome.

Karel Weijand Lion & Lamb Courtyard, Farnham, Surrey GU9 7LL. *Tel*: 0252 726215. *Open*: Mon to Sat 10am to 5pm. Or by appointment. Fine selections Oriental rugs/carpets; over 30 years' experience. Valuations, restorations, cleaning.
Also at: Odiham Gallery, 78 High Street, Odiham, Hants. *Tel*: 0256 703415. *Open*: Mon to Sat 10am to 5pm. Closed Wed.

Mail Order

Simon Boosey The Tun House, High Street, Whitwell, Herts SG4 8AG. *Tel*: 043 887 563. Leaflet. Anti-creep underlays for rugs on carpets/hard floors.

9/SCREENS

An old-fashioned screen provides privacy, hides ugly features, and adds an atmosphere of mystery.

All Districts

Laura Ashley Home See **Furnishing Stores**. Choice of screens in co-ordinated furnishing fabrics.

Futon Palace See **Bedrooms 11/Futons**. Traditional serene Japanese shoji screens.

Screens Gallery The Malt House, Bridgefoot Rd, Emsworth. *Tel*: 0243 377334. *Open*: by appointment. One-off designer screens: special paint techniques, wood-carving, sandblasting, screen-printing. Also tables, mirrors, frames, fabrics.

London Postal Districts

Bibelots 180 Wandsworth Bridge Road, SW6 2UF. (*10 mins Fulham Broadway/Parsons Green tubes*). *Tel*: 01-736 3112. *Open*: Mon to Sat 10am to 5.30pm. Folding fabric-covered screens to order; also antique decorative accessories.

Kate Blee Textile Workshop and Design Studio, 54 Rivington Street, EC2 3QP. *Tel*: 01-729 5591. *Open*: Open: by appointment. Screens, hangings, upholstery, cushions, curtains, inlaid marble floors. Rich colours with images and textures abstracted from nature.

The Cartoon Carpet Company 4 Short's Garden, Covent Garden WC2. (*5 mins Covent Garden/Leicester Square tubes*). *Tel*: 01-240 5745. Quality (80/20 wool/nylon pile) Axminster rugs featuring Mickey Mouse, Snow White, Thunderbirds, Captain Scarlet, Noddy, Flintstones et al.

The Dormy House See **Soft Furnishings 6/Tables & Cloths**. Screens to cover in your own fabrics.

Lead & Light See **Windows 2/Stained & Decorative Glass**. Stained glass screens.

Robert & Colleen Bery Designs See **Furniture 8/Painted**. Intricately stencilled screens in wonderful colourings; stock or to order.

Screens 41 Thornhill Road, N1 1JS. (*10 mins Highbury & Islington/Caledonian Road tubes*). *Tel*: 01-607 5575. *Open*: by appointment. Mary Cooke offers asymmetric outlines, geometric designs, and painted colours for full-size/medium height/fire-screens.

Zadah Persian Carpets 29 Conduit Street, W1R 9TA. (*5 mins Oxford Circus tube*). *Tel*: 01-493 2622. *Open*: Mon to Fri 10am to 5.30pm. Sat by appointment. Stock of around 1,000 fine old carpets for decoration or investment. Family business: Lida and her brother Alex Zadah are second generation.

Mail Order

A Taste of America (Mailbox) Home Farm, Swinfen, near Lichfield, Staffs WS14 9QR. *Tel*: 0543 481612. Hand-loomed printed machine-washable cotton rugs; 13 original designs: geese, cats, ducks, shells, hearts etc; 2? by 40in. Also scrubbable doormats in same style. Colour catalogue features American Colonial country furnishings.

10/GENERAL

Why not give your home a present? See what's on offer below.

London Postal Districts

Anvil 89 Dulwich Village, SE21 7BJ. (*West Dulwich or North Dulwich BR*). *Tel*: 01-299 1000/3000. *Open*: Mon to Sat 10am to 5.30pm. Liberty designs, Waterford crystal, Dartington glass, Bodum plastic and glass. Inspired ideas for interiors and gifts.

The British Museum Shop Great Russell Street, WC1B 3DG. (*5 mins Russell Square/Holborn tubes*). *Tel*: 01-323 8613. *Open*: Mon to Sat 10am to 5pm. Sun 2pm to 6pm. Wonderful replicas of internationally famous museum pieces. Striking Eygptian black cats; and copies of Greek marbles.

Casa Fina 9 Central Avenue, The Market, Covent Garden WC2E 8AH. (*5 mins Covent Garden tube*). *Tel*: 01-836 0289. *Open*: Mon to Fri 10am to 7.30pm. Sat 11.30am to 6pm. Distinctive Casa Fina look linking all shops is ornate: ceramics, rugs, lighting: pretty colours and white furniture from Spain. Gift wrapping. Wedding lists. *Also at*: 132 Notting Hill Gate, W11 3OG. *Tel*: 01-221 9112.

Celebrations 70 Fulham Palace Road, W6 9PL. (*10 mins Hammersmith tube*). *Tel*: 01-748 4697. *Open*: Mon to Sat 10am to 6pm. Fun shop for parties and gifts.

The Covent Garden General Store 111 Long Acre, WC2. (*Immediately opposite Covent Garden tube*). *Tel*: 01-240 0331. *Open*: Mon to Sat 10am to 11.30pm. Sunday 11am to 7pm. Note late closing times – handy for emergency gifts. Three floors packed with fun ceramics, pictures, books, decorative tinware, prettily packed food/toiletries. Unfortunately tourist trap with rugger scrum atmosphere and heavies rather than assistants. Café at back: salad bar. *Also at*: 20 Shaftesbury Avenue, Piccadilly W1. *Open*: Mon to Sat 10am to 12pm. Sun 12am to 8pm. *And at*: Sideshow, Victoria Palace (*above Victoria Station*), SW1. *Open*: Mon to Sat 9am to to 8pm.

FFWD (Fast Forward) 14a Newburgh Street, W1V 4LF. (*5 mins Oxford Circus tube*). *Tel*: 01-439 0091. *Open*: (both branches): Mon to Sat 10am to 7pm. As the name says, the shop that's always racing ahead of trends/fashion. Mark Schofield and partner Marion Wilson have been all over (even to China) "sourcing" their always innovative, frequently amusing and often decorative stock, which ranges from ceramics/glassware to clocks, telephones, gifts. My favourites: traditional blue Polish glass in exclusive modern shapes.

The General Trading Company 144 Sloane Street, SW1X 9BL. (*2 mins Sloane Square tube*). *Tel*: 01-730 0411. *Open*: Mon to Fri 9am to 5.30pm. Sat 9am to 2pm. Late night Wed 7pm. Difficult to classify this genteel and gracious store, which holds 4 Royal warrants. Charmingly crowded with all kinds of furnishings/gifts in 11 departments. Antiques, furniture, rugs, cookware, books, beautiful artificial and dried flowers.

Graham & Green 4 & 7 Elgin Crescent, W11 2JA. (*8 mins Notting Hill Gate tube*). *Tel*: 01-727 4594. *Open*: Mon to Sat 10am to 6pm. Unusual accessories/gifts. New/antique furniture, bedspreads, rugs, cushions, china, kitchenware. Browsing well rewarded.

The Green Parrot 2 Turnpin Lane, SE10 9JA. (*Private lane, off Greenwich Church Street*). *Tel*: 01-858 6690. *Open*: Wed to Sun 10.30am to 5.30pm. Dedicated owner offers collector's items, antique and new. Pottery, handcrafted glass, mobiles; pocket-money gifts.

The New Etcetera 47 Golders Green Road, NW11 8EL. (*10 mins Golders Green tube*). *Tel*: 01-455 3441. *Open*: Mon to Sat 9.30am to 6pm. Sun 10am to 5.30pm. Lalique glass, Royal Worcester china, up-market gifts. *Also at*: 37 St John's Wood High Street, NW8 7NL. *Tel*: 01-586 8959. *Open*: Mon to Sat 9.30am to 6pm.

Ogetti 101 Jermyn Street, SW1 6EE. (*3 mins Piccadilly Circus tube*). *Tel*: 01-930 4694. *Open*: (both branches): Mon to Sat 9.30am to 6pm. New store over 2 floors is a haunt for London's home design cognoscenti; wide ranging stock of furnishing accessories, including tableware, rugs, cushions. "We aim to focus attention on quality design and manufacture for everyday objects; we promote new designers alongside 20th-century classics." *Also at*: 133 Fulham Road, SW3 6RT. (*10 mins South Kensington tube*). *Tel*: 01-581 8088. Smaller selections in Ogetti's first branch.

Quinto of Marylebone 83 Marylebone High Street, W1. (*10 mins Bond Street tube*). *Tel*: 01-935 9303. *Open*: Mon to Sat 9am to 6pm. Antique/second-hand books in decorative bindings for impressive shelves!

Saville Edells 25 Walton Street, SW3 2HU. (*5 mins Knightsbridge/South Kensington tubes*). *Tel*: 01-584 4398. *Open*: Mon to Sat 9.30am to 6pm. Handcoloured framed prints, hand-painted mirrors and ceramics. Photo frames: burr walnut, glass, crystal, silver. Small silver antiques. Vases, plant holders. Free mail order catalogue from shops, or £2.50 by phone: 01-248 1192, £3 redeemable on first order. *Also at*: 41 Queen Victoria Street, EC4N 4SA. *Tel*: 01-248 1192. *And at*: Simpson, 203 Piccadilly, W1. *Tel*: 01-734 2002.

4 Sight Design 128 Lower Richmond Road, Putney SW15 1LN. *Tel*: 01-789 0073. *Open*: Tues to Sat 10am to 5pm. Original furnishing accessories in peaceful showroom. Lamps, mirrors, china etc. from all over the world. Plus cushions, French/Italian chairs, handmade sofas, occasional furniture. Downstairs: co-ordinated furnishing collections; interior-design service.

Tessa Fantoni 24 Abbeyville Road, Clapham, SW4 9NH. (*6 mins Clapham Junction BR*). *Tel*: 01-673 1253. *Open*: Mon 2pm to 6pm. Tues to Thurs 11am to 6pm. Fri 11am to 7pm. Sat 10.30am to 6pm. Visitors' books, photograph albums and blank books made from marbled paper and handbound.

Wimbles 39a High Street, Wimbledon Village SW19 5BY. (*Wimbledon tube/BR*). *Tel*: 01-947 4899. *Open*: Mon to Sat 9.30am to 5.30pm. Sun 12am to 5pm. Everything from pocket-money gifts and stocking fillers to substantial presents and home ideas. *Also at*: **Wimbles and Daughters**, 37 High Street, Wimbledon Village SW19 5BY. *Tel*: 01-946 5437. *Open*: Mon to Sat 9.30am to 5.30pm.

Outer Ring

Ditto 22 Croydon Road, Caterham,

Surrey CR3 6QB. (*Caterham BR*). *Tel*: 0883 45866. *Open*: Mon to Sat 9.30am to 5.30pm. Frequently-changing displays of gift ideas/home accessories.

Helios 1 Grace Reynolds Walk, Camberley, Surrey. (*10 mins Camberley BR*). *Tel*: 0276 27076. *Open*: Mon to Sat 9am to 5.30pm. Porcelain, crystal, glass and woodware, pottery, gifts.

MacDonalds 71/73 High Street, Camberley, Surrey GU15 3RB. (*10 mins Camberley BR*). *Tel*: 0276 23005. *Open*: Mon to Sat 9am to 5.30pm. Glass, lighting, pine/cane furniture, rugs, terraria. Picture framing.

Quelque Chose 9 King Street, Richmond, Surrey TW9 1ND. (*10 mins Richmond tube/BR*). *Tel*: 01-948 3036. *Open*: Mon to Sat 9.30am to 5.30pm. Handmade ceramics, basketware, bedspreads, cushions, vases, dried and silk flowers. Ideas abound from its creative owners.

Rainbows End 126 High Street, Epsom, Surrey KT19 8BT. *Tel*: 03727 23434. See London Postal Districts above under Wimbles.

Stoneleigh Galleries 9 The Broadway, Stoneleigh, Epsom, Surrey KT17 2JA. (*2 mins Stoneleigh BR*). *Tel*: 01-393 0424. *Open*: Mon to Sat 9.30am to 5.30pm. Wed to 1pm. Ceramics, lace/satins, glass, enamel. Gift wrapping service.

Home Counties/S.East

The Aspidistra 29 Sun Street, Hitchin, Herts SG5 1AH. (*Opposite Sun Hotel*). *Tel*: 0462 53817. *Open*: Mon to Sat 9.30am to 5.30pm. Victorian bric-a-brac, modern crafts, lace, feathers, unusual gifts.

Sharbooks *Tel*: 04896 267. (*7 miles Winchester*). *Open*: by appointment only. Customer collection service from Winchester BR. Leather-bound books for elegant shelves. Half-bound (spine only) or full leather binding. Cleaned/restored. Wide selection/reasonable prices.

Mail Order

Erme Wood Forge See **Heating 4/Fireside accessories**. Substantial bootscraper – with or without boot remover!

The Manor Bindery Fawley, Hants SO4 1BB. *Tel*: 0703 894488. Leaflet. "Display" books, made in units from board with leather-grained covering material and gold detailing.

SECURITY

So nice to come home to . . . but not if the burglar got there first. Take to the barricades with the help of specialist lock/alarm stores.

London Postal Districts

AKP Security Services 88 Wilton Road, SW1V 1DN. (*10 mins Victoria tube*). *Tel*: 01-821 1991. *Open*: Mon to Fri 8.30am to 6pm. All security products. Expert advice, installations.

The Alarm Shop 110 Balls Pond Road, Islington N1 4AG. *Tel*: 01-241 5680.

Banham Patent Locks 233/235 Kensington High Street, W8. (*5 mins Kensington High Street tube*). *Tel*: 01-937 4311. *Open* (both branches): Mon to Fri 9am to 5pm. Sat 9am to 12.30pm. Full security services from this famous name. Locks, alarms, grilles, window bars, folding door gates. 24-hour emergency alarm service.
Also at: 11 Lillie Road, SW6 7TX. (*West Brompton tube*). *Tel*: 01-385 3822.

Barrs Security 329 Fulham Palace Road, SW6. (*10 mins Putney Bridge tube*). *Tel*: 01-736 7668/2918. *Open*: Mon to Fri 9am to 5.30pm. In stock: most makes locks/safes; workshop at rear for special orders. Installations. 24-hour emergency locksmith service.

Barry Bros 121/123 Praed Street, W2 1RL. (*5 mins Paddington tube*). *Tel*: 01-723 9663. *Open*: Mon to Sat 9am to 5pm. Established 1945, now run by founder's sons. All security devices: safes, fire extinguishers, burglar

alarms, fire escape equipment, fireproof- and gun-cabinets. Huge range of locks. Trained staff. Full fitting service.

A Buckenham (Locksmiths) Rear of 158 Blackstock Road, Highbury N5 1HA. (*5 mins Arsenal tube*). *Tel*: 01-226 8734. *Open*: Mon to Fri 9am to 5pm. Family firm, trading for over 30 years. Speedy, friendly service. High security locks. Advice, fitting.

FGW (City) Locksmiths 129 Whitecross Street, EC1 8JL. (*Barbican/Moorgate/Old Street tubes*). *Tel*: 01-253 9454/9721. *Open*: Mon to Fri 6.30am to 3.30pm. Family firm trading for over 100 years. Locks, tools, alarms, security bars. Trained staff. Installations.

Finch DIY Stores 329/333 Regents Park Road, Finchley N3 1DP. (*Near corner of Hendon Lane/Regents Park Road*). *Tel*: 01-346 4417. *Open*: Mon to Fri 8.15am to 6pm. Sat 8.30am to 6pm. Sun 9.30am to 1.30pm. Trading for over 25 years. Locks for doors, windows, patio doors, etc. Security devices, property-marking kits. Lockfitting, key cutting.

Dennis Lock and Key Services 139 Wood Street, Walthamstow E17 3LX. (*Walthamstow Central tube*). *Tel*: 01-520 7450/521 2444. After-hours emergencies: 01-529 0223. *Open*: Mon to Fri 9am to 5.30pm. Sat 9am to 2.30pm.

Safe engineers, security specialists, key cutters. Friendly, knowledgeable family firm.

Market Lock and Safe 251A East India Dock Road, E14 0EG. (*All Saints Docklands Light Railway*). *Tel*: 01-515 2121/987 5757. *Open*: Mon to Fri 9am to 5pm. Sat 9.30am to 4.30pm. Small family locksmith. Advice, outside repairs, 24-hour emergency service. Safes, key cutting, installations.

Modern Alarms 259 City Road, Islington EC1. *Tel*: 01-251 1616.

Multisecure Brent Terrace, Tilling Road, Brent Cross NW2 1LJ. (*10 mins Brent Cross tube*). *Tel*: 01-208 1766. *Open*: Mon to Fri 9am to 5.30pm. Supply/install high security locks/doors.

PA Alarms 3 Raleigh House, Admirals Way, Docklands E14 9SN. *Tel*: 01-583 0630. After hours emergencies: 01-538 5599.

J Reeder Lock & Safe Co Ltd 587 Barking Road, Plaistow E13 9EX. (*Plaistow tube*). *Tel*: 01-472 3431. *Open*: Mon to Fri 8am to 5.30pm. Sat 8am to 1pm. Safe engineer, specialist locksmith. Expert advice. All locks supplied and fitted.

R & R Security Services 167 South Ealing Road, W5 4NT. (*1 min South Ealing tube*). *Tel*: 01-847 3129/847

4404. *Open*: Mon to Fri 9am to 6pm. Sat 9am to 5pm. Locks, alarms, safes, grilles, supplied and fitted. Key specialists. Fire protection. Burglary prevention.

Saxon Security Locks 208 Mitcham Road, Amen Corner SW17 9NN. (*Between Tooting Broadway tube/Tooting BR*). *Tel*: 01-767 6281. *Open*: Mon to Fri 8.30am to 5.30pm. Sat 10am to 4pm. Expert advice, speedy fitting, made-to-measure sliding gates and grilles. Safes. Registered key system. *Also at*: 332 Balham High Road, SW17 7AA. *Tel*: 01-416 0417.

Young & Marten Grove Crescent Road, Stratford E15 1BT. *Tel*: 01-534 6630. *Open*: Mon to Fri 8am to 5pm. Sat 9am to 4pm. Expert advice. All security supplies/services.

Outer Ring

A1 Security Systems 168 Pinner Road, Harrow HA1 4JP. *Tel*: 01-427 1993.

Richardsons 6/7 Rochester Parade, High Street, Feltham, Middx TW13 4DX. *Tel*: 01-890 4399. *Open*: Mon to Sat 9am to 5.30pm. Four partners: efficient uniformed family business. All keys cut. Safes, boxes, locks. Chubb Lock Centre. Window grilles. Security surveys.
Also at: 128 The Centre, Feltham, Middx TW13 4BN. *Tel*: 01-890 9946.

Young & Marten 634 Hanworth Road, Hounslow TW4 5NP. *Tel*: 01-755 4455. See London Postal Districts above.

Home Counties/S.East

Young & Marten 73 High Street, Clacton-on-Sea, Essex CO15 6PW. *Tel*: 0255 425241.
Also at: Greenstead Road, Essex CM5 9HQ. *Tel*: 0277 362231.
And at: No 2 The Candlemakers,

Temple Farm Industrial Estate, Sutton Road, Southend-on-Sea, Essex SS2 5RT. *Tel*: 0702 63292. See London Postal Districts above.

The following firms also supply/fit quality locks:

Angel Lock & Safe Co 372 Caledonian Road, NW1. *Tel*: 01-837 8506/0269

WD Bishop & Sons 9 Park Road, Hornsey N8. *Tel*: 01-341 0859.

Crown Security Locksmiths 6 Crown Passage, Pall Mall SW1Y 6PP. *Tel*: 01-839 3253/9.
Also at: 34 Station Approach, London Bridge SE1 9RS.

Trafalgar Lock & Key Co 36 Kennington Road, SE1. *Tel*: 01-928 0796. *Also at*: 110 Trafalgar Road, Greenwich SE10. *Tel*: 01-853 3614.

Willet & Sons 87/89 Loampit Vale, Lewisham SE13. *Tel*: 01-692 1080.

GARDENS & OUTSIDE

From city yard to country estate, the earth is waiting to help furnish every inch of your property with colour and design. Decorate the exterior with the tender loving care you expend inside, and your home is truly complete.

1/GARDEN CENTRES

*Along with **DIY Superstores** garden centres are (aptly) a major growth industry. Conveniently collected together on often spacious sites is everything you need to furnish your garden from soil and plants to pavings and barbecues. Sunday trading is the norm and shopping becomes a weekend treat. Below are a few of my favourites.*

London Postal Districts

The Chelsea Gardener 125 Sydney Street, SW3. (*10 mins Sloane Square tube*). *Tel*: 01-352 5656. *Open*: Mon to Sat 10.30am to 6pm. Sun 10.30am to 5pm. Everything for the fashionable gardens of the area. Shrubs/herbs/perennials/annuals: helpfully arranged for shade/sun. Display gardens for inspiration. Also good selection exotic plants. Temples, gazebos, topiary, urns, statues. Bookshop/pictures. Interior landscaping.

Clifton Nurseries 5a Clifton Villas, W9 2PH. (*2 mins Warwick Avenue tube*). *Tel*: 0289 6851. *Open*(Winter): Mon to Sat 8.30am to 5.30pm. Summer: Mon to Sat 8.30am to 6pm. Sun 9.30am to 4pm. Clifton brings the decorator touch to garden merchandise with lots of pretty accessories besides extensive plant/tree stocks.

Antique statues/ornaments. Trellis/pots/garden furniture. Conservatory furniture/planters.

The Garden Centre Alexandra Palace N22 4BB. (*Alexandra Palace BR; plentiful free parking*). *Tel*: 01-444 2555. *Open*: Mon to Fri 9.30am to 5.30pm. Sat Sun & bank holidays 10am to 6pm. Breathe bracing Ally Pally air and wander around expansive 2.3 acre site. Wildlife Garden, Study Centre. Pet Superstore with aviary, aquarium, videos on pet care; visiting weekend vet. Advice Centre: professional designers/horticulturists. Planting ideas/stock guarantees. Centre Shop has imaginative house/conservatory plants. Organic materials. French garden furniture with designer names; Chinese/Italian/English pots, tubs, windowboxes. Tools/books. Barbecue Equipment Demonstration Area. Find birds and bees in the Wildlife Garden; explore a happy habitat for butterflies. Herb/water gardens. Cafe. Play area.

C Rassell 80 Earls Court Road, W8. (*7 mins Earls Court tube*). *Tel*: 01-937 0481. *Open*: Mon to Sat 9am to 5.30pm. Late night Thurs 6.30pm. Dignified shop, old-fashioned in best sense; for decades stalwart stand-by of green-starved flat dwellers. Out front: houseplants, cut flowers: trained florists for bouquets. Out back, spacious area for outdoor plants. Camellias a speciality.Soils/fertilisers/insecti-cides. Tools/watering equipment/stakes/trellis. Chinese decorative canes. Toughs/pots/urns in wood/glass fibre/terracotta/stone. And everything for that definitive Kensington window box . . .

World's End Nurseries 441/457 King's Road, SW10. (*Sloane Square tube plus bus*). *Tel*: 01-351 3343. *Open*: Mon to Sat 9am to 6.30pm. Sun 10am to 5pm. An acre of landscaped garden in one of London's most densely domesticated areas. Green positively flows from the fingers of founder/owner James Lotery. Plants are helpfully grouped: shady, sunny, perfumed, climbing and so on. Herbs, heathers, alpines. Large greenhouse with forest of Kentia palms. Plant hospital. Trained staff.

2/TRELLIS

All Districts

WH Newson See **Home Improvement Specialists.** New white painted designer squared trellis in standard panels from stock: diamond cut-outs, curved/arched tops.

Wickes See **Home Improvement Specialists.** Instructions/planed timber components for attractive timber decking with overhead pergola.

London Postal Districts

Artech Unit 15, Burmah Workshops, Marsden Street, NW5. *Tel*: 01-482 2181. *Open*: by appointment. Trelliswork, planters, benches, pavilions, garden design.

Lloyd Christie Garden Architecture Unit 10, Acorn Product Centre, 105 Blundell Street, N7. *Tel*: 01-609 3498. Designer trellis.

Worth a Trip

Trellisworks West Mead Nursery, Clay Lane, Fishbourne, Chichester. (*15 mins Chichester BR; customer collection service*). *Tel*: 0243 774238/01-567 3862. *Open*: Mon to Fri 7am to 4.30pm. Phone for appointment, directions, brochure. Designer trellis. *Mail order.*

3/ GARDEN FURNITURE

All Districts

B & Q and **Texas**, see **DIY Superstores**, carry summer selections of attractive budget garden furniture in plastics and coated metal tubing with pretty plain and mostly floral upholstery, with chairs, loungers, swingseats, and tables. Also simple designs in plain wood that can be left out all year. Shop early in season for best selections.

London Postal Districts

Astrohome See **Furniture 1/General**. Spanish Casa collection designed for out-of-doors cafes. Fashionable/ stylish. Polished aluminium tube; weather-resistant seats in plastic-coated nylon cord, or black/silver slats. Burnished textured stainless steel table tops.

John Lewis, Harrods, Peter Jones and **Selfridges** (see **Department Stores**), all stock attractive selections of garden furniture. But shop early in the season for best selections: or wait for summer sales for Bargains!

Louise Gilbert Scott 7 Curtain Road, EC2A 3LT. *Tel*: 01-674 7785. *Open*: by appointment. A range of individually made and brightly painted planters, garden tables and large platters. Garden furniture particularly suitable for balconies, conservatories and small gardens. Commissions welcomed.

Home Counties/S.East

Andrew Crace Designs Bourne Lane, Much Hadham, Herts SG10 6ER. (*E of B1004, North of Widford, South of Much Hadham, signed to Perry Green and Green Tye*). *Tel*: 027984 2685. *Open*: by appointment. Superbly ornamental garden furniture re-interpreting past themes (Chinoiserie, Windsor, Indian Lattice) for present effect. Splendid benches, octagonal tables. Iroko hardwood in gloss white, or any colour micro-porous matt paint. All-weather swing seats in wood/galvanised metal. Tree seats. Love seats.

St Pier Street Farm Workshops, Acton Turville, Avon GL9 1HH. *Tel*: 045 421 736. *Open*: by appointment. Elegant curving modern interpretation of classic slatted iroko/teak garden benches.

John Wyndham Designs Westgates, Muddles Green, Chiddingly, Lewes, East Sussex BN8 6HW. *Tel*: 0825 872036/872764. Sculptural modern shapes handmade by traditional methods in kiln-dried oak, stained/ coloured.

4/ ORNAMENTS & TUBS

London Postal Districts

Architectural Ceramics Unit 120, Building A, Raleigh Wharf, 8/12 Creekside, SE8 3DX. (*Deptford BR*). *Tel*: 01-692 7287. *Open*: by appointment. Art school graduates have perfected terracotta techniques for large garden ornaments: urns, wall fountains, and even a sphinx!

Colours: from ivory to traditional brick red.

Stephen Dixon 145 Pancras Road, NW1. *Tel*: 01-387 6230. *Open*: by appointment. Hand-pressed ornately-moulded planters, urns, fountains; limited editions, traditional motifs.

The Ecology Shop 21 Endell Street, WC2H 9BJ. (*5 mins Covent Garden tube*). *Tel*: 01-379 3108. *Open*: Mon to Sat 10am to 6pm. Ecologically sound bird tables and feeders – and bat boxes (for an endangered species)!

Garden Crafts 158 New King's Road, Fulham SW6 4LZ. (*2 mins Putney Bridge tube*). *Tel*: 01-736 1615. *Open*: Mon to Sat 9am to 5.30pm. Sat 10am to 5pm. Garden ornaments/furniture. Arresting outdoor displays of classical reproductions.

Anthony de Grey Garden Construction 1 Cambridge Road, SW11 4RT. (*Sloane Square tube plus bus*). *Tel*: 01-228 8808. *Open*: Mon to Fri 8am to 6pm. Small garden centre under direction of imaginative landscape artist. Own range planters, tubs, Versaille boxes. Reproduction Victorian garden flower bed edges, including twisted rope design. Pavings, patios.

Sundials Studio 22, Acme Studios, 105 Carpenters Road, E15 2DY. *Tel*: 01-221 5319. *Open*: by appointment. Working sundials. Colour brochure.

Outer Ring

Crowther of Syon Lodge London Road, Isleworth, Middx TW7 5BH. (*Back of Syon Park; M4 Junction 2*). *Tel*: 01-560 7978. *Open*: Mon to Fri 9am to 5pm. Sat & Sun 11am to 4pm. Garden crammed with splendid antique sculptures, fountains, urns, benches. Also antique panelling/ chimneypieces. World famous but very expensive.

Home Counties/S.East

Hannah Peschar Gallery Black and White Cottage, Standon Lane, Ockley, Surrey. *Tel*: 030679 677. *Open*

4 / Ornaments & Tubs

May to Oct: Fri & Sat 11am to 6pm. Sun 2pm to 6pm. Other times by appointment. Modern sculptures/ceramics for gardens/exteriors displayed in wonderfully-landscaped semi-wild garden, where the wilderness is carefully ordered to create visionary vistas. Essential viewing for garden/fine art lovers.

Tiger Developments Millwards, Laughton, Lewes, East Sussex. *Tel*: 0825 872555. *Open*: by appointment. Breathtaking bridges in painted steel: not just water-crossings but works of art/sculpture. Also cast iron bridges Regency/Gothic/Victorian styles. Colour brochure shows grand commissions, but individual home owners welcome. Gazebos, steel fencing, pergolas.

Pots and Pithoi Grange Farm, Turners Hill Road, Crawley Down, West Sussex. *Enquiries to*: Bankton Cottage, Turners Hill Road, Crawley Down, West Sussex RH10 4EY. (*M23, A264, turn right at Dukes Head pub into B2028*). *Tel*: Copthorne 714793. *Open*: dawn to dusk, 7 days. Terracotta pots up to 95cm tall, made by hand in Crete and imported. See them set amidst a working farm, with sales office next door.

Mail Order

R Bleasdale See **Staircases 2/Spiral.** Cast iron reproduction railings, balconies, balustrades.

Erme Wood Forge See **Heating 4/Fireside Accessories.** Weather vanes topped by delicate outline in wrought iron of charming choice of farmyard animals.

Roseney Farm Designs Lanlivery, Bodmin, Cornwall. *Tel*: 0208 872664. Well-detailed and stylish dovecotes/wild bird houses made to order.

5/LIGHTING

With garden lighting, enjoy your garden from inside on chilly days, and sit outside on warmer evenings. Check projects out carefully for safety: all wiring must conform to safety standards. Use a competent electrician. The effects are magical . . .

All Districts

Wickes See **DIY Superstores.** Exterior lighting range/weatherproof fittings for installation. Attractive globes for wall mounting/columns for low-level lighting, or practical floods on spikes.

Christopher Wray's Lighting Emporium See **Lighting 2/Traditional.** Good selection traditional reproduction lamps/posts, including Aldgate post with ladder bar lamplighters used when streetlighting was fuelled by gas.

London Postal Districts

The Garden Lighting Company 352 Old York Road, SW18 1SS. (*2 mins Wandsworth Town BR*). *Tel*: 01-877 0144. *Open*: Mon to Fri 10am to 5pm. Sat 9.30am to 12.30pm. Unique showroom for exterior lighting. Wall fittings; decorative lighting for gardens, drives, pathways, security. Design/install.

Mail Order

The English Street Furniture Company Pastures Drive, Caxton, Cambs CB3 8PF. *Tel*: 09544 637. Colour brochure. Faithful reproductions of 19th-century gas street lamps (gaslights were first patented by Frederick Winsor in 1803). Lamp-posts/wall/pedestal lanterns crafted from old blueprints and hand-finished in copper/brass. Exclusive electric "Gasbulbs" simulate warm qualities of traditional gas.

Gebron Technical Services 34 Bridge Street, Walton-on-Thames, Surrey KT12 1AJ. *Tel*: 0932 223183. Traditional and classic lanterns, lamp-posts and wall lanterns.

6/CONSERVATORIES

Conservatories that do not exceed "permitted development" do not require planning permission: check with your local authority. Approval under Building Regulations is not needed provided floor area is less than 30 sq m. Most firms below will help battle bureaucracies.

Abbeydale Conservatories Trenton Works, Hewell Road, Redditch, Worcs B97 6AR. *Tel*: Redditch 64200. Custom-built hardwood in stylish shapes.

Alexander Bartholomew Conservatories 277 Putney Bridge Road, SW15 2PT. *Tel*: 01-785 7263.

Clear Span Freepost, Greenfield, Oldham, Lancashire OL3 7BR. *Tel*: 04577 3244/5/6. Lean-to or freestanding greenhouses.

Imperial Cornerstones Farndon Road, Market Harborough, Leicestershire LE16 9NP. *Tel*: 0858 65051. Freephone. Competitive prices, range of styles.

Lifestyle Conservatories TGP House, Cobham, High Street, Surrey KT11 3DP. *Tel*: 0932 64463 (24 hours). Handbuilt conservatories.

New England Conservatories Whitney Road, Daneshill East, Basingstoke RG24 0NS. *Tel*: 0256 468896. Range of styles for professional or DIY installations; bronze-tinted polycarbonate insulating roof.

Palm Rooms Unit 9, Sheddington Industrial Estate, Burgess Hill, West Sussex RH15 8QY. *Tel*: 0444 870633. Elegant styles in white finished aluminium.

Rooks Mist PO Box 6, Huntingdon, Cambridgeshire PE17 2DN. *Tel*: 0480 61912. Victorian and traditional styles with modern engineering and full installation service.

Teknek Cromwell Road, Ellesmere Port L65 4DS. *Tel*: 051-356 1806. Modern boxy no-nonsense shapes with aluminium frames in choice of finishes.

Traditional British Conservatories

Halls Homes and Gardens, Church Road, Paddock Wood, Kent TN12 6EU. *Tel*: 089283 4647. Based on original Victorian styles, durable cedar and mahogany combined with modern assets such as double glazing.

White Diamond 42 South Street, Stanground, Peterborough PE2 8HA. *Tel*: 0733 52055. White, elegant architect-designed frames in traditional styles.

PART TWO

WHERE TO BUY WHAT

DEPARTMENT STORES

London's department stores are a magnet for visitors from all over the world. As specialist shops multiply, furnishings strengths of the giant stores are sometimes overlooked. But they are well worth getting to know. Avoid if possible peak periods: weekends, lunch hours, late nights. Enjoy a total service: variety, value, deliveries, credit, restaurants, cafés, toilets.

London Postal Districts

Fenwick Brent Cross Shopping Centre, Hendon NW4 3FN. (*Hendon Central/Brent Cross tubes plus bus*). *Tel*: 01-202 8200. *Open*: Mon to Fri 10am to 8pm. Sat 9am to 6pm. Furniture, electrical appliances, soft furnishings, lighting, glass, cookshop, kitchenware, linens.
Also at: 63 New Bond Street, W1A 3BS. *Tel*: 01-629 9161.

Harrods 87/135 Brompton Road, Knightsbridge SW1X 7XL. (*5 mins Knightsbridge tube; own car park*). *Tel*: 01-730 1234. *Open*: Mon Tues Thurs to Sat 9am to 6pm. Wed 9.30am to 7pm. Premier international tourist attraction: but don't be put off! Motto: *Omnia Omnibus Ubique*: all things for all people everywhere. Ambience is unsurpassed: original plaster ceilings, 1930s light fittings, wonderful blue-and-white tiles in the meat department of the celebrated Food Hall. Famous terracotta facade completed 1900/05. 6 storeys, 5 selling floors, 72 window displays. 2nd floor: linens, with monogramming service; interior design; cookshop with advice from resident home economist; Smallbone, Wrighton, Bosch kitchens with free design service; radio/TV; glass engraving on the spot (Wed 9.30am to lpm). 3rd floor: furniture, trad./mod.; pianos, posters, prints, picture framing, drycleaning. 5 restaurants, 5 bars.

Harvey Nichols Knightsbridge SW1X 7RJ. (*1 min Knightsbridge tube*). *Tel*: 01-235 5000. *Open*: Mon to Fri 10am to 7pm. Sat 10am to 6pm. Part of The Burton Group but with own identity. Modest beginnings as small linen store of 1813. Now 7 floors high-quality fashion/design. Reputation: most elegant store in Europe. Three Royal warrants. Atmosphere of elegance and luxury. Accessories (china, glass, silverware, linens, lighting, gifts, bathroom): 4th floor. Oriental carpets: 5th. Wedding lists: 3rd. Toilets: 3rd; baby changing/nurse: 4th. Meals, snacks, drinks: Harveys At The Top, 5th; Zone Café, basement.

House of Fraser *Tel* (nearest branch/general enquiries): 01-834 1515. Extensive refurbishment taking place throughout House of Fraser with ultimately all stores being revamped and given H of F name. Own-brand merchandise is Allender label. Star Store: The House of Fraser, Oxford Street, W1. (*5 mins Oxford Circus tube*). *Tel*: 01-629 8800. *Open*: Mon to Sat 9.30am to 6pm. Late night Thurs 8pm. Formerly DH Evans, this store now bears the new group stag logo, and extends over 7 floors. You have to get to 3rd before you find any furnishings. 3rd: audio & TV; major electricals; haberdashery; The Bath Shop; soft furnishing. 4th: silverware; china/glass; gifts; housewares. 5th: art gallery; furniture; carpets; beds. Gift wrapping: 4th. The River Restaurant: 6th. Coffee shop: Lower Ground. Toilets: 5th.
Also at: House of Fraser Kensington, Kensington High Street, W8. (*3 mins Kensington High Street tube*). *Tel*: 01-937 5432. *Open*: Mon to Sat 9.30am to 6pm. Late night Thurs 8pm. What many of us knew and loved as Barkers has shrunk to 4 floors (including basement) with newspaper offices above. (Pontings and Derry & Toms have long since vanished, of course, except for the famous D & T roof garden.) Lower Ground: furniture; carpets; soft furnishings; haberdashery; lighting. 2nd: silverware; gifts; radio/TV; electrics; china and glass. Restaurant: 2nd.
Also at: Army & Navy, Victoria Street, SW1. (*5 mins Victoria tube*). *Tel*: 01-834 1234. Currently under refurbishment.
Also at (still trading as Army & Navy): Lewisham, Gravesend, Bromley, Guildford, Camberley, Basildon, Wood Green.

The John Lewis Partnership 22 stores nationwide. Staff are "partners", share profits. Good value, relatively keen prices. "Never knowingly undersold": If you can buy cheaper elsewhere, they will refund price difference. Jonelle own brand: good value/design. Jonelle fabrics: outstanding designs/colours, quality, price. Extensive making-up services all soft furnishings (own workshops). Home Service for carpets: measure/estimate/lay within 14 days. Loose covers: cut in home on furniture. Kitchen planning: £30 refundable. No credit cards except own: lowest APR of all store groups.

John Lewis Oxford Street, W1A 1EX. (*5 mins Oxford Circus tube*). *Tel*:01-629 7711. *Open*: Mon to Sat 9am to 5.30pm. Thurs 9.30am to 8pm. Flagship store. Furnishing fabrics, soft furnishings, carpets, flooring, linens: 2nd floor. Furniture: 3rd. Wallcoverings, paints, paint mixing: 3rd. China, glass, cutlery, lighting, kitchens, appliances, picture framing: basement. Coffee Shop: 4th. Place to Eat (licensed): 3rd. Ladies: basement, 1st, 2nd, 3rd, 4th floors. Gents: 2nd & 3rd. Invalid toilets: 2nd. Babies changing room: 4th.

Liberty 210/220 Regent Street, W1R 6AH. (*3 mins Oxford Circus tube*). *Tel*: 01-734 1234. *Open*: Mon to Sat 9.30am to 6pm. Late night Thurs 7.30pm. Distinctive Tudor-style building, dating back to 1875, complete with linenfold panelling in lifts! Best known for wonderful furnishing fabrics. 3rd floor: Upholstery/curtain-making services, quilt commissions. Basement: glass engraving, modern crafts, John Hungerford custom-made kitchens/bathrooms. Ground floor: pictures/prints, framing. Restaurant. 4th floor: furniture, including Liberty Guild reproductions.

Peter Jones Sloane Square, SW1W 8EL. (*2 mins Sloane Square tube*). *Tel*: 01-730 3434. *Open*: Mon to Sat 9am to 5.30pm. Wed 9.30am to 7pm. Reputation particularly for soft furnishings, plus antique/repro furniture. Furnishing fabrics, soft furnishings, linens,

pictures, picture framing, china, glass: ground floor. Carpets, flooring: 5th. Antiques/reproduction furniture: 4th. Lighting, wallcoverings, paint: basement. Coffee shop: 5th. Crockpot (licensed): 4th. Ladies: 2nd, 4th, 5th. Gents: 4th. Mother and baby room: 3rd.
Also at: John Lewis, Brent Cross Shopping Centre, NW4 3FL. *Tel*: 01-202 6535. *Open*: Mon to Fri 10am to 8pm. Sat 9am to 4.30pm.
And at: Jones Brothers, 340-366 Holloway Road, N7 6NY. *Tel*: 01-607 2727. *Open*: Tues to Sat 9am to 5.30pm. Wed 9.30am to 7.30pm.
And at: Pratts, 210 Streatham High Road, SW16 1BD. *Tel*: 01-769 4450. Open as for Jones Bros.

Selfridges 400 Oxford Street, W1A 1AB. (*5 mins Marble Arch/Bond Street tubes; own car park*). *Tel*: 01-629 1234. Rivals Harrods in size. 1st floor: soft furnishings, extensive selections ready-made curtains, plus made-to-measure. Interior design service; linens, including monogramming; furniture. 4th: garden furniture during summer. Basement: fabulous range DIY products/tools/materials; lighting. Hamper service/deliveries from ground floor Food Hall. Snack bars: ground, basement, 2nd. Restaurant: 3rd.

Outer Ring

Allders The Whitgift Centre, Croydon, Surrey CR9 1NN. (*East Croydon BR; Dingwall Avenue multi-storey car park*). *Tel*: 01-681 2577. *Open*: Mon to Sat 9am to 6pm. Tues 9.30am to 6pm. Late night Thurs 9pm. 3rd largest department store in UK, after Harrods and Selfridges. 5 floors; strong emphasis on home furnishings; own-brands. Basement: housewares; electrical (largest department of its kind in Europe). Ground: carpets (free measuring/fitting); china/glass. 1st: soft furnishings, linens. 2nd: beds/furniture; interior design. 4th: audio/TV. Tea/coffee/snacks: basement, ground, 1st. Restaurants: 3rd, 4th. Mother-and-baby room: 3rd.
Also at: Arding & Hobbs, Clapham Junction SW11 1QL. *Tel*: 01-228 8877.
And at: Eastgate Centre, Basildon,

Essex SS14 1HR. *Tel*: 0268 27858.
And at: High Street, Bromley, Kent BR1 1HJ. *Tel*: 01-464 6533.
And at: High Street, Camberley, Surrey. *Tel*: 0276 692122.
And at: High Street, Chatham, Kent. *Tel*: 0634 407377.
And at: High Street, Eltham SE9 1TP. *Tel*: 01-850 9911.
And at: High Street, Sutton, Surrey SM1 1ES. *Tel*: 01-642 6000.

Bentalls Wood Street, Kingston-upon-Thames KT1 1TX. (*5 mins Kingston BR*). *Tel*: 01-546 1001. *Open*: Mon to Fri 9am to 5.30pm. Sat 6pm. Late night Thurs 9pm. Strong furnishings emphasis. Good selections branded furniture 3rd floor: Derwent, G-Plan, Collins & Hayes, Nathan etc. 2nd floor: carpets (good choice Orientals); furnishing fabrics, ready-made-curtains. Full made-to-measure soft furnishings service; bed linens, including own New Nights brand. Lower ground: electrical appliances; china/ glass, including concessions: Wedgwood, Royal Doulton, Edinburgh Crystal, Royal Worcester. Restaurants: 1st, 2nd, 3rd. Home Service. Furnishing advisory department: free in-home interior design advice. Free laying carpets over £200.
Also at: Ealing Broadway Centre, W5 5JY. *Tel*: 01-567 3040.
And at: High Street, Bracknell, Berks RG12 1DW. *Tel*: 0344 424 678.
Also at: Angel Centre, Angel Lane, Tonbridge, Kent TN9 1SF. *Tel*:0732 771177.
And at: South Street, Worthing, West Sussex BN11 3AN. *Tel*: 0903 31801.

Home Counties/S.East

Harrison Gibson 193/207 High Road, Ilford, Essex IG1 1LZ. (*5 mins Ilford BR; own car park Clements Road*). *Tel*: 01-478 4455. *Open*: Mon to Fri 9am to 5.30pm. Sat 9am to 6pm. Recent £2.5 million re-vamp by Gillow Group. Ritzy glass facade/sophisticated interiors spreading 97,000 sq ft. Nursery furniture, domestic appliances, hi-fi/radios/TVs/videos: 1st floor. Also on 1st: lighting, garden furniture, framed prints, mirrors. Concession shops: Knobs & Knockers, Edinburgh Crystal, Chinacraft,

Casa Pupo. On 2nd: excellent carpets, keen prices through Gillow Group bulk buys. Also fitted kitchens, furnishing fabrics, beds, bedroom furniture. 3rd floor: furniture (many famous brands); all-day restaurant. 4th floor: more furniture.

John Lewis Furnishing & Leisure Holmers Farm Way, Cressex Centre, High Wycombe, Bucks HP12 4NW. (*Easily accessible from M40; parking 600 cars*). *Tel*: 0494 462666. *Open*: Tues to Fri 10am to 8pm. Sat 9am to 6pm. See entry under London Postal Districts above. Two floors uncluttered furnishings displays in purpose-built premises. Fullest showing for most merchandise outside Oxford Street.

CHAIN STORES

A familiar feature on every High Street, the British chain stores are a national institution. Get to know their furnishing strengths, and profit from keen prices, good value, convenience and accessibility, together, increasingly, with good design. At major stores benefit from extended opening hours. On the minus side, you will miss out on service and expert advice.

BhS Nearest branch/General enquiries: *Tel*: 01-262 3288. Star store: 252/258 Oxford Street, W1N 9DD. (*2 mins Oxford Circus tube*). *Tel*: 01-629 2011. *Open*: Mon to Sat 9am to 6pm. Wed 9.15am to 7pm. Late nights Thurs 8pm Fri 7pm. Since BhS (formerly Britsh Home Stores) was acquired by Sir Terence Conran's Storehouse Group, merchandise style has been steadily improving. Already established as a premier source for light fittings, traditional and modern, BhS now offers attractive co-ordinated collections for tableware, and household linens. Bed linens and ready-made curtain are also substantially improved, and linking design themes help towards the creation of a total look. Full furnishings selections are only carried by larger stores, so you may have to visit a nearby town.

Marks & Spencer Nearest branch/General enquiries: *Tel*: 01-935 4422. Star store: 458 Oxford Street, W1N 0AP (*4 mins Marble Arch tube*). *Tel*: 01-935 7954. *Open*: Mon to Fri 9am to 8pm. Sat 9am to 6pm. Here you can find full roomsettings for furnishing ranges which are becoming increasingly sophisticated. Up-to-the-minute themes are continued through merchandise ranging from wallcoverings and bed linens to saucepans and tableware. Furniture is also included, of the highest quality. Prices are not cheap, but value and quality is assured.
Also at: Brookfield Centre, Half Hide Lane, Cheshunt, Herts. (*Cheshunt BR; ample free parking*). *Tel*: 0992 36441. *Open*: Mon to Thurs 9am to 8pm. Fri 9am to 9pm. Sat 8am to 8pm. M&S's finest furnishing displays: full roomsettings all on one level. Merchandise includes carpets. Services include cut fabric and make-up; customer information desk; and instant credit.

Woolworth Nearest branch: *Tel*: 01-262 1222. Star store: 168/176 Edgware Road, W2 2DX. (*5 mins Edgware Road tube*). *Tel*: 01-723 2980. *Open*: Mon to Sat 9am to 8pm. Late night Fri 9pm. With a merchandise range drastically pruned in an attempt to achieve profitability, selections seem thin on the ground compared with times past. However, still a useful port of call for kitchen and DIY basics. *Also at*: 115/119 High Street, Camden Town NW1 7JS. (*5 mins Camden Town tube*). *Tel*: 01-485 3932. *Open*: Mon to Fri 9am to 5.30pm. Sat 9am to 6pm.

Littlewoods Nearest branch: *Tel*: 051-235 2673. Star store: 207 Oxford Street, W1N 9LA. (*3 mins Oxford Circus tube*). *Tel*: 01-434 4301. *Open*: Mon to Sat 9.30am to 6pm. Late night Thurs 8pm. Inside Story is the name to watch for. This chic department is gradually being introduced into major Littlewoods branches. Stylish selections of French cookware, china and glass, with British furniture and linens. Definitely worth investigation. *Also at*: Clarence Street, Kingston-upon-Thames KT1 1RF. (*5 mins Kingston BR*). *Tel*: 01-549 8877. *Open*: Mon to Sat 9am to 6pm.

FURNISHING STORES

1/INDIVIDUAL STORES

London Postal Districts

The Conran Shop 81 Fulham Road, SW3 6RD. (*8 mins South Kensington tube*). *Tel*: 01-589 7401. *Open*: Mon to Sat 9.30am to 6pm. Tues 10am to 6pm. Opposite site of very first Habitat, in splendidly restored Michelin building. Atmosphere of cool elegance; exquisite merchandise garnered by Priscilla Carluccio, Sir Terence Conran's sister-in-law. 22,000 sq ft. Fabrics. International furniture, many classics: exclusive PEL 1930s tubular steel. Carpets/fabulous rugs; beds/linens. Also china/glass; Food Shop: utensils for every cuisine. All soft-furnishing services. Wedding lists, gift wrapping, glass engraving.

Heal's 196 Tottenham Court Road, W1P 9LD. (*2 mins Goodge Street tube*). *Tel*: 01-636 1666. *Open*: Mon 10am to 6pm. Tues to Sat 9.30am to 6pm. Late night Thurs 7.30pm. Open Sat 9am. Part of Storehouse group, but retains own identity, although pruned to 3 floors. Royal warrant for handmade bedding (2nd floor, with linens/Bath Shop). Latest international furniture designs: ground floor. Also on ground: lighting, china/glass, carpets/rugs, fabrics, accessories, Kitchen Shop. 1st floor: interior design, fitted furniture, Humpherson kitchens/bathrooms. Full range carpet/soft furnishing services. Restaurant.

Charles Page 61 Fairfax Road, Swiss Cottage NW6 4EE. (*5 mins Swiss Cottage tube*). *Tel*: 01-328 9851. *Open*: Mon to Sat 9.30am to 5.30pm. Latest international furniture, selected for good design/value/quality. Bedrooms, dining rooms, living rooms, including beds, fitted furniture. Full interior design service.
Also at: 93/94 Lower Level Churchill Square, Brighton. (*15 mins Brighton BR*). *Tel*: 0273 737055.

Outer Ring

Stockwell & Oxford 16 Katharine Street, Croydon CR9 1JY. (*5 mins East Croydon BR*). *Tel*: 01-688 5521. *Open*: Mon to Sat 9am to 5.30pm. Family firm founded 1891, friendly personal service. Wide range modern furniture, living rooms, dining rooms, bedrooms. Carpets, soft furnishings.

Trend Interiors 8 Richmond Hill, Richmond, Surrey TW10 6QX. (*10 mins Richmond tube/BR*). *Tel*: 01-940 7261. *Open*: Tues to Sat 9.30am to 6pm. Owner/buyer Mrs Pat Street promotes quality modern furniture from Germany, Italy, Scandinavia and so on. Full interior-design service: lots of fabric/paper samples, all top makes.

Home Counties/S.East

Beadle & Crome 32 Oxford Street, High Wycombe HP11 2DJ. (*Car park at rear*). *Tel*: 0494 23249. *Open*: Mon to Sat 9am to 5.30pm. Personal service from family business trading for 62 years. Quality furniture: G-Plan and other famous makes. Danish & German fitted wardrobes; rosewood/teak dining furniture. Classic upholstery.
Also at: 53 The Broad Street Mall, Reading RG1 7QE. (*Car park over store*). *Tel*: 0734 581356.

Bennett & Brown 181/183 Windmill Street, Gravesend, Kent DA12 1AJ. *Tel*: 0474 352235. *Open*: Mon to Sat 9am to 5.30pm. Roomsets over 4 floors display upholstery, cabinet furniture, curtains and carpets.

Clement Joscelyne Market Square, Bishop's Stortford, Herts CM23 3XA. (*Town centre, adjacent car parks*). *Tel*: 0279 506731. *Open*: Mon to Sat 9am to 5.30pm. Captivating atmosphere. Family firm established 1879 dedicated to quality and good design. Collection of old buildings, some dating back to Elizabethan times. Floor space now around 12,000 sq ft. International furniture selections. Hulsta, Grange, Titchmarsh & Goodwin. Interior design service. Own workroom for curtain making.

Fishpools 115 High Street, Waltham Cross, Herts EN8 7AL. (*10 mins*

Waltham Cross/Theobalds BRs). Tel: 0992 31911. *Open:* Mon to Fri 9am to 5.30pm. Closed Thurs. Sat 9am to 6pm. Family firm, founded 1899. Friendly personal service, with experienced staff. 42,000 sq ft, plus offices/warehouses. Compete furnishers: furniture, lighting, china/glass. Interior design department: fabrics, wallpapers, carpets, soft furnishings. G-Plan, Ercol, and international furniture, including German, Belgian, Italian, Scandinavian in natural ash/oak. Coffee shop. *Also at:* 24/26 Market Street, Watford WD1 7AD. (*On Ring Road*). *Tel:* 0923 221844. *Open:* as above, but closed Wed.

Holmes of Reading Chatham Street, Reading RG1 7JX. (*Own car park; adjacent multi-storey car park*). *Tel:* 0734 586421. *Open:* Tues to Sat 9am to 5.30pm. Late night Thurs 9.30am to 8pm. Founded 1815: present family management took over in 1920. 13,000 sq ft over 2 floors. 8,500 sq ft of furniture displays. Flexible/versatile Hulsta German wall furniture, in elegant wood/coloured finishes. Home Service: design/install. French country house designs, American Shaker range, Scandinavian classics in solid woods, Italian dining ranges. interior design section: fabric/wallcoverings, carpets, soft furnishings. Finishing touches department: cushions, rugs, mirrors, plants. Coffee shop.

Interior Concepts Unit N, Turnpike Way, Cressex Industrial Estate, High Wycombe, Bucks. *Tel:* 0494 27379. *Open:* Mon to Sat 9am to 5.30pm. Early closing Wed 1pm. Sun 10am to 4pm. Independent 4th generation furnishing business going places: just moved to large edge-of-town premises. Lots of display ideas for furnishings/co-ordination. Italian leather/British upholstery. German bedroom/Danish dining room furniture. British fabrics/curtains. Scandinavian carpets. American paintings. Flexible personal service, ranging from in-store consultations to full scale interior design.

Peter Knight 45 London End, Beaconsfield HP9 2HP. (*A40 from London*). *Tel:* 0494 5561/4. *Open:* Mon to Sat 9am to 5.30pm. Closed all day Wed. Complete interior furnishers. Merchandise/service reflects enthusiasm of owner, who founded store 25 years ago. Attractive showrooms created from 3 Victorian houses. Classic furniture/ upholstery, fabrics, Oriental rugs, lighting, china, glass, gifts. Full interior-design service.

JP Lucas & Co 7 Friars Square, Aylesbury, Bucks HP20 2SS. (*Town centre*). *Tel:* 0296 86255. *Open:* Mon to Sat 9am to 5.30pm. Traditional "house furnishers". Furniture, carpets, curtains but not lights, chinaware etc.

2/MULTIPLE STORES

Allied Carpets and Furnishings Nearest branch. *Tel:* Teledata 01-200 0200. Star store: County Oak Retail Park, London Road, Crawley. *Tel:* 0293 541162. *Open:* Mon, Thurs & Fri 10am to 8pm. Tues, Wed & Sat 10am to 6pm. Sun 12am to 4pm. 98 stores nationwide, including Marble Arch, Putney, Wood Green, Wembley. Floorcoverings, curtains, linens, upholstery, beds, bedroom furniture. Around 3,000 carpets; 2,700 curtain fabrics. 2,000 ready-made curtains, from inexpensive light-weights to rich velvets. Over 700 fabrics for free made-to-measure. Branded beds include Silentnight, Myers, Sleepeezee. Fully-fitted, semi-fitted, freestanding bedroom furniture; free planning. Low price guarantee. Free fitting on carpets over £6.99 sq yd; fitting guarantee for 12 months. Wearability guarantee. Home Service. Free product selection advice.

Laura Ashley Home Nearest branch. *Tel:* 0628 770345. Star store: 7/9 Harriet Street, SW1. (*3 mins Knightsbridge tube*). *Tel:* 01-235 9797. *Open:* Mon to Sat 9.30am to 6pm. *Also at:* Brighton, Windsor, Oxford, Croydon, Kingston. New concept: expands familiar Laura Ashley decorating merchandise to everything for home: furniture, beds, china/glass, cookware etc.

Laura Ashley by Post: Freephone 0800 868100. Catalogue £2.75.

Perrings Home Furnishing Nearest branch. *Tel:* 01-337 0951. Branches: Basingstoke, Bedford, Bexhill, Bournemouth, Brighton, Canterbury, Crawley, Ealing, Eastbourne, Guildford, Kingston, Oxford, Reading, Southend, Staines, Uxbridge, Watford, Working, Worcester Park. Family firm still with Perrings in charge. Well-known furniture brands, including upholstery in your fabric or theirs. Co-ordinating curtains. Full soft furnishing service. Carpets. Tableware themed around pretty colour combinations. Coffee shops in larger stores.

The Gillow Group Nearest branch. *Tel:* 01-387 7000. Amalgamation of Maples, Waring & Gillow, Wades, Kingsbury. Middle-market branded furnishings: bedroom furniture, beds, upholstery, dining and occasional ranges. Central buying makes carpets excellent value.

Next Interiors 54/60 Kensington High Street, W8. (*5 mins Kensington High Street tube*). *Tel:* 01-938 42112. *Also at:* 160 Regent Street, W1. *Tel:* 01-434 2515. *Open* (both branches): Mon to Sat 9.30am to 6pm. Late night Thurs 8pm. Co-ordinated fabrics, papers, borders, upholstery, sold alongside fashions in 42 stores nationwide. Particularly good for accessories: china/glass, vases, etc. *Mail order Next Directory:* 0345 100500. £3 refundable.

The Reject Shop Nearest branch. *Tel:* 01-736 7474. The Plaza, 116/128 Oxford Street, W1. *Tel:* 01-255 2240. *Open:* Mon to Fri 10am to 8pm. Sat 10am to 7pm. *Also at:* 209 Tottenham Court Road, W19 9AF; *Tel:* 01-580 2895; 243 King's Road, SW3 5UA; *Tel:* 01-352 0307/2750/2820; 245/249 Brompton Road, SW3 2BY; *Tel:* 01-584 7611. *And at:* Brighton, Bromley, Kingston, Watford. Misleading title: smart merchandise, low prices. Good selections modern furniture, mostly from stock.

Also china, glass, cookware, etc.

3/FURNISHING SUPERSTORES

Courts Mammoth Staples Corner, off Edgware Road, NW2. (*Brent Cross/Cricklewood tubes*). *Tel*: 01-450 9538. *Open*: Mon to Fri 9am to 8pm. Sat 9am to 6pm. Sun 11am to 5pm. Vast selection branded furniture, bedding, carpets, accessories. The China Shoppe, Curtains and Co-ordinates, fitted kitchens, bathrooms.
Also at: Canterbury, Maidstone, Shoreham, Southend, West Thurrock.

Habitat Out of Town Nearest branch. *Tel*: 0491 35000. Alliance Road, Western Avenue, Acton W5. (*10 mins Hanger Lane tube; free car park*). *Tel*: 01-993 8261. *Open*: Mon Tues & Sat 10am to 6pm. Wed to Fri 10am to 8pm. Sun 10am to 5pm.
Also at: Drury Crescent, Purley Way, Croydon; *Tel*: 01-681 3818. Knaves Beech, Loudwater, High Wycombe, Bucks HP10 7QW; *Tel*: 06285 31142.

Seacourt Tower Retail Park, Westway, Botley, Oxon OX2 0JJ; *Tel*: 0865 790313.
And at: Hatfield, Basingstoke, West Thurrock, Epsom, Havant. Habitat, pioneers of High Street design, now have superstores. Roomsettings display kitchens, dining rooms, bedrooms, living rooms. Made-to-measure soft furnishings. Take away furniture. Lighting, including low voltage. Accessories. Café. Children's play areas.

Furnitureland Nearest branch. *Tel*: 01-698 6625. Unit A2, Lakeside Retail Park, West Thurrock, Essex RM16 1WU. (*Grays BR plus bus; free car park*). *Tel*: 0708 867194. *Open*: Mon to Fri 9am to 8pm. Wed & Sat 9am to 6pm.
Also at: Catford, Finchley, Goodmayes, Merton, Stevenage, Wembley. Branded furniture for bedrooms, dining rooms, living rooms. Carpets, curtains, accessories. Emphasis on good service, competitive prices.

Ikea Drury Way, North Circular Road, NW10 0JQ. (*10 mins Neasden tube; free car park*). *Tel*: 01-451 5611. *Open*: Mon to Fri 10am to 8pm. Sat 9am to 6pm. Swedish megastore: over half goods come from Sweden. Wonderful value in self-assembly furniture. Also beds/linens, lighting, floorings (including wood strip), china/tableware, cookware. Bathroom fittings, including fitted furniture. Kitchens. All furniture carries "mobelfakta" information (furniture facts), and is tested to rigorous standards of Swedish Furniture Institute. Free catalogue. Café. Children's play areas (inside and out).

MFI Furniture Centres Nearest branch. *Tel*: teledata 01-200 0200. Star store: Victoria Road, Ruislip, Middx. (*Eastcote/Ruislip Manor tube plus bus*). *Tel*: 01-423 6884. *Open*: Mon to Sat 9am to 6pm. Late nights Mon, Thurs & Fri 8pm. MFI is getting a new look. Improved layouts, products, at keen prices. Free planning for kitchens, bedrooms, bathrooms. Installations. Deliveries.

DIY SUPERSTORES

The recent expansion of the DIY Superstores (or "sheds", depending on your point of view), has been explosive. This retail phenomenon is based on a welcome upgrading of product quality and design, combined with new "user-friendly" service attitudes.

B & Q Nearest branch. *Tel*: Teledata 01-200 0200. Star stores: Hayes Bridge, Uxbridge Road, Hayes UB4 0JU. (*Southall tube plus bus; 207 stops outside*). *Tel*: 01-848 1898. *Open* (all branches): Mon to Sat 8am to 9pm.
Also at: 2 Larch Drive, Gunnersbury Avenue, Chiswick Roundabout, W4. (*5 mins Gunnersbury tube*). *Tel*: 01-995 8028.
Also at: Sutton Court Road, Sutton, Surrey SM1 4RQ. (*5 mins Sutton BR; bus station opposite*). *Tel*:01-643 8933. B&Q stocks over 25,000 lines. Banquet kitchens; free planning. Bathrooms in 13 colours. Fitted bedrooms. Own-brand paints. Wallcoverings, tiles, floorings. DIY materials, tools, tool hire. Free delivery. Telephone ordering. Guaranteed lowest prices. Garden design.

Do It All Nearest branch. *Tel*: Teledata 01-200 0200. Unit 1, Boulevard Park 25, Borehamwood, Essex. (*5 mins Elstree/Boreham Wood BR*). *Tel*: 01-207 5277.
Also at: 113/117 Farnham Road, Slough, Berks. (*5 mins Slough BR*). *Tel*: 0753 822905.
Also at: Alliance Road, Western

Avenue, Park Royal W3. (*Park Royal tube*). *Tel*: 01-992 5097. *Open*: Mon to Fri 9am to 8pm. Sat & Sun 9am to 6pm. Prettiest of the Superstores: usual DIY stocks plus furniture and soft furnishing co-ordinates. Over 23,000 lines. Own brands for tiles, wallcoverings, textiles, tools, paint. Free DIY leaflets.

Homebase Nearest branch. *Tel*: 01-773 3155. Star stores: Syon Lane, Isleworth, Middx PW7 5NP. (*Syon Lane BR*). *Tel*: 01-847 3687.
And at: Warwick Road, Kensington W14 8PU. (*5 mins Earls Court tube*). *Tel*: 01-603 6397.
And at: Weir Road, off Dunsford Road, Wimbledon SW19. (*Wimbledon Park tube/Haydons Road BR*). *Tel*: 01-944 1044. Fresh, clean approach to DIY. Light, airy stores. High display standards. Minimum 18,000 lines. Wide range decorative products, DIY materials, tools etc. Outside stores for building materials. Outstanding house plants/garden centres, with resident horticulturists for advice. Laura Ashley boutiques. Tool hire. Timber/glass cutting. Paint mixing service. Deliveries. Information desks. Free DIY Project Planners. Extra Service for special/custom-made products to order. (Basingstoke, Brentford, Catford, Colchester, Croydon, Hatfield, Kensington, Luton, New Southgate, Rayleigh Weir, Reading, Rochester, Romford, Walthamstow, Watford, Wimble-

don). Interior design schemes: £5.

Magnet Nearest branch. *Tel*: 0535 661133. Star stores: 245/259 Kensington High Street, W8 6SA. (*7 mins Kensington High Street tube*). *Tel*: 01-938 3377. *Open* (all branches): Mon to Sat 9am to 6pm. Late night Thurs & Fri 8pm.
Also at: Pinkham Way, North Circular Road, New Southgate N11 2UT. *Tel*: 01-368 5919.
And at: 2/8 The High Street, Staines, Middx TW18 4EE. *Tel*: 0784 51313.
And at: Longfield Road, North Farm Industrial Estate, Tunbridge Wells, Kent TN2 3UR. *Tel*: 0892 511088.
And at: St Mary's Cray, Near Orpington, Kent BR5 3PU. *Tel*: 0689 77021. Formerly a joinery firm, Magnet are particularly strong in windows/doors. Impressive kitchen range; computer-aided planning/installations. Also fitted bathrooms/bedrooms. Attractive free colour catalogue.

Payless DIY Nearest branch. *Tel*: 0732 460000. Star stores: 330 Purley way, Croydon, Surrey. (*East Croydon BR*). *Tel*: 01-680 0165. *Open* (all branches): Mon to Sat 8am to 8pm.
Also at: Botley Road, Oxford. (*Oxford BR*). *Tel*: 0865 790415. Wide range decorative products, DIY/heavy building materials, including own brands. Free loan roof racks. Free DIY leaflets. DIY Doctor gives advice on 0800 289119 (freephone) Mon to Sat 9am to 8pm. Sun 9am to 5pm.

DIY Superstores

Guaranteed lowest prices. Free plug with electrical appliances.

Texas Homecare Nearest branch. *Tel*: Teledata 01-200 0200. Star stores: Luton Road, Dunstable, Beds LU5 4JN. (*M1, junction 11*). *Tel*: 0582 472028.
And at: County Oak Retail Park, Crawley, Sussex. (*A23, South of Gatwick*). *Tel*: 0293 511551.
Also at: Lakeside Retail Park, West Thurrock, Essex RM16 1WR. (*M25*). *Tel*: 0708 865766. *Open* (all branches): Mon to Sat 9am to 8pm. Open Tues 9.30am. Open bank holidays. Around 30 kitchen ranges, plus bathrooms; freestanding bedrooms. Planning. Free central heating planning. Some 360 wallcovering patterns; vinyl, cork, carpet, ceramic tiles. Hand/power tools, ladders, decorative materials, ironmongery. Housewares, small electrical appliances. Square Deal paint/wood finishes. Own-brand Match-Point co-ordinated soft furnishings. Dulux Paint studios for ideas/advice. (Dunstable, High Wycombe, West Thurrock, Tunbridge Wells, Crawley). Information bar, trained staff. Texas Pantry for refreshments. Children's play area, video shows/rides. Free wood cutting service.

Wickes Nearest branch: *Tel*: 01-863 5696. Star stores: Weldale Street, Reading RG1 7BX. (*5 mins Reading BR*). *Tel*: 0734 588288. *Open* (all branches): Mon to Sat 8am to 8pm.
Also at: High Road, Chadwell Heath, Essex RM6 4HX. (*5 mins Goodmayes BR*). *Tel*: 01-590 1116.
Also at: 1 Rat Lane, Rayleigh, Essex SS6 7UP. (*5 mins Rayleigh BR*). *Tel*: 0268 776262. Timber, building materials, ceramic tiles, bathrooms, kitchens, paint, electrical goods, plumbing, windows, doors, conservatories – even swimming pools! Made-to-measure doors/windows. Free Project Planners for creative DIY. Free catalogues. Deliveries with help from forklift trucks. Tool hire for large projects at Catford (01-314 5831); Cricklewood (01-450 9888); Edmonton (01-884 0059); Farnborough (0252 513340); Hanwell (01-567 2003); Reading (0734 588288); Ruislip (01-423 4309); Wimbledon (01-946 9951).

HOME IMPROVEMENT SPECIALISTS

The old-fashioned builders'/timber merchant is the mainstay of the British home improvements industry, standing up well against DIY Superstore competition. Many are now glamorous Home Improvement Centres. Frequently family firms, they offer the inestimable attraction of one-to-one advice/service.

BJ Brown (London) 681/689 Holloway Road, N19 5SE. (*5 mins Archway tube*). *Tel*: 01-263 7283. *Open*: Mon to Sat 9.30am to 6pm. One of new image up-market "designer" builders' merchants. Luxury kitchen displays by Italian Schiffini/British Rossini. Worktops: Corian, laminate, solid wood, tiles, granite. Ceramic/ marble floor tiles. Built-in kitchen appliances. Kitchen/bathroom planning. Bathroom sanitaryware. Best brands sinks/taps. Builders'/DIY supplies: plumbing, heating, rainwater drainage. Tools, ironmongery.
Also at (trade counter): 53/59 Hargrave Road, N19 5SH. *Tel*: 01-272 2157/6418 & 01-263 7283.

CP Hart & Sons Newnham Terrace, Hercules Road, SE1 7DR. (*5 mins Lambeth North tube/Waterloo tube/ BR*). *Tel*: 01-928 5866. *Open*: Mon to Fri 8.30am to 5.30pm. Sat 8.30am to 5pm. Sophisticated showroom "underneath the arches" for kitchen/bathroom roomsettings. Tiles, sinks, taps. All plumbing requirements. Kitchen/bathroom planning. Personal service; prompt deliveries. Catalogue.

W H Newson 61 Pimlico Road, SW1W 8NF. (*7 mins Sloane Square tube*). *Tel*: 01-730 6262. *Open*: Mon to Fri 8am to 5pm. Sat 8am to 12 noon. Timber/DIY specialists trading for over 100 years. Fine timber/mouldings, doors/windows, fencing, hardware, home improvement materials, for trade/private customers. Mouldings matched to any specification. Trained staff. Speedy free deliveries. Fat free colour catalogue: a DIY essential.
Also at: 491 Battersea Park Road, SW11 4NH. *Tel*: 01-223 4411.
And at: 7 East Hill, Wandsworth SW18 2HT. *Tel*: 01-874 7085.
And at: 61-79 Norwood High Street, SE27 9JS. *Tel*: 01-670 0112.
And at: 19 Station Road, Sunbury-on-Thames, Middx TW16 6SB. *Tel*: 0932 780633.
And at: Heathside House, Brighton Road, Burgh Heath, Surrey KT20 6BE. *Tel*: 0737 362111.
And at: All Saints Industrial Estate, All Saints Avenue, Margate, Kent CT9 5TJ. *Tel*: 0843 227697.
And at: Burr Street, Luton LU2 0HN. *Tel*: 0582 21707.

Poores of Acton 230/234 Acton High Street, W3 8EX. (*15 mins Acton Town tube, 207 bus stops outside*). *Tel*: 01-992 1177/1179. *Open*: Mon to Fri 8am to 5.30pm. Sat 8.30am to 5.30pm. Open bank holidays. Old-established family firm; 7,500 sq ft rambling buildings. Tools, hardware, paints, security, garden, household. Service counter at back: helpful expert advice. Friendly staff.

Smith & Sons Anvil House, Matthias Road, N16 8NU. (*Arsenal/Manor House tubes plus bus; 5 mins Newington Green BR*). *Tel*: 01-254 1200. *Open*: Mon to Fri 8am to 5.30pm. Sat 8.30am to 4.30pm. Family firm with 120 years' experience: "The Professionals' Professional" - but they welcome home owners. Over 17,000 items under one rambling roof. 20 kitchen displays: SieMatic, Elizabeth Ann, Grovewood, Neff, De Dietrich, Franke, Leisure. Sinks, tiles, taps. Planning/installation. Interior design. Bathroom, shower, tile centre. Paint, gas, plumbing departments. Personal service; prompt deliveries.

Travis Perkins Bathroom and Kitchen Design Centre 22 Praed Street, W2 1NH. (*5 mins Edgware Road/Paddington tubes/Paddington BR*). *Tel*: 01-723 9229. *Open*: Mon to Fri 8.30am to 5pm. Sat 8.30am to 12 noon. New designer look for Sandell Perkins, familiar builders' merchants, which opened doors January 1989. Kitchens/bathrooms in exclusive ranges from leading manufacturers; complete interior design products. Tiles, taps, bathroom accessories, mirrors, showers, wallcovering and fabrics. One of the largest showrooms in London: over 7,000 Sq ft. "Everything under one roof" is their admirable aim. Most stock available within a week: some designer ranges take longer. Kitchens by Siematic/Poggenpohl. Bathroom sanitaryware/fittings from Villeroy & Boch/Habs Grohe. Majestic/Ideal-Standard/Twyford/ Armitage Shanks. Co-ordinated fabrics/wallcoverings by Parkertex/ Hill Knowles/GP & J Baker/JAB International. Own special value Ultimate Kitchen Collection. Tel. for free brochure, plus free literature for all products in showroom.

ARCADES & MARKETS

1/ARCADES

Arcades are better known to tourists than to London shoppers, quite inexplicably. Definitely the 'upmarket' places to shop, not only are they architecturally attractive, they are of historical interest too. Burlington arcade for example, tucked away in Piccadilly almost opposite the Ritz, was opened in 1819, just after the Battle of Waterloo. When the strip of wasteland was being cleared for building, forty tons of oyster shells were discovered. Food for thought there perhaps? The shops, fun to visit, usually offer excellent quality goods and services.

Brompton Arcade SW3

(*Green Park/Piccadilly Circus tubes*). Runs off the Brompton Road through to Basil Street. It's quiet and peaceful compared to the frenzied activity of Knightsbridge – nice to get away from the general rush of the main street for a while.

Camilla Hepper *Tel*: 01-225 0188. *Open*: Mon to Sat 10am to 6.30pm. Wed 10am to 7pm. A general main theme of cats and other animals. Purrfect kitchen additions consist of oven stoves, mugs and catty coasters. They also stock tea-pot stands, mirrors, framed prints, gold plated toothbrush mugs, soap dishes and pretty hand made tissue boxes, bins etc. (lace un-

limited). Fill your room with fresh flowery fragrance, courtesy of modern technology: an electric room 'perfumier' heats your own choice of essential oils. Death of the traditional bunch of red roses perhaps?

The Italian Paper Shop *Tel*: 01-589 1668. *Open*: Mon to Sat 9.30am to 7pm. Wed 9.30 to 5.30. Rare hand marbled paper from Il Papiro, Florence. Gift boxes of various shapes. Marbled in-out trays with lids, letter racks to match. Unusual lamps: a small hand marbled shade designed to go with a brass holder that fits on top of a candle. Slides down as the candle burns. Not only a bright idea but a saving on electricity too.

Jarrolds *Tel*: 01-581 7975. *Open*: Mon to Sat 9am to 5.30pm. An enormous choice of photo frames of different shapes and sizes and you can even have them specially made to order to match your decor. A vast array of leather goods including leather bound visitors and address books are on sale here and you can have a gold stamp with your name and/or address if you wish (it takes approximately four days to be done). Table mats with designs of African animals, London scenes and Japanese prints, or special designs of your choice can be made to order. A range of brushes with mock ivory handles. Services include rebristling of brushes and restringing of pearls.

Burlington Arcade W1

(*Piccadilly Circus tube*). Burlington Arcade is a joy to wander through – and wander or at least stroll you should, because if you run or hurtle through, the Beadles will get you. They'll also stop you if you whistle or sing. Resplendent in their three-quarter length grey frock coats, decorated with gilt buttons and rows of gold braid around the cuffs (three rows for the head beadle and two for the others) the Beadles do not tolerate any bad behaviour and are quick to stop anyone who attempts to ruffle the serene surroundings. Their duty is to act as guards, to keep a protective and watchful eye on the shoppers and shops, but they are also very amiable characters, often willing to chat to interested visitors about the arcade.

Charles Clemments *Tel*: 01-493 3923. *Open*: Mon to Fri 9am to 5.30pm. Sat 9am to 4.30pm. Stock various bits and pieces for both dedicated and novice wine buffs, including wine thermometers and clip-on bottle parasols. A selection of shaving brushes, wallets, drinking flasks and embroidery scissors. Will rebristle your handmade brushes.

Demas *Tel*: 01-493 9496. *Open*: Mon to Fri 10am to 4.45pm. Sat 10.30 to 1pm. Informal but interesting and informed sales staff selling, amongst other things like jewellery and so on,

Art Deco chinaware.

Edmonds *Tel*: 01-495 3127. *Fax*: 0273-26627. *Open*: Mon to Fri 9.30am to 5.30pm. Sat 9.30am to 4.30pm. Took over this shop in December 1988 but far from being newcomers to the trade, Edmonds have been in this business for over twenty years, in The Lanes in Brighton. They sell antique gold and silver and jewellery, stocking items that date from 1700s up to 1950s. A Fax machine pours out requests, orders and instructions from their many overseas customers. Service includes engraving.

Irish Linen Co *Tel*: 01-493 8949. *Open*: Mon to Fri 9am to 5.30pm. Sat 9am to 4.30pm. Established in 1875 and has a long tradition of supplying bed and table were made of pure Irish linen. Heavy damask table linens are this shops speciality. Also stock a wide range of sheets and handkerchiefs. Monograms, appliqué and embroidered patterns are available. Framed testimonials from Buckingham Palace, the Athens Royal Palace and the Agents of Charles Chaplin adorn the walls.

The Pewter Shop *Tel*: 01-493 1730. *Open*: Mon to Fri 9am to 5.30pm. Sat 9am to 4.30pm. The Americans love it and so do the French. The Germans take it seriously but many of the English, it seems, have yet to appreciate the beauty of this silvery metal. Pewter is the fourth most precious of the world's commonly used metals after platinum, gold and silver. It ages gracefully without the need to be polished, and is ideal as a drinking vessel as it doesn't taint. The Pewter Shop stocks both antique and modern pewter including plates, candlesticks, tankards and flagons with lids.

Pickett *Tel*: 01-493 8939. *Open*: Mon to Fri 9am to 5.30pm. Sat 9am to 4.30pm. A shop that specialises in British-made goods. Hand silk-screen printed scarves, robes, ties, waistcoats by designer Georgina von Etzdorf. Leather goods include visitors books, desk sets, note books, jewellery boxes. Services include monogramming, gold blocking and cornering.

Piccadilly Arcade W1

(*Piccadilly Circus tube*). Immediately opposite Burlington Arcade, this smaller and less grand affair is nevertheless worth a visit.

Waterford Wedgwood *Tel*: 01-629 2614. *Open*: Mon to Fri 9am to 6pm. Sat 9am to 4pm. A good selection of lovely fine bone china and earthenware. Has loads of ideas for gifts (for yourself as well as for others).

Princes Arcade W1

(*Piccadilly Circus tube*). Situated near Fortnum and Mason, the original building here was opened in 1883 and the arcade created in the 1930s.

Coleridge *Tel*: 01-437 0106. *Open*: Mon to Sat 10.30am to 6pm. An impressive shop which sells beautiful handmade glass. It has the widest selection of good quality British contemporary glass in the world. Coleridge provide a major outlet for new talent. Worth a visit, if not to buy, at least to look.

John English Gifts *Tel*: 01-437 2082. *Open*: Mon to Fri 9am to 6pm. Sat 9am to 5pm. Emphasis on British made goods. Sells enamel boxes, handmade scent bottles, Scottish jewellery and Moorcroft handmade pottery with its typically dark blue glazed backgrounds and magnolia designs.

2/MARKETS

This little piggy went to market, This little piggy stayed at home ... I'm afraid that a domesticated piggy would miss the unequalled thrill of shopping at the market. You never know what you might find. Not just the usual things, pretty things and let's face it, the basic motivation, cheap things, but also wit, sparkle and thrills galore from the traders themselves and other shoppers. But do be careful, you might get your wallet pinched, or handbag snatched, but in my experience, you never get short-changed. Markets are legion and built into the British way of life. They are also top tourist attractions so I'm afraid you'll just have to put up with top tourists. But they too can be interesting and you never know who you're going to meet. My book is concerned with the home, as you must have realised by now so below I have highlighted markets in London and the South East that offer home merchandise ... if it isn't raining.

London Markets

Bell Street Market Bell Street, Lisson Grove NW1. (*Edgware Rd tube*). *Open*: Mon to Sat. Junk, second hand furniture, antiques.

Beresford Square Woolwich, SE18. (*Woolwich BR*). *Open*: Tue to Sat 9am to 5pm. Thurs 9am to 1pm. Variety of general items and household goods at reasonable prices.

Bermondsey Market Bermondsey Square, SE1. (*London Bridge tube/BR*). *Open*: Fri 3 am to 4pm. Antique market. Main venue for dealers in London and South East. 250 stalls selling furniture, silver, stuffed animals, glass, porcelain, pictures.

Brick Lane Shoreditch, E1 and E2. (*Liverpool Street, Aldgate East, Old Street tubes; Liverpool Street BR*) *Open*: Sun am. One of the more popular markets. Serious collectors have been, shopped and gone before 9am. Antiques, crockery, electrical equipment, furniture, carpets.

Brixton Market Electric Avenue, Popes Road, Brixton Station Road, SW9. (*Brixton BR*). *Open*: Mon to Sat 8am to 6pm. Wed 8am to 1pm. Household, haberdashery, bric-a-brac.

Camden Lock Chalk Farm Road, NW1. (*Camden Town tube*). *Open*: Sat and Sun 9am to 6pm. Art deco and antiques, rugs, secondhand furniture, paintings.

Camden Passage Camden Passage, Islington N1. (*Angel tube*). *Open*: Wed 6.30am to 4pm and Sat 8am to 4pm. Antiques, art nouveau, art deco, clocks, maps and prints, antique toys.

Church Street Market Church Street, W2. (*Edgware Road tube*). *Open*: Tues to Sat. Household goods, junk, antiques, bric-a-brac.

Deptford Market High Street, Douglas Way, Deptford SE8. (*New Cross tube; Deptford BR*). General household, bric-a-brac, second hand, wicker work, lamp shades.

Earls Court Market Lillie Road, SW6. (*Earls Court tube*). *Open*: Sun 8am to 1pm. Bed linen, electrical goods, general household.

Greenwich Market Church Street, Greenwich High Rd, SE10. (*Greenwich BR. Boat from Charing Cross or Westminster*). *Open*: Sat and Sun. Books, crafts, antiques, bric-a-brac.

Inverness Street Camden, NW1. (*Camden Town tube*). *Open*: Mon to Sat (except Thurs pm). Bric-a-brac, junk, general household.

Jubilee Market Covent Garden, WC2. (*Covent Garden tube*). *Open*: Sat to Mon. Bric-a-brac and antiques Mon. Crafts, ceramics Sat and Sun.

Kingsland Waste Market Kingsland Road, E8. (*Dalston Junction BR*). *Open*: Mon to Sat. A large market selling a diversity mixture of goods. DIY tools, house paints, electrical goods, second hand furniture.

Lambeth Walk Market Lambeth Walk, SE11. (*Vauxhall, Lambeth North tubes*). *Open*: Mon to Sat 8am to 6pm. Thurs 8am to 1pm. Household goods.

London Silver Vaults Chancery Lane, EC2. (*Chancery Lane tube*). *Open*: Mon to Fri, Sat am. Modern and antique silver.

Lower Marsh Lambeth, SE1. (*Waterloo tube/BR*). *Open*: Mon to Sat 10.45am to 3pm. General household goods.

Northcote Road Market Northcote Road, SW11. (*Clapham Common BR*). *Open*: Mon to Sat 7am to 6.15pm. General Household goods.

North End Road Market North End Road, SW6. (*Fulham Broadway tube*). *Open*: Mon to Sat 9am to 5pm. Thurs 9am to 1pm. Hardware, electrical goods, kitchen/bathroom ware, bed linen, haberdashery.

Portobello Road Market Portobello Road, W10 and W11. (*Notting Hill Gate/Ladbroke Grove tubes*). *Open*: Sat. Bric-a-brac, junk, antiques.

Putney Flea Market Putney Hill, SW15. (*East Putney tube/Putney BR*). *Open*: Fri, Sat. Bric-a-brac, junk.

Shepherd's Bush Market Uxbridge and Goldhawk Roads, W12. (*Goldhawk Road tube*). *Open*: Mon to Sat 9am to 4.30pm. Thurs 9am to 1pm. Crockery, bric-a-brac, kitchen utensils, carpets, rugs, vinyl flooring, bedding, furnishing fabrics, electrical goods, haberdashery.

Walthamstow Market High Street, Walthamstow E17. (*Walthamstow Central tube/Walthamstow Queens Road BR*). *Open*: Thurs, Fri, Sat. Kitchen ware, good quality crystal.

Well Street Market Well Street, Hackney E9. (*Hackney Central/London Fields BR*). General household.

Wembley Market Wembley Stadium Car Park, Middlesex. (*Wembley Park Tube/Wembley Complex BR*). *Open*: Sun am. Large market. One of the busiest. Linens, general household, hardware.

Berkshire

The Emporium Merchants Place, Reading. *Open*: Mon to Sat. Junk, bric-a-brac, antiques.

General Retail Market Hosier Street, Reading. *Open*: Wed, Fri, Sat. Household goods, bric-a-brac, second hand.

General Retail Market Rear of Town Hall, Wokingham. *Open*: Tues, Thurs, Fri, Sat. General household items.

Buckinghamshire

General Retail Market Friars Square, New Town Centre, Aylesbury. *Open*: Wed, Fri, Sat 8am to 5pm. Large outdoor area and a covered underground section, stocking general household items, electrical goods, bric-a-brac.

Cambridgeshire

Ely Market Market Place, Ely. *Open*: Thurs 9.30 to 4.30. China, crockery, bric-a-brac, fabric, garden equipment.

Essex

General Retail Market Market Road, Chelmsford. *Open*: Thurs. In the town centre, sells second hand items.

General Retail Market High Steet, Colchester. *Open*: Sat. General household goods.

Romford market Market Place, Romford. *Open*: Wed, Fri, Sat. Antiques, bric-a-brac.

Hertfordshire

General Market St Peter's Street, St Albans. *Open*: Wed, Sat. Bric-a-brac, bed linens, general household goods.

Kent

General Retail Market Kingsmead Road, Canterbury. *Open*: Wed, Sat. Large market stocking general household goods, haberdashery, bedding, towels, bric-a-brac, furnishing fabrics.

Ivy Lane Canterbury. *Open*: Mon to Sat. Bric-a-brac.

Sydney Cooper Centre St Peter Street, Canterbury. *Open*: Sat 9.30 to 5pm. Antiques and crafts.

The Brookman Chatham. *Open*: Sat 9am to 5pm. General household goods.

General Retail Market King's Road, Herne Bay. *Open*: Sat 9am to 4pm. General household goods, furnishings, bric-a-brac, bedding.

Corporation St Rochester. *Open*: Sat 9am to 1pm. Fleamarket and Antiques.

Maidstone Market Maidstone *Open*: Tues. Large market with indoor and outdoor area. Popular hunting ground for dealers from all over the country. Antiques, bric-a-brac.

Surrey

St Peters Street Indoor Market St Peters Hall, Ledbury Road, South Croydon. *Open*: Fri 10am to 4pm. Antiques, Household items.

The Covered Market High Street, Epsom. *Open*: Mon to Sat except Wed 9am to 4.30pm. Wicker work, crockery, cooking utensils, carpets, pictures, bric-a-brac, towels, linens, dried flowers.

East Sussex

Saturday Market Upper Gardiner Street, Brighton. *Open*: Sat morn. Antiques, junk, furniture, china, glassware.

Sunday Market British Rail Car Park, Brighton. *Open*: Sun 9am to 2pm. Various household items plus junk/treasures, antiques, furniture, pictures, bric-a-brac.

West Sussex

General Market Central Car Park, Burgess Hill. *Open*: Wed, Sat. Antiques.

SHOPPING CENTRES

London Postal Districts

Brent Cross Shopping Centre Hendon, NW4 3FP. (*Brent Cross/Hendon Central tubes: buses 16a, 26, 112, 113, 142, 182, 266, C11. Free car park: 5217 spaces. Easy access from M1 and North Circular Road.*) *Tel*: 01-202 8095. *Open*: Mon to Fri 10am to 8pm. Sat 9am to 6pm. Enclosed shoppers' world likely to be refurbished and extended soon. Floors are clean, paved with marble or carpeted, fountains play under huge dome of coloured lights. Wander around 82 stores protected from the weather. Fashion predominates. Find **Burtons, Laura Ashley, John Kent, Miss Selfridge, Next, Wallis, Dorothy Perkins, Coles, Benetton** and shoe shops like **Ravel, Lilley & Skinner, K Shoes.**
The Centre is on two levels connected by escalators. In **John Lewis** (*Tel*: 01-202 6535) find china and glass in front; to right, traditional and modern lighting. Good bedlinens, plus Jonelle furnishing fabrics unparalleled for value and style. 'Place To Eat' caters for all tastes. **BhS Lighting** (*Tel*: 01-202 4562) For traditional homes, Victorian styles, or Art Deco or Art Nouveau designs. Spotlights in all colours. **Fenwick** (*Tel*: 01-202 8200) opposite end from John Lewis, bright and breezy, full of fashions and home goods. **Marks & Spencer** (*Tel*: 01-202 0711) accessible from lower level, excellent home furnishings department. Get their Home Furnishings Collection catalogue: includes room settings as well as practical guidance with size charts for bedlinen, curtains and towels. Customer order service for goods in catalogue. **Boots Cookshop** (*Tel*: 01-202 5256) at lower level. Stylish low-cost glassware: everything for basic kitchen.

The Ealing Broadway Centre The Broadway W5 5JY. (*3 mins Ealing Broadway tube. Car park 1,000 spaces.*) *Tel*: 01-567 3453. *Open*: generally 9am/9.30am to 5.30pm/6pm, late night Thursday, closing times vary. Part pedestrian street, part covered walkways. Spectacular architecture: pitched slate roofs, tall towers, rustic red brick, Portland stone. Mirrors, glass, fountains and globe lamps to illuminate the trees and plants. Endearing bronze horse sculpture. This centre caters for all needs, but the emphasis is fashion. **Miss Selfridge, Blowsy, Benetton, Chelsea Girl, Dorothy Perkins, Evans, Principles: Salisbury's** bags and leather goods. For men **Hepworth, Burton, Horne's, Zy, Orbit.** Recent newcomers **Wallis, Warehouse, Dash** and **Olympus. Bentalls** packed with fashion. Post Office, North Games Gas Showroom. Also **Boots** and **Superdrug: Curry, Dixon** and **Lasky.** Large **Safeway** for late night shopping till 9pm Thurs. Snack bars/restaurants: Gatsby's in balcony area, Deux Pigeons and Olivers. **John Sanders** department store adjoins the Centre and includes **John Perrings** furnishings with good selection of sofas/furniture.

Surrey Quays Shopping Centre Redriff Road, SE16 1LL. (*Surrey Docks tube. Car parking for 1,500 cars.*) *Tel*: 01-237 5282. *Open*: 9am to 5.30pm: late Thurs/Fri. In the Surrey Docks region of the London Docklands Development Corporation: new town centre shopping for Rotherhithe and Southwark, immediately south of Rotherhithe Tunnel. In 22 acre landscaped waterside setting. High fashion content. **BhS,** shops-within-a-shop **Mothercare** and **Richards,** plus **River Island, Top Shop/Top Man, Dorothy Perkins, Evans** and **Burton: Tie Rack, Ravel, Body Shop, Salisbury's, Samuels.** On home side, **Curry, Athena, Magnet.** Food court around central atrium on first floor with seven different types of branded foods.

Outer Ring

The Ashley Centre/Kings Shade Walk High Street, Epsom, Surrey KT18 5DB. (*2 mins Epsom BR: multistorey car parking.*) *Tel*: 03727 42548. The Ashley Centre, built in 1959, now refurbished. Kings Shade Walk links it to Epsom High Street. 16 shops and stores include **Dickins & Jones, Marks & Spencer, Dorothy Perkins, Etam, Solo, Principles** and **Waitrose** supermarket. For soft furnishings, see **Shalets.**

Shopping Centres

Broadway Shopping Centre Broadway, Bexleyheath, Kent DA16 7JN. (*1m Bexley/Bexleyheath/BR. Parking for 1,000 cars, free after 5.30pm for late night shopping Thurs till 9pm.*) *Tel*: 01-301 2956. High quality malls, marble floors, copper-clad ceilings. Thousands of plants in sunken central square with trees. 58 shops are planned. Now seven major high street stores: **BhS, Marks & Spencer, Boots, Woolworth, Mothercare, Smiths** and **Safeway.** Soft furnishings from **BhS** and **Harveys.**

St Ann's St Ann's Road, Harrow HA1 1AR. (*2 mins Harrow on the Hill tube/Harrow BR. Parking 950 cars.*) *Tel*: 01-861 2282. *Open*: 9am to 6pm. Late night Thurs to 8pm. Single-level main mall connecting main square overlooked by restaurant gallery. Distinctive roofs cap lift and stair towers, dramatic entrances to College and St Ann's Road, festive look. Big stores include **BhS, C&A, Marks & Spencer** (satellite store), **WH Smith** with fashion stores like **Miss Selfridge, Richards, Benetton, Wallis, Principles for Men, Olympus Sports** and speciality shops for chocolates, rings and beauty.

The Whitgift Centre North End, Croydon, Surrey CR0 0XB. (*Multistorey parking for 2,800 cars.*) *Open*: 9am to 5.30pm. Late eve. Thurs till 9pm. Built in the 60s, now refurbished under glass-domed roof: half under cover. Over 12 acres on two levels with 125 shops. Good emphasis on furnishings including **Reject Shop, Oriental Carpets, GKD** bedrooms, **Wallspan** fitted bedrooms, **Danish Guild.** Adjoins **Allders** store at one end where more furnishings to be seen. Third largest **Marks & Spencer** (no furnishings), **Boots, Woolworth, BhS, Mothercare,** fashion including **Next** and **Principles for Men, Ratners** the jewellers.

Home Counties/S.East

Milton Keynes Shopping Centre Central Milton Keynes, Beds MK9 3ES. (*One hour Euston BR; taxi ranks at north end of Acorn Walk/south end of Borough Walk. Racks for 250 cycles next to all main entrances. Free parking for 10,000 cars in perimeter streets. Special spaces for the disabled.*) *Tel*: 0908 678641. *Open* (shops): Mon, Tues, Wed, Sat 9am/9.30am to 6pm. Late night Thurs & Fri 8pm. John Lewis closed Mon. No dogs except guide dogs for the blind and hearing dogs for the deaf. Shopping information centre opposite the open market provides advice on shopping and travel plus news of events taking place in the locality. *Tel*: 0908 670231. People come from as far away as Carlisle and South Wales, often in coach loads to this edifice of shops and services, unique not only in the UK but also in Europe. The sheer size takes your breath away. Over 150 traders with room for an average 100,000 visitors on Saturdays alone strolling down the half mile walkway. On going through one of 22 entrances, you can remain completely under cover, protected from rain or sun, unless you choose to walk, sit or picnic in the central open air square with its grass, lake and fountains. The glass vaulted ceilings to the covered walkways create a conservatory-like atmosphere, enhanced by marble floors and an abundance of exotic shrubs. Milton Keynes Shopping Centre boasts the largest mobility shop in the UK owning 60 electric wheelchairs powered specially to accommodate people weighing up to 20 stone, and averaging about 8,000 per annum. To reserve a chair, which can be brought to a specific entrance by a security guard, *Tel*: 0908 670866. Well known stores include **John Lewis, Habitat, C&A, Marks & Spencer, BhS, Mothercare, Boots** and **WH Smith. Dickins & Jones,** destroyed by fire, is being rebuilt. For fashions, find **Chelsea Girl, Dorothy Perkins, Etam, Evans, Hennes, Miss Selfridge, Next, Richard Shops** and others, shoe shops like **Dolcis, Faith Shoes, Freeman Hardy & Willis, John Farmer, Peter Lord, Ravel** and **Style Barrett.** For electrical goods, try **Curry, Dixon** and **Rumbelow.** There are banks, a Post Office, Citizens Advice Bureau and a "resource centre" for information on voluntary organisations as well as numerous food stores and shops with restaurants. Free leaflet with map, list of shops and facilities from CMK Shopping Management, 96 Midsummer Arcade, Secklow Gate West, Central Milton Keynes MK9 3ES.

West Gate Shopping Centre Stevenage, Herts SG1 1QR. (*2 mins Stevenage BR: 20 mins King's Cross. Parking for 395 cars.*) *Tel*: 0438 740696. *Open*: 9am to 5.30pm: no regular late night except at Christmas. Opened 1988, enclosed centre arranged round impressive 55ft high central atrium with 33 shops. Panoramic lifts. A striking interior: crystalline dome and curving external form of building distinguishes West Gate from its surroundings. Fashion oriented inc. **Principles, Top Man, Dorothy Perkins, Chelsea Girl, Wrygges, Suit Co.** No big department stores.

Worth a Trip

The Quadrant Centre St Peter's Road, Bournemouth BH1 2AB. (*Bournemouth BR. Car parking.*) *Tel*: 0202 298315. *Open*: 9am to 5.30pm. The Quadrant Shopping Centre lies in the heart of Bournemouth on the Old Christchurch Road. It is Britain's first Shopping Centre devoted exclusively to House and Home and at present has about 20 shops over three interlinked levels under one roof. It is not just the theme of the Centre which is different but also the overall feel of the place. With carpeted floors, soft lighting and gentle colours it is easy for the shopper to forget the noise and hustle of the normal shopping centre and relax to concentrate on the merchandise. The shops pride themselves on providing a wide and varied range of goods but, above all, on the service they offer. **John Perrings,** the furnishers, are prominent here, with **Strachan Studios** who specialise in fitted bedrooms. There is also a picture gallery called **Quadrant.** Also see **And So To Bed** who have very elegant beds, **Sofa Workshop, Lighting Workshop, Stacks** pine and cane furniture and **Curtain Dreams.** Refresh yourself at Hartley's Café and Bar.

AUCTIONS

Viewing is essential: find out viewing times and make thorough inspections. Check catalogue descriptions of lot numbers against goods. Many catalogues are available by mail order/ subscription. Beware of description AF: this stands for "as found" but may be a warning that something is wrong. A valuation list may give price guidance, or consult a member of staff. Fix an upper limit firmly in your mind and stick to it.

Take a tape measure and plans/ measurements of the rooms you are furnishing.

Read carefully conditions of sale. Buyer's commission is prevalent, usually at 10%. VAT is charged on this, making a total of 11.5% on whole item. Find out latest date for collection: after that you may be charged storage.

Bid by raising catalogue/programme. But call out a price from the floor if you wish. Bids progress in £2, £5, or even jumps according to value, but may creep up by £1 when approaching a competitive conclusion. Don't worry about dealers and special signs: let them get on with it. Blow your nose if you want to!

The following firms hold regular London auctions. In all cases, please phone to check details.

Bonhams Auctioneers 65/69 Lots Road, SW10. (*10 mins Fulham Broadway tube*). *Tel*: 01-351 7111. Tues 10.30am: sales general goods. Viewing: Sat 10.30am to 1pm; Mon 9am to 7pm. Phone to check details.

Frank G Bowen 15 Greek Street, W1V 6NY. (*3 mins Tottenham Court Road tube*). *Tel*: 01-437 3244. Thurs: every 2/3 weeks sales of household furniture/pics etc. Phone to check details.

Dowell Lloyd & Co 118 Putney Bridge Road, SW15 2NQ. (*10 mins East Putney tube*). *Tel*: 01-788 7777. Sat 9.30am to 3pm: fortnightly sales of general goods. Viewing: Fri 9am to 7.45pm.

General Auctions 63/65 Garrett Lane, SW18 4AA. (*Tooting Broadway tube/Earlsfield BR plus bus*). *Tel*: 01-870 3909. Mon 11am to 3.30pm: household furniture. Viewing: Fri 10am to 4pm; Sat 10am to 3pm.

RF Greasby (London) 211 Longley Road, SW17. (*7 mins Tooting Broadway tube; opposite Tooting BR*). *Tel*: 01-672 2972. Mon 10am: fortnightly miscellaneous sales, including lost property for London Transport, and confiscated goods from Customs & Excise!

Forrest & Co 79/85 Cobbold Road, E11 3NS. (*Leyton tube plus bus*). *Tel*: 01-534 2931. Thurs 11am: fortnightly sales of "general goods" plus occasional sales of antiques. Viewing: Tues 10am to 5pm.

Lots Road Galleries 71 Lots Road, SW10 0RN. *Tel*: 01-352 2349. (*10 mins Fulham Broadway tube*). Mon 4pm: contemporary furniture, paintings, objects. Mon 6pm: antique/traditional furniture, rugs, paintings, works of art. Viewing: Fri 10am to 3pm; Sat Sun 10am to 1pm. Mon 10am to 6pm.

North West London Auctions Lodge House, Lodge Lane, N12. *Tel*: 01-445 9000. Mon 5pm: general antiques. Viewing: Sun 9am to 1pm; Mon 9am to 5pm.

Rosan & Co 144/150 London Road, Croydon Surrey CR0 2TD. (*Adjoins Croydon General Hospital; 5 mins West Croydon BR*). *Tel*: 01-688 1123. Sat 10am to 2pm: sale of general goods including furniture and antiques. Viewing: Fri 9am to 5pm; Sat 9 to 10am.

Rosebery's 3/4 Hardwick Street, EC1. (*5 mins Angel tube*). *Tel*: 01-837 3418. Wed once a month: antiques/ works of art/fine furnishings. *Also at*: The Old Booking Hall, Crystal Palace Station Road, SE19. (*Situated in Crystal Palace station*). *Tel*: 01-778 4024. Sat: fortnightly auctions. Phone to check details.

SERVICES

1/CHINA MENDING

Ashton-Bostock 21 Charlwood Street, SW1V 2EA. *Tel*: 01-828 3656.

China Repairers 64 Charles Lane, St John's Wood NW8 7SB. *Tel*: 01-722 8407.

Judith Larney The Studios, 1A Sangora Road, SW11 1RL. *Tel*: 01-350 1002.

Studio ID 1d Kensington Church Walk, W8 4NB. *Tel*: 01-937 7583.

2/CLEANING: GENERAL

Cleantime 9/11 Kensington High Street, W8 5NP. *Tel*: 01-450 2231/01-938 3405. Complete spring-cleaning service. Carpets/upholstery/curtains.

The German Bedding Centre 138 Marylebone Road, NW1. *Tel*: 01-935 0196. Cleaning/renovation all continental quilts.

Kingcome Cleaning 40 Kyrle Road, Battersea SW11. *Tel*: 01-223 9354. Wallcoverings, chandeliers, lamps. Curtains/festoon blinds taken down, cleaned, rehung. Rugs cleaned in special workshop. Total spring-clean.

Poppies Domestic Cleaning Agencies Local agency. *Tel*: 0325 488699. Everyday cleaning/domestic help.

Service Master in the Capital 24 Neasden Lane, NW10. *Tel*: 01-459 6274. Curtains, walls, hard floors, leather. Emergency service for floods/fire. Stain-proofing. Anti-static treatments. Upholstery/carpet repairs, French polishing.

3/CLEANING: CARPETS & UPHOLSTERY

Many firms advertise. But carpets/upholstery can be ruined by inexpert cleaning, so choose with care. Contact:

The Carpet Cleaners Association For nearest branch. *Tel*: 0533 554352. Membership guarantees professional standards; arbitration service for complaints. Firms licensing cleaners to use equipment/methods/chemicals oversee standards.

Fiber-Seal (UK) *Tel*: 0628 771066.

Prochem *Tel*: 01-549 0927.

Safeclean/Safeproof *Tel*: 0235 833022.

Scotchcare Services (Scotchgard) *Tel*: 0494 463825/463752.

ServiceMaster For nearest branch. *Tel*: 0533 610761. Hot water extraction (aka steam cleaning) is the newest method for carpet cleaning. Machines can be hired.

Trewax (Hydro-Mist machines) *Tel*: 0582 599571.

Vibra Vac (Rug Doctor) *Tel*: 0903 32019.

Bissell (Carpet Butler Deep Clean) *Tel*: 01-531 7241.

Firms listed below clean carpets/upholstery in home/factory.

London Postal Districts

Abacus Cleaning 7 Lewisham Way, SE14. *Tel*: 01-691 4518. Flood damage service; carpet laying.

Abbey Cleaning 6 Station Road, Winchmore Hill N21. *Tel*:01-360 9541. Flood damage service; carpet re-fixing.

A Cleaner Carpet 90 Wilton Road, SW1. *Tel*: 01-821 1221.

Cleaningmasters 64 Coombe Lane, SW20. *Tel*: 01-879 1200. Flood damage service; carpet relaying.

The Cleanteam 9 Lonsdale Road, NW6. *Tel*: 01-586 0005.

Cleaningwise 211 Upper Richmond Road, Putney SW15.*Tel*: 0l-789 2133/ 01-785 2552. Wet/flooded carpet service. Carpet fitting.

EMG Cleaning Services 1121B London Road, Norbury SW16. *Tel*: 01-679 2569. Oriental rugs. Emergency treatment for wet/flooded carpets; carpet fitting.

Four Corners 217c Victoria Park Road, Hackney E9 7HD. *Tel*: 01-533 3241/986 7357. Carpet/upholstery/ soft furnishings. Carpet repairs including split seams, uneven wear, aged/discoloured underlay.

Kleentex Ltd 60 Woodberry Avenue, Winchmore Hill N21 3LD. *Tel*: 01-886 7602.

Magic Carpet 47 Colebrook Avenue, Ealing W13 8JZ. *Tel*:01-997 3374. Emergency service wet/flooded carpets; carpet fitting.

Pilgrim Payne Latimer Place, Latimer Road, W10. *Tel*: 01-960 5656. Holder of the Royal warrant. All cleaning to highest standards.

Permaclean (UK) Unit 31, Sleaford Street Ind. Est., Sleaford Road, SW8. *Tel*:01-622 0151. Service for wet/ flooded carpets. Stain-proofing.

ServiceMaster by Jenkins 500 Chesham House, 150 Regent Street, W1. *Tel*: 01-734 5351.

ServiceMaster (SW1/SW3) Abbey Farmhouse, Winkfield Lane, Winkfield, Windsor, Berks. *Tel*: 01-584 3187.

ServiceMaster St John 38 Crawford Street, W1. *Tel*: 01-722 3550.

Supreme Carpet Cleaning Services 42 Epple Road, SW6. *Tel*: 01-736 3680. Emergency service for floods. Orientals rugs; carpet re-laying.

Sutherland Cleaning Service 17 Morella Road, SW12. *Tel*:01-673 2475.

Outer Ring

A-Z Cleancare Crompton House, Ullswater Crescent, Coulsden, Surrey CR3 2HR. *Tel*: 01-688 4188. Carpets/ upholstery/curtains. Carpet/fabric protection treatments.

ServiceMaster (Kingston) 92 Richmond Road, Kingston-upon-Thames, Surrey. *Tel*: 01-546 7494.

ServiceMaster by Four 26 Epsom Road, Croydon, Surrey. *Tel*: 01-680 4101.

ServiceMaster (Croydon) Rear of 14/16 High Street, Sutton, Surrey. *Tel*: 01-661 2170.

Home Counties/S.East

ServiceMaster by Knight 7 Upper Path, Goodwins, Dorking, Surrey. *Tel*: 01-937 9801; 0306 886027.

ServiceMaster (Westway) 71 Chartdowns, Dorking, Surrey. *Tel*: 01-573 8777; 0306 888502.

4/CLEANING: ORIENTAL RUGS

Many firms below can also clean carpets/upholstery. See also 7/Restoration, 7/Textiles below.

London Postal Districts

Abercorn Carpet Specialists Abercorn Place, St Johns Wood NW8. *Tel*:01- 624 8365. Oriental carpets/ rugs.

Aquaclean AC House, 4/8 Loveridge Mews, NW6. *Tel*: 01-328 2212. Oriental rugs.

David Banks Services 20 Filmer Road, SW6. *Tel*: 01-385 9759/5701. Carpet relaid; Oriental carpets/rugs.

Samuel Behar & Son The Alban Building, St Alban's Place, Upper Street, N1 0NX. *Tel*: 01-226 0144.

David Black Oriental Carpets 96 Portland Road, Holland Park W11

4LM. *Tel*: 01-727 2566. Embroideries, knotted carpets, flat weaves and tapestries.

Clean Interiors 61 Nightingale Lane, SW12. *Tel*: 01-673 8623. Specialist cleaners valuable/Oriental carpets.

ML Waroujian 110/112 Hammersmith Road, W6 7JP. *Tel*: 01-748 7509.

Outer ring

Bestway Group rear of 14/16 High Street, Sutton, Surrey. *Tel*: 01-661 2170. Oriental rugs handwashed; restoration/repairs including refringing.

Home Counties/S.East

Thames Carpet Cleaners 48/56 Reading Road, Henley-on-Thames, Oxon. *Tel*: 0491 574676. Specialists cleaning/restoring Oriental rugs.

5/CLEANING: CURTAINS

Many firms listed under 3/Carpets & Upholstery above can clean curtains. As can drycleaners:

Sketchley Nearest branch. *Tel*: 0455 38133.

Bollom Nearest branch. *Tel*: 0273 41211.

The Drycleaning Information Bureau *Tel*: 01-863 8658. Can recommend cleaners for specific problems.

The Cadogan Company 95 Scrubs Lane, NW10 6QU. *Tel*:01-960 8020. All types cleaning/restoration including unique service for reglazing chintz.

Cibenze Fabric Care 173 Hollydale Road, SE15. *Tel*: 01-639 4913. Curtains/all furnishing fabrics/rugs.

K's of Mill Hill 62 The Broadway, Mill Hill NW7 3TE. *Tel*: 01-959 6996/ 7066. Curtains/blinds (all types): take down, clean, repair, alter, reline/ adapt, rehang.

Services

5/Cleaning: Curtains

6/DYEING

Thuro Clean 55 Bondway, SW8. *Tel:* 01-582 6033. Furnishings/carpet dyers.

Chalfont Cleaners & Dyers 222 Baker Street, NW1. *Tel:* 01-935 7316. 18 standard colours, or can match colour samples. Soft furnishings, but no carpets.

7/GLASS REPAIRS

China Repairers See entry under **1/China Mending** above. Grinding, polishing, sticking.

R Wilkinson 5 Catford Hill, SE6 4NU. *Tel:* 01-314 1080. Repair/restoration all glassware. Chips ground out; stems replaced.

8/HIRING

*Wickes, B&Q, and Homebase offer tool hire. See **DIY Superstores**. The HSS Shops provide a comprehensive hire service. Branches in London/SE, with telephone numbers:*

Acton: 01-992 0101. Barking: 01-594 1042. Barnet: 01-440 3157. Beckenham: 01-658 5877. Cheam: 01-664 0026. Croydon: 01-689 3443. Eltham: 01-859 2017. Fulham: 01-736 1769. Greenwich: 01-853 4114. Hackney: 01-533 3428. Hammersmith: 01-748 6740. Hayes: 01-573 1188. Hendon: 01-202 7671. Kenton: 01-907 3614. Kilburn: 01-328 1798. Kingston: 01-546 1538. Lewisham: 01-690 7116. Leytonstone: 01-555 0293. Notting Hill: 01-727 0897. Purley: 01-660 6485. Richmond: 01-940 8441. Shepherds Bush: 01-743 6300. Stockwell: 01-720 6524. Tooting: 01-767 3127. Tottenham: 01-801 3261. Welling: 01-304 5528.

9/KITCHENWARE

The Copper Shop See **Kitchens 9/Kitchenware**. Copper pan relining.

Divertimenti See **Kitchens 9/Kitchenware**. Pan relining. Knife sharpening.

Leon Jaeggi & Sons See **Kitchens 9/Kitchenware**. Pan mending. Copper saucepan relining. Repolishing. Silver plating.

10/RESTORATION: FURNITURE/ GENERAL

The following firms carry out general restorations; specialities as listed.

London Postal Districts

The Chair Man 1 Baronsmead Road, SW13. *Tel:* 01-748 6816. Chairs; small new parts constructed, carving/inlays replaced. No caning/rushwork, or upholstery. Collection/delivery.

Alexandre Kidd 63 The Grove, W5. *Tel:* 01-840 2019. Gilding/lacquer work.

K Restorations 1/3 Ferdinand Street, NW1 8ES. *Tel:* 01-482 4021. French polishing, desk/table leathering, traditional/old furniture reupholstered, cane/rush repairs, oak liming. Collection/delivery. DIY mail order releathering kit.

Brian O'Donnell Antiques Restorer 1 Waterfall Road, Colliers Wood SW19. *Tel:* 01-543 1369/01-648 2684. Wood-turning.

Max E Ott 1a Southcote Road, N19. *Tel:* 01-607 1384. Copies/restorations.

J Wolff & Son 82 Troutbeck, Albany Street, N21. *Tel:* 01-388 3588. Fine cabinet repairs, carving, gilding.

Outer Ring.

Barry L Cole 7 Blossom Waye, Heston, Middx TW5 9HB. *Tel:* 01-570 8275. Veneering, wood-turning, polishing.

Home Counties/S. East

Manor Antiques 2 The New Shops, High Street, Old Woking, Surrey GU22 9JW. *Tel:* 04862 24666. French polishing, leather tops. Caning, seagrass, rush; pine stripping.

Sage Antiques & Interiors High Street, Ripley, Surrey GU23 6BB. *Tel:* 0483 224396.

Michael Schryver Antiques The Granary, North Street, Dorking, Surrey. *Tel:* 0306 881110. Cabinetmaking, polishing, upholstery.

Youngs Unit 24, Hewitt Industrial Estate, Elmbridge Road, Cranleigh, Surrey. *Tel:* 0483 274965. Cabinet work, French polishing.

11/RESTORATION: FURNITURE/ CANING & RUSHING

M & F Caners 10 Derby Road, South Woodford, E18 2DU. *Tel:* 01-505 0198. Caning only. Fortnightly collection/delivery.

12/RESTORATION: LEATHER

*Leather cleaning/restoration. See **Restoration 1/Furniture** above.*

Connolly Bros (Curriers) Wandle Bank, SW19. *Tel:* 01-542 5251/01-543 4611. Workshop cleaning/repairs for upholstered leather furniture.

13/RESTORATION: METALS

Dreams See **Bedrooms 5/Brass Beds**. 34 Chalk Farm Road, NW1. *Tel:* 01-267 8107. Restoration metal bedsteads.

144

T Smith & Co 35 Clerkenwell Close, EC1. *Tel:* 01-253 7314. Mending, repolishing, replating: all metal work.

Verdigris Art Metalwork Restorers 31 Clerkenwell Close, EC1. *Tel:* 01-253 7788. Repairs/fine cleaning for pewter, brass, bronze, copper and spelter (lead/zinc mix). Repair/cleaning bronze sculptures. Repairs for old chandeliers/light fittings.

Voysey & Knapp 20 Goodge Place, W1. *Tel:* 01-636 8741. Repairs for bronze, copper, silver: speciality is brass. Chandeliers, lanterns, coffee tables, wall brackets.

14/RESTORATION: PICTURES & FRAMES

*Many firms below are also specialist picture framers. See also **Accessories 2/Frames**.*

London Postal Districts

Blackman Harvey 36 Great Queen Street, WC2B 5AA. *Tel:* 01-836 1904. All picture/frame restoration. Expert/comprehensive framing service. Murals. Limited edition prints/reproductions. DIY framing materials.

John Campbell Picture Frames 164 Walton Street, SW3 2JL. *Tel:* 01-584 9268. Conservation/restoration carved/moulded frames. Gilding.

Kate Colleran 17 Frognal, NW3 6AR. *Tel:* 01-435 4652. Conservation/restoration all b&w/coloured prints, watercolours, drawings, posters.

Alexander G Ley & Son The House, 13 Brecknock Road, N7 0BL. *Tel:* 01-267 3645.

The Rowley Gallery 115 Kensington Church Street, W8 7LN. *Tel:* 01-727 6495.

John Tanous 115 Harwood Road, SW6. *Tel:* 01-736 7999.

Outer Ring

The Hampton Hill Gallery 203/205 High Street, Hampton Hill, Middx TW12 1NP. *Tel:* 01-977 5273/1379.

Naive and Fantasy Paintings Studio House, 46 Selborne Road, Park Hill Village, Croydon CR0 5JQ. *Tel:* 01-686 9971. Picture restoration.

Opal Frames 114 Imperial Parade, Brighton Road, Purley, Surrey CR2 4DB. *Tel:* 01-668 8606. Oils, watercolours, etchings, lithographs, drawings, posters, prints.

Home Counties/S.East

Knight's Gallery 59/61 Guildford Street, Luton, Beds LU1 2NL. *Tel:* 0582 36266.

Jennifer Scott Coach Hill House, Burley Street, Ringwood, Hants BH24 4HN. *Tel:* 04253 3361. Oriental paintings paper/silk.

15/RESTORATION: STONE & MARBLE

*Firms listed under **Heating 2/Fireplaces** and **Architectural Salvage** may also carry out stone/marble repairs.*

Architectural Castings 59 The Arches, New King's Road, SW6. *Tel:* 01-731 7172.

HW Poulter 279 Fulham Road, SW10 9PZ. *Tel:* 01-352 7268.

Poyner & Weatherley The Stoneyard, Dorset Road, N15. *Tel:* 01-800 4559.

16/RESTORATION: TEXTILES

Samuel Behar & Son The Alban Building, St Albans Place, Upper Street, N1 0NX. *Tel:* 01-226 0144. All tapestries, textiles, Oriental rugs.

Janie Lightfoot 24 Cholmondeley Avenue, NW10. *Tel:* 01-961 5469. All textile restoration, including oriental rugs.

Christian Potter 63 Carthew Road, Hammersmith W6 0DU. *Tel:* 01-741 9842. Tapestries, canvas, flat weave/pile rugs.

The Royal School of Needlework Apartment 38, Hampton Court Palace, East Moseley, Surrey KT8 9AU. *Tel:* 01-943 1432. Callers strictly by appointment. Quality textile restorations for needlepoint, tapestry, lace and so on.

17/REUPHOLSTERY

All Districts

The Association of Master Upholsterers 564 North Circular Road, Neasden, NW2 7QB. *Tel:* 01-452 4469. Send sae for list of members in your area.

London Postal Districts

Michael Angell Upholstery Wellsbach House, The Business Village, Broomhill Road, Wandsworth SW18 4JG. (*20 mins Wandsworth Town BR*). *Tel:* 01-871 5140/01-876 2157. *Open*: Mon to Sat 8.30am to 6pm. Reupholstery, recovering. Antique/modern furniture repairs. Free local collection/delivery.

The Choumert Upholstery Co 131 Bellenden Road, SE15 4QY. *Tel:* 01-679 1775. *Open*: Mon to Fri 9am to 5.30pm. Sat 9am to 12 noon. Reupholstery; new upholstered furniture to order.

AV Fowldes & Sons 3 Addington Square, Camberwell SE5. (*Elephant & Castle/Oval tubes plus bus*). *Tel:* 01-703 2686. Established in 1870; traditional reupholstery service for Camberwell area.

Refurbish Partnership 52 River Avenue, N13 5RN. *Tel:* 01-886 6433. Mr and Mrs Watts undertake all furniture reupholstery/restoration/curtain making with no additional help. Services cover London/Northern Home Counties.

Jill Saunders See **Furniture 4/Classics & Reproduction.** Upholstery specialists; also range of reproduction Victorian/Edwardian upholstery. Plus furniture restoration, including French polishing, recaning and rerushing.

Tulleys of Chelsea 289/297 Fulham Road, SW10 9PZ. (*South Kensington tube*). *Tel*: 01-352 1078. *Open*: Mon to Fri 9am to 5.30pm. For other branches see **Livingrooms 2/Upholstery.** Replacement seat/back cushions made-to-measure. Any shape, 4in deep. Feather or Dacron filling. Takes about 3 to 4 weeks. *Mail order.*

Mail Order

Foam for Comfort 401 Otley Old Road, Cookridge, Leeds LS16 7DF. *Tel*: 0532 678281 or 673770. Mail order service for replacement fire-retardant foam: soft/medium/firm. Existing covers can be refilled. Colour brochure.

18/STRIPPING WOOD & METAL

All Districts

In Situ 13 Orleans Road, Twickenham, Middx TW1 3BJ. *Tel*: 01-891 2539. On site stripping service for woodwork/floors.

London Postal Districts

Victorian Pine See **Doors 11/General.** Stripping service for wood/metal.

Outer Ring

Strippers 41 Leicester Road, New Barnet, Herts EN5 2PD. *Tel*: 01-441 2944. *Open*: Mon to Fri 9am to 5.30pm. Sat 9am to 1pm. Stripping service for removing paint/varnish from doors/fire surrounds/furniture etc.

19/BUILDING

Many people choose to extend rather than move. The following firms specialise in extensions at ground level, or in the loft.

All Districts

Aristocast Loft Conversions Freepost, Sheffield S9 3TW. *Tel*: 01-891 6326. Established national company for 16 years; estimate and survey free. Fitters usually finished in one week.

The Brick Centre Trustbrick, Brimington Road North, Pottery Lane, Chesterfield S41 9BH. *Tel*: 0246 451197. Specialist brick matching service so that extensions blend with existing house. Post them a sample brick and they will match/send back sample/deliver nationwide. Any size/shape/colour: 6,000 types on file. Range of handmade bricks. Suppliers to B&Q/Texas (see **DIY Superstores**).

Crescourt Loft Conversions Freepost, Roebuck Lane, West Bromwich, West Midlands B70 6QR. *Tel*: 021-553 4131. *London Office*: 01-874 5645.

Room Plus Freepost, Bond Street, Sheffield S9 3TW. *Tel*: 0742 430413/01-891 6380.

London Postal Districts

Home Design Centre Freepost, 170 Byron Way, Northolt, Middx UB5 4BR. *Tel*: 01-841 8951.

Outer Ring

The Loft Shop Progress Way, Purley Way, Croydon, Surrey CR0 4XD. (*A23 from Central London*). *Tel*: 01-681 4060. *Open*: Mon to Sat 8am to 5.30pm. Not a building firm as such, but suppliers of everything needed for a loft conversion. Walkround room-settings demonstrate your loft's potential, providing ideas to discuss with your builder. Advice; informative free fact sheets on regulations/materials/finance. Recommendations to professional builders/installers. Quality products, competitive prices. Windows/stairs/ladders. Floors/walls/ceilings. Insulation. Loan scheme. Next day deliveries.

HELP!

1/YOUR RIGHTS

Shops

You will be more effective as a shopper if you know your rights under the law. The Sale of Goods Act 1979 covers all goods (including food) bought from any form of trader – whether from shops, street markets, doorstep salesmen, in sales, at parties in private homes, or by mail order.

The Act applies whether goods are bought for cash or by credit. Once the seller accepts your offer to buy (whether made verbally or in writing), a contract has been made. Under this contract, you have the right to receive goods of "merchantable quality" and fit for their normal purpose, bearing in mind the price paid, the nature of the goods, and how they were described. The goods must be "fit for any particular purpose" indicated by the seller, and they must be "as described".

If the seller has not fulfilled any of these obligations, your contract has been broken, and you are entitled to your money back or compensation.

Make your complaint to the seller not the manufacturer, as it is the seller that is responsible (whatever shops sometimes say). But see note below on manufacturer's liability.

Bear in mind the following points:

You don't have to have a receipt to make a complaint. But obviously, matters run more smoothly if you have, so keep all bills/receipts carefully in a special place.

When a complaint is justified, you are entitled to your money back. You do not have to accept an exchange, or a credit note. But once you take a credit note, you cannot ask for your money back later.

Your rights apply even during sales. Notices that say "No goods exchanged; no money refunded" are illegal. But if the shop has drawn your attention to imperfections (with a "seconds" sign, for example) the onus is on you to make a good inspection of the goods before buying.

Make complaints politely and calmly to the department or shop manager. Keep carefully copies of any correspondence. If you need help/advice, go to your local Citizens Advice Bureau, or consult the Trading Standards Department at your town hall.

Manufacturers

The Consumer Protection Act 1987 makes manufacturers and importers liable for injury and damage caused wholly or partly by a defective product made after 1 March 1988. In the case of injury, or death, anyone can claim, not just the purchaser. Seek advice if you have been harmed by a product.

2/CREDIT

Used sensibly, credit is a valuable aid, especially as a means to buying better-quality longer-lasting furnishings than you could otherwise afford. (This particularly applies to carpets, upholstery and beds.)

But make sure you know the full cost of any credit you are offered, and in particular compare the APR – Annual Percentage Rate. If you sign a credit agreement in a shop, garage or finance company office, it is legally binding. But if you sign a credit agreement in your own home, you have five days in which to cancel or change your mind.

3/BUYING BY MAIL ORDER

In this book, mail order describes goods that are ordered by post or the telephone. They may then be delivered by post, carrier, the supplier's own transport, and so on.

Shopping from home by mail order can be comfortable and convenient. Some merchandise is only available by mail order. And some goods may be cheaper bought this way.

On the other hand, you cannot inspect before you buy. Illustrations can be deceiving. Brochure colours may not be accurate. You may not get a fair idea of scale – of furniture in particular. And quality is hard to assess.

Help!

Upholstery and beds pose special problems: it is important with these items to "try before you buy"; to assess for personal comfort.

Goods may get damaged in transit. It may be difficult for you to find a time convenient to receive goods. Packing goods up again to return them (if need be) can be troublesome.

Here is some basic guidance for readers following up mail order sources in this book. Keep a copy of any order and note its date. When telephoning, make a note of the date of the conversation, and the name of the person with whom you spoke.

Never send cash through the post. Send cheques, postal orders etc. with orders only if you are asked to pay in advance, and keep carefully stubs and counterfoils. Note that payment by cheque may delay your order, for cheques take upwards of a week to be cleared. Ordering by phone and paying by credit card is often quicker.

If you need goods urgently, make this clear from the start. The supplier must know when you will be available to receive goods by post or carrier. Add your daytime telephone number to your order. Keep packaging safely until you are sure you do not want to return goods. Keep guarantees safely with copies of original order etc. If returning goods, get certificates of posting, or receipts from carriers.

4/WHAT TO READ/ WHERE TO GO

Free leaflets on consumer rights are available from your local library, or from The Office of Fair Trading, Field House, Bream's Buildings, EC4A 1PR. "Fair Deal" is a useful paperback published by HMSO for £1.95.

Like any other subject, furnishing repays homework. Frustrating though it is, shops often do not have good stocks of manufacturers' literature/ samples. Write off for these yourself. Get in contact with manufacturers before making major buys. A recommended stockist may offer the best service (see, for example, the Solutions bathroom stockists). Make the effort to get to manufacturers' showrooms: you cannot buy direct, but sight of the full product range and access to specialist advice is always helpful.

Specialist monthly magazines are numerous, and contain the very latest news of suppliers. *Which?* published by the Consumers' Association (2 Marylebone Road, NW1 4DX. *Tel*: 01-486 5544) gives monthly comparitive reports on tested products; you can consult back numbers at your local library.

A long browse in a specialist bookshop is well worthwhile. I recommend The Design Centre Bookshop, at 28 Haymarket, SW1, and The Building Bookshop, at The Building Centre, 26 Store Street, WC1E 7BT. *Tel*: 01-637 3151.

Both the above organisations are in themselves worth visiting. The Design Council can help on product selection, with displays, addresses, and an information service. The Building Centre has extensive displays of products and materials (including bathrooms and kitchens, tiles, floorings, electrical equipment, and bricks, to name just a few), with an information/ product leaflet service.

5/LEAFLETS

Informative/inspirationalleaflets/ booklets are published by many trade organisations and makers of home furnishing/decorative products/equipment. Below is a small selection (available 1989).

Colour scheming

Colour scheming/painting. Leaflets. Crown Paints, PO Box 37, Crown House, Hollins Road, Darwen, Lancs BB3 0BG.

Leaflets on colour scheming/painting techniques. Dulux, ICI Paints Division, Wexham Road, Slough SL2 5DS.

Planning & furnishings

Consumer leaflets on choosing a new bed/sofabed. Free (34p stamp). National Bed Federation, 251 Brompton Road, SW3 2EZ.

Good Furniture Guide; Furnishing for the Future. Free consumer advice leaflets. Sae. British Home Furnishing Bureau, Bury House, 126/128 Cromwell Road, SW7 4ET.

Basic Bathroom Planning Kit. Free. Ideal-Standard, PO Box 60, National Avenue, Hull HU5 4JE.

Details of Kitchen Specialists Association (KSA) consumer protection scheme. KSA Information Office, 8 St Barnards Crescent, Edinburgh EH4 1NP. *Tel*: 031-332 8884.

Free planning leaflets on kitchens, bathrooms, bedrooms. Advice on replacement doors and windows. Magnet, Royd Ings Avenue, Keighley, West Yorks BD21.

Your Bathroom Planner: help with drawing your bathroom out to scale. Move-around cut-outs represent various bathroom fittings. Free. Stelrad Bathroom Products, Whieldon Road, Stoke-on-Trent ST4 4HN.

Hints/tips equipping a bathroom. Free. British Bathroom Council, Federation House, Stoke-on-Trent ST4 2RT.

Floors & Carpets

The Ronseal Book of Colouring Wood: colourful ideas for floors, panelling and furniture. Free. Consumer Services, Stirling Roncroft, 15 Churchfield Court, Churchfield, Barnsley S70 2LJ.

Carpet Facts: hints/tips on buying carpets; stain removal. SAE. British Carpet Manufacturers Association, Royalty House, 72 Dean Street, W1J 5HB. *Tel*: 01-734 9853.

Soft Furnishings

Curtain/track style guidance. 95p. Antiference, Bicester Road, Aylesbury, Bucks HP19 3BJ.

Curtain making/style details. £1. Practical Matters, Rufflette, Thomas French, Sharston, Wythenshawe, Manchester M22 4TH.

Fact sheets on stencilling cushions, blinds, furniture and so on. Large sae The Stencilling Advisory Bureau, PO Box 1609, London W8 7TN.

Colour booklet: ideas for dressing windows with nets. Free. The Curtain Net Advisory Bureau, 68 Knightsbridge, SW1X 7LN.

Fireplaces

The Book of Fireplace Ideas, Countryside, ECC Quarries, PO Box 130, Swindon, Wilts SN1 4LG.

DIY

Free leaflets on all DIY projects. 1. Branches of Homebase. 2. Branches of Payless. See **DIY Superstores.**

Step-by-step DIY instructions for panelling a wall, building a shelving unit, etc. Free. The Home Woodwork Campaign, 21/25 Carolgate, Retford, Notts DN22 6BZ.

Home Security

Guide to home security fittings. Free: please send 22p stamp. The Security Lock Association, Penfold House, Brent Street, NW4 2EU.

Symbols

Explanation of washing symbols. Free. The British Apparel Centre, 7 Swallow Place, London W1R 7AA.

Doors & Windows

Free leaflets on double-glazing, safety-glazing, and mirrors. Glass and Glazing Federation, 44/48 Borough High Street, SE1 1XB. *Tel*: 01-403 7177. Plus regional lists of members, including double-glazing firms whose trading practices are governed by the GGF's Code of Practice.

Free leaflets on replacing doors and windows. Magnet, Royd Ings Avenue, Keighley, West Yorks BD21.

The Good Door Guide. Free hints/tips on choosing/fitting interior and exterior doors. Crosby Doors, National Distribution Centre, Groundwell Industrial Estate, Swindon, Wilts SN2 5BQ.

INDEX OF PRODUCTS

Index of Products

INDEX OF SHOPS & OUTLETS

Index of Shops & Outlets

Index of Shops & Outlets

Index of Shops & Outlets